DEFENDER OF MINORITIES: PAUL SCHIEMANN, 1876–1944

Paul Schiemann, early 1920s

JOHN HIDEN

Defender of Minorities

Paul Schiemann, 1876–1944

HURST & COMPANY, LONDON

For Juliet

First published in the United Kingdom by
C. Hurst & Co. (Publishers) Ltd,
38 King Street, London WC2E 8JZ

Printed in India

A Cataloguing-in-Publication data record for this book is available from the British Library.

ISBN 1–85065–751–3

Contents

Illustrations

Preface

I first heard of Paul Schiemann when researching a doctorate in the 1960s on Germany and the Baltic states. All that interested me then was his role in the evolution of German *Ostpolitik* after the First World War. Still, I discovered enough to make me think vaguely of finding a lot more about the man and his ideas at some stage. It has taken me all this time to get round to it, and the present book is the result.

Most general readers and more than a few historians of modern Europe will never have come across this remarkable Baltic German journalist, politician and minorities' spokesman. For one thing, he lived much of his life in Latvia—a country that with neighbouring Estonia and Lithuania seems to attract only fitful, if sometimes intense interest from the rest of the world. Certainly, the media spotlight bathing these three states during and immediately after the break-up of the Soviet Union has long since been turned off. Soviet tanks in Vilnius, Tallinn or Riga have instant public appeal; reconstruction, democratisation, privatisation and the peaceful management of ethnic conflict have not. Yet precisely the non-violence of the 'Baltic model' of transition is what makes it of interest to Europe's future, as Paul Schiemann argued long ago in different circumstances.

Actually, in important respects the circumstances were not that different. A mighty Russian empire had disintegrated; newly-independent Baltic countries were struggling successfully to manage the transition from economic structures and large scale enterprise, once serving Russian markets now lost through the dictates of Soviet economic practice; small and medium enterprises were slowly emerging to meet other European and regional needs; a new generation of small farmers struggled into being, profiting from the break-up of vast landed estates in Estonia and Latvia; Baltic countries were looking with determination for a place in the post-war European security system that would keep them out of Russia's realm; and finally in Estonia and Latvia a once all-powerful ruling minority—the Baltic Germans—had to cede power in 1919 to the indigenous populations, just as Russians did after the formal end of Soviet rule in the Baltic countries in 1991.

No more than those did the conservative Baltic German nobility and urban élites who governed the Baltic provinces autonomously on behalf of Tsarist Russia readily accept the loss of power and their 'turn of fate' in the winter of 1918. Most refused even to acknowledge the new Latvia until it became unavoidable in the second half of 1919. They were fortunate, although most failed to see it, that the political leadership of their community at this point fell to Paul Schiemann. Long before 1914—and in the face of ferocious criticism and wounding personal attacks from the all-powerful conservative camp—Schiemann had campaigned passionately as a journalist for reform of the provincial administration and for the right of Estonians and Latvians to manage their own lands. His belief that the very future of Baltic Germandom was at risk from its refusal to involve Estonians and Latvians in governance had become by the end of the war an absolute commitment to independent Baltic countries.

Although relatively favoured among Baltic Germans by Latvia's new leaders, Paul Schiemann eschewed the easy road to personal political advancement. Instead he sought compromise with the same authoritarian conservative forces that had attacked him. He worked to engage them, as chairman of the group of German parties in the Latvian parliament (Saeima), in the active rebuilding of the state on a democratic basis. The resistance this encountered from the former Baltic German leadership caste, convinced of the case for special treatment because of its historic role, remained a punishing constant in Schiemann's political life. Reactionary elements in the Latvian German community continued to find it hard to reconcile themselves—in Schiemann's words—'to being the minority to which history has condemned us.' The stark reality, he insisted, was that if Latvia collapsed it would mean the end of Baltic Germandom too.

It was this conviction—that there could be no meaningful life for Baltic Germans *as* Baltic Germans outside their historic homelands—which prompted Schiemann to insist on the absolute loyalty of the German minority to the Latvian state. Of course, there was another side to this bargain. If history, Schiemann admitted, gave Baltic Germans no right to rule, it *did* give them the right—like other established minority groups in Latvia—to live and work in their home on equal terms with the Latvian majority, as well as the right to observe their own culture and language. Manifestly, the precondition for having minority rights is the *existence* of a minority, so that Schiemann also wanted Baltic German émigrés to return in order to help with what he insisted was the privileged task of state building.

Not surprisingly, Schiemann was virtually predestined to become a fighter for minority rights. What makes his theoretical work in this field so interesting is that it arose not from detached study but from an intensely active life as a practising politician and newspaper editor. In addition he became a leading campaigner on the European stage for cultural autonomy, through the Nationalities Congress that he helped to set up in Geneva in 1925. From his work in this forum arose too his compelling vision of a future Europe as a collection of nations rather than nation states, the rich cultural diversity of the continent made all the more secure by what he became convinced would be a progressive decline in the importance of its territorial borders. Far from being Utopian, as his nationalist critics charged, Schiemann was ahead of his time, seeing the looming war in 1939 as additional proof that forceful solutions to nationality disputes could never be lasting ones.

It adds to the charm and attraction of this resolute, but in his era somewhat lone enemy of the sovereignty-fixated nation state that Schiemann resisted all forms of nationalism. He was therefore an early, unrelenting and principled opponent of National Socialism. Not least he fought against its progressive infiltration of German minorities in Europe—the *Auslandsdeutschen*—and the attempt to transform them into adjuncts to the policies of the Third Reich. Even when forced to give up his work in Latvia in 1933, through a combination of Nazi pressures and ill health, he continued from Vienna, through the pages of the anti-nazi newspaper, *Der Deutsche in Polen*, relentlessly to criticise Hitler's efforts to 'coordinate' German minorities. When German troops entered Austria in 1938, Schiemann went back to Riga to escape the concentration camp.

Sadly, he returned to a German community wholly enamoured of Germany's 'national renewal' under Hitler and seeing the Third

Reich as their best defence against further decline in a Latvia firmly under control of Karlis Ulmanis and nationalist forces. True to his beliefs, Schiemann did not join in 1939/40 the mass re-settlement of Baltic Germans on land taken from Poland by German armed forces. By opting for German citizenship and resettlement Baltic Germans 'removed themselves from history'—thereby in Schiemann's view depriving those unable or unwilling to leave Latvia of their rights as a minority. He subsequently endured and wrote about the very first experience of a westernised society exposed to Bolshevik rule, 1940–1. His now extreme illness and inability to move far from his home in a Riga suburb spared him a worse fate when Germany occupied the Baltic area in 1941. Although monitored by the Gestapo, Schiemann's private resistance continued through his illicit help to those persecuted and through secretly collecting information on Jews killed in Latvia. He died in 1944, only weeks before the Soviets returned to expel the German forces.

Understanding the vanished world of Baltic Germandom is fraught with difficulties to the outsider, and I have a huge debt to those who have helped me. They include Gert von Pistohlkors, who was instrumental in engaging me in the activities of the German Baltische Historische Kommission. Among its members the Schiemann expert Helmuth Kause has answered queries and directed me to sources, as have Wilhelm Lenz and Dietrich Loeber. Michael Garleff, the leading historian of Baltic Germans between the wars, has gone far beyond the call of duty by looking through my manuscript and in general offering support and advice. For this I am especially grateful. Eduard Mühle, the director of the Herder-Institut at Marburg, and his staff, notably Peter Wörster and Dr Jürgen Warmbrunn, have been immensely supportive during my research trips there.

In Riga I must thank Sarmite Šāvēja at the Latvian State Archive, for helping me locate and use relevant material, and especially Sarmite Pijola. Valters Scerbinskis also kindly sent me photocopies of interesting documents on Paul Schiemann, as well as tracking down relevant photographs. Viesturs Zanders, of the Latvian National Library, whose duties include managing the Baltic collection located in R. Vagnera Street in Riga, brought to my attention many important items when I was working there on the Schiemann papers. In addition he provided me with prints of photographs of Paul

Schiemann. So too did Silvija Voite at the Museum of the History of Riga and Navigation. The photograph of Herder Square and the Café Otto Schwarz in Riga are reproduced by courtesy of that Museum. The potrait of Schiemann reproduced on the last page of the illustration section facing page 127 was made available by the Baltic Central Library in Riga. I also owe a debt to Leo Dribins and his colleagues at the Latvian Academy of Sciences for including me in their conference in September 2000, celebrating Paul Schiemann's recognition by Israel as Righteous Among the People. During my spells of work in Riga I was fortunate to have the support of a succession of staff members at the British Council Offices, as well as hospitality from the British Embassy. Of the ambassadors, Nicholas Jarrold and his wife Anna not only regularly extended their hospitality to me but also took a direct interest in Paul Schiemann.

In the course of researching this book several private individuals have given generously in terms of information or materials. Ingeborg Baumann allowed me to look through the papers of her father, Hans Donath, the former colleague of Schiemann's, who late in life laboured at his own cost to produce the invaluable collection of Schiemann editorials and other writings, typed or photocopied from originals. Ms Baumann and her brother Christian Donath helped me to acquire the full collection for my own library. Monika von Hirschheydt sent me a copy of an unpublished section of Wilhelm von Rüdiger's memoirs, as well as photographs of Paul and Lotte Schiemann. Ruth Schiemann-Gostic gave me a copy of Lotte Schiemann's personal memoir of her visit to her husband during the First World War. Their generosity is much appreciated. Interesting personal insights into my themes have come from private correspondence with Leonore von Skerst and Brigitte von Ungern-Sternberg, both of Baltic German origin.

Valentina Freimane, the last living witness to Schiemann's final days, has given unstintingly of her time in answering letters, and was good enough to let me interview her extensively in her Riga home. It was a privilege to hear not only her account of life with Paul and Lotte Schiemann, but her own extraordinary story. Of colleagues at Bradford University who have been exceptionally responsive to discussions of Baltic and minority issues and have therefore helped me to clarify my own ideas I would single out David Smith, Martyn

Housden and Gabor Batonyi. None of these, and certainly not the Baltic German specialists mentioned earlier, bear responsibility for whatever mistakes might be found in my book. These are definitely all my own work. I am enormously grateful too for a British Academy Small Research Grant enabling me to carry out archive work in Latvia and Germany. Finally, I must admit once more the huge debt owed to the person to whom this book is dedicated.

Burley in Wharfedale, April 2004 JOHN HIDEN

1. The Making of a Democrat

In his modest house in a suburb of Nazi-occupied Riga, the Baltic German, Paul Schiemann, began to dictate to a young Jewish girl—concealed in their home by him and his wife Charlotte—a memoir of his crowded life as a politician, newspaper editor and European minority leader. His intention was to take his extraordinary chronicle to the year 1933—when he finally gave up his seat in the Latvian parliament and relinquished his post as editor-in-chief of the *Rigasche Rundschau*. The plan was frustrated by his death in 1944. He managed to complete only an account of the years 1903–19, posthumously published as 'Between Two Eras'.[1]

The idea of displacement is not unique in the biographical literature of early twentieth-century Europe. Germany's first two foreign ministers after the First World War were both characterised as 'wanderers between two worlds'—between monarchy and republicanism, between stability and revolution.[2] Schiemann experienced all this, as well as the sea-change from ruler to ruled, when the formation of independent Baltic states at the end of the War finally destroyed the historic foundations of Baltic German power. There had been portents of this catastrophe awaiting the Germans in the Baltic, yet Schiemann came to maturity in an environment still bearing the hallmarks of a late colonial society, built up over time by the descendants of the Germanic Crusader knights, missionaries and merchants who arrived in the region from the late twelfth century onwards.

When the medieval Ordenstaat of Old Livonia fell into the threefold division of Estonia, Livonia and Courland towards the end of the sixteenth century, a succession of foreign powers, culminating with Russia, secured the governing of the territories by recognising the special position of the German element. The nobility belonging to the four knightly orders (*Ritterschaften*) of Estonia, Livonia, Courland and Oesel ruled through their exclusive provincial assemblies

(*Landtage*) and monopolised appointments to the important posts in law, the police and the administration of church and school. Property-owning German burghers, organised in Great and Small Guilds, administered Riga and the other towns. Such was the influence of the German minority that people came to refer to the *German* Baltic provinces of Russia. At the bottom of this feudal and stratified social order sat the Estonian and Latvian populations, mostly, until the early nineteenth century, tied in as serfs to the existing order for the greater good of Baltic Germans.[3] Even then, hairline cracks were being exposed in the edifice of power.

Ironically, they were caused in part by the influx during the second part of the eighteenth century of more Germans, this time in the form of teachers, pastors, lawyers and other academics. Together they comprised the so-called '*Literaten*', and in social—if not strictly legal—terms constituted a fourth estate, alongside the German aristocracy, merchants and craftsmen. Enlightened *Literaten* encouraged native Baltic languages and culture. In criticising the repression of Estonians and Latvians they stimulated liberal elements in the *Ritterschaften* to bring serfdom to an end in the Baltic provinces between 1816 and 1819. The land problem remained to be solved, but the personal freedom given to serfs further eroded the feudal order and was a major precondition for the later development of Latvian nationhood.[4] For the time being at least the relationship with the Russian throne remained the defining one for all Baltic Germans, including *Literaten*. Into this latter 'caste' Paul Schiemann was born.[5]

He could trace his family line in Courland back for two centuries. Jelgava (Mitau), where he lived as a boy, had since the 1770s been an important intellectual centre in its own right. His father, Julius, a lawyer, was closely involved in his youth with liberal movements in the Baltic German community, campaigning against the predominance of the aristocracy in the courts and administration. He was naturally excited by Bismarck's *Reich*—united five years before his son Paul's birth in 1876. The fact that Julius Schiemann was a citizen of the Russian Empire did not prevent him from being 'a German patriot in the first instance'.[6] However, reconciling the two positions became increasingly problematic from the 1870s onwards as the Russian government steadily chipped away at the autonomy of its Baltic provinces.

The process accelerated when Alexander III's accession to the throne in 1881 brought greater centralisation of education and justice. In 1885–6 elementary schooling was placed under the Russian Ministry of Education, and in April 1887 Russian became the language of instruction in secondary schools. Laws of 1888 and 1889 deprived the *Ritterschaften* of their rights to staff the offices of justice and police authorities. If this was modernisation, it had a national edge to it, visible enough in the warning of the celebrated Slavophil author Iurii Samarin, that the Baltic provinces were 'not an advance post of Germany …but a western maritime borderland of Russia'.[7] Perhaps inevitably, the Baltic German community perceived the centralising reforms as 'Russification' and reacted accordingly.[8]

Where Paul Schiemann first experienced change was in his schooling. Education in the Baltic provinces had naturally profited from the influx of intellectuals from East Prussia, Saxony and Thuringia from the second half of the eighteenth century. Names on a long and illustrious list included Johann Gottfried Herder, who taught at the Domschule in Riga between 1764 and 1769, as well as Johann Friedrich Hartknoch, the first book dealer in the Baltic provinces, who published in Riga the first four editions of Immanuel Kant's *Critique of Pure Reason*. A defining moment for the German minority was the re-founding of the University of Dorpat (Tartu) by Alexander I as an autonomous German-speaking institution. The traditions at Tartu—'the true heart of their country'—reinforced the independent spirit in Baltic German society noticed by Herder. Tartu University schooled those individuals staffing the autonomous corporations in town and countryside, incidentally promoting a closer relationship between *Literaten* and *Ritterschaften*. Both Schiemann's father and grandfather had studied at Tartu. When it too succumbed to Russification, becoming the University of Iurev in 1893, Baltic Germans felt that a decisive blow had been struck at their position.[9]

The changing times meant that after completing the third form of the private German primary school run by Karl Stavenhagen, Paul Schiemann and his older brother Oscar had to take the examination for entry to the now Russified secondary school. Yet for the next two years—against regulations—they continued with private tuition, alongside six sons of the Courland nobility and the youngest child of a wealthy privy councillor. 'Underground' lessons, taught by the very

German teachers dismissed by the Russian authorities, were in either Schiemann's or the privy councillor's house. Schiemann specifically recalled a brilliant Latin master. The high cost of private tuition underlined the priority given to education in the Baltic German community, and Julius Schiemann strictly monitored progress at 'school' through lunchtime conversations with his sons, displaying extreme displeasure at signs of slackness. He abandoned the daily inquisition only when the two boys finally joined the top form of the Gymnasium, for he shared the contempt of his fellow *Literaten* for Russian schools.[10] Paul and Oscar continued their private study of Greek, Latin and French, and eventually in 1893 were transferred to the top class of the secondary school at Elberfeld in Germany.

Apart from his conviction of the superiority of German schooling, Julius Schiemann hoped that his sons would find a new fatherland to make up for the one they had 'lost' through Russification. He was dismayed as Russians steadily displaced German teachers, judges and administrators during the 1880s and 1890s, finally convincing himself that the basis for any meaningful future for the German element in the Baltic provinces had been eroded. Like many other *Literaten*, Julius Schiemann lost heart in trying to reform provincial government. Instead he devoted his energies to supporting the *Ritterschaften* in the belief that the resolute defence of their traditions and privilege now provided the only guarantee for the survival of Baltic Germandom as a whole.[11] The self-isolation to which this ultimately condemned the Baltic Germans is best encapsulated in Carl Schirren's famous reply to Juri Samarin: 'Our action will be to stand fast; to survive will be the sum of our policy.'[12]

Julius Schiemann's sons, however, continued to imbibe liberal values in the dynamic new Germany, where the head of their Elberfeld boarding house, Dr Hermann Rassow, was brother-in-law to the influential Hans Delbrück and Adolf Harnack, and where the Schiemann brothers were introduced to and attracted by the thinking of Friedrich Naumann. Paul Schiemann completed his School Leaving Certificate in 1895 before opting to study law and embarking on a higher education journey through Berlin, Marburg, Munich and Bonn. His university education was temporarily broken by a year's military service in the Caucasus in 1896, and in the summer of 1898 by a spell of officer training in Lithuania. Student life for him culminated with a doctorate in Greifswald in 1902: 'The legal position of public banks in war—together with an appendix containing official documentary material concerning the branches of the Bank of France situated in Alsace-Lorraine during the German-French war.' The mundane title wholly belied the sharp mind and colourful personality behind it. Schiemann's intelligence was honed by an avid pursuit at university of other disciplines alongside his legal studies, evident in the intellectual rigour that later marked all that he wrote. He was naturally drawn to literature, quite apart from his attendance at classes in philosophy, history and economics. Anyone later coming across his sustained critique of Bolshevism will readily see that he certainly did 'swot up' on Karl Marx's *Das Kapital* while studying in Munich in 1897–8.[13]

In Munich Schiemann also had his passionate and lifelong interest aroused 'in everything connected with the theatre', after being introduced into the city's artistic circles through various personal and family friends. Indeed his student days were charmed and eased by numerous influential contacts of this kind. Typically he was able for his dissertation to draw on materials from the Auswärtiges Amt (German Foreign Ministry), thanks to his uncle, the eminent conservative historian Theodor Schiemann. The latter was one of 100 or so prominent Baltic Germans leaving their homeland in the first wave of disgruntled emigration following the onset of Russification. They were to be influential in forming a hostile picture of Russia and slowly arousing more interest in the Baltic Germans among the Reich's policy-makers, particularly after 1905. Theodor Schiemann arrived in Berlin in 1897 and thereafter became a well-known journalist, and a friend and adviser to Kaiser Wilhelm II. Paul Schiemann's 'Uncle Theodor' also dedicated himself to convincing the German government of the menace that Russia constituted and the advantages to be gained by weakening it permanently.[14]

Against such a privileged background it is easier to understand the intellectual and social confidence which, as many of Paul Schiemann's contemporaries testified, gave him something of the demeanor of the Baltic German aristocracy, notwithstanding his distaste for their political priorities. The impression was heightened by Schiemann's strong sense of personal honour and readiness to defend principles in which he believed, to the point at times of risk to life and limb. The trait expressed itself most dramatically within the duelling conventions of German student corporations. Schiemann's fearlessness was what first attracted his later co-worker, the conservative Baltic German leader Baron von Fircks.[15] Channelled by maturity and experience, Schiemann's remarkable courage also informed his political speeches and journalism, giving them great power. His charm, however, was that he combined seriousness of purpose with an absence of pettiness and an enormous appetite for social life, a trait that emerged firmly during his student days.

Paul Schiemann was endowed with a constitution that allowed him to drink and smoke heavily while conversing into the small hours, and be at his desk promptly the following morning. His lifestyle became and remained markedly bohemian. From his early studies in Berlin he remembered 'a seemingly endless spree'. Of his liaisons with the theatrical world Schiemann in later life specifically recalled a tumultuous affair with the Berlin actress Herta Weeren. When in Bonn writing his thesis he determinedly enjoyed the generous hospitality of the headquarters of the 'Academic Jurists Association', to which he was introduced by an old school friend from Elberfeld. In Greifswald he fell in with a high-living group of Mecklenburg aristocrats lodging at the Hotel Deutsches Haus. He soon broke into the money provided by his family for graduation expenses. For the first and last time in his life he took part in a gambling session with high stakes to recover his losses. During the game one of the Mecklenburgers lost 30,000 marks, but Schiemann's modest win enabled him to pay the 800 marks required by the university before he underwent the oral examination. Characteristically, he survived this—'rather well prepared'—*magna cum laude.*[16]

With his doctorate finished, practical career issues took priority. An application to be released from Russian citizenship was rejected, notwithstanding the interjection on his behalf of a 'celebrated lady in waiting', on the grounds that he was a Tsarist reserve officer. As a foreigner in Germany he could not practise at the bar. 'There remained', he recorded, 'journalism, of which in essence I had always dreamed.'[17] He was driven by a conviction that it, like the profession of law or indeed politics, entailed defending justice. His thinking on the subject was amplified in the late 1920s during a lecture on the role of the press. 'To be a real journalist one needs a definite calling, an inner compulsion, which sooner or later declares itself, and which can no longer be contained within the confines of a rigid career.' It is doubtful if Schiemann had reached such a pitch in 1902, in so far as he linked the 'inner compulsion' specifically to the overwhelming urge to comment on events of the day.[18] In contrast to his now decisive acceptance of all that was modern in literature and the arts, his political commitments were still forming.

Within him, he recorded of that period, social élitism battled with oppositional inclinations. Friedrich Naumann, with his vision of a 'social monarchy' overcoming the historic cleavage between liberalism and the working class, continued to appeal to Schiemann.[19] He had also decided that he could admire none of the parties in the German Reichstag; for him the patriotic brouhaha in the German Empire held no charms. Even so, his political engagement was not yet such as to prevent him from accepting the patronage of his ultra-conservative Uncle Theodor, who regarded working for the liberal press as a sickness. He secured for his nephew a promise of the editorship of an official German publication in Yokohoma, and in preparing for the post Paul Schiemann became a voluntary helper in the editorial offices of the *Norddeutsche Allgemeine Zeitung* and took English classes at the Berlitz School. He was later dismissive of his contribution, recalling a review of a play and a few volumes of the *Gotha Kalender*; a longer article on Max Klinger's memorial to Beethoven was spiked. In addition he had a piece accepted for the *Deutsche Monatsheft*. As ever, Schiemann's contacts with the art world flourished, following an invitation to the monthly dinner of the Literary Society at the Hôtel de Rome.

In the event Theodor Schiemann's plans for his nephew were foiled by the rising tension between Russia and Japan; the Auswärtiges Amt did not wish to risk having a young Russian reserve officer running an official German journal.[20] The setback was just as well, for Schiemann was discovering a political goal to engage him emotionally as well as intellectually. He came to realise that his most valued social contacts were in fact fellow students from his own homeland and grew to admire their absolute resolve to return to work for the Baltic German community. Aware of his father's own pessimism on that score, Paul Schiemann could not imagine 150,000-strong minorities abandoning the Baltic provinces *en masse*. He even began to feel like a deserter himself, so that when the Yokohama posting fell through, the moral imperative to return home to complete his training became irresistible. Another personal factor in his decision was the need he felt to escape the torrid relationship with Herta Weeren so that he could honour the engagement he had promised a young girl from Jelgava on completion of his doctorate.[21]

Once in Tartu in the spring of 1903, aged twenty-seven, Schiemann in fact pushed jurisprudence aside, having discovered that new Russian regulations made it impossible to complete training for the magistracy without several more years of intensive study. Meanwhile he immersed himself in reading literature and economics in the University library. A piece or two of his appeared in the *Dünazeitung* and an analysis of contemporary women's literature was written for the *Baltische Monatsschrift*, when, 'suddenly', he wrote later, 'I was also drama critic for the *Nordlivländische Zeitung*.' The unexpected visit to Tartu of his Berlin lover, Herta, resulted in a whirlwind of drinking and socialising lasting several weeks, which left him feeling unwell and with a distinctly bad conscience. The outcome of his behaviour, duly marked in the small world of Baltic German society, was the end of his engagement and of his affair with Herta. As luck would have it, the liberal poet and editor-in-chief of the *Revalsche Zeitung*, Christoph Mickwitz, had casually mentioned an opening to Schiemann, who now left for Reval (Tallinn) to become an assistant to Mickwitz and theatre critic on his paper. Once more the remarkably long-suffering father settled his son's large student debt from Bonn, adding to Paul Schiemann's sense of making a clean break.

He could hardly have been more excited on joining the *Revalsche Zeitung*, particularly given his great love of the theatre. Mickwitz had hired Schiemann precisely because he felt the paper needed a younger voice in tune with modern trends in the performing arts. Not only was Schiemann given a completely free hand as a critic, but Mickwitz, in his capacity as Chairman of the Theatre Committee in Tallinn, took his younger colleague's advice in staging more contemporary drama. In a predominantly conservative Baltic German society Schiemann's commitment to modernity itself gave his theatrical criticism a political resonance. His work also reflected the Russian government's censorship of overt political commentary in the German-language press. Ultimately 'The job of [theatre] criticism offered the chance one way or the other to discuss every aspect of existence, and to voice ideas that would seem to be wholly precluded in editorials.'[22] Within a short time stories began to circulate in German journalist circles in Russia, about a rebellious and 'fresh young spirit' on the *Revalsche Zeitung*, writing interesting political articles and theatrical criticism 'with verve'.[23] Plainly Schiemann's earliest sustained journalism was integral to his awakening to politics and vice versa.

In Tallinn Schiemann directly experienced for himself the beleaguered mood among his fellow countrymen, now comprising 180,000 of the 2 million inhabitants of the Baltic provinces. The *Ritterschaften* still had their estates and their provincial assemblies, but Russification and reforms of local government were inexorably weakening their grip on rural affairs. German management of the towns and cities had been affected by the replacement of German lawyers, judges and teachers with Russians. There were other pressures. Rapid industrialisation and urbanisation from the late 19th century onwards went hand in hand in the Baltic provinces, while the abolition of compulsory guild membership, together with legislation allowing all citizens to pursue a trade, 'paved the way for the emergence of an indigenous middle class composed of businessmen and craftsmen.'

Conservative-nationalist, liberal and social democratic political parties materialised among the majority Baltic peoples. More significant than the merging of various associations to form the Latvian Social Democratic Party in 1904 were the aspirations to national autonomy coming from the so called 'New Current' of young international Marxist Latvian intellectuals. These were inspired by the group of Latvian political émigrés around Mikelis Valters in Switzerland.[24] Unlike earlier Latvian nationalists, the new generation was just as opposed to social advancement through Germanisation as to Tsarism.[25] For all the differences between the Latvian political groups it was difficult to disguise their shared dislike of the German element and their rejection of the historic Baltic German claim to speak for the Baltic provinces as a whole.

Schiemann's character, beliefs and lifestyle inevitably predisposed him against the rigid social stratification that continued, even in the towns, to keep a 'wall' between Baltic German and majority populations. Stratification clearly gave a dangerous social edge to the mounting nationality conflict in the Baltic provinces.[26] Yet Schiemann continued to hope that a peaceful solution could be reached through timely reforms of the regional self-administration, bringing in changes in the composition of the provincial assemblies to reduce the nobility's control of them, as well as liquidating the remaining feudal privileges of the landed élites. These can now be seen to have been proposals that would never have satisfied the majority Baltic peoples in the long run. Schiemann himself later admitted his slowness in forging political alliances with the Estonians and Latvians. However, what struck him at the time, in the early 1900s, was that 'Baltic Germandom essentially found only enemies in the land, and it is surely understandable that a young German journalist had to see, and saw, his essential duty in deflecting this hostility.'[27] Schiemann's first priority, as a journalist, was to tackle the differences between sectors of the German community, the better to promote its overall self-defence.

He was daily reminded of the almost hermetically sealed divisions within Baltic German society by the mutual exclusiveness of the four major German clubs in Tallinn, respectively for the nobility, the middle class and *Literaten*, the merchants, and finally the artisans and skilled craftsmen. Only Mickwitz was a member of all four clubs and warmly welcomed in them. That impressed Schiemann greatly, as did his long list of extra duties within the German community; he saw Mickwitz's paramount achievement as being the prevention among the Estonian Germans of the bitterness which developed between conservative and liberal Baltic German groups in Livonia and Courland. Accordingly Schiemann set out to overcome the limits imposed on his own understanding by his hitherto more or less exclusive contact with the upper reaches of society. In Tallinn he began dropping in to talk to traders and merchants, as well as businessmen, augmenting his overview through meeting artisans, small shopkeepers and other petit bourgeois, who showed sympathy for his arguments, but their 'liberalism' was best characterised as objection to the social predominance and exclusivity of the higher classes, the pride of the nobility, the superciliousness of the *Literaten* and the reserve of the big merchants and factory-owners. What they loved most was the 'unaffected humanity' of Mickwitz, very evidently an early role-model for Paul Schiemann, the politician in waiting.[28]

Schiemann's personal soundings convinced him that the Baltic German bourgeoisie had to be educated out of an inclination to leave politics to the traditional élites, to 'those chosen for it'. The same industrial and urban growth that generated new challenges from Latvians and Estonians also strengthened the power-base of the Baltic German bourgeoisie. Until the end of the First World War, however, politics remained the preserve of the nobility, whose leaders focused on direct diplomatic representations in St Petersburg and were 'never active politicians in the full sense'. They too needed the help of the press, Schiemann reasoned, not least to make the fact that some at least were contemplating reforms more widely known. Moreover, the impression of indifference to the 'worth' of Estonians and Latvians—which Schiemann felt was a potent source of anti-German hatred—had to be dispelled at all costs. He dated his 'battle against the publicity-shyness' of the *Ritterschaften* from the spring of 1905, following Baron Eduard Stackelberg's denigration of Baltic German papers in the *St Petersburger Zeitung*. Equally Schiemann devoted time and effort to detailed rebuttals of 'pitiless' Latvian and Estonian press attacks, as well as various 'utterly senseless denunciations' of German landlords, priests and other 'authorities'. There was more than enough for the campaigning young journalist to be getting on with.[29]

By now the Baltic Germans had suffered their first election defeats in four smaller cities in Latvia—after a long and successful rearguard action, fought by Baltic German conservative and liberal alike, following the introduction of Russian municipal statutes in 1870. The first major Baltic city where Baltic Germans lost at the polls, in 1904, was Tallinn. The feeling that something was in the air could not be banished; that 'decisive events' were inescapable; 'that there would have to be either timely reform or revolution.'[30] The latter came in 1905, spreading rapidly into the cities and towns in the Baltic provinces after the shooting of peaceful demonstrators by Tsarist troops in January in St Petersburg. The growing influence of the Estonian and above all Latvian left was attested by strikes called in Baltic cities. Schiemann watched buildings burning in Tallinn and endured the loss of electricity, gas and water. Living now with the actress Anita Remani, and drinking schnapps and beer by the light of kerosene lamps, he first experienced the masses as an 'elemental force'.

Schiemann did not forget the lesson, or that the mood had been inflamed by the Latvian Social Democrats, against whom he angrily railed in an article at the end of October titled 'It is Enough'.[31] He was upset that the Tsar's manifesto of 17 October, with its offer of a parliament (Duma), had neither stemmed the violence nor curtailed the influence of the extreme left. Eventually mass unrest climaxed in October and November, after spreading to the countryside. Here the savage attacks against Baltic German estates, and in due course the participation of individual German landlords in brutal Russian reprisals, left a legacy of mutual hatred profoundly inimical to organic reform.[32]

Nevertheless, Schiemann continued to argue that the most had to be made of the changed situation; that the act of *becoming* a constitutional monarchy committed Russia to the principle of equality for all citizens, precluding material preferences for some of them and placing the onus on individual citizens to collaborate, both within and between national communities. He now added to his growing duties the post of secretary to the newly-formed Deutsche Schulverein (German School Association—soon referred to simply as the Association). Like its sister associations in Courland and Livonia, the Estonian organization capitalised on language concessions as a result of 1905 and embarked on the rebuilding of German schooling. The Association also tried intermittently to break down social barriers within the Baltic German community. In that cause Schiemann endured some 'extremely stilted discourse' arising from the mingling of classes at functions held in the Black Heads House, normally the exclusive domain of the great merchants.[33]

More important, Schiemann also became one of the two secretaries of the new Constitutional Party in Estonia (a sister formation of the Baltische Konstitutionelle Partei—BKP—in Riga). A moderate liberal party founded by Baltic Germans and chaired by Mickwitz, the Constitutional Party in Estonia aimed expressly to appeal to all classes and nationalities. When the party opened a new office in Tallinn's Town Hall Square, Schiemann also ran that and indeed slept there, helping to prepare for the elections to the First Duma. However, the Estonians regarded the party as the product of 'reactionary Germandom' and no Baltic German was elected to the first Duma. 'Estonian voters did not reject a programme on Tuesday', Schiemann reflected bitterly, 'but community with us, with their German compatriots. Not the politician, but the *German* within me complains, casting about in vain for a friendly hand, willing to work jointly with him in the heavy task of political recovery for our home.'[34]

Clearly Estonian and Latvian activists did not distinguish in any significant way between Baltic German liberalism and the conservative forces that for so long had sustained Baltic German dominance. Julius Schiemann's own 'conversion' to the *Ritterschaften's* cause suggests that their instincts were generally correct, as did the outcome of the Estonian Provincial Council convened under the Russian Governor late in October 1906. It was conceived as part of the mechanism for generating reform of the provincial administration. With its cross-section of landed, farming and urban interests, including selected Estonians and Latvians, it was the nearest thing yet to a representative assembly. Schiemann, who attended every session, emphasised the point by parodying previous administrative practice: 'The estate-owner had his Landtag, in which regional policy was essentially made, and from which the towns were carefully excluded; the burgher played at politics in his town assembly; the farmer had his parish council and last but not least his newspaper, which concocted its own special world picture for him.'[35]

His optimism was short-lived. Even the cautious proposals emanating from the conference in Estonia found no echo in Courland and Livonia. Here the *Ritterschaften* set out from 1905 to offset the absence of a German peasantry by recruiting German settlers, adding to the resentment of Latvians. When the Russian Premier Stoylpin's dissolution of the Second Duma on 3 June 1907 signalled the return of reaction, the Baltic German leaders reneged on commitments made in the heat of 1905, gripped by the stubborn fear that the concession of any privilege would bring down the whole edifice of self-government.[36] Very few voices were raised within the *Ritterschaften* against reaction. It has been aptly said that the liberalism of the Baltic German *Literaten* was silenced by the combined menace of Estonian/Latvian and Russian nationalism.[37] The self-perception of Baltic Germans under threat is captured in the assertion that from 1881 'the Germans said to them: you are Russians and shall remain so for eternity; and the Russians cried: you are German, and therefore ought to disappear from the earth.'[38]

The liberalism of the Baltic Germans in fact focused primarily on achieving civil liberties and greater co-operation between the region's disparate cultures, rather than on greater democratisation of the franchise—either in the towns or in the new Russian state Duma. Paul Schiemann, clinging to the belief that fulfilling the Tsar's October manifesto would promote peaceful and organic change, shared liberal fears that far-reaching democratisation with more power to the left would completely sweep Baltic German influence aside. However, he had no illusions that over a period of time—and this was crucial—'a change in our regional constitution is a necessity, a matter of natural evolution.'[39] This, and his sense of justice, drove him to make an increasingly pointed and sustained assault on the stubborn obstruction of the *Ritterschaften*. Since they still wielded considerable social and economic influence even after 1905 and were highly effective at mobilising hostility against their critics within the German community, Schiemann's bid to capture the moral high ground was a particularly courageous political act.

The increasingly sharp tone of his editorials was signalled in a pointed attack in June on the 'wretched error' of following the Russian premier Stoylpin's example and retreating from change. 'So far', Schiemann warned, 'revolution has deprived us only of material wealth. But our intellectual inheritance has always been threatened most fiercely and brutishly by reaction.'[40] It was not by chance that his battle of words against the traditional Baltic German leadership suddenly became fiercer from 1907—the year of his move to Riga.

Richard Ruetz, publisher of the *Rigasche Rundschau*, also the official organ of the Baltic Constitutional Party, had already appointed a liberal campaigner, Axel Schmidt, as its first political editor. Ruetz's action was a direct response to most of the other German dailies being committed to the right—the *Dünazeitung*, the new *Rigasche Zeitung*, the *Baltische Post* and the morning paper, the *Rigaer Tageblatt*. Now Schiemann, with a fast-growing reputation, was also invited to join Ruetz's editorial team. As well as theatrical criticism he was asked to write political leading articles. It was an offer he could not refuse: first, it improved his material position, offering a salary of 250 roubles a month. In addition he was paid 15 roubles (25 if Ruetz was particularly pleased) for each of his twice-weekly editorials. The move at once opened up for him a much bigger sphere of influence.[41]

Of Schiemann's relocation to Riga a contemporary observed succinctly: 'Here began his rise.'[42] Anybody who has made the train journey even today from the village—like atmosphere of Tallinn, to emerge from the station at Riga some hours later, will appreciate the quickening of spirits experienced by Schiemann on his arrival in the city around July 1907. Riga had become a major metropolis, absorbing most of the rural-to-urban migration of Latvians. In complete contrast to 1867, when Germans made up 42.9 per cent of Riga's population and Latvians only 23.6 per cent, by 1913 the figures were, respectively, 16.7 and 39.6 per cent. The city as a whole was five times larger than it had been in the mid-1860s. From its 'narrow inward-turning medieval heart'—now the 'historic' area—the city limits had expanded rapidly, absorbing suburbs, spawning modern buildings and wide streets.[43]

The city was busy and prosperous—with flourishing industry and commerce and a third of Russia's trade with Europe passing through it. It was cosmopolitan, embracing—apart from Germans and Latvians-Russians, Jews and, by 1913, significant Lithuanian and Polish minorities. The Riga Polytechnic was increasingly becoming the focus of higher education for Latvians. If the latter were still only slowly winning seats on the city council after 1905, Riga was nonetheless the real centre of Latvian nationalism—an engine of Latvian cultural growth—sustaining many newspapers and Latvian writers. In an understatement Paul Schiemann recorded of Riga: 'I could almost say that it was here that I first experienced a politically charged atmosphere.'[44]

He found the differences between communities more intractable by far than anything he had yet experienced in Estonia. In Courland and Livonia there had been greater violence between lord and tenant in 1905. To Schiemann it seemed that rural Baltic German society had abandoned hope of reconciliation with the Latvian peasantry surrounding them—hence the recruitment of German settlers or, as the Latvians viewed them, 'colonists'. To an anonymous brochure preaching reaction Schiemann responded by cataloguing the short-sighted assumptions of Baltic German conservatism in Courland and Livonia: namely, that revolution had been caused by Estonians and Latvians, not by the loyal Germans; that their loyalty and their historic past gave Germans special cultural rights; that any German compromising with Estonian and Latvian wishes was a weakling and a traitor to his people's cause; and that German domination in the region could be preserved by co-operating with Russian reactionaries.[45]

Schiemann saw in such attitudes 'the negation of long-term policy' arising from panic. They did not take into account the rejection of Baltic German corporate privileges implicit in the reforms of 1905. These signified that constitutional rights, rather than nationality, would ultimately determine the political and communal influence of individuals. Thus wholly new questions had to be urgently addressed: which factors of public life, which groups of taxpayers would have most influence in the state? Unless the German minority systematically competed with the growing enterprise of the Latvians—and, above all, until it educated its youth in the harsh new realities—its economic power base would decline. Schiemann neatly summarised the dilemma in the sentence 'Our national strength is dependent on our political strength—our political strength, however, will depend on our economic strength.'[46]

Economic arguments added force to his insistence that the BKP remain in principle a truly national party and not just a formation for Baltic Germans. Only after arriving in Riga did Schiemann perceive 'ever more clearly' an underlying and essential community of interest between Latvians and Germans in defending their own cultural identities in the face of Russian nationalism. The realisation opened up a new line of attack on Baltic German conservatives, in that Schiemann began to expose the fallacy that the Baltic German national and cultural privileges *could* originate in 200-year-old treaties with a bygone ruler of Russia. Instead, he reasoned, culture and nationality necessarily derived from free choice. He made his point by positing a parallel with religion, which had been decided by earlier despots for their subjects. But just as religion came to be seen in civilised societies as purely a matter of personal conviction, so too was the right to 'practise' one's nationality and culture. The theme was to become central to his thinking on minority issues between the World Wars.

Schiemann's move to Riga thus brought to an end the harmony he had once enjoyed with leading Baltic German circles. He accepted in his own mind the inevitability of a showdown with Baltic German reactionaries. After his crushing repudiation of articles published in the conservative *Rigasche Zeitung*, which had deeply offended him by mocking the 'ideal of freedom', Schiemann finally drew upon himself the full force of conservative displeasure. He endured from then on not only virulent press attacks and the overt hostility of leading Baltic German circles, but social ostracism and even an attempt at an organized boycott of the *Rigasche Rundschau*. His father was consoled for the 'loss' of a son. 'Red Schiemann' virtually became a 'bogeyman'. Unrepentant, Schiemann' looked back in his end-of-year editorial on 'frightened conservatism', obsessed with its past, slowly trying to revive itself, its own press tirelessly crooning 'the lullaby of its superiority'. He ended cuttingly: 'Self-awareness is a necessary and strong companion in life's struggles. But it cannot be replaced by complacency.'[47]

Such was the pressure mobilised by Schiemann's enemies that even the BKP executive became alarmed. Richard Ruetz, still not financially independent, was persuaded to have Schiemann's political articles for the paper vetted in future by the party secretary—something decidedly unwelcome to their author. However, his conviction that the very future of Baltic German society depended on it uniting as an electoral body behind a moderate liberal programme gave him no alternative to staying with the *Rigasche Rundschau*. In any case his own articles—he wrote 600 between 1907 and 1914,—were a major factor in the paper's rising circulation figures during those same years, from 6,000 to 20,000.

In 1907 Schiemann also replaced Axel Schmidt—'who wielded a rather leaden pen'—as first political editor. Characteristically he kept on good terms with his predecessor, even when Schmidt founded a new liberal paper, *Rigasche Neueste Nachrichten*, and Ruetz's financial backers banned its mention in the *Rigasche Rundschau*. Schiemann considered resigning at this point and joining Schmidt's venture but his father dissuaded him. Although Julius Schiemann remained personally convinced that the *Ritterschaften* had to be supported, he scrupulously respected his son's right to a different opinion. He therefore persuaded Paul not to risk his career in journalism as well as the ruin of his political ambitions in his own homeland by leaving Ruetz for a paper that would almost certainly collapse.[48]

Julius Schiemann was also shrewd enough to stress that he set great store by his son continuing with his drama criticism, which was something dear to Paul Schiemann himself. He managed during this period to complete an extensive study of nineteenth-century drama, yielding seven public lectures in the winter of 1911. These eventually appeared as a book in 1912, *On the Road towards a New Drama*, where he explored how specific problems of destiny and character development in drama were affected by the spirit of any given epoch. Schiemann's theatrical writing continued to compensate to some extent for the curtailment of overt political commentary on Baltic issues as a result of the increasingly nationalist and reactionary mood in St Petersburg. All the more lively was the debate in the paper on the intellectual and moral life of Baltic Germandom, marked by the vitality of Schiemann's own style and a capacity for finding the *mot juste*.

In so far as political undertones coloured his every article he had indirect political influence through the readership of the *Rigasche Rundschau*.[49] However, Schiemann had no prospect of direct participation in the political processes as a mere thirty-year-old 'burdened with liberal views'. He inhabited a society where the influential élites saw no need for a political press except at election time. Richard Ruetz also insisted that a political journalist had to retain his independence of judgement by not being a politician, just as in his view a theatre critic should neither act in nor help manage a theatre. Schiemann had to be content, apart from the odd speeches at party meetings, with working for a section of the Association concerned with literature and art.

Even in theatrical matters Schiemann ran foul of the forces of reaction in Riga. While his drama reviews were admired in authoritative circles, he could not avoid criticising the management of the theatre from time to time. Behind this, however, stood the theatre committee of the socially exclusive Great Guild. This now had a more decorative role, being increasingly concerned with charity and preserving its traditions, but doubtless for this reason it regarded itself as a bastion of the good old days. 'And woe betide anybody', Schiemann recalled, 'who voiced a contrary opinion of this institution.'[50] That is precisely what he did during a dispute over the new management of the theatre in 1908. As a result representatives from the Great Guild demanded that Schiemann cease to be theatre critic. Ruetz refused, and the *Rigasche Rundschau*'s two concessionary seats were duly withdrawn.

By now Schiemann fully and finally acknowledged that he had 'completely fallen foul of that sector of Germandom categorised as the good society'.[51] His lifestyle in Riga, where Anita Remani lived with him from time to time, and where he enjoyed the city's colourful night life in the company of other actresses and entertainers, did not endear him to the Baltic German establishment, which duly subjected him to the ignominy of being publicly blackballed from membership in the city's exclusive German club, *Der Musse*. Schiemann felt this calculated slight from his social peers deeply, attributing to it his subsequent reticence in the company of strangers.[52]

Not long after, on 4 March 1911, Paul Schiemann's father died on a visit to Riga, a few days after suffering a stroke during lunch with his son and daughter, Leonore Rüdiger. The inevitable sadness that Paul Schiemann felt was compounded by the knowledge that both he and his brothers Julius and Oscar had caused their father so many sleepless nights through their behaviour. He also regretted that a strict regime in childhood had made it difficult for him and his brothers to get closer to their father as grown men. Julius Schiemann was at least spared seeing his son Paul being badly injured in the side the following year, having been provoked into a duel by two men at a nearby table in a restaurant. As Schiemann dryly recorded of his pre-war years in Riga, 'There was no shortage of escapades.'[53] Changes came during the summer of 1913, when he met a promising young Munich actress, Charlotte Schüler. The two were married on 2 February 1914, after Schiemann had parted amicably from Anita Remani. Not surprisingly he remembered too the 'satiated pre-war atmosphere' and 'its comfort, recklessness and peace'. The Schiemanns moved into a larger house and 'the glorious summer of 1914 had begun'.[54] In emotional terms Schiemann was not between two eras but had made an important transition.

That could also be said of his political and intellectual convictions. 'Whoever works for the future must free himself from the dreams of the past,' Schiemann had urged in 1911.[55] He had certainly met this test. Personal abuse and attacks from his own class and people, as well as from Latvians, failed to deflect him from the pursuit of moderate liberal reform. In 1913 he reiterated his certainty that the only obstacle to the German minority renewing itself 'in the sunlight of political freedom' was its refusal to give other citizens the rights it claimed for itself.[56] This was still some way from the degree of political democratisation characteristic of Western Europe, but even so Schiemann's pleas were ignored. Georg von Rauch tellingly wrote: 'There are no historical grounds for assuming that from 1905 onwards the German upper class was seriously thinking of subjecting the essentially aristocratic constitution of the Baltic territories to a complete overhaul along democratic lines.'[57] That Baltic nationalists would not have been content even with this was evident from their branding as treachery any practical co-operation with Germans in city elections.[58] Still, Schiemann clung to his hopes of forging a multi-national liberal grouping. For example he initiated the first of two Baltic press congresses in 1910 between liberal Baltic German and Latvian journalists: no real collegiality developed between the two camps but they did endorse Schiemann's resolution pledging them not to attack the cultural efforts of each nationality.[59]

Rapprochement between nationalities had already become the focal point of Schiemann's efforts. Almost every second article he wrote before 1914 was coloured by explicit or implicit warnings against nationalism, whether of the Russian, German, Latvian or any other variety. In truth, the influential forces at work within both the Baltic German and Latvian communities before 1914 offered little hope of change. Ironically, neither Baltic German nor Latvian nationalists at that stage seriously envisaged an independent Latvian state. Apart from the left wing of the Latvian underground movement, there was little in the way of effective political organisation or mobilisation for national ends, despite the remarkable cultural and economic developments among the majority population.[60] The matter at issue was the administration and government of the Baltic provinces, and on that there was no prospect of consensus, particularly once the Russian government quietly shelved regional reform projects. The *Ritterschaften* stayed loyal to the Tsar, and the idea of switching allegiance to the Kaiser actively appealed to only a small minority of Baltic Germans.[61] War soon changed this.

2. Leaving Russia

Few would have predicted at the outbreak of war in 1914 that the conflict could bring about the end of the mighty Russian Empire, and Paul Schiemann reasoned that disloyalty to the Tsar would have brought disaster on Baltic Germans. Although he deplored all war as a reversion to barbarism, he could not see how military service could be refused. 'Once war came, the individual had to share the common fate and do his duty. War can only be opposed in times of peace.'[1] Schiemann duly reported as a reserve officer to an echelon of a dragoon regiment of the 12th Cavalry Division. His misgivings were compounded by the presence of his older brother in the opposing German army. In the event Paul Schiemann was posted to the Turkish and Austrian theatres in the early months of the fighting.

He had three weeks training before going to the front and wrote to his wife asking if she wished to visit him, 'but the journey is long and you know no Russian, so it would be dangerous for you.' Lotte Schiemann felt depressed at being left alone in Riga so soon after their marriage and rose to the challenge. She arrived in Mirgorod after an eventful journey, posing sometimes as an Englishwoman and relying when necessary on her one Russian phrase, 'I am an officer's wife.'[2] The pair were next re-united after Schiemann received a severe shrapnel wound in the upper arm early in 1915 and went back to Riga for a brief convalescence. He had already been decorated for bravery, his commander stressing Schiemann's *sang-froid* in battle. Schiemann himself dismissively ascribed this impression to his inability, even during the fighting, not to smoke one cigarette after another.[3] He now found in the inflamed patriotism at home a startling contrast to the easy camaraderie he had experienced among the different nationalities at the front.

Hostility to the Baltic Germans was overt and actively encouraged by the Russian Governor-General. Schiemann's mother Anna, whose name appeared on a list of deportees bound for Siberia because she had a son in the German army, was reprieved only because he was a decorated Russian officer. The civic life of the Baltic German minority had been virtually suspended, their language was banned in public, their associations were dissolved, and their schools and newspapers closed.[4] That fate befell the *Rigasche Rundschau* during Schiemann's leave, which coincided with the fatal heart attack of the paper's proprietor, Richard Ruetz, whose son Alfred, was only able to continue with the paper for a while as a Russian-language publication. Overnight the *Rundschau* became the *Rishkoje Obosrenij*.[5]

In the paper's editorial offices at 7 Domplatz the novelist and St Petersburg journalist Oscar Grosberg, who settled in Riga during the War and later worked on the *Rigasche Rundschau* himself, came across an armed Paul Schiemann, his shoulder in a sling, putting in a brief editorial spell and firmly controlling his feelings as a Baltic German surrounded by Russians.[6] Disapproval from the Baltic German leaders was the price Schiemann was prepared to pay to ensure a semblance of objective war reporting in an environment otherwise publishing virulently anti-German accounts.[7] He found solace as ever in the company of close friends, for the wartime ban on alcohol consumption was circumvented in Riga by serving schnapps and wine in coffee jugs in the restaurants. In private officers could have what they wanted.[8]

Like Schiemann himself, Baltic Germans as a whole were reluctant to break with the Tsar while he occupied the throne, but the cumulative hostility towards the German element during the war undermined its loyalty to the Empire. In Schiemann's words, hearts had long since crossed the frontier. He might have added, bodies too, given the large exodus of Baltic Germans to the Reich after 1914. A turning-point came with the occupation of Lithuania and the subsequent incorporation of Courland in 1915, under Major Alfred von Gossler, into the German army's administrative unit for the conquered Baltic territories, Land Ober-Ost. The émigré Baltische Vertrauensrat in Berlin insisted that Baltic Germans faced the stark choice of being 'annexed by Germany or massacred by Russia'.[9] They found willing helpers in the German Army High Command (OHL), bent on weakening Russia permanently by rolling back its borders, a goal endorsed by the Kaiser and a swathe of reactionary and pan-German political sentiment in the Reich.

For different reasons a number of German liberal politicians and intellectuals were also not averse to seeing the Baltic provinces detached from Russia. These 'ethical imperialists' envisaged war eventually bringing a full-scale reordering of the multinational region between Russia and the West but nevertheless still firmly under German tutelage, if enlightened—a vision of *Mitteleuropa* famously articulated in the book that Friedrich Naumann published in 1915.[10] Russia's vulnerability on the nationalities issue also prompted the Auswärtiges Amt to appeal to neutral opinion by calling the Liga der fremdvölker Russlands (League of Foreign Nationalities of Russia) into being in 1916 under the Lithuanian German, Baron von der Ropp.[11] What seemed on the surface a broad political consensus in the Reich to deprive Russia of its border provinces in truth barely concealed an underlying fragility of purpose, but this was only fully exposed when separation of the region became reality in 1918.

Schiemann's own experience of the war and his entrenched dislike of extreme nationalism made him desire a peace where no single power would be triumphant. He had witnessed the start of the 'senseless evacuation' of Riga's industry by the worried Russians before his leave ended in 1915 when, at the instigation of his old friend General Lieutenant Aljoscha Dellingshausen, he headed a small mounted detachment and found himself on patrol between Vilnius and the front. He was soon decorated for the second time after coming under fire. He then served briefly as adjutant in a special formation evacuating Vilnius before resuming sentry duties in Polozk. Once more he was united with Charlotte. She remained with her husband for much of 1916 and early 1917, when Schiemann's unit shifted to trench duty in Viborg in Finland, in anticipation of war with Sweden. The worst that Schiemann recalled of the period was a flurry of anxiety over his wife's 'serious abdominal operation'. With the outbreak of revolution in Russia in February 1917 he was relocated to Dünaburg, only to fall ill with pneumonia. The prognosis from a doctor attached to a nearby Cossack regiment was gloomy, yet his health improved when Charlotte came to nurse him and he soon resumed smoking. Nothing could part him for long from the cigarette packet.[12]

Against the daily background of military routines the contours of Schiemann's future political career also emerged. The Russian Provisional Government formed in February 1917 nominally ended the historic threefold division of the Baltic provinces with a law of 30 March. It created two new self-governing units of Estonia (Northern Livonia and Estonia) and Latvia (Southern Livonia and Courland). Expectation of further reforms ran high among liberals. The party Schiemann was to lead after the war, the German Balt Democratic Party, first surfaced as the Democratic Party of Russian Citizens of German Nationality. In the charged atmosphere it grew rapidly following its inaugural meeting under Roman Schlachat on 23 April 1917. At the invitation of the chairman, Johannes von Eckardt, Schiemann took special leave to head the party's list for the Riga elections on 13 August, when he duly became a city councillor. While the Democratic Party anticipated 'an era of democratic change', it was divided over how moderate or radical reforms would be.[13] Schiemann only had time to contribute a pamphlet to the debate in July, where he advocated greater intervention in the economy.[14] In 1917 his attention was in fact devoted less to the detail of policy than to the overall reform of Russia. On that his doubts had deepened. To help pass the long winter evenings in Finland he had translated aloud from the major nineteenth-century Russian literary and critical texts for his wife's benefit, and was struck by the 'characteristic inflexibility' of the Russian intelligentsia.[15]

The arguments inside the Democratic Party were suspended when it was banned under the German occupation of Riga from 3 September 1917. Schiemann recalled the event being noisily hailed as a liberation by most inhabitants of the city, although he personally had returned to the front.[16] The youngest Schiemann, Julius, now joined his brother Paul's unit, shortly after the execution of officers in his own infantry regiment by revolutionary order. Soldiers had the right after the Bolshevik coup in October 1917 to reduce unpopular officers to the ranks and to elect their chosen leaders, but Paul Schiemann's men endorsed his command.[17] Nevertheless, by December, as Lenin's regime opened peace talks with Germany, Schiemann sensed that Russia's new masters no longer valued the existing army. The likelihood of further military action was discounted and 'brotherhood was celebrated' in the German trenches. Had Schiemann not chosen to remain with his younger brother, he could have expected early discharge on grounds of seniority. Danger came from elsewhere and for officers not favoured by the troops the situation could be grim.

Schiemann personally discovered the risks after an unpleasant grilling from a 'brutal looking commissar-soldier', where he parried questions about his attitude to Lenin and Trotsky by feigning lack of interest in politics.[18] Soon the disappearance of the unit's money supply—stolen by the soldiers themselves as it later transpired—again brought the Schiemann brothers for interrogation before the same hostile commissar. In spite of a formal deposition of support and trust from Schiemann's men, he and Julius faced the likelihood of a people's tribunal when their military service eventually ended. Schiemann had often calculated the risk of being shot as a political enemy, but found unbearable the prospect of execution as a common criminal. Using a trusted contact in an infantry regiment in Dünaburg, Adam von Gernet, the Schiemanns escaped by sledge and then foot across the German front line, subsequently travelling with immense relief to Riga. Paul Schiemann felt real fear for the first and only time in his life during this escapade, haunted by the 'gruesome' thought of being caught by Bolsheviks as a thief on the run.[19] It was now March 1918.

Lotte Schiemann had enjoyed theatrical success in German—occupied Riga but was staying with her parents in Bavaria at the time of her husband's return to the city. His financial position was parlous, relieved marginally by the fact that clothes originally purchased for his wedding were still at the home of his sister Leonore and brother-in-law, Wilhelm von Rüdiger. Alfred Ruetz—who had prospered and owned substantial property on the Domplatz—failed to honour his father's commitments; Schiemann extracted only a small sum from him and the promise of employment if the *Rigasche Rundschau* reopened. Luckily he found room in the house of an old friend, Baron Fritz von Stromberg. Schiemann promptly set to work expanding his study of Russian intellectuals into an investigation of the psychological causes of 1917. A major factor, he believed, was the Russian intellectual tradition's ill-judged belief in the innate goodness of the masses and a resultant failure to raise political awareness. October 1917 suggested to Schiemann that the domination of the proletariat, arising from the combination of rapid democratisation and political immaturity, could only lead to anarchy. Socialism—of the Russian variety—placed the economic construction of the state 'in the hands of those with nothing to lose', whereas the 'social idea' presupposed a strong economy and state for its realisation. Schiemann was thinking less of centralisation than of some form of institutionalised collaboration between different economic interest groups within a parliamentary democracy respecting the individual; indifference to the latter 'leads to the state of drones.'[20]

While Schiemann was working at his book, the German military authorities suddenly arrested him. The incident was not unrelated to the fact that his return to Riga coincided with the advance of the German forces into Estonia and the conclusion of the German-Soviet Treaty of Brest-Litovsk in March 1918. Estonians and Latvians had responded to the Bolshevik coup with the first clear calls for independence, and since both Lenin and the Allied leaders acknowledged the principle of national self-determination, the German government also had to pay lip-service. When Brest-Litovsk, together with supplementary clauses appended in August, detached Russia's Baltic provinces and placed them under German tutelage, it was stipulated that their future be determined 'in agreement with their populations'. In reality the Estonian declaration of a republic on 24 February—the day between the departure of Soviet troops and the arrival of the Germans—was ignored by the Reich government. Had the Latvians been able to voice their wishes most would have echoed the call from the newly-formed Latvian Provisional National Council. At its inaugural meeting in non-German—occupied territory in mid-November 1917 the council insisted that the future of 'Latvia'—embracing Vidzeme (Livland), Kurzeme (Courland) and Latgale (Lettgallia)—would have to be decided by a constitutional assembly elected by the *Latvian* people.[21]

Instead the German occupation authorities chose to 'consult' a General Provincial Assembly, containing a smattering of compliant Estonians and Latvians but dominated by the traditional Baltic German élites. On 12 April the assembly appealed to the Kaiser to make a German protectorate of a united 'Baltic state', opening the way for a future personal union with the Prussian crown.[22] The strategy immediately met strong resistance from the reformist 'majority parties' in the Reichstag-liberals, centrists and social democrats—who were engaged in trying to reduce monarchical power. 'Germany can only make this peace treaty last', the Centre Party spokesman Matthias Erzberger argued, 'if it uses the time between now and the general peace settlement to promote the general contentment of Russia's western border nations.'[23] The efforts to implement Brest-Litovsk's provisions for self-determination and dissolve the military occupation authorities effectively linked the future of the Baltic provinces with the outcome of the mounting struggle for democratisation in Germany.[24] For the time being, however, events in Estonia, Livonia and Courland remained under the control of the OHL and their Baltic German collaborators.

These did not welcome Schiemann's return to Riga. He made an immediate impact on political discussions, contacting all elements of German society, accepting numerous speaking engagements, visiting landed estates, responding to visits from delegates from Latvian parties as well as Jewish representatives, and going to Tartu and Tallinn for discussions with Germans and non-Germans alike.[25] It was all too much for one of his old adversaries, Livonian Privy Councillor Max von Sivers Roemershof, the man who instigated Schiemann's imprisonment on the grounds that he was a spy and pro-Latvian.[26] Fortunately, Schiemann was released after ten days through the good offices of brother-in-law Wilhelm von Rüdiger and a City Elder, Wilhelm Reimers, both advisers on city affairs to the German military administration. The stipulation was that Schiemann should leave the occupied area and meanwhile refrain from journalism and politics. A military police officer detailed to keep observation on him complained of being kept out until 5 o'clock every morning, but his charge somehow finished his manuscript on Russian intellectuals. It was dispatched immediately to the famous uncle, together with an urgent request to arrange an entry visa for the Reich. Funding was still desperately needed.[27] Schiemann had a small advance as the Berlin correspondent of the liberal paper tolerated by the military administration, the *Baltische Zeitung.* Its 'talented and progressive' editor, Wilhelm Baum, saw Schiemann as a valuable link between liberal circles in Berlin and Riga.[28] Schiemann had already written for the paper as 'Civis', a subterfuge abandoned in mid-August 1918, when he was formally commissioned to write four articles a month for 40 marks each.[29]

The move to Germany was finally made possible, however, through the generosity of a new acquaintance, a young Baltic German from Estonia, Ewald Ammende. Because his father was an avid reader of the pre-war *Rigasche Rundschau*, Ammende had encountered and been inspired as a schoolboy by Schiemann's ideas. Ammende went on to study economics at Cologne before working for his father's export business in Pärnu during the war. At the time of the Bolshevik coup he was in German—occupied Ukraine, trying to organise four wagonloads of sugar for Riga. Only one got through, but the profits were enough to support Ammende's gregarious style of life in the city. His offer of an interest-free loan enabled Schiemann to leave Latvian territory in June, collecting Lotte from Bavaria *en route* to Berlin. His finances were boosted by 1,000 marks on the publication of his *Fiasco of Russian Democracy.* It had a laudatory foreword by Theodor Schiemann, recently appointed Rector to the University of Tartu. Additional income trickled in from his political writing for the *Frankfurter Zeitung*, the weekly *Korrespondenz Osteuropa* and the *Preussische Jahrbücher.*[30] He also resumed theatre criticism for *Welt am Montag*, but only briefly; he realised that war had blunted his sensibilities and he 'was no longer the theatre critic he had once been'.[31] Politics now wholly absorbed him since in Berlin he had reached at long last a receptive audience for his ideas.

Schiemann's initial contact with a charmed and influential circle of German liberal academics, politicians and publicists came via Hans von Eckardt (son of Schiemann's liberal colleague from Riga, Johannes von Eckardt) and Baron von der Ropp. They engaged him to cover Estonian and Latvian issues in their unofficial-Bureau für Ostpolitik and soon introduced him to the Weber brothers: Alfred, persistent critic of German's annexationist war aims and a key figure among liberal politicians associated with the *Berliner Tageblatt*, and Max, eminent sociologist and incidentally a formative influence on Schiemann's self-confessed pre-war intellectual mentor Friedrich Naumann.[32] Other liberal politicians he met, apart from Naumann and the Webers, were Theodor Heuss and Hans Delbrück.

Delbrück was also Professor of History in Berlin and editor of the *Preussische Jahrbücher.* He opened more doors for Schiemann by inviting him to his political discussion evenings.[33] Guests included State Secretary Bernhard Derburg, Professors Adolf Harnack and

Friedrich Meinecke, Paul Rohrbach, Otto Gessler—the future Reichswehr Minister—and senior army officers.[34] Through Ropp, Schiemann also forged ties with a number of Auswärtiges Amt officials later involved with Germany's post-war Baltic policy; Herbert von Dircksen, Baron von Thermann (son-in-law to Wilhelm Reimers) and the highly intelligent future head of the Eastern Department of the Auswärtiges Amt, Baron Ago von Maltzan.[35]

Ironically, then, Schiemann's political enemies in Riga did his political career a service and their own cause harm by bundling him off to Germany in the summer of 1918. The setbacks following Germany's unsuccessful spring offensive in the West made all the more urgent the need for durable solutions in the East, where the impact of military occupation was prompting Estonians and Latvians to turn increasingly towards 'the arbitration of Europe and America'.[36] To mounting concerns in Berlin about German influence declining in the border states were added worries about long-term damage to German-Russian relations arising from the OHL's 'forward policy'.[37] Doubtless the Webers, Naumann and others in their circle still felt that stability for Russia's lost border states depended on them remaining within the framework of a German—dominated Mitteleuropa. Even so they were committed to national tolerance and greater democratisation in East Central Europe whatever happened.[38]

Such figures could hardly fail to value deep knowledge of Baltic affairs of a man like Paul Schiemann, untainted by occupation politics and known for his fiercely independent journalism and advocacy of multi-national politics. Soon after Delbrück met Schiemann he commissioned him to write a major article for his *Preussische Jahrbücher* on Baltic issues. This intellectual rationale of the ethical imperialist view of Brest-Litovsk catches Schiemann inexorably transmuting from an advocate of greater national cooperation in the Baltic provinces to the supporter of independent Estonia and Latvia which he undoubtedly was by autumn 1918.[39] In his opinion a sufficient legal basis for creating a united Baltic state from the three Baltic provinces already existed in the terms of Brest-Litovsk, in conjunction with the Bolshevik decree of November 1917 on the right of national self-determination. He never again countenanced suggestions that Russia's wellbeing depended in any way on controlling

Baltic ports, and roundly dismissed arguments in favour of revising Brest-Litovsk merely to placate Russia. To do so was an error reflecting 'past preconditions no longer applicable' and 'future combinations, which are speculative'.

With the case for leaving Russia made, Schiemann argued that a further expression of local political will was needed to determine what sort of unitary Baltic state would be built. The residual distrust he felt concerning the impact of mass politics and the radicalisation of the Latvian Social Democratic Party was very evident. 'I tried to prove [in *The Fiasco of Russian Democracy*] that an absolute democracy, in attempting to control social upheavals, must founder on the apolitical nature of the masses and generate lasting manifestations of disorder, making Bolshevism with its anarchy seem merely an inevitable continuation of democratic revolution.' To Schiemann this danger justified the Reich's continuing engagement in the process. He reasoned first that Germany could not meet its treaty obligation to maintain order by sanctioning political systems likely to produce *dis*order. It therefore had to use its presence to redress what today would be categorised as the democratic deficit, by politically educating broad sectors of the Baltic population before it was too late. He saw this as the key to persuading Baltic populations to identify their interests as a whole with Germany's policy on *Mitteleuropa*.[40]

Schiemann's views on the political immaturity of the Estonian and Latvian masses appear today distinctly patrician. However, in endorsing the move towards Baltic independence in the fullness of time he attacked the premisses on which the Baltic German aristocracy still operated. While their rigged provincial assemblies engaged with Reich authorities in drafting political and economic conventions to tie the provinces permanently to the Kaiser's Germany, Schiemann concentrated on how best to give immediate expression to the national aspirations of Estonians and Latvians.[41] Specifically, he recommended democratic elections within three separate curias, respectively for Latvians, Estonians and Baltic Germans. This, and the suggestion that the national parliament be constituted only by the three curia meeting together, would ensure national parity for Baltic Germandom in the lengthy interim before full democracy could be risked.

Schiemann's commitment to winning over the Baltic populations was absolute. It would 'blunt any attacks from our enemies at the eventual peace conference and must be incomparably more effective than the tepid backing of a weak Russia, burdened by a thousand cares, and won over only at the cost of all our successes in the East.' Germanisation was rejected in the lapidary phrase: 'Every restriction on national self-development means a decline in the standing of the German Reich in the eastern zone.'[42] Not surprisingly the gradualist thrust of Schiemann's article in the *Preussische Jahrbücher* met with the approval and support of Delbrück and other German liberals.[43]

That Baltic German conservatives recognised the threat to their own plans from Schiemann's activities in Berlin is clear from the Baltische Vertrauensrat's immediate resort to personal smears to keep their adversary out of politics.[44] Vertrauensrat members still smarted under Schiemann's diatribe in early August against those 'who could not conceive of a Baltic without preserving German Balt domination.' This outburst also marked the beginning of an emotional correspondence from August to October 1918 with his uncle Theodor.[45] In a blunt opening missive on 17 August the uncle regretted ever introducing his nephew to a wider public, urging him to keep out of politics and to stick to the theatre and Russian literature. The 'advice' was rejected with an impassioned reference by Paul Schiemann to his 'life's purpose', namely 'to unite my fellow countrymen in a political community assuring our homeland the fortune of a peaceful cultural development'. His realisation that this was the only route Baltic Germandom *could* follow, given the course of the war and the Reich's declared political programme, appeared so overwhelmingly important 'that the petty intrigues of my political enemies, evident as soon as I got back from Russia, can neither embitter me nor dissuade me from my purpose.' He added later that he was so 'accustomed to Balt conservatives always resorting to personal calumny and dishonourable attacks to make their political case, that I would feel something amiss if the tone from this camp suddenly changed.'[46]

Schiemann also took heart from the realisation that his ideas were 'more than ever shared' by those Baltic and Reich Germans familiar with developments in the Border States. The only people behaving in a way likely to endanger the future of Germandom in the Baltic provinces, as well as Germany's standing in the East, were the 'little gaggle of Sivers' followers'. If this remark illustrated Schiemann's capacity to shoot from the hip, Theodor Schiemann's graceless reference to what his late brother Julius might have thought merited merely dignified dismissal: 'We agreed', said Paul Schiemann of his father, 'on two important points, respect for the individual and the right to free development for every national culture.' On this the gulf between uncle and nephew was starkly revealed as unbridgeable. The former claimed after 1905 to distrust not only Latvians—'a disloyal, treacherous, brutish race'—but Jews and, 'to a lesser extent', Estonians. 'To allow these people equality in the coming Baltic state is, I think, as harmful and dangerous to the future of the Baltic Germans as it is to the future of the German Reich.' Completing the inversion of his nephew's arguments, Theodor Schiemann favoured thorough Germanisation of the Baltic provinces.

It was his nephew's analysis that was vindicated as September wore on, bringing adverse reports from the battlefronts and generating an increasingly critical and assertive tone in the Reichstag debates. By the middle of the month Schiemann was confidently reassuring an anxious inquirer that his connections with the Reichstag majority convinced him that 'under no circumstances' would a violation of the national or political rights of the Latvian people be allowed.[47] During September Schiemann also did his best to make sure that the Reichstag heard a clear and united voice from Baltic German liberals at least.[48] In the Auswärtiges Amt frustration slowly gave way to a more determined mood. There were signs of greater forcefulness in representing the office's viewpoint with the OHL.[49] Thus Schiemann interceded successfully through his contact with Under State Secretary von Rechenberg for the release by the German occupying authorities of several political figures, including the future president of Estonia, Konstantin Päts.[50]

Then, suddenly, the entire situation was dramatically transformed by the Army's insistence at the end of September on an immediate armistice to prevent a military disaster for Germany. There followed the formation on 3 October of Prince Max of Baden's government—the first in Germany's history responsible to parliament. The projected time—scale for political reforms in the East receded to the realm of fiction.

Schiemann seized the opportunity in *Hour of Crisis*, published on the day Prince Max's government was formed, to warn that the changes within Germany would deprive Baltic Germans of the support they had during the war, making it all the more urgent that they join in the construction of a new state and thus thwart the 'enemy of all culture'—Bolshevism. 'We can no longer go back to Russia. Even if a viable state again arises from the present chaos, it will be so weakened culturally and economically that being part of it will not strengthen but seriously damage our economic, political and intellectual interests.' Baltic Germans must finally 'abandon unrealisable and to that extent unjustified claims'. Since the majority Baltic peoples needed to exercise for themselves the freedom won (from Russia) through Brest-Litovsk, Baltic Germans would have to secure their cultural rights acting as a minority, 'to which the history of this land condemns us'.[51] It was Schiemann, together with Ropp, who provided the decisive push in Berlin for a new Baltic policy, in a jointly written memorandum handed over to Prince Max on 7 October 1918.[52] In it the dangers of Bolshevism again loomed large.

The threat from the East to 'freedom, culture, life and property' should persuade all, irrespective of nationality and class, to put up with the German occupation for a bit longer, but only until local police and military forces could be formed as a matter of 'dire necessity'. Meanwhile, Schiemann and Ropp proposed immediate changes to the nature of occupation in a seven-point plan, which included transferring overall responsibility for Baltic affairs from the Reich Interior Ministry to the Auswärtiges Amt and the creation of three organisational committees, each representing the various nationalities. The committees would then carry out wide-ranging soundings in the Estonian, Latvian and Lithuanian parts of the Baltic before convening three regional assemblies. These would then prepare for elections. Polling would preferably be through electoral curia to cater for minority interests. Alternatively, three provisional governments might be appointed, each with a German adviser responsible for Reich officials until their replacement by native officers. Restoration of the local self-governing bodies in the Baltic provinces would be a further guarantee that the military authorities would be quickly dismantled.[53]

Events thus finally conspired with conviction in Schiemann's call for establishing independent Baltic states as the only way to prevent chaos in the region and lasting hostility to Germany. Prince Max's government, under the watchful eye of the Reichstag majority, was already searching for new directions in foreign policy. Schiemann's plea therefore fell on fertile ground. The advantages were quickly seen of opening a dialogue with local peoples before the Baltic question came up at the armistice and peace talks.[54] Schiemann had the satisfaction of being told by a social democrat Reichstag deputy and under state secretary at the Auswärtiges Amt, Eduard David, that his proposals would be acted on. He was assigned to accompany the Progressive People's Party politician, Professor Gerhart von Schulze-Gaevernitz, on a fact-finding visit to Tallinn and Riga. They were to make initial soundings with Estonians and Latvians about setting up two republics.[55] Schiemann lost no time writing to enlist Alfred Ruetz' help in publicising the forthcoming visit. He suggested that Ruetz should be the representative of the Baltic German bourgeoisie on the planned organisation committee, alongside Nikolai von Klot as spokesman for the nobility, the lawyer Paul Mintz for the Jews, and for the Latvians Mikelis Valters.[56]

Ruetz was also informed of another initiative useful to 'our young states', aiming to set up an organization to promote the idea of the League of Nations, the East European Association for the Foundation of the League of Nations (Osteuropäisches Verband zur Begründung des Völkerbundes). On 15 October, only days before travelling to Riga, Schiemann became a founding member of this 'free association of citizens of the people, states and areas once belonging to the former Russian Empire'. Envisaged as a successor to the Liga der Fremdvölker—now virtually defunct as a result of the Empire's break-up—the new body propagated the idea of the League of Nations and eventual League membership for independent border states ruled by governments with 'genuine popular support'. Schiemann had already taken over from Ropp the burdensome *Neutral Correspondence* and promoting the new East European Association added greatly to his growing workload, even though the organization foundered eventually on differences between the border states themselves. Ironically, although the episode drove Uncle Theodor to voice shame at sharing the same family name as his nephew, the Ukrainians at first objected to working with 'Schiemann' in the new association because they assumed the person in question to be the Kaiser's celebrated but heartily disliked personal adviser.[57]

When Paul Schiemann left with Schulze-Gaevernitz for the Baltic provinces on 18 October he was hopeful that the time left to the Reich before the withdrawal of troops from the border states could be put to constructive effect. The Provincial Assembly leaders had discovered the general drift of Schiemann's proposals and, once more, disappointment was his reward. On 20 October 1918, the very day that an Auswärtiges Amt directive marked the dramatic shift in Ostpolitik by formally abandoning the concept of a personal union, the Baltic German leaders insisted on their corporations being the only properly constituted representatives of the Baltic lands.[58] Schulze-Gaevernitz and Schiemann were received as unwelcome guests at the party in Riga, but at least the occupation authorities treated the German parliamentarian with the minimum courtesies. Not so Schiemann, who was again placed under police observation. The idea of preparing for Baltic independence was branded as treachery, and press coverage of the visit was banned.

Under these conditions no progress was made, either with setting up the planned organisational committees, or with promoting the League. Schiemann reassured Arveds Bergs and V. Zāmuels that the German government's policy would prevail sooner or later, only to discover preparations being made by the Latvians themselves to form a representative assembly on the basis of agreements between different political groupings and organisations. The proposed Latvian National Council would reportedly be open only to properly constituted political parties, including those of the national minorities.[59] Schiemann at once agreed, in discussions with his close friend and future parliamentary colleague Lothar Schoeler, the importance of founding a German party.[60] When he finally reached Tallinn—after wiring Berlin to circumvent visa obstacles imposed by the German military authority in Riga—he listened to the demand of Estonian leaders for German recognition of the republic they had already proclaimed in February 1918. He promised to do what he could to arrange for an Estonian delegation to come to Berlin, although in the event neither he nor the Auswärtiges Amt could persuade the OHL to issue the relevant visas.[61]

This behaviour is less astonishing than it seems. Admittedly the German representatives in Riga were officially informed by the Auswärtiges Amt on 1 November of the new focus on the majority populations and the 'hope for governments to be created which will survive the peace conference'.[62] Moreover, Ludendorff's successor from 26 October, General Wilhelm Groener, believed that helping the Latvians and Estonians set up their own defences might yet deter them from moving further towards the Allied camp. Schiemann also did not doubt the German government's will, but he did observe that the overriding preoccupation in Berlin with high policy throughout October and early November made for reluctance to shake up the Baltic provinces too much before the Armistice negotiations.[63] The resulting delay in appointing a civilian head to begin winding up the German occupation authorities left Major Gossler and his officials in place until December. Their response to policy directives was dilatory; latitude was taken in interpreting the German government's commitment to securing cultural and economic rights for the Baltic German element. This much is clear from Schiemann's report of his Baltic visit. According to this, not only was Latvian and Estonian sympathy for the newly—democratised Germany being eroded by the military's failure to abandon its old aims, but the OHL was deliberately exploiting fears of Bolshevik invasion to force the indigenous populations to acknowledge the 'hopelessly compromised provincial councils' and their policy. Schiemann urged re-staffing all key German administrative posts with personnel of 'democratic conviction', as well as lifting restrictions in the Baltic provinces on the press, right of assembly and the movement of individuals. These constraints were making any meaningful political life 'virtually impossible'.[64]

Paul Schiemann's commitment to independent Baltic states was now complete. It is best appreciated against the prevailing international scepticism on the subject. Close to the surface of Western thinking on intervention against Bolshevism was the idea that the Baltic territories might again become part of a re-constituted 'white' Russia. Schiemann did not expect such a Russia to reappear. Because the 'very purpose' of his work was to secure Baltic independence, his chief fear was that if 'the German administration and the Baltic German representatives continue to maintain their old standpoint, there will inevitably be divisions within the state bearing forces in the land.' The 'unavoidable consequence' would be a Bolshevik upheaval.[65] Schiemann's experience in Russia, as well as his early intellectual engagement in *Fiasco of Russian Democracy*, convinced him that Bolshevism would stay in Russia for the foreseeable future. In his journalism, in pamphlets and in his correspondence he felt driven to fight, not against the socialist economic programme as such, 'but against wilful and arbitrary socialisation, against the lust for dictatorship, inimical to all free exchange of opinion, against the overthrow of ideas of justice and rule by prescription'.[66] The critique that Schiemann developed in 1918–19 commands attention both in its own right and for the key it provides to his alternative view of society and to his subsequent work in independent Latvia.

Schiemann had two brochures published by the Anti-Bolshevik League, a body sponsored by German heavy industry: *Grief of the Masses* and *Asiatisation of Europe*, and his analysis of what Lenin was forging in Russia was far removed from the crude anti-Red diatribes common at the time. One might dispute *Grief*'s rosy view of liberal reform prospects in Russia before the Bolsheviks wrecked all with 'the simplest propaganda in the world', but its dissection of Bolshevik thinking—particularly on economics—was prescient. On the assumption that the existing economic order had relied on force alone, the Bolsheviks had decided that only through force could another system be put in its place. Wreaking revenge on the representatives of capitalism was the only socialist promise the Bolsheviks had kept. The autonomy of local soviets resulted in economic mismanagement; the suffering endured by the urban masses exceeded anything experienced in Tsarist times; the nationalisation of banks and industries made the state both creditor and debtor—in sum, Bolshevik economic reforms had been a disaster.[67]

Schiemann also elaborated on the differences he had earlier indicated in his *Fiasco of Russian Democracy* between western social democracy and the socialism 'imported' into Russia. Its veneration for the 'secret, higher wisdom' of the masses helped to explain why Lenin waged class war simply to destroy the upper class rather than to educate the proletariat. Lenin was 'the communist of a coming generation' moving towards future common ownership 'through a sea of blood, unfreedom, hunger and misery'.[68] Lenin was no social democrat because he was prepared to allow the ruin of the products of capitalist culture, whereas Marx had envisaged these being taken over by the people. 'Socialism stands for fairness, not equality, or at least only for social equality, not for equality of the clever and stupid, industrious and idle, good and bad. Socialism desires cultural and economic growth. Only the communists want a levelling down.'[69] This deadening process, Schiemann argued in *Asiatisation*, deprived work of meaning and in so doing prevented the individual's development. He deduced from this the novel conclusion that the nature of class struggle under Bolshevism was not in fact economic but cultural.[70]

These views also need to be set against Schiemann's expectation—shared by many at the time—that the era of unrestrained capitalism was drawing to an end, its bankruptcy exposed by the war. Whether socialism or bolshevism delivered the final push for change, he reasoned, was therefore critical to the world's future. The fact that so few of his contemporaries had fully grasped that socialism and Bolshevism were diametrically opposed ideas systems alarmed Schiemann. That Bolshevism was not merely a radical socialist variant he underlined by pointing to the Asiatic notion of power that the Bolsheviks were bringing towards Europe.[71] Since Schiemann saw parliamentary democracy as the only way to combat the 'Asiatisation of Europe', more imaginative ways of mitigating class war had to be found to avoid destroying trust in parliaments. Schiemann's answer was to create—alongside parliamentary assemblies, elected by direct, secret, proportional voting—some form of administrative apparatus representing the economic and cultural interests of all social strata. This would help to separate 'class' from economic power, and governments could draw intellectual and moral force from it.

Schiemann's plea for apolitical, professional expertise in alliance with government has a modern air, as does his extended justification of his proposals. Thus he reasoned: 'For resolving the class struggle economic socialisation is of secondary importance. The most important and imperative precondition for resolving class conflict is rather the state's recognition of the right of all citizens to realise their potential.' Once the state had assumed the costs of educating its children according to their needs, 'class war in today's meaning of the word disappears.' Elsewhere he wrote: 'In place of proletarianisation of culture we put the cultivation of the proletariat.'[72] These ideas were to recur in Schiemann's future work in independent Latvia. They further crystallised in November and December 1918 around the concept of 'national solidarity', during informal discussions he had with Eduard Stadtler, at that time linked with the Centre Party, the social democrat Oskar Müller, and others.

The group elaborated a programme for an Association for National Solidarity. Luckily the suggested name—National Socialist Association—never took hold and the members invariably called themselves simply 'solidarists'.[73] They envisaged a social economy, where individuals' right to realise their potential was firmly coupled with duties to the whole, but also a policy of international conciliation between all peoples and states in Europe.[74] At forty-two, Schiemann was already two years older than the cut-off date permitted for membership of the association—and he was not a German citizen—but he was involved in all its board and committee meetings. In the event he failed to agree to the association's full social programme, but thereafter he never abandoned the concept of social solidarity.[75]

It was not a term that could be applied to the Baltic German community as a whole in November 1918. The stream of innuendo directed towards Schiemann from the Baltische Vertrauensrat had reached such a pitch as to make him doubt if he would ever be able to resume political journalism in his homeland. Yet he had another important indicator of the fundamental soundness of his policy line to sustain him. His uncle Theodor, a man who had arguably done more than any single individual to influence the Kaiser to take over the Baltic provinces, and had tried so hard to dislodge his nephew from politics in the second half of 1918, capitulated in a way that Schiemann was never to forget by writing on 8 November: 'My dear Paul, I have read your letter with its enclosures and have been convinced by it that you are right and I am wrong. Until now I had no such detailed insight into the actual realities. Best thanks. Uncle Theodor.'[76] The following day the German revolution broke out abruptly terminating plans for a careful phasing out of German occupation and leading to the declaration of independent Baltic states.

3. Joining Latvia

The revolution that ended the German Empire and gave birth to a new republic under a socialist government on 9 November should have buried Baltic German hopes of controlling the Baltic provinces. German social democracy had long urged the transfer of power to the majority populations. Another pillar of Balt authority crumbled when the Armistice was signed between Germany and the Allied Powers on 11 November 1918. Among other things it declared Brest-Litovsk and its supplementary agreements to be null and void. Two days later the Soviet leaders, anticipating the retreat of German troops and preparing their own advance, also rejected Brest-Litovsk. Finally, on 18 November, Latvian political parties, with the exception of the Bolsheviks, met in German—occupied Riga to form their National Council. It promptly proclaimed an independent Latvia under a provisional government led by Kārlis Ulmanis. Schiemann welcomed the event in an article for the *Libauische Zeitung*, calling on Baltic Germans to accept the new state.[1]

Astonishingly, a further eight months were to pass before this call was answered by the German community as a whole. Shock at the speed of the 'turn of fate' in the long history of Baltic German hegemony undoubtedly brought disorientation in the winter and spring of 1918–19. A fierce critic of the *Ritterschaften* and their allies, Baron Eduard Rosenberg, portrayed them as 'helpless and wretched'—like children seeing their 'painfully constructed house of cards wrecked by a gust of wind'.[2] More sympathetic observers saw the 'rudderless' response of the German community as evidence that hitherto energies had focused exclusively on surviving (*Ausharren*) under the leadership of the *Ritterschaften*.[3] In fact their influence on policy endured for a critical period through the new Baltic German 'National Committee'. Formed on 9/10 November, it represented numerous organizations, including the political groupings crystallising among the Baltic Germans as war ended. The National Committee aspired to co-ordinate the actions of the entire Baltic German community. Schiemann described it as 'a sort of association of associations' under the leadership of the *Ritterschaften* and backed by Riga's German upper middle classes.[4]

Parties incorporating such 'old Balt' values on the National Committee included the German Balts Union (Deutsche Baltenbund) and the reactionary National Liberal Party. In the words of one of its leaders, Woldemar Wulffius, it faced 'enmity, distrust and hatred' and lacked the 'protecting hand of the Fatherland, which must abandon its oldest colony.'[5] Overt resistance to this mind-set came from Eduard Rosenberg's Progressive Party, the first new German party to form in November, as well as from the Liepāja Young Balt Union (Libauer Jungbaltenbund).[6] Both distanced themselves pointedly from previous tradition, with the former agreeing to send delegates to the Baltic German National Committee only to reduce strife.[7] Absent hitherto were the disciplined organisations and mass followings normally associated with political parties.[8] That was also true of the group Schiemann would later lead, the liberal German Balt Democratic Party, which formally constituted itself successor to the Democratic Party of Russian Citizens of German Nationality on 8 December 1918.[9]

Schiemann's first inclination in November was to join the *Landeswehr* being formed on the National Committee's initiative to defend the Latvian homeland from Bolshevik attacks, though he doubted if its leaders would welcome him. In the end economic realities prevailed; he had to support himself and his wife through paid employment. In addition to his activities for the Anti-Bolshevik League, he had taken over the running of Ropp's East European Bureau, and it soon absorbed much of his energy, becoming a meeting-point for the stream of refugees from Latvia—Russians and Jews as well as Latvians—passing through Berlin. With backing from the Auswärtiges Amt Schiemann arranged for refugees who produced his personal signed recommendation to be given residence permits. As well as his official links he exploited his longstanding connection with the theatrical world to help raise funds for an association he founded with Baltic German, Latvian and Jewish fellow-countrymen to free Riga from the Bolsheviks. Schiemann concluded with friends in Delbrück's circle that for the time being he should remain where he was,[10] and it proved to be the right decision. His office was the only effective counterweight in Berlin to the Baltische Vertrauensrat and his circle formed a nucleus of practical, multi-ethnic collaboration.

That aspect was crucially important. Only Latvian parties founded the new state, but their joint 'Political Platform' of 18 November promised to observe the national and cultural rights of the *people* of Latvia. Accordingly it offered proportional parliamentary representation for minorities. A disgruntled Wolfgang Wachtsmuth, a co-worker of Schiemann's in the 1920s, confessed in old age to astonishment at how little chauvinism was initially apparent in Latvia, although he cynically ascribed this to the country's uncertainty about surviving and its need for German support.[11] Aspirations to build a Latvia for the Latvians were certainly held in check by anxieties over the external world, but other Latvian political figures believed strongly that a multi-ethnic solution would offer the best, if not the only guarantee of their state's future viability. It was to encourage such tendencies that Schiemann and his co-workers in Berlin were bent on displaying solidarity with the Latvians in their country's 'darkest hour'.[12]

However, the Baltic German National Committee took Latvia's precariousness as an opportunity to try to secure special treatment for the German-speaking population. In talks at Riga's Hotel Rome (22–24 November) its leaders demanded that political representation of the German community, rather than its size, should reflect its 'cultural and economic significance'. There was also a bid to pre-empt legislation by calling for detailed elaboration of the Latvian promise to respect national and cultural rights. A list of National Committee 'conditions' for accepting Latvia was defiantly published in the *Baltische Zeitung* on 26 November. In effect the national parity advocated by Schiemann before 1914 was endorsed by Baltic German conservatives only when the cause was hopeless. Unsurprisingly, the Latvians rejected what amounted to a claim by the Baltic Germans to be treated as equal co-founders of the new state. For its part the National Committee continued to profess willingness to co-operate with but not yet to recognize 'Latvia'.[13] The fragility of this position was underlined by Germany's *de facto* recognition of Latvia on the very day the *Baltische Zeitung* article appeared.[14]

The uneasy co-existence to which National Committee policy condemned Baltic Germans and Latvians, before reality broke through in summer 1919, made future reconciliation extremely difficult, as Schiemann forcefully reminded his colleagues.[15] The existing political divisions within Baltic Germandom were further exacerbated by the policy of 'wait and see'. This proved too much for Eduard Rosenberg, who accepted Latvia's 'Political Platform' on 30 November, pending the convening of a constituent assembly. His party duly occupied five of the eight seats allocated to the German minority on the Latvian National Council.[16] Rosenberg and A. von Klot-Engelhardtshof became respectively State Controller and Ministerial Aid to the Trade and Industry Ministry in the Provisional Government. A week later the inaugural session of the German Balt Democratic Party also formally acknowledged the Latvian political platform. On 3 December the National Committee designated one of its members, Karl Keller, for the third government post on offer, as adjunct to the Ministry of Education. It was considered vital to the cause of German schooling.[17]

The National Committee's overall position on the Latvian state stubbornly remained that of the reluctant suitor; it wouldn't say yes and it wouldn't say no. As things stood, the precondition of *any* Baltic German policy remained the defence of Baltic territory, for on 14 December Latvian Bolshevik Peter Stučka declared a Latvian Soviet Republic. By the beginning of the New Year, Bolshevik forces held all but a strip of Courland, including Liepāja. It was here, after Riga fell on 3 January 1919, that the Ulmanis government and a reconstituted National Committee resumed their political fencing-match.[18] Notwithstanding growing opposition within its ranks, the German committee was still dominated by the old élites; the fourteen-point programme for negotiating with the Latvians was virtually indistinguishable from the demands published the previous November in Riga. The plain fact was that the German camp held the trump card—the *Landeswehr.*

Unlike the Baltenregiment in Estonia, which had at once thrown its weight behind the new state, the *Landeswehr* was not immediately integrated into Latvia's defences. It contained few Latvians and remained a predominantly Baltic German force, equipped with German materials, its officers trained by occupying German 8th Army staff. Commanded by Major Fletcher, it soon had Reich Germans alongside and mingling with it. Their presence derived from the provision in the Armistice that for the time being German troops defend 'former Russian territory'—used by Reich officials as an excuse for the replacement of exhausted regulars with fresh volunteers.[19] August Winning, social democrat and former trade union leader, transmuting to German nationalist, prepared the ground.[20] As Reich plenipotentiary entrusted with handing over the administrative reins in the Baltic lands, Winning pressured Ulmanis on 29 December into agreeing citizenship for German fighters for Latvia. The agreement was duly interpreted by Reich recruitment offices as implying offers of land, costing Ulmanis the support of the Latvian Social Democrats.[21] Inevitably, the National Committee felt its star rising as General Rüdiger von der Goltz arrived in Liepāja on 2 February 1919 to assume overall command of the German forces in the field.

Schiemann's general view of these developments derived inexorably from his critique of the *Ritterschaften*'s wrong-headedness. The policy they had pursued under German occupation had failed because it was 'inherently flawed' and not just because of Germany's military collapse. The National Committee's Achilles Heel remained its reliance on élitist, feudal principles. Schiemann saw the precondition for successful co-operation with a Latvian state as being 'a downward displacement of the social centre of gravity in our own ranks'.[22] It was not for one moment that he disputed the need to fight Bolshevism; he recorded in a letter to his mother on 9 February his considerable pleasure at the German advance.[23] In Berlin he gave talks to troops, arranged anti-Bolshevik street propaganda and distributed leaflets, writing, as we have seen, two important tracts on communism in Russia. What worried him was that General von der Goltz treated Baltic Germandom as 'but one element of his plan for Germany's recovery in the East'.[24]

That could be said of other Reich nationalists. The commander of the volunteer 'Iron Brigade', Max Bischoff, wrote of the Baltic campaign: 'Once succeed in opening the way to Russia and in co-operating resolutely with the still well-organized anti-Bolshevik circles there, then the threatened containment of Germany would be broken.'[25] In the name of this cause von der Goltz showed scant sympathy for the nationhood of small states. He once dubbed the Baltic countries 'three wholly non-viable northern state formations'.[26] Yet on the folly of such thinking Brest-Litovsk had foundered. Amid revolution and preparations for peace talks Berlin clearly allowed too much latitude on the distant Baltic front, making the campaign all the more difficult to liquidate later. The German government nonetheless remained aware that Germany's military presence in the Baltic depended ultimately on the agreement and good will of the Allied Powers. Notwithstanding the prevarication of Winnig, the defence minister Gustav Noske, a few other officials and above all von der Goltz, the German government had already accepted the idea of independent Baltic states.[27]

Schiemann worked hard in Berlin to promote awareness of these underlying realities among Baltic Germans. Slowly even the Baltische Vertrauensrat began to succumb to his constant representations and to regard a Latvian state as inevitable, inviting Schiemann to talk about Baltic Germandom's future. Together with Professor W. Sokolowski, he urged national autonomy, backed by Baltic German propertied wealth. Soon after, in early April 1919, he travelled to Liepāja with Ropp at the Vertrauensrat's request to address the National Committee on the same subject. Scant regard was shown for such 'communist' ideas in these circles. The focus of attention in Liepāja—following Jelgava's recapture on 23 March—was on freeing Riga. Schiemann heard from a beleaguered Kārlis Ulmanis that von der Goltz was preventing Latvians from mobilising on the grounds of their alleged Bolshevism. In fact Colonel Janis Balodis' Latvian brigade had already helped to clear Courland. Schiemann, himself prone to remarking on affinities between Bolshevism and Latvian social democracy, vehemently objected to tarring Latvian middle-class parties, let alone Latvians as a whole, with the same brush. 'Men like Ulmanis, the Interior Minister Valters and the ultra-chauvinistic War Minister Sahlit were no less embittered enemies of Bolshevism than the Balts themselves. A victory for Bolshevism meant for them the destruction of their life's work.' Schiemann was forced to conclude that Valters was 'genuinely concerned to reach understanding with Baltic Germandom'.[28]

Instead *Landeswehr* shock troops led by Baron Hans von Manteuffel suddenly toppled the struggling Ulmanis government on

16 April and installed a pro-German administration under Pastor Andrievs Niedra. Young *Landeswehr* recruits subsequently assured Schiemann in Berlin that they had no option but to take action to overcome Latvian resistance to an advance on Riga. Broadly that rationale informed Baltic German accounts thereafter, where the move against Ulmanis was ascribed to his alleged refusal to guarantee the political, cultural and economic rights of the German minority; or to 'the desire to see in the place of the chauvinist government a more moderate one, in which Germans were represented'.[29] At the very least, the judgement obscures the intrigues linking von der Goltz indirectly to the episode.[30] Latvians recently described the April coup as nothing less than a bid to erect a bi-national German-Latvian republic against the wishes of the majority.[31]

The view finds support in a passage struck from the original manuscript of Schiemann's memoir: 'At a time when the whole of Europe was alive with democratic slogans, when communist notions of shaking up the entire existing state were not yet played out' it was impossible to try to establish 'a German-aristocratic oligarchy' and to avoid agrarian reform.[32] He also dryly recorded of the National Committee's fourteen points that they 'could only with difficulty be reconciled with the concept of an independent democratic state'.[33] Significantly, only one of the Baltic Germans on Niedra's team, Karl Keller, went on to play an important political role in independent Latvia.

For much of April Schiemann was constantly 'between trains' in Germany. After a lecture in Halle and another following almost immediately in Bremen—netting a much-needed 360 marks in all—the German government asked him to address individual *Freikorps* units, to take part in anti-Spartacist undertakings and ensure balanced press coverage of them. So he found himself lecturing in Magdeburg at Easter, and on returning to Berlin he immediately left for Dresden. 'Tomorrow I am speaking here twice,' he wrote to his mother, 'once in the morning and once in the evening. Tuesday I have to be back in Berlin and may stay there on Wednesday, because that is Lotte's birthday.'[34] During this characteristic display of energy Schiemann never moved his focus far from the Baltic. He persuaded the Riga Jews, 'who still love me', to give substantial support to his relief committee for Riga. American Jews also provided funds and even the Vertrauensrat sent representatives to the relief committee meetings. Its work intensified with the liberation of Riga on 22 May, which was marred by the violent and ugly reprisals exacted by a small but significant minority of Baltic Germans, shamefully overlooked to this day in Baltic German historical writing.[35]

Riga's recapture inevitably brought Schiemann into closer contact with the Baltic German National Committee, and he had 'political conferences' in Berlin with one of its more intelligent leaders, Arthur Reusner.[36] Neither guessed just how soon the National Committee's political route would have to converge with that followed by Schiemann. April's events abruptly re-awakened Allied fears of a new German power base in eastern Europe, triggering the departure to the Baltic of a stream of Allied missions and aid. The conflict between German and Latvian leaders thus 'became an international issue', intensifying pressure on Baltic German leaders to negotiate with the legitimate Latvian government.[37]

The standing of the Ulmanis team naturally improved with the re-establishment of Latvian rule in liberated Riga. Niedra's cabinet remained 'an appendage to further German intrigues.'[38] Just as Niedra owed his sudden elevation to German arms, so their failure ended his short acquaintance with high office. Soviet forces had been driven from Estonia by February, which facilitated the formation of a Latvian army unit on Estonian territory. Ulmanis had been mobilising from late May in northern districts of Latvia already freed with Estonia's help. The first inclination Schiemann had of impending catastrophe for the *Landeswehr* was the news of fresh skirmishes as it advanced beyond Riga with the National Committee's blessing. He realised to his dismay that battle was being engaged not with the Bolsheviks but with native forces; that the fight would be 'against the Latvian majority, against the National Council and government, that is to say, civil war'. He and Ewald Ammende promptly telegraphed the National Committee, warning against further military adventures and calling in vain for talks with Ulmanis.[39]

A month to the day after Riga's liberation a combined Latvian and Estonian force repulsed German troops at Cēsis—which, ironically, had once been an important residential, administrative and military centre for the Livonian Order. Schiemann gave in to the urge to get back to Riga and entered the city to find the decisive battle over but in time to see an armistice concluded under the auspices of the Allied powers. The Cēsis agreement of 3 July finally disentangled Landeswehr and Reich German units, compelling both to evacuate Riga by 5 July and placing the *Landeswehr* at Latvia's disposal as an independent unit under an English commander, Colonel Alexander. Schiemann, whose brother Julius was adjutant to Major Fletcher, confessed to have been saddened at the spectacle of the demoralised *Landeswehr*, to which 'almost all my friends and acquaintances belonged'.[40] Nonetheless, the dramatic event precipitated his return to Latvian politics. Nothing better symbolised the collapse of old Balt positions against which he had struggled than the fact that Stephen Tallents, the English governor temporarily appointed to restore order in Riga, was residing in the Ritterhaus.[41]

The armistice had followed a decisive shift in the leadership of the Baltic German National Committee, brought about by the ill-fated advance and by pressure from an increasingly confident liberal opposition. On 21 June, a prominent and respected conservative, Baron Wilhelm von Fircks, was nominated in his absence to the presidency of the National Committee. It was he who selected the delegates to negotiate with the Allies and with the Ulmanis government—restored in Liepāja on 27 June, and triumphantly back in Riga on 8 July.[42] Whether Ulmanis would have welcomed to his second cabinet Edwin Magnus and Robert Erhardt, respectively Justice Minister and Finance Minister, without the prompting of the Allied representatives remains an open question. They thought well of the administrative abilities of the Baltic Germans and of Fircks himself.[43] Ulmanis was uneasily aware too of the National Committee's influence over the *Landeswehr.* Apart from the disgruntled German *Freikorps,* which was deeply reluctant to evacuate Latvia, 'White' Russian anti-Bolshevik forces were also gathering in the Baltic. In truth the signature of the Versailles Peace Treaty, together with the armistice at Cēsis and the re-convening of the Latvian National Council on 15 July 1919, ended all illusions of preserving Baltic German hegemony.

This decisive 'turn of fate' brought fully into conjunction the two parliamentary leaders credited in the annals of Baltic German historiography since 1945 with ensuring the future of Baltic Germandom in independent Latvia: Fircks and Schiemann. The partnership was less unlikely than it seemed to be at first glance. Fircks exemplified the values of an aristocratic Courlander.[44] His florid and sentimental memoir is imbued with a patrician nostalgia and sense of loss, doubtless replicated in the breasts of all Baltic German estate-holders fearfully anticipating radical agrarian reform in the new states.[45] He spoke and continued to speak for the former aristocracy. Yet he had been trained as a mining engineer and worked in German East Africa as well as in Serbia and Spain till 1916. His long absence from Latvia left him, like Schiemann, untainted by Baltic German intrigues at home and therefore more acceptable to Latvian politicians than might otherwise have been the case. The youngest son of an impoverished branch of an ancient Courland noble family, Fircks personally became rich enough to return in 1913 and buy back the estate at Warwen bei Windau, only to suffer financial ruin when war deprived him of his large Russian currency reserves. After Latvia's agrarian reform took away his lands too, he was poorer than ever. Something in this predicament spoke to Schiemann, himself never free of nagging money worries.

Their personalities engaged at other levels. The father of 'Willy Fircks', as Schiemann referred to his political ally, had made a name for himself as a lyricist; the son Wilhelm duly married a daughter of a family of *Literaten* from Jelgava. The thin, ascetic, melancholy-looking and lightly bearded Fircks peering out of contemporary photographs, for whom even the cost of a new suit became virtually unthinkable, could hardly have looked out of place in the bohemian environment favoured by Schiemann. He found himself attracted to Schiemann's principled arguments and strong personality, his willingness to confront all challenges, and his refusal to compromise over fundamental values. 'What captivated me about Schiemann from the very beginning', Fircks later admitted, 'was his absolute courage. The man knows no fear.'[46] As to Fircks, he impressed the French General Henri Niessel, who was supervising the German evacuation of the Baltic region in 1919: 'Of German race but reasonable and of a most moderate tendency, extremely loyal to the Latvian government.'[47] Schiemann too, looking back on his life, charitably described Fircks' conservatism as less a product of doctrine than of emotion, held in check by a grasp of the practical. He also recalled, however, that friendship with Fircks 'grew slowly' and chiefly from 'shared work and shared worry'.[48] Others observed 'explosive' disagreements between the two leaders in the course of their working relationship.[49]

Schiemann, leader of the German Balt Democratic Party from early August 1919, could hardly always see eye to eye with Fircks, head of the conservative German Balt People's Party, formally constituted in January 1920. Fircks had as much criticism from his own camp for working with Schiemann as Schiemann did for collaborating with him. While Fircks's approval was vital in nursing a deeply resentful conservative Baltic Germandom towards acknowledging Latvia, his task was eased by the gloomy resignation among the old élites in the summer of 1919 that their game was played out. However, a great deal more was demanded of Schiemann in order for the compromise with conservatism to work. He was under strong pressure from his own party for a liberal merger and a joint Schiemann-Rosenberg leadership of a loyal German fraction in the Latvian National Council.[50] Baltic German Liberals still distrusted the National Committee and its 'misconceived' policy from the April coup onwards. Rosenberg again roundly attacked it in '*All hands on deck!*' after his return from political refuge in England in early June.[51] Schiemann had briefly contemplated a merger of liberal forces but he eventually constrained the radical wing of his party and opted 'resolutely' against such a fusion.[52]

In doing so he eschewed the obvious and easy route to immediate personal advancement in Latvian politics. His clashes of personality with Fircks were only one factor in his thinking. His later assessment of Rosenberg as 'consumed by personal ambition' partly mirrored the attack on his own person and politics in Rosenberg's vitriolic memoir. Yet both friends and opponents of Schiemann testify that he was rarely driven solely by such considerations. He freely acknowledged Rosenberg's early acceptance of Latvia as 'timely' but could 'scarcely speak of [the Progressive Party] having genuine political ideas beyond working with the Latvians'. Far from accepting Rosenberg's view of the Progressive Party as a bridge for other Baltic Germans to the new state, Schiemann felt that his rival was courting success by pointedly setting himself apart from the German community.[53] Like members of Riga's pre-war Liberal Club, whose resentment of ruling cliques appeared stronger than genuine convictions, Rosenberg's actions created a splinter group, which could have no lasting influence in a parliamentary system once the Latvians ceased to need its backing.[54]

For Schiemann that consideration was ultimately decisive. He could hardly now envisage Baltic Germans adopting a common political programme but that made agreement on a common purpose—namely 'to remain in the homeland, to remain German and, within the given realities, to win a position for the German community worthy of our past'—all the more important.[55] This sentiment provides the key to his opposition to a liberal merger. In the *Rigasche Rundschau* on 14 November 1919 he resolutely rejected demands in the Latvian press for Baltic German parties to abandon their National Committee. Obliquely indicting the Progressives, Schiemann reiterated that his own party 'had always supported a policy of co-operation with the Latvian people, not merely to secure the goodwill of fellow Latvian citizens, but because this policy was regarded as the most appropriate for the whole country and for all Balts in it. We have more reason today than ever not to lose the connection to our fellow Baltic Germans, and to help them adapt to the new times. Deserting the National Committee would be to break up the cultural community and thereby destroy our own cultural existence.'[56]

His principled, politically far-sighted decision to work with the conservatives demanded nothing less than conciliation of the very personalities and forces who had been attacking him over the preceding two decades. However, unity within the Baltic German community remained for him, as always, only one side of the coin; the other side the need to show communal unity with the Latvians. The essential continuity of this theme with his pre-war writing was immediately revealed on his assumption of the editorship of the *Rigasche Rundschau* in the summer of 1919. That demanding role he filled with short breaks till 1933, combining it with his hectic new career as a national politician and (till 1925) membership of the Riga City Council—an achievement unusual for any statesman. His remarkable editorials were integral to his standing as a political leader, while his output in the first six months of returning home confirmed him beyond doubt as the intellectual force behind the parliamentary strategy of 'solidarity' that underpinned his collaboration with Fircks. Although contact with 'solidarists' in Berlin late in 1918 was a factor in Schiemann's thinking, his specific Baltic experience had already formed his broader vision of national and social cohesion, as well as his hostility towards narrow class interests.[57] These were already central themes of his campaigning journalism early in the century.[58]

A strong sense of place coloured Schiemann's vision of solidarity. One of his first post-war editorials, calling Baltic German émigrés home to re-build Latvia, eloquently argued that they had no future, as Baltic Germans, outside their homeland. 'Whoever abandons his position in the country today loses his standing in the world.'[59] It was a patriotic duty of the emigrant to return and build a new order with the Latvians. 'This realisation, that our deepest interest is intimately bound up with that of the Latvian state, must be more firmly rooted in the perceptions of the entire Balt community.'[60] Schiemann's displeasure was reserved not for those genuinely finding leaving Germany materially difficult, but for émigrés waiting 'on the sidelines', who could not or would not forget the past.[61] 'Each Balt labouring here daily under difficult conditions does more for his people than any emigrant.' Anybody 'outside' hindering the policy 'on which we have embarked' by 'promulgating pan-German slogans' and 'trying on the martyr's crown' was 'a wrecker (Schädling) and our foe'.[62]

Schiemann's concept of social solidarity informed and was formed by his critique of Marxism, energetically resumed in the pages of the *Rigasche Rundschau*. Promoting social solidarity exposed the reality behind 'the theory and practice of Bolshevism'—to use the title of Bertrand Russell's famous book, which appeared three years after Schiemann's *Fiasco of Russian Democracy*. The course of the German revolution convinced Schiemann that full-scale socialisation was not yet practicable and that 'most could be achieved in social policy through patience, married to resolution.' Communists, however, refused to wait.[63] Schiemann parodied their preoccupation with materialist explanations in biblical terms: 'In the beginning was the interest.'[64] He objected vehemently to Marxists making social awareness the prerogative of one class, arguing nearer to home that Latvian social democrats, while certainly no Bolsheviks, fostered social envy by singing 'all the old songs from 1905'. As so often, Schiemann deployed paradox to imply that obsession with past glories of

Latvian social democrats like Kalnins, Menders and Zehlen, made them 'essentially more conservative than the most troublesome Junkers of East Prussia or of our home'.[65]

What was worse, such class bias seriously impeded the solution to 'the problem of the Latvian state', which was 'above all' an economic one. 'We cannot just wait for the Russian state, shattered with contemptible frivolity, to be built up again over years, and then to offer us a pitiful shelter.' Latvia had to acknowledge its dependence on the trust of international capital. Socialists, Schiemann wryly observed, were forgetting that 'the precondition of socialisation is capitalism. A state which does not posses adequate means of production to nourish its people, and then wants to socialise those means of production, is just as ludicrous as a debtor besieged by a thousand creditors who makes his "wealth" available to the poor.'[66] Privatisation thus neatly legitimised the avoidance of narrow party interest, the pursuit of social solidarity and hostility towards Bolshevik Russia. Finally, Schiemann's reasoning naturally took in the physical location of the Baltic countries between capitalism and communism. 'If we are fighting for Europe', he warned early in 1920, 'then the whole of Europe has to view this fight as a common cause and give us much more extensive support than has been the case so far.'[67]

For Schiemann nationality disputes endangered the pursuit of solidarity as much as, if not more than, class differences. At the time when he entered Latvian politics a nationalities commission, set up by the Latvians in December 1918 to implement the national and cultural rights promised in their Political Platform, was considering a radical proposal from the Jewish Union. It advocated removing the management of cultural affairs from the state's remit and broadly followed the thinking of the Austrian Socialists Karl Renner, who as 'Synopticus' published *State and Nation* in 1899, and Otto Bauer. Schiemann's 26 July editorial 'Overcoming national hatred', nailed his own flag firmly to the mast: 'I do not doubt for a moment that the idea [of cultural autonomy] will be realised in the course of the coming decades as the basis of state law throughout the civilised world, and that in conjunction with the League of Nations it will become the guiding principle internationally for implementing that right to self-determination which the World War has failed to achieve.'[68]

Although taken by the notion that Latvia might be the first to practise the ideals in post-war Europe, Schiemann was equally sure that the 'party papacies' would long resist autonomy as creating a 'state within a state'. That was precisely the reason given by Latvian Education Minister, Kārlis Kaspersons, for holding up the draft autonomy and language law submitted in August 1919 by the nationalities commission.[69] Still, Schiemann and his fellow Baltic German politicians were quickly able to make a distinctive contribution to the practice of minority rights in the field of education.

Exposure to arbitrary state intervention in schooling—not only in the Russian Empire but also under German occupation during the First World War, when Prussification loomed—made Baltic Germans fully alive to the importance of Karl Keller's post as adviser to the Latvian Education Minister. Keller and three experts designated by the German Balt Teacher's Association, Wolfgang Wachtsmuth, Max von Radecki and Friedrich Demme, whose own influential drafts provided the discussion framework, aimed to help mould Latvia's education policy and to incorporate an autonomous Baltic German education body within the state authority.[70] With the ending of Bolshevik occupation, a revised draft in the form of a law was handed over to Ulmanis on 15 July 1919 for consideration by the Latvian National Council. Edwin Magnus and Karl Keller, supported by Rosenberg, were prominent in the ensuing exchanges with the Latvian side; Magnus and Robert Erhardt, still at that stage respectively Ministers of Justice and Finance, also joined a special government commission examining the German, Russian and Jewish draft school autonomy projects from late August.[71] Since Ulmanis was sympathetic to the project, there were obvious advantages in capitalising on current political circumstances, which could easily change for the worse.[72]

Schiemann, who assumed the chair of the nationalities commission at this juncture, played a central role in the effort to find a legal basis for the rebuilding of German schooling. He initially directed his fire at the Latvian Education Association, following his declaration in the *Rigasche Rundschau* on 20 August 1919 that national autonomy and school autonomy were the 'precondition of a democratic nationalities policy'. A week later he responded sharply to Latvian charges that his view was undemocratic by reiterating that with school autonomy the question of 'our cultural existence, of being or not being' was at stake. 'All of us who have made ourselves available to the state, in any form—as government representatives, as members of parliament, as public servants—must know that this state of ours has no wish to condemn us to cultural deprivation. So without menace or any trace of national agitation but with deep resolve we ask the [Latvian] National Council to secure the foundation of our cultural work by accepting the draft for school autonomy during the present session.'[73] He failed to dispel the reservations of Kaspersons and his colleagues about the extent of self-regulation envisaged in the German scheme. The cabinet eventually opted on 22 August for a general provision covering all minorities.

Nevertheless, Schiemann's personal weight ensured the inclusion of key elements of autonomy in the short 'Law on the Schooling of Minorities in Latvia', eventually approved at the same time as a general Latvian school law, on 8 December 1919.[74] Henceforth the state undertook to provide primary schooling for every thirty children of a minority and instruction was to be in the mother-tongue of the minority (article 39). In the case of secondary schooling such instruction was merely permissible. Furthermore, each minority was to have, within the Latvian Education Ministry and responsible to the Education Minister, its own department, with officials paid by the state but appointed by the minority's parliamentary fraction. The German education authority began operations on 2 January 1920. Its director, who also had an advisory role in the cabinet on the overall cultural affairs of the minority in question, was Karl Keller. Schiemann also secured the insertion of a clause allowing existing arrangements to stand until the elected bodies envisaged for the management of the cultural affairs of the national minorities eventually came into being.[75]

Schiemann instantly hailed the law of December 1919 a 'break in the circle of antagonism'. Moreover, he saw it as 'an act of outstanding importance for our political life in general, which is never more threatened than by national antagonism, giving the social conflict its sharpness too.'[76] Other Baltic Germans were not so generous in analysing Latvian motives. Wolfgang Wachtsmuth's view—influential for subsequent historians—was that the Latvian government merely wanted to create a favourable reception for its bid to join the League of Nations. Wachtsmuth also suggested that Ulmanis was concerned to discourage the *Landeswehr* from taking part in the abortive attack on Riga that General Bermondt-Avalov's ill-organised White Russian and renegade German troops launched in October.[77] However, since that episode provoked fresh anti-German hostility it was scarcely helpful to the negotiations over schooling.[78] (While Fircks managed to keep the *Landeswehr* neutral during the Bermondt campaign, Latvian press and public hostility was precisely what had prompted Schiemann, as we have seen, to defend the Baltic German National Committee in mid-November.)

Indeed, with Bermondt's defeat and the last remnants of the German *Freikorps* leaving Courland during December, Ulmanis even denied the National Committee the right to nominate ministers to his new administration. The political sea-change was all too evident from Rosenberg's exclusion from all discussions. His journey towards the political wilderness accelerated with a diatribe in the Latvian National Council on 5 December, not only attacking the Baltic German National Committee but accusing Ulmanis' government of ignoring the Progressives—the 'one loyal German party'.[79] In other words the school laws were passed as the arc of Latvian confidence rose, indicating not just anxiety on the part of the government but readiness in spite of everything to contemplate a multinational future.

Schiemann caught something of that mood in his 'New Year's Eve' editorial on Baltic Germandom's struggle against hardship and chauvinism. 'But is it not an advantage of our time that we *can* conduct such a campaign? That we have an inalienable right to make our opinion felt in the [Latvian] National Council, in the press, in public meetings? That we can strengthen our position by peaceful political activity, build firmer bases for our interests by voting together? Here the new democratic era, which in some ways has impoverished us, brings a treasure that it would be criminal to undervalue, a treasure we must preserve and protect, not only against the spirit of reaction but above all against the menacing anti-democratic wave from the East, which recognises no personal freedom.'[80]

The immediate background to this rousing call was Ulmanis' insistence in December that only political parties could contest seats for the Constituent Assembly, scheduled to replace the un-elected Latvian National Council in April 1920. Thus the Baltic German

National Committee at last faced complete oblivion. Within the German community three parties were founded early in 1920: Edwin Magnus' moderate centre right German Balt Reform Party; the right-wing conservative German Balt People's Party led by Fircks; and Egon Ropp's Libau Unity Party, politically not dissimilar to the Reform party, if further to the left.[81] These now joined those led by Schiemann and Rosenberg in the run-up to the Constituent Assembly elections. However, Baltic Germans and Latvians alike had much to learn about parliamentary practice.[82] Schiemann brought his energy to bear on the task of political education in the weeks leading up to Latvia's first democratic elections, determined to use the pages of the *Rigasche Rundschau* to air political programmes and to foster political debate.[83]

The emergence of other parliamentarians within the German community under the pressure of events in no way diminishes Schiemann's definitive contribution, both to the intellectual rationale for different Baltic German parties and to the intensely practical task of co-ordinating work between them at the beginning of 1920. He had emphasised the vital importance of voting processes as such in December, by representing the Riga City Council elections as an 'examination'—giving Baltic Germans the chance to demonstrate that their contribution did not depend solely on ownership of land. 'Never, since Riga's old walls were built, have the fortunes of our city been so completely in the hands of its combined citizenry as today. Never have elections had such comprehensive and decisive importance for our entire economic and cultural future.' In Schiemann's view, any Baltic German, Jew or Russian not voting was 'committing suicide'.[84] Those professing to have no party failed to grasp that in a democratic state parties were a precondition of influencing policy.[85]

Schiemann set an example by presenting his own party's manifesto at an open Sunday meeting in the building of the Johannes Guild. Shortly after, on 12 January 1920, the 'Guidelines for the work of the German Baltic Democratic Party of Latvia' appeared in the *Rigasche Rundschau*. The document has been justly described as Schiemann's 'entirely personal work'.[86] The first part rejected rights related merely to birth and property, as well as condemning the class conflict preached by Bolshevism. In addition to a parliament chosen by proportional representation, Schiemann advocated a second chamber incorporating the intellectual and practical expertise essential to the construction of the state. Its representatives were to be chosen by the different professional sectors. Exemplifying social solidarity in its very composition, it was to draft economic and social legislation. However, the undefined constitutional relationship between the two bodies suggests that the 'Chamber of Work' was expected to sway the party-political 'parliament of ideas' through advice and persuasion.

Such corporate elements, as well as distaste for selfish party politics, reveal Schiemann's lingering doubts over the *sort* of parliamentary democracy that might arise in Latvia. Nevertheless, his promotion of the interests of the whole remains a striking feature of the guidelines.[87] The concept of 'social solidarity' was fleshed out by proposals for an equitable and economically sound land reform, the development of the co-operative movement, changes in shareholding legislation to benefit those actually doing the work, as well as other plans for health care and welfare. Moreover, the call in the second part of the guidelines for autonomy in national and cultural affairs for Baltic Germans in Latvia was securely premised on their 'unqualified co-operation' in building Latvia. 'The party is striving to realise its political and national aims within the bounds of an independent Latvian state.'

Thus, joining Latvia meant in the first instance contesting the elections to the Constituent Assembly. As early as August 1919 Schiemann had argued that proposals—which eventually became law—to divide Latvia into five electoral districts damaged the principle of proportional representation in the case of minorities scattered across the country, splitting up an already small German community.[88] Close coordination between the different Baltic German parties clearly had to be the order of the day. In the same month therefore Schiemann first proposed regular meetings between the German representatives on the Latvian National Council, German city councillors and the heads of various expert groups within the parties. However, the initiative did not really bear fruit until New Year 1920 when preparations for the Constituent Assembly elections gave it fresh impetus. Preliminary discussions between Democrats and Progressives in late January were followed by several weeks of preparation leading to the publication in the *Rigasche Rundschau* on 13 February 1920 of the 'Proclamation and Guidelines of the Committee of German Balt Parties'. It was signed by Schiemann (Democrats), P. Kluge (Progressives), E. Magnus (Reform Party) and Fircks (People's Party). The distinction between the new body and the old National Committee was deliberately underlined, in the face of Latvian suspicions, with emphasis placed primarily on working for the minority's cultural wellbeing.[89]

The dominance of the German Balt Democratic Party and of Schiemann personally could scarcely be concealed. He also chaired the central election committee set up by the Committee of German Balt Parties (CGBP) at the beginning of February 1920. At the CGBP meeting on 6 February 1920 he successfully made the case for Rosenberg's Progressive Party to allocate one of its five seats in the Latvian National Council to Fircks' new People's Party, thus further implicating recalcitrant conservative forces in the new democratic order.[90] Inevitably they were as anxious as the progressives not to lose influence, and the CGBP's board was made up of one from each of the four member—delegations elected by the individual parties to the full CGBP. Its chairmanship was to rotate on a six-monthly basis between the parties. Finally, only resolutions unanimously approved by all the parties could be carried out in the committee's name, each party being entitled to act in its own right in the event of dissension.[91] Nevertheless, the Democratic Party's expectations of increasing its influence over Baltic German policy were fulfilled. The CGBP's very existence, rationale and guidelines betray Schiemann's political thinking in every single line, as did the fact that the different Baltic German parties combined to form a single list of candidates.

No more telling evidence is wanted of Schiemann's paramount position in the overall political leadership of the Baltic Germans in Latvia after the War than the CGBP's call to émigré Baltic Germans: 'The German Balt parties of Latvia, which in their Committee incorporate the united will of our people remaining in the homeland, conceive of it as their duty to inform their brethren currently living abroad, on the basis of better knowledge of local circumstances, that participation by the German Balt population in the rebuilding of the homeland, in the context of the Latvian state, is possible and urgently necessary. In spite of the variety of our political views, we have no doubt that only on the basis of Latvian statehood will we be able to gain and preserve the rights guaranteeing a thriving development of our national existence within the state.'[92]

Not that Schiemann himself had any illusions about the scale of the tasks ahead. He freely acknowledged in mid-March 1920 that it would not be difficult to destroy the German minority. But he also warned: 'At the very moment when the last German ceases to feel himself a Latvian citizen, where we have mentally to withdraw from the society of our home, Latvia's fate must and will be decided.'[93]

4. Practising Democracy

By the early months of 1920 all hostile troops had left Latvian soil, and with the winding-down of Allied intervention and the signing of Soviet-Baltic treaties in the summer peace came at last. Many doubted the motives of Lenin's regime. Yet the armistice with the Soviets on 1 February and the ensuing peace treaty on 11 August showed 'that there was indeed a Latvian state with a Latvian government.'[1] By becoming the first major power to accept Baltic independence in 1920, Russia exposed the disappointing Allied prevarication on recognition. A year earlier Schiemann had cautioned against Soviet peace overtures. His dislike of Bolshevism was undiminished, but he used the occasion of Latvian-Soviet talks to stress that security would not come through involvement in anti-Soviet combinations.[2] He focused instead on the practicalities of co-existence; treating the view that Russia needed to recover its lost Baltic ports as a product of pre-war thought categories. 'If we stay imprisoned in these maxims, then we revert completely to the origins and ideas which for their part made the catastrophe of World War unavoidable and [would] provoke similar misfortune in future.' A Russia made aware that building anew would come not by restoring past borders but only through 'work within' would eventually cease to resent the independence of the Baltic countries.[3]

They too faced daunting tasks of reconstruction. Apart from the depredations of war and the impact of the Allied blockade of Russia, the very act of creating three separate economic units through Baltic independence compounded problems. Once great Baltic industries now languished in enforced idleness, depleted from 1915 onwards of labour, equipment and resources by Tsarist evacuation policies. Pre-war markets practically vanished with the onset of Bolshevism in Russia, and commercial banks and financial organisations in the Baltic suffered the destruction of their records and the withdrawal of liquid assets by the St Petersburg parent companies as the result of the war. Naturally, no Baltic central banks yet existed and in Latvia—as in the other two Baltic states—a mixture of German occupation currency and near-worthless Russian roubles still circulated. The lapidary description of Latvian independence as based on ruined industries, empty coffers and largely agrarian economies was apt.[4]

Small wonder that European observers felt 'the component parts of the old Russian Empire are bound to come together again, but this time in a strictly limited economic federalism, and decentralised politically to the fullest extent.'[5] However, Schiemann drew the opposite conclusion; that the 'spiritual well-being' of the Russian people was dependent on their old state continuing to fall into its component parts, and that the Baltic states 'must show the world how necessary we are'.[6] Baltic Germans had no choice but to take part in this demonstration. For Schiemann the interdependence of majority and minorities alike in the new Latvia was axiomatic. He again warned Baltic German sceptics in *At the Cross-roads* in August 1920: 'If this state collapses and we are thrown into complete chaos, then that is the end for our specific nationality.'[7]

As it was, the German minority's future in independent Latvia was already circumscribed by long-term sociological and occupational shifts. Russification, revolution in 1905, the fear of Bolshevik invasion in 1918–19, agrarian reform—all drove many Baltic Germans to the Reich or to a lesser extent overseas. Not all returned with peace. At the outbreak of the First World War 162,000 Baltic Germans lived on territory later comprising Estonia and Latvia. Only 76,432 of them remained in 1920. 58,113 were in Latvia, rising to 70,964 (3.8 per cent of the population) by the 1925 census. Yet the long-feared agrarian laws, pushed through the Constituent Assembly on 16 September 1920, dealt the fateful blow. The result was that of the 2,721,503 hectares formerly in German hands, only 65,771 hectares were not appropriated by the state land fund for redistribution.

To emphasise the fact that this draconian land reform threatened not just estate-holders but the very existence of Baltic Germandom, Schiemann spoke of a *Kulturkampf*.[8] Most obviously, agrarian reform accelerated the relocation of Baltic Germans to the towns, already marked before 1914. It was not just the former propertied élites staying on in Latvia who sought new opportunities, once they abandoned what remained of their land as not being viable. The German agricultural *Mittelstand* dependent on the estates, in so far as it was not Latvianised, also drifted townwards and virtually 'disappeared'. The 17 per cent or so of Germans ekeing out a rural existence in the 1920s were mainly so-called 'colonists', originally mostly settled on some of the Courland estates from 1905–6.[9] By 1925 no fewer than 82.81 per cent of Baltic Germans in Latvia lived in towns, 62 per cent of them in Riga.[10]

Here, of course, the German element, owning or managing some 85 per cent of Latvia's pre-war industry, was already bearing the brunt of industrial collapse. Moreover Latvia's currency law of 8 March 1920 re-valued pre-war rouble debts, generally to the benefit of heavily mortgaged Latvian land and householders, mainly at the expense of German creditors. The latter could now hope to recover only a fifth of their original outlay. What provoked Schiemann almost as much as the act itself was the Latvian press onslaught when he dared to criticise a 'swindle' being elevated into law by the state. 'Where is the connection here', he asked, 'with democracy and its values?'[11] He was eventually to calculate that Baltic Germans had lost 90 per cent of their former wealth.[12] Many continued to harbour the bitter feeling that they had been asked to make a disproportionate sacrifice to their new masters. While Schiemann's own rise mirrored the inexorable shift of influence towards the urban middle classes, the socio-economic dislocation within the German community during and after the war manifestly did not ease the task of political leadership.

To some extent the voice from the left of the Baltic German political spectrum was weakened for the moment by Rosenberg's continuing fall from grace. Under a new chairman from 1923, Fröhlich, the depleted Progressive Party eventually made its uneasy peace with the CGBP. More problematic was to be the German Workers' Party of Latvia, founded by Robert Riedel in April 1924 (chapter 5). On the other hand, Schiemann benefited from the support of the moderate right German Balt Reform Party of Edwin Magnus and, thanks to Fircks, of some conservatives. Although both committed themselves to the new state, they remained close to the interests of traditional élites, Magnus' party targeting the better off urban bourgeoisie and Fircks voicing landowners' concerns.[13] Fircks also had good standing within the *Ritterschaften*, which were reduced to being charitable associations (*Gemeinnützige Verbände*) after their dissolution in 1920. Indeed he chaired the Courland association. In spite of his personal authority he was still struggling two years after the Latvian state was founded against elements in his party who believed 'the worse it goes for the [Latvian] state, the better will the German element fare.'[14] Far too many Baltic German conservatives remained resentful at having had to make the journey from dominion to parliamentarianism—'from Seraphim to Schiemann', in the words of one disaffected contributor to the *Rigasche Rundschau*.[15]

The arrogance of such 'old Balt mentalities', particularly in émigré circles, was neatly caught in the complaint: 'We were older than these states, whose passports we were one day favoured with.'[16] A contemporary Latvian polemic described such people as 'doubting, intolerant' and longing for the Eastern question to be re-opened.[17] Their nostalgia showed itself in disdain for Baltic German party politics and a desire to return to an all-embracing organisation for Baltic Germandom, eschewing parliament.[18] Instead, they had to live with an organization predicated on parliament, the Committee of German Balt Parties (CGBP). This body spanned committed democrats and arch-conservatives, its constituency embracing the desperately poor and the relatively affluent, addressing urban workers and scattered subsistence farmers and, from 1924, including not just parties but *all* Baltic German political organisations in Latvia, and it was primarily through its agency that Baltic German parliamentary practice in Latvia was moulded.[19]

The CGBP's activities were first extensively catalogued in the 1950s, if episodically, in the three-volume work of Wolfgang Wachtsmuth, a co-worker with Schiemann. Michael Garleff's excellent standard account of Baltic German politics in both Estonia and Latvia between the wars is also indebted to Wachtsmuth's trilogy, at least in overall organisation and general content.[20] Both writers enshrine the same memory; that of a tightly-disciplined committee, where at the regular weekly meetings representatives of the five different Baltic German parties thrashed out the strategy and voting tactics they would jointly pursue in the parliamentary arena. There the overriding test of any action was to be not what served narrow sectional or individual party interest but what promoted the wellbeing of Baltic

Germandom in the new conditions; where endless *ad hoc* commissions were spawned to raise funding to rebuild a shattered existence; where precision campaigning won more deputies' seats for the Baltic Germans at national and municipal elections than their percentage of the population appeared to warrant; where what was in fact a fraction comprising different German parties, but answerable from 1922 to the CGBP, was dubbed by Latvians the 'German party'. Tellingly, when the duration of the CGBP's rotating chairmanship was eventually fixed in December 1922 at six months, Schiemann's 'term' was to last almost continuously until the end of Latvia's parliamentary period. It was not unusual to hear the German fraction described as 'Schiemann's party'.[21]

In spite of this, the full extent of his achievement was never widely appreciated during the 1920s, partly because of the continuing hostility of Baltic German conservatism and later the dominance of the extreme right in the shape of the Baltic German *Bewegung* in the 1930s. The wholesale Baltic German resettlement (*Umsiedlung*) to the Reich in 1939 threatened to consign Schiemann and his legacy to oblivion. However, with National Socialism totally defeated in 1945, documenting the labours of the Baltic German parliamentary fraction helped to rehabilitate a painful past. In the process the fundamental political principles separating Schiemann from his erstwhile enemies were often reduced to clashes of personality and life style. In this way Paul Schiemann was finally 'reclaimed' for the Baltic German gallery of historic personalities.[22] The judgement is harsh but recently Schiemann's 'portrait' was again flanked not only by one of Ewald Ammende, with whom he had a good deal in common as well as later fundamental differences, but of the Estonian German, Werner von Hasselblatt, who ultimately trod a political path Schiemann could never under any imaginable circumstances have taken.[23]

What might be viewed as the relativisation of Schiemann as a political leader in the historiography of the Baltic German minority may partly be the outcome of his own deliberate emphasis on the collectivity of the German parliamentary fraction. It purported not to represent 'specific political or ideological positions, economic or other interest groups of their voters, unlike the parties of the majority population and also some minorities. As opposed to a grouping of the population in horizontal sectors, the main purpose of any representation of a class interest, Latvian Germandom was an expressly "vertical construct", which combined within it all sectors of the population "from the proletariat to the most educated and most wealthy" and in itself wrought a shared ideal from the numerous conflicts within it.'[24] Perhaps unsurprisingly, hostile Latvian commentators regarded the purpose of Schiemann's political leadership as being to adapt the corporatist traditions of Baltic Germandom to the new political order. In this spirit too the Latvian press frequently lampooned Schiemann as 'the Barons' serf'.[25]

The charges indicate the difficult path Schiemann had to tread as a politician. On the one hand he responded by accusing Latvia's public figures of not recognising that they had broken the power of the Barons for ever through land reform, attributing their failure to credit the new Baltic German leadership for its support of Latvia to a lack of moral courage.[26] On the other hand, given the immediate difficulty of achieving political consensus among the Baltic German community, Schiemann was perfectly aware of the value of appealing to its corporate traditions to reinforce the case for a highly organised defence of the minority's truly parlous position after the War. Nevertheless, the implication of Schiemann's leadership strategy remained a wholesale politicisation and democratisation of the German community—as conservative Baltic German circles realised only too well. Important as Schiemann's fellow Baltic German parliamentary deputies were to the overall cause, not one of them could match his political inspiration and drive.

Even the bloodless protocols of the CGBP weekly meetings confirm Schiemann as anything but *primus inter pares.* There were no fewer than 171 meetings in the two years covered by the Latvian Constituent Assembly, and Schiemann attended almost every session. His return after occasional absences is often noticeable in the minutes from an immediate prioritisation of issues under review.[27] Needless to say, his formidable energy and stamina stood him in good stead. Apart from political initiatives that stemmed directly from him he had a major personal input into the 130 laws and seventy-three parliamentary amendments and submissions drafted by the CGBP between 1920 and 1922. He also did not disdain the humdrum work of the sub-committees spawned by the CGBP to generate extra funds for the hard-pressed Baltic German community. Scratch the surface of almost any sphere of Baltic German activity in the 1920s and Schiemann's name is rarely far below it. Somehow the sheer scale of the personal struggle he waged on many levels to nurture and consolidate Baltic German parliamentarism has slipped from view in the detailed narrative descriptions we currently have of the CGBP.

Inevitably, the battle in the parliamentary arena was fierce. Schiemann, together with the five other deputies making up the German fraction, entered a hostile Constituent Assembly on 1 May 1920. If any declaration of intent hung metaphorically over their heads it was surely Schiemann's *cri de coeur*: 'We [Baltic Germans] are not colonists, not foreigners on foreign soil but citizens and look for support from non-Germans too. And all citizens of Latvia, to whom the well being of our home is dearer than the narrow desires of cliques, should support us.'[28] The message was formidably difficult to put across in the 150-strong assembly, where the Baltic German fraction took its place with numerous other political parties, groups and individuals. Here was testimony not just to the fledgling stage of party formation but also to an electoral system where any group of citizens over the age of twenty-one could propose candidate lists in Latvia's five electoral districts. A closer look reveals the existence of a recognisable and persistent pattern.

Significantly the only two big parties, the Social Democratic Workers' Party, with 38.7 per cent of the vote in 1920 and the Farmers' Union with 17.8 per cent already had a pre-war existence on which to build. With two brief exceptions, the social democrats, eventually to split between moderates, led by Margeris Skujenieks and R. Dukurs, and an extreme left-wing preaching class warfare, tended to favour opposition. While remaining the largest party in the Latvian parliament till 1934 the social democrats were to see their share of the vote decline throughout the 1920s, losing ground to the bourgeois camp. The Farmers' Union on the other hand became the backbone of the bourgeois coalitions ruling Latvia in the 1920s; Latvia's first prime ministers, Kārlis Ulmanis and Zigfrīds Meierovics, came from its ranks. Further to the right of the Farmers' Union was the National Centre Party founded by Arvēds Bergs in 1921.

The shifting middle ground in what Georg von Rauch described as a 'tripartite system' was held by a mixture of national liberal parties representing the Latvian intelligentsia, a number of individual politicians and some small regional groups.[29] Of these the deputies of particularist parties from the eastern Latvian province of Latgale exerted disproportionate influence. Unlike Livonia and Courland, which over the course of time had been subject respectively to Swedish and German dominion, Latgale had been under direct Polish rule for a long period before 1772, when it was administered, separately from its sister Baltic provinces, as part of the Vitebsk gouvernement. Latvians in Latgale also differed in being largely Catholic while the province was at a lower level of development economically and culturally than Livonia or Courland.[30] Within such a system Latvia's national minorities, commanding between them some 10.27 % at the polls in 1920, rising to almost 19 per cent by 1931, had the potential to influence coalition-building.

The German community as a whole, particularly its conservative wing, was not enthusiastic about minority party cooperation, arguing that because of their historic importance the Baltic Germans had more in common with the Latvians than the other national minorities, but Schiemann placed a premium on working with those minorities, particularly in the early years of the new state. He reasoned that unless minority parliamentary deputies voted together they would cease to be a political factor, and took the initiative during the Constituent Assembly elections in drawing up a nine-point action programme on essential minority rights. They included national autonomy, with powers of self-taxation, unrestricted use of the mother-tongue and school autonomy to be anchored in the constitution. It was a week into the Constituent Assembly, on 8 May 1920, before the Baltic German, Jewish and Russian representatives were able to set up the Minorities Committee of Latvia, with its own information office. There were further delays before Schiemann was elected chairman by 9 votes to 2 on 13 May. He was to be flanked by a Russian deputy, A. Bocagov, and a Jewish one Moritz Mintz.[31]

The influence of the CGBP model was obvious. Among other things, the Minorities Committee tried to agree over the allocation of minority representation on the parliamentary sub-commissions. It also formed an economic council, which met weekly to discuss proposed legislation.[32] However, the nationality mixture was far more complex and volatile in Latvia than in Estonia. Delays in Schiemann's election as chairman of the Minorities Committee already revealed underlying differences in the priorities of the different national groups.

The strongest numerically was the Russian minority of 92,000, compactly settled but divided in religion between Orthodox, Old Russian and Catholic. There were also tensions between the large body of Russian farmers and the small élite of former Russian officials and merchants. As a result, the mostly upper-class Russian politicians were unable either to rally their voters with a programme for all social groups or to form a common front. The relationship between Russians and Latvians was in Schiemann's words mutually 'without enmity and without love'—which, he suggested, compounded the Russians' predisposition against intensive political organisation.[33] As a result, a Russian minority making up 12.6 per cent of the population of Latvia had only three deputies elected to the first Latvian parliament in 1922.

In the case of the Jews there were three distinct groups, in Courland, Latgale and Livonia, of which the Riga Jewry was the most important.[34] A basic division between Zionist and non-Zionist factions was further complicated by their distribution between four groups: those associating themselves with either German or Russian culture, and those inclined to speak either Hebrew or Yiddish. Ultimately the Jewish education administration had to cope in its schools with four languages. Naturally there were marked political divisions within Latvia's Jewish community. Five Jewish parties between them represented Orthodox Jews (Agudas Isroel), under Morduch Dubin; a bourgeois group (Zeire Agudas Isroel), under J. Baranchik; the Zionist organization Misrachi, whose best known member was Professor Max Laserson; and finally a socialist workers' party, the Jewish Bund, joining the Latvian social democrats in 1923 as an autonomous group. Not surprisingly, at the 1922 parliamentary polls 80,000 Jews managed to have only six deputies elected. By comparison, the 52,000 Poles captured one seat. Baltic Germans, with their six seats in parliament, were unique in achieving over-representation for their proportion of the total population.[35]

The thin fabric of co-operation between Latvia's national minorities was soon tested by differences over interpreting the 1919 school law. In its generality there was scope for both minorities and government to determine—for good or ill—the *practice* of autonomous schooling. By the autumn of 1920 a carefully worked-out, 400-page programme for the management of German schooling was already available for the Minister of Education's approval.[36] A German Parents' Association had also been founded in the same year to raise funds for schooling where state and communal resources were not adequate. Generally, the disciplined German fraction aimed to implement its preferences while the Latvians themselves were trying to build a new state system.

As things stood, German schools were open to pupils whose family language was German, including many Latvians and, above all, Jews attracted by the quality of the education on offer. Schiemann personally saw in such 'mixed' schooling the promise of greater support in time for the German community as a whole, but others, including Karl Keller, were unhappy. His proposal at a meeting of the Minorities Committee on 5 August 1920 that nationality rather than language should determine school entry appears to have caused surprise, but although supported by the Russians Keller's actions ultimately failed to bring about a change in prevailing legislation and achieved little besides upsetting Jewish leaders. More disturbing were the calls from some Russians in December 1920 to have their own education chief removed by the government. To the Germans this was the equivalent of taking an axe to the very principle of autonomy. Schiemann blocked the action through the Minorities Committee.[37]

Concern that the uncertain signals given by the other minority education authorities might encourage state aspirations to rescind school autonomy had already driven the CGBP to protest formally in the Minorities Committee. The Germans stressed the grave disadvantages of what they took to be the 'apolitical stance' of the Russians and Jews.[38] Equally, Schiemann was troubled from an early date by the poor attendance of the Russian and Jewish deputies at minorities' meetings—he naturally deplored the failure of the national groups to win more seats through tighter political organisation.[39] The omission reduced the influence a compact minorities bloc might otherwise have expected in the prevailing parliamentary balance, where socialists were not strong enough to govern alone and where the disparate bourgeois groups invariably had difficulty in putting together cohesive coalitions.

Schiemann acknowledged the obvious political affinities between Baltic Germandom and the Latvian bourgeois groups, even though his fraction's commitment to national solidarity often required it to be more progressive than Latvian conservatives over the defence of important civil rights and of the poorest elements in society. In these areas *ad hoc* accommodation with the social democrats became part of Baltic German parliamentary strategy. Cooperation was still restricted, in Schiemann's view, by Latvian social democrats not having experienced the shifts forced on their counterparts in the west. As a result, they had yet to develop political responsibility and end their addiction to extending state controls over economic life. These 'natural' differences between liberalism and socialism Schiemann saw as particularly damaging in Latvia, which had yet to construct its economic and legal system.[40] Such considerations reinforced the German fraction's natural inclination to work with Latvia's bourgeois governments. So too did hostile demands from the left in the Constituent Assembly to expropriate the big estates without compensation even before legislation was in place.[41]

That very issue, however, exposed the limits within which any minorities' bloc could expect to manoeuvre. Land reform had been long dreaded in Baltic German society but in the new democratic order had to be accepted by the German fraction. Fircks himself, as parliamentary spokesman for the big landowners, acknowledged that the expansion of smallholding would necessarily be at the expense of the large estates. However, instead of land being immediately appropriated to a state land 'fund' for later reallocation, Fircks proposed that estate holders voluntarily relinquish land only as and when required, against suitable compensation. Schiemann's public acceptance of reform in August 1919 took more into account the political and social imperatives driving land redistribution. Among these he heartily shared the desire to deprive communism of its appeal. Yet he was essentially in agreement with Fircks in arguing that the aim of agrarian reform had to be 'to create a strong small farm holding and not the destruction of the large estates'.[42] However, for most Latvians the sharp memory of *Ritterschaften* hostility, the harsh experience of German occupation policy and the ill-starred Bermondt adventure made the erosion of Baltic German wealth far from unwelcome.

Under the circumstances the Ulmanis administration rejected the German offer. What the intensive personal lobbying of Schiemann and Fircks could achieve was to make a dire situation fractionally less so; the government eventually agreed to leave a 'remainder' of 50 hectares for each estate and to postpone a decision on the emotive issue of compensation. It hardly guaranteed a rosy future for the big landowners, but even so it infuriated the social democrats, who stormed out of the chamber before the vote was taken. On the grounds that Ulmanis had behaved honourably, Schiemann opposed exploiting the cabinet's difficulties with the economy to bring it down. The German fraction voted for the agrarian legislation passed on 16 September 1920. Whether it *needed* to do so—in that the withdrawal of the social democrats guaranteed in any case that Ulmanis' 'moderate' proposals would win acceptance—long preoccupied Baltic German conservatives thereafter, fuelling the myth of Schiemann being against the estate owners. In fact his assurance to the CGBP after the vote—that 'Any other response would have been at best a gesture'—was well founded. Henceforth the German element had to live with the grim situation summarised earlier.[43]

Schiemann's admission that agrarian reform was necessary did not prevent him from depicting its execution as the deployment of a 'chauvinistic weapon'.[44] The reaction followed his general assessment of the Constituent Assembly's economic policy as 'a series of experiments determined by national antagonism'. His judgement was broadly consistent with the hostile reactions of Western governments at the time to the emergency decrees and state intervention characteristic of all three Baltic republics till well into 1921.[45] Schiemann had anticipated from the chauvinism displayed during the elections that the Constituent Assembly would be short on business acumen.[46] His earlier plea for Baltic Germans to come home aimed among other things at maximising the chances of their know-how being used in parliamentary commissions. Here, he maintained, the real work of state-building would take place.

This conviction also lay behind the CGBP's decision to select candidates for the German list for the first parliament in 1922 on the basis of scarce expertise, rather than party affiliation. Agriculture, education, economics and law were identified as priority skills in demand from the government.[47] Schiemann's own review of the

CGBP's activity confirms that during the first Saeima individual Baltic Germans sat on the commissions for agriculture, finance, social policy, justice, education, public law and foreign affairs.[48] It was to extend the expertise available to the state that Schiemann also unsuccessfully floated his idea for an upper house of professionals to the Constituent Assembly's constitutional commission, of which he was also a member.[49]

Baltic German participation on parliamentary commissions was integral to Schiemann's quest for the parliamentary moral high ground, serving as tangible proof of the German deputies' commitment to Latvia's good. Equally, he depicted his fraction's reconciliation of conflicts within the German community as the very model of how coalitions *ought* to behave. He had the advantage of being able to hammer his points home in the stream of editorials that issued from the *Rigasche Rundschau*'s premises in the shadow of the massive German Dom. The paper's pages were open to all the parties represented in the CGBP, but Schiemann's liberal values firmly set the overall tone. Moreover, his convictions on the calling of journalism did not allow the paper to become just the German fraction's mouthpiece. Its editorials had resonance far beyond the Baltic German community, as could be seen from the frequency with which Latvian politicians and newspapers took up the gauntlets that Schiemann threw down. He reserved particular dislike in his editorials for 'leaders' who slavishly followed popular opinion rather than educating it, thereby undermining liberalism by inverting the democratic principle. As he warned the Latvian Interior Minister, Arvēds Bergs, in January 1922, 'the danger of liberal thinking being wholly displaced by democratic dogma has never been so acute as today.'[50]

One of Schiemann's favourite taunts in the Constituent Assembly was to accuse the government of behaving with the arbitrariness of the Old Russian rulers. Certainly, by the close of 1920 a cumulatively revealing series of official acts testified to determination to forge a Latvian nation state. Measures included the replacement in summer of Riga's famous triple-language street plaques with Latvian—only signs—compared by Schiemann to putting a Chinese wall around the city. It was symptomatic of a wider assault on the use of German and Russian in the public space, as well as in the state administrative and judicial apparatus.[51] In addition, the German minority suffered Riga City Council's decision in August to support only one of the five German middle schools in Riga, as well as the government's determination to secure the large Stock Exchange school building for an art school. There were also planned cuts in the German schooling budget under Education Minister Plahkis, the man who forbad the use of Riga's second and smaller theatre by the minorities.[52] To the catalogue of woe was added the difficulty of the German 'colonists' (as former inhabitants of the now defunct wartime Ober Ost) in securing Latvian citizenship, and that of other Baltic Germans in getting permission to return to their homes.[53]

This makes all the more impressive the air of resilience rising from records of the CGBP and its sub-committees—labouring on into 1921 to raise funding and to rationalise the collection mechanisms, debating how best to influence the implementation of land reform, trying to ensure prompt processing of the citizenship applications by 'colonists' and to delay the partitioning of their land pending the state's rulings, drafting proposals for autonomy, and struggling to resist the evacuation of German school buildings in Riga until alternative premises were provided. 'How does [school] autonomy help us', Schiemann asked the Constituent Assembly in the spring of 1921, 'if you evict us from the schools and deprive us of the opportunity to teach?'[54] Yet there was no immediate sign that the key concerns troubling the German community would be resolved. Rather, CGBP meetings by May 1921 recorded Schiemann's intention formally to protest at the rising chauvinism in the Constituent Assembly.[55]

At least the faintest glimmer of light was beginning to filter through from the international arena. The West's *de jure* recognition of Latvia and Estonia on 26 January 1921 inevitably encouraged nation-state aspirations but it also signalled the end of Western intervention and a switch from isolating communism to trading with it. The reintroduction of elements of capitalism into Soviet planning under Lenin's New Economic Policy (NEP) stimulated a European-wide 'race' for Russia. It naturally engaged Germany, where in January 1921 the government convened talks between German industrial and commercial interest groups specifically to publicise the advantages of Latvia as the major commercial 'bridge' to Russia.[56] Once the state of war between Germany and Latvia arising from Bermondt's campaign formally ended with the treaty of 15 July

1920, preparations intensified for trade agreements. The Reich expected the 'power of economic facts' to help it draw a line under its wartime policies and to recover influence in the Baltic through active friendship.[57] Germany's *de jure* recognition of Latvia and Estonia in February 1921 crowned the policy that Schiemann had personally helped to launch in the autumn of 1918. For him recognition signalled that Russia was at last to be left to sort itself out, making the Baltic countries 'Europe's wall against Asiatisation'.[58]

He immediately exploited the idea of increasing pressure on the government to resolve the country's internal conflicts, to capitalise better on the increased credit-worthiness expected to flow from *de jure* recognition.[59] One promising sign was the appointment in March 1921 of Ringolds Kalnins as Finance Minister. A wealthy business man—physically fearsome, with gleaming gold-filled teeth—Kalnins was set on rolling back the state, ending monopolies and emergency legislation, founding a central bank and issuing a stable currency—in sum wrenching the country on to a privatisation course.[60] The Latvian Minorities' Economic Council, discussing the situation on the evening of 2 April under Schiemann's chairmanship, broadly welcomed the proposed changes. It was particularly pleased about the issue of a new currency, the Lat, to be secured against gold reserves. It 'should give our economic life the foundation it lacks'.[61] Not all CGBP members were happy with such fiscal stringency, but Schiemann was.[62] All the same, the dominant motif inside Latvia remained distrust of minorities, Baltic Germans above all.

Conditions worsened in May with Latvian opposition charges that Ulmanis' administration was relying too much on the minorities' bloc, causing unacceptable delays in breaking up the landed estates. The opposition watchword—'Free from the minorities'—said it all. The mood deepened Schiemann's concern at the failure of the Jewish and Russian groups to emulate the political organisation of the Baltic German minority. Meanwhile the persistent difficulties in persuading the non-German groups to pay their share of the Minorities' Information Office brought matters to crisis point in April. The organisation was wound up and re-launched as the Information Office of the CGBP, under the management of the novelist and journalist, Oskar Grosberg. In truth, the shortage of funds mirrored the lack of genuine agreement between the different national minorities.[63] They continued to preserve a semblance of unity through *ad hoc* cooperation but were not well placed to counter the chauvinism washing through the Constituent Assembly from the spring of 1921. All the more space was left for the small Latvian centre forces—the Democrats, Small Farmers and, last but not least, the deputies from Latgale—to broker deals.[64]

These groups, in Schiemann's harsh assessment, had neither statesmen nor political principles, only 'careerists'—keen 'to bring their little flock in from the cold by wooing the chauvinistic interests of the street'.[65] His view of the Latgale deputies was also coloured by press leaks in March 1921 that the government planned to hand over the Lutheran Jakobkirche to a new Catholic Bishop of Riga. The intention was to bind Polish-influenced Latgale (whose incorporation into Latvia increased its Catholic population to 22 per cent) closer to Riga. In Schiemann's view the Latgalers were in thrall to the Catholic Church, pursuing the narrow 'parish pump interests' of their 'culturally retarded stock' and ready to side with either left or right 'as long as their account was credited'.[66] Following one such deal and a hostile interpolation from the Latgale deputy, Kindsul, Ulmanis fell to a no-confidence vote at the beginning of June 1921, backed by the social democrats. What depressed Schiemann about the 'new course' was not only that these sanctioned the new coalition, nor that the new government promised to root out corruption from an inflated state apparatus; it was rather that the socialists conspired with the Latgale Farmer's Union leader Kindsul, 'who from the cultural and social viewpoint has only ever represented regressive principles' and as far as the economy went 'was loath to look beyond the fence of his own chicken-pen or pig-sty'.[67]

Schiemann's concern that the political shift would accentuate the negative qualities in Latvian social democracy was deepened by the regime's slogan 'Latvia for the Latvians'. Yet he treated as a compliment the taunt, made in the debate on the new government's programme on 17 June, that the minorities themselves voted sometimes with the left, sometimes with the right. What distinguished this from the mere opportunism of the small centre parties, Schiemann countered, was that the minorities kept practical considerations to the fore. Ultimately, they had 'regard more for the state's well being than the dictates of a programme'.[68] However, what mattered to those toppling Ulmanis was 'not for Latvia to bloom again economically, but simply to prevent a single non-Latvian from prospering. Whether or not the state collapses, it must above all live or die a *Latvian* state.'[69] The minorities registered their misgivings by abstaining from the vote on 17 June for the new cabinet of Zigfrīds Meierovics. Schiemann welcomed its promises to manage the economy more effectively but admitted gloomily that two solid years of constructive work had not advanced Baltic German wellbeing by a single step.[70]

In spite of these setbacks he saw 'no other route than that we have taken'. Baltic Germans in Latvia could not abandon 'the right way'.[71] His words also contained an implicit warning against a possible Baltic German backlash, one more reminder of the many fronts Schiemann had to engage with in order to sustain his fraction's work. It was to discourage the 'pointless hope' of help from outside that Fircks and Schiemann were authorised by the CGBP to tackle the fresh surge of disapproval coming from the émigré community in the Reich. Together the two Baltic German leaders visited Germany in August 1921.

By now the influence of the Baltische Vertrauensrat had declined. Its secretary, Georg von Freymann, focused largely on émigré welfare. Nevertheless, the Vertrauensrat co-operated with the association where the real post-war work centred, the Baltenverband. This emerged during 1919–20 from the collaboration of local refugee committees. Its managers, together with representatives of the Balt Red Cross in Danzig and the Principal Association of Balt Students, were to form the Balt Working Group in Berlin in 1922. To this forum the Vertrauensrat eventually attached itself in 1926, as did the Balt Women's Association two years later. The branches of the Members of the Couronian, Estonian and Livonian Nobles Society, which conceived itself as preserving the traditions of the *Ritterschaften*, ostensibly worked independently of these organisations. Last but not least was the newly-formed secret society, 'X'.[72] Though not manifesting its public face as the Balt Brotherhood till 1929, comparisons of the membership of the Balt Association and Balt Working Group with that of the Brotherhood confirm the Brotherhood's early infiltration of the other organisations.[73]

Much of this lay in the future but Schiemann saw from his visit to Germany that in spite of differences between the émigrés their leadership was still centred on the former ruling élites and the 'old *Literatentum*'. He found his Berlin meetings poorly attended. Those who turned up angrily attacked CGBP 'inaction' on land reform, arguing: 'Since the nobility's property is destroyed there can be no Germandom and so it is necessary to work for the destruction of the Latvian state.' Schiemann also found contempt for his fraction's policy on schooling now that the *Ritterschaften* were no longer in charge. 'Dearest friend,' he later wrote to Nicolai von Berg, 'you pose the rather difficult question: have our brethren learnt anything? For the moment the situation is that most of those who have learnt nothing remain abroad, fulminate and bear false witness, as is the nature of émigrés. Those staying here have admittedly yielded to dire necessity and to some extent brought to reason …and accept me as an unavoidable evil.'[74] At the same time he registered disbelief at the publication *Deutsches Land in Feindes Hand* by emigrants in Berlin. 'We have good reason to say'. Schiemann railed in the *Rigasche Rundschau*, 'Lord, protect us from our friends.'[75] Small wonder that Latvians had difficulty believing that the leopard had changed its spots.

It was vital to the credibility of the German fraction's work to counter disinformation outside. Unless the émigrés were made to accept the CGBP's explicit renunciation of the pre-war *status quo* they would not realise the opportunities for building a new existence in Latvia and Estonia, based on small and medium private enterprise rather than land ownership. At the same time, a bad press deterred potential Reich German investors. Schiemann managed at a meeting in Berlin on 12 August 1921 to get the émigré community to agree to the CGBP setting up its own information office in Berlin, which was functioning by early September of that year. Among its duties was the preparation of accurate economic information on Latvia,[76] and it became the approved channel for information which hitherto had trickled into Germany from a bewildering variety of German Balt organisations.

The development could not have been more timely for German-Baltic economic relations. Although Berlin could directly represent only Reich Germans resident in Latvia and Estonia, it envisaged the provisional Baltic trade treaties being negotiated in 1921–2 as helping the entire German community. Conversely, viable German minorities acting as trade intermediaries promised the Reich a competitive edge in the race to expand commerce eastwards. The strategy depended on Baltic Germandom's self-help, augmented by the limited Reich subsidies that Baltic governments tolerated for minority cultural and schooling needs. Here, for the Weimar Republic, weakened and constrained by the peace settlement, considerations of cost-effectiveness and political expediency coincided in the matter of discharging moral obligations to Baltic Germandom incurred during the war—as to *Auslandsdeutschen* elsewhere.[77]

There was an obvious congruence between this effort and Schiemann's argument to the Constituent Assembly, that the wellbeing of minorities was not 'a threat against the state ideal but the logical outcome of it'. That was the line he followed in the constitutional commission of the Constituent Assembly when it considered the Minorities Committee draft on autonomy on 28 April 1921. Unfortunately the event roughly coincided with the political moves leading to the fall of Ulmanis. However, with help from the social democrat member on the constitutional commission Schiemann secured a one-vote majority in favour of national autonomy being incorporated in the final constitution. A separate parliamentary commission was to elaborate appropriate provisions in more detail, making it imperative for the minorities to feed their thinking into the process. By June the CGBP had formed its own nine-member cross-party 'autonomy commission'. Chaired by Lothar Schoeler, it naturally included Schiemann, as well as the school chief Karl Keller.[78] Mounting disillusionment with the indecisiveness and lax organisation of the other minorities reinforced the German fraction's inclination to concentrate on its own project. The other large minorities were to do the same but all agreed to exchange drafts and for the minorities' deputies to endorse the separate proposals in due course.[79]

The process was not unconnected with Latvia's entry to the League of Nations on 22 September 1921. This committed the country to explore with the League Council the 'scope and details of the application of [Latvia's] international obligations for the protection of minorities'.[80] Schiemann hailed the event as rounding off the 'outward structure of the state' and allowing unhindered response to the 'challenges posed by the state's internal development'.[81] These included the demands of Latvia's nationality groups, which

Schiemann formulated at the request of the Minorities Committee. The points covered citizenship rights, entry visas for those anxious to return to Latvia, the inviolability of property serving cultural needs (schools, churches—no reference to estates) and equal language treatment. Pointedly linking international and domestic issues, Schiemann argued that all minorities, especially in states joining the League of Nations, had 'not only the right but a duty' to make their experience available to the wider cause. In this spirit he was deputed by the Minorities Committee (after his own nominee, the Jewish deputy Paul Mintz, had declined) to make representations at the forthcoming meeting of European minority associations in Vienna. The meeting was timed to follow an international sociology congress and a conference of the central council of the Federation of League of Nations Associations.[82]

Schiemann left for Vienna on the evening of Sunday 8 October, first drawing attention in a press interview to the broad agreement between Latvia's minorities, particularly over autonomy.[83] In keeping with the strategy of the German fraction he deliberately excluded from his presentation, as 'against the law and therefore also against the state', attacks on land reform as such.[84] The approach contrasted sharply with that of the Baltic German lawyer, Baron Alphons Heyking, spokesman of the Berlin-based Association of Latvian Minorities. Heyking's earlier private petition to the League, in a bid for international sympathy for the dispossessed German estate-holders, had attacked the 'anti-democratic tribalism' and 'Bolshevik leanings' of the Estonians and Latvians.[85] His tactics greatly pleased the émigrés as well as many Baltic Germans in Estonia and Latvia, including Fircks. However, Schiemann was at pains to distance the German minorities inside Latvia from Heyking's confrontational strategy; hence his specific remit from his fellow minority deputies in Riga, his dissociation from Heyking's own submissions to the conference, his complete openness to the Latvian media before leaving for Vienna, and his subsequent public disavowal—in the face of hostile Latvian press reports—of any sinister connection between the Berlin Association and minorities in Latvia.[86]

In Vienna Schiemann felt himself present at the infancy of a Europe-wide quest to define what minority rights were, with a view to influencing the practice of the League of Nations. [87] Similar considerations prompted him to campaign with Paul Mintz and others for Latvia to form a 'League of Nations Association'.[88] Schiemann again pointedly highlighted the parallels between these efforts and Latvia's ongoing discussions in Geneva on how to implement its general promise on minority protection.[89] 'As in other states', he wrote on returning from Vienna, 'the citizens of Latvia also need to engage with the far-reaching ideas of the League of Nations by forming an association. Latvia's minorities wish to take part in this effort too, especially, if at all possible, with the Latvian majority. But Latvia's minorities will in all circumstances act only within the bounds of Latvian statehood.'[90] In fact the Latvian League of Nations Association, constituted a few months later, merely agreed provisionally that there could be a minorities' section, but it was not till the following December that a 'Riga section' was at last acknowledged.[91] The German fraction's suggestion that the Latvian parliament send representatives to the European Inter Parliamentary Union was also taken up

Nevertheless, Schiemann's foray to Vienna was interpreted at the time as critical of the Latvian government, a form of disloyalty even, and thus the affair added to the feeling of oppression among Latvian Germans. Shortly after leaving the intellectual excitement of Vienna Schiemann found himself in the very different turmoil of an enlarged CGBP session. The sixty-strong meeting was convened on 29 October 1921 to consider the suggestion of Professors W. Sokolowsky, chairman of the recently constituted Herder Society, and Karl Kupffer, that the German fraction should finally show its displeasure by withdrawing from a hostile Constituent Assembly.

The specific grievances the two professors listed included almost a third of Evangelical pastorates being left vacant in the wake of agrarian reform, as well as the feared confiscation of the Jakobkirche. Sokolowsky in addition bitterly resented 22 June (the battle of Cēsis) being designated a national holiday. This issue incidentally prompted the formal dissolution of the Minorities Committee, after the Jewish fraction failed to back the German standpoint on 20 September 1921. However, Fircks spoke for his fellow parliamentary deputies in declaring resignation from their seats in the Constituent Assembly wholly 'unthinkable'. Schiemann's analysis clinched the argument. Seriously as he took the threat to the Jakobkirche and the provocative Latvian celebration of Cēsis, he wanted nothing to jeopardise autonomy—an issue of an altogether higher order. 'Our future National Council [envisaged under autonomy] is anchored in the constitution currently under discussion. It would be an error to give up helping with the constitution for the sake of a gesture. Such an act would only be permissible if we were to be placed in circumstances that were utterly hopeless. (Applause)'[92] That was manifestly not the case.

The discussion Schiemann referred to had been under way since the opening of the fourth session of the Constituent Assembly on 20 September. He failed to win support either for a second chamber of professions or a popularly elected head of state as additional checks on party infighting. However, his personal input to the constitutional commission led to the inclusion of two crucial provisions in the second part of the document dealing with basic rights. Article 115 acknowledged a right to the unhindered use of minority languages, and article 116 allowed minorities to set up for cultural purposes autonomous associations at public law (the legal basis for any national council).[93] Schiemann was encouraged by the incorporation of 'our [minorities] paragraphs' in the final constitution of 7 February 1922, but this had yet to be passed by the Constituent Assembly. A 'vital step forwards' had been taken but theory had to be converted into reality; 'everyone in Latvia' knew the regime was 'riding roughshod over this fundamental provision with sovereign disregard'.[94]

He had in mind the fresh wave of political gloom in the wake of a parliamentary outburst by the Latvian Interior Minister Alberts Kviesis on 28 October, in which he accused the Baltic Germans of promoting 'fanaticism' in their public campaign against government plans for the Jakobkirche. More worryingly, Kviesis ranked the Jakobkirche campaign alongside Schiemann's visit to Vienna as part of 'a chain of political weaponry'.[95] 'Anyone reading Latvian newspapers today', Schiemann responded, 'and then hearing of the brutal manner in which the Interior Minister spoke out against Latvian Balts must think a battle of life and death is in progress in our homeland.' He consoled himself with the thought that in truth the conflict was not 'rooted in the consciousness of the people'. Instead he placed the blame squarely on Latvian politicians. That the present government had been formed solely from a desire to be 'free' from its minorities made it prone, 'whenever it seems advisable, according to the favour or disfavour of political pettifoggers, to take action against the minorities, without any rational political reason'.[96] One such example was the dismissal of 100 German employees by the Riga City Council on the grounds of insufficient skill in Latvian, prompting a mass protest by Baltic Germans in Riga on Sunday 22 January 1922.[97]

Against this background the CGBP rounded off an extensive consultation process within the German community on its draft law, 'National Cultural Autonomy for Germans in Latvia'. It had benefited from exchanges of ideas between the CGBP's autonomy commission and German leaders in Lithuania and Estonia, particularly the latter, as well as from 'extensive discussions' with the Jewish representatives, above all Mintz.[98] On Schiemann's express advice, the draft excluded minority social welfare needs (except where state or municipal provision was poor), so as not to offend Latvians. Most of his effort in presenting the proposal to Baltic Germandom during the hectic winter of 1921–2 aimed at overcoming resistance to suggestions for implementing article 116 of the constitution. Neither the Progressive Party nor the Manufacturers' Association was happy with the idea of self-taxation for cultural purposes, fearing tax avoidance. The Progressive Party also opposed compulsory enrolment on a national community register.[99] Only after Schiemann addressed a volatile meeting of an enlarged CGBP on 5 March 1922 (p…) were objections grudgingly withdrawn, largely for the sake of Baltic German unity. The German draft law was handed over on 25 March 1922 to Latvian president Janis Čakste.

As the Constituent Assembly moved to a close amid preparations for Latvia's first full parliamentary elections, Schiemann remained critical of the failure of the 'new course'—launched the previous June 'amid the acclaim of the left and of all the country's chauvinists'—to deliver its promises to cut back on state expenditure and corruption. He acknowledged the success of Zigfrīds Meierovics in getting into his cabinet a number of 'most worthy men' but personalities alone could never overcome the coalition's inner contradictions.[100] He identified the inability of Latvian socialist and bourgeois parties to reconcile their views on agriculture or to agree social policy priorities as the most glaring of these. The first explained 'the hopeless decline of our rural economy'. The second manifested itself in bitter internal disagreement over the length of the working day and the right to strike. Indeed, the refusal of the social democrats to accept limitations on the right to strike caused the entire second part of the Latvian constitution to lapse after it failed, at its third reading on 5 April, to secure a majority in the Constituent Assembly.[101]

It was in the second part of the constitution, with its extensive catalogue of civic and other rights, that national autonomy was to have been anchored. The vote on 5 April therefore left the minorities with no constitutional guarantee that promises would be kept. What is more, the government continued to be reluctant to spell out in detail the minority protection it had agreed to as a condition of Latvia's membership of the League of Nations. The feeling prevailed in Baltic German quarters that Latvia's politicians were only now becoming aware of what they might have committed themselves to in endorsing the principle of autonomy in 1919, and were having second thoughts. That the Constituent Assembly failed to complete the very foundations on which Latvia was to be erected—that there was only, in Schiemann's words, a 'rump constitution'—contributed to the unusually sombre note of his 'Easter wishes' in the Sunday edition of the *Riga Rundschau* on 15 April 1922.[102]

5. A Place Within

At the close of the Constituent Assembly's last sitting on 20 July 1922 Schiemann voiced the hope for better things from the coming elections to Latvia's first parliament (Saeima). He had deflected yet another attack on Baltic German 'aristocracy' from the social democrats, likening them to those who had once persecuted Huguenots.[1] For him the 'real reactionaries' remained not those branded by social democrat Mārģeris Skujenieks during the election campaign as of 'foreign origin'—and who seemed likely to capture almost a fifth of the seats in the Saeima—but Latvian politicians trapped in the past. The thrust was pointed, given Skujenieks active participation in the 1905 revolution in Latvia, which allowed Schiemann to emphasise once more the German fraction's concern with the present.[2]

The building images to which he reverted were prominent in an editorial marking the 'historic transition' from Constituent Assembly to the Saeima, opening on 7 November 1922 'to the peaceful sound of bells and the heroic thunder of canons'. While the (state) 'edifice' had thankfully been roofed under difficult conditions, it still awaited the furbishing of the interior and the strengthening of its walls 'to withstand storm and the weather'. Mundanely, 'what the National Council began under heavy foreign menace and the Constituent Assembly encouraged, parliament now must finish.'[3] His insistence that the completion of the job required the labour of 'all citizens of Latvia without regard to nationality' was yet another reminder to fellow Baltic Germans that 'Whoever helps to build [the state] will also find a place within it.'[4]

In Latvia's first full parliament Paul Schiemann, Wilhelm Fircks, Karl Keller, Egon Knopp, John Karl Hahn and Manfred von Wegesack certainly found places. Their achievement was the greater in that political passions were aroused to 'white heat' during the election. Moreover the Saeima had only 100 seats, fifty fewer than the

Constituent Assembly. The broad political cleavage already observed by Schiemann still held. Arrayed against thirty-seven socialists were forty-seven bourgeois deputies, spread between the influential Farmers' Union (17) and parties further to the right—Christian Nationals (4) and the Arved Berg group (4)—as well as a centre group made up of the Democrats (6), Small Farmers (3) and various Latgalers [13]. Noteworthy in the longer run was the emergence of the Democratic Centre in 1922. It included the Democratic Party, the Radical Democratic Party and the People's Party. It was above all the voice—not always united—of Latvian nationalism, speaking through the country's largest daily, the *Jaunākās Ziņas*.

Fears about the threat to Central and Eastern Europe arising from France's occupation of the Ruhr in January 1923 for the moment predisposed even socialists to support a 'great coalition' under Janis Pauļuks (Farmers' Union). The arrangement barely outlasted the foreign policy crisis but until it collapsed in late June 1923 Pauļuks was inclined to dispense with support from the minorities and to rely heavily on the small centre parties.[5] Among other portents for the German fraction, three more deputies from Latgale joined Pastor Francis Trasuns. His determination to see the Jakobkirche handed over to the Catholics continued to attract the sharp end of Schiemann's pen.[6] The minorities' deputies saw no option other than to vote against the new administration.[7]

Neither the machinations of the bourgeois parties nor Latvian social democracy's 'addiction to programme'—in day-to-day politics 'perhaps the greatest evil of all'—dented Schiemann's faith in parliamentary systems.[8] He believed that coalitions would eventually be the European norm, even in Britain, and viewed the conduct, of parties, not their number, as the litmus test of parliamentary health. Only liberal parliamentary systems could ward off the ideological oligarchies of Bolshevik Russia and, most recently, Italy where fascism had come to power. Both regimes claimed to act for the masses, but to Schiemann they were merely perverting democracy by subjugating the individual.[9] Equally, he launched an early attack on the infant German variant of fascism for its anti-Semitism. In an extended analysis of the 'Jewish question' in July 1922 he dismissed the 'ludicrous' notion of a Zionist conspiracy as a misreading of the help offered by Germany's assimilated Jewry to their brethren arriving from the ghettos of Eastern Central Europe in the second half of the nineteenth century. 'Every aggressive nationalism', he warned, 'can have only a fruitless and negative impact on one's *own* people and one's own state.'[10] It was with communism that he was most immediately concerned at this critical juncture of Latvia's statehood, even though the government banned the communist party.

Reflecting in June 1922 on Lenin's illness and on how Bolshevism had replaced the dominance of an aristocracy of birth with an aristocracy of party, Schiemann predicted the system outlasting its leader with the phrase: 'The Russia of Bucharin or Trotsky will doubtless remain the Russia of Lenin.'[11] Two considerations followed for the Baltic states in his reading. First, economic relations had to be resumed with Russia; secondly, Baltic governments must avoid international combinations hostile to Moscow. Interestingly, Schiemann saw both goals move nearer with the German-Soviet treaty of Rapallo in April 1922, notwithstanding its adverse impact on European opinion. He too regretted its timing—it proved to be the last nail in the coffin of the world economic conference at Genoa, the first ever between communist and capitalist systems.[12] At the same time he dismissed widespread suspicions of a hidden German threat behind Rapallo on the grounds that the Weimar Republic could only pursue economic policy for the foreseeable future.[13] In this respect the new treaty undoubtedly gave advantage to German industry but, as Schiemann pointed out, the Reich could hardly rebuild Russia without the Western powers. Furthermore, 'The independence of the Baltic states and the maintenance of their democratic development is a precondition for any productive work in solving the Russian problem.'[14]

His emphasis on the 'horizontal' relationship between Germany, the Baltic states and Russia pointedly questioned the 'vertical' axis claimed for Latvian policy by Meierovics immediately before the Genoa conference, when Latvia, Estonia, Finland and Poland signed a defensive accord in Warsaw.[15] Schiemann was not opposed to regional blocs as such but only to those harmful to Baltic independence. With the words 'The Baltic bloc is dead—long live the Baltic', he read Finland's failure to ratify the accord (and here Rapallo had its impact) not as indifference but as a turning away from the dance of the great powers towards the ideal of a neutral Baltic sea.[16] 'If we accept this function of our own geographical position, then a wealth of mutual economic and political interests automatically arises, which we could encompass in an independent policy, to be construed not as a French, German or Russian orientation but as a purely Baltic, northern orientation.'[17] Closer ties with the Scandinavian states offered the only way 'to create a power factor which every state interested in north eastern Europe would have to reckon with'.[18] Schiemann identified the precondition for the Baltic states joining the Scandinavian sphere as being an intensification of their own economic activity. With this he returned to the struggle to promote the liberal ideals he believed essential to enterprise in Latvia.

The prospects were no better for his idea of a parallel 'business parliament' to liberate the Latvian economy from party tyranny. Yet he clung tenaciously to the principle of dispersing state functions to appropriate work and business 'associations'. The process seemed to him an essential part of a new armoury needed by liberals to 'fight for human freedoms'. Throughout his life Schiemann retained the conviction that only liberalism—which he characterised as undogmatic, rooted in the present, and tolerant of state form as long as it allowed the individual to develop—stood against the excesses of state power. The latter was 'never so threatening as it is today, now that monarchical absolutism is finally vanquished'.[19] His 'corporatism' thus had nothing in common with the ideas then being explored in Mussolini's Italy but rather envisaged economic restructuring as a check on the power of central government, whose seemingly unlimited growth he came to see as inimical itself to parliamentary democracy. Inexorably, this line of reasoning converged with his advocacy of autonomy for Latvia's minorities.

'Culture' appeared to him a prime candidate for central government divesting itself of responsibilities. He could not, for example, imagine a national Latvian entity dedicated to its own cultural values being equally committed to promoting those of the German, Russian and Jewish communities. The alternative to being imprisoned by the nation-state framework was for minorities to manage their own cultural affairs. On this subject Schiemann always took pains to credit the innovative thinking of the Austro-socialists Renner and Bauer. They had first seen the inequality and repression of national minorities as a barrier to the goal of bringing social and political freedom and equality for the individual, and had initiated moves away from the older precept of autonomy applied to compactly settled territories towards one based on *persons*, in an attempt to facilitate self-administration for the scattered national groups of Austria-Hungary. Apart from isolated ventures—notably the Moravian compromise of November 1905, fixing German and Czech language in the autonomous administration and creating separate national school authorities—the doctrine made little headway outside left-wing circles. However, the onset of the First World War and the ensuing calls for self-determination, culminating in the formation of new nation states in Central and Eastern Europe after 1918, stimulated a wider European awareness of the need to protect minorities.[20]

An influential document circulating at the Paris Peace Conference was the Viennese international lawyer Rudolf Laun's 'Draft of an international treaty for the protection of national minorities'. Among other things it demanded national equality of citizenship; nationality to be determined by free choice; a regular national census and the creation of a national register (Kataster); autonomy to be embodied in a national corporation owning and managing its own resources and with rights of self-taxation; and schooling in the mother-tongue. Laun's draft directly inspired Baltic German activists for cultural autonomy, particularly Ewald Ammende and Werner Hasselblatt in Estonia, as well as Paul Schiemann. He too stressed as preconditions for personal autonomy a share of state resources for a minority's cultural needs, the enrolment of its members on a national register, and the setting-up of a public law administrative body for the minority concerned. Such a 'national council' would subsequently enjoy regulatory and taxation rights in all cultural matters.[21]

Compared with pre-war autonomy campaigners, Schiemann was to have the advantage of prolonged and practical engagement with the issue as a working politician and journalist in Latvia. Here, during 1922, he declared: 'The essence of autonomy consists of according the right to a minority to administer independently, albeit under the state umbrella, a defined area of state duties, primarily cultural, and to receive for this purpose a percentage of state funding proportionate to its [the minority's] size.' Since private corporations enjoyed no entitlement to state support, it was felt essential for the minority to be constituted as a public law corporation.[22]

Obligatory enrolment on the national register was central to the concept. Schiemann warned the Riga Parents' Association: 'The moment we cease to regard the German national community as the actual body of all citizens of Latvia of German nationality, and declare instead that anybody can both be German and yet not a member of the national community, we forgo the hard-won substance of autonomy; we degrade the national community to a private association'—allowing it to sink to the level of a 'choral society'.[23] From the choice of nationality, once freely made, ineluctably flowed the obligations as well as the benefits of that decision. Schiemann's words indirectly rebuked circles who only reluctantly endorsed the original German autonomy project to preserve an appearance of unity. Their brooding presence made him anxious in a climate where he sensed a government preparing a crusade against the cultural heritage of minorities, in particular their schooling.

The 1919 law obliged local authorities to provide primary classes for every thirty children of a minority, but middle and higher minority schools were only entitled to a percentage of their costs from state funds. The German middle school in Riga, for example, needed an extra 1.5 million lats from private resources in 1922 alone.[24] In the Baltic German community regular collections and the work of the German Parents' Association, particularly in the countryside, helped to meet additional need.[25] Schiemann was therefore irritated by Latvian claims that middle schools were being given to the German minority. The management of education was another matter. Here the German community profited from ambiguities in the 1919 law, as well as the goodwill of individual Latvian education ministers, to enshrine the practice of self-inspection. It was subject only to review by central Ministry of Education officials. When budget cuts eliminated one state-funded Baltic German inspector as early as 1920, the German community promptly appointed two 'honorary inspectors'. German was also used in the conduct of education authority business, although the original legislation referred only to instruction in the mother-tongue.

All this was threatened by a decree of the new Education Minister, M. Gailits, on 5 February 1923. His draconian measures proposed to eliminate the minorities' inspectorate, relegate minority education chiefs to lower salary grades, and enforce the use of Latvian in the conduct of all school administration.[26] For Schiemann this struck at the very heart of school autonomy, 'the one genuinely significant success of recent times for Latvia's minorities'.[27] These readily agreed on the nature of the threat. However, a widespread perception that Baltic Germans enjoyed more leeway over schooling than either Russians or Jews added to the familiar obstacles to coordinating minority policy responses.[28] Schiemann's offer to resign from the board of the Minorities' Committee was refused, but both he and Fircks insisted on making direct representations to Gailits, advising other minority deputies to do the same.[29] The German fraction chose not to withdraw Karl Keller as German education chief pending a more favourable political constellation for fear of harming German youth. By remaining on the Saiema's education commission Keller could intensify doubts within the ruling coalition about the legality of Gailits' proposals.[30]

Such doubts, also exploited by Schiemann and Fircks in direct talks with Gailits, as well as with the Farmers' Union and other parties, produced a compromise in late March 1923. Private assurances were given to the German fraction that Latvian inspectors would only gather information, and not issue directives. The arrangement permitted German inspectors to continue in a semi-official capacity—no longer as civil servants but as 'school councillors of the [Baltic German] Parent's Association'.[31] Within a few months the anticipated defection of the socialists from the ruling coalition, the inception of a new Meierovics administration on 26 June 1923, and Latvia's preparations to sign a League declaration on minority protection combined to bring marginal improvement in the bargaining position of the minorities.[32] Gailits tacitly accepted the practice of dual language documentation for school governance. Additional Baltic German pressure overturned requirements for obligatory Latvian language exams for teachers and administrative staff in minorities' schools. Only after Meierovics' own precarious cabinet was replaced by one under Voldemār Zāmuēls in January 1924 could the Russian and Jewish representatives in the new government secure a firm agreement not to enforce the decree.[33] German school councillor Max von Radecki noted with relief that the outcome of the struggle left Latvia's minorities opportunities to develop schooling 'undreamt of in Tsarist Russia'.[34]

Schiemann agreed with the sentiment, but the need for vigilance amid the whims and dictates of Latvian parliamentary politics remained. Even Zīgfrids Meierovics'—a politician increasingly admired by Schiemann as a principled exception proving the rule—had pressed on with legislation for the confiscation of the Jakobkirche, as well as enforced sharing with Latvian Lutherans of the Domkirche, historically the preserve of the German community alone. The fate of the Jakobkirche provoked Schiemann to comparisons with the Thirty Years War and a fierce parliamentary outburst in April 1923 for which he was called to order. 'With today's law', he insisted, 'you abandon the principles of a state of culture and of law… Make sure that the day never comes when your party bargaining is in full bloom but the state, to whose leadership you are essentially called, is ruined.'[35]

Schiemann and his co-workers mobilised considerable domestic and international sympathy for legislation protecting the Church from the state in the course of 1923. Their campaigning culminated impressively—but in honourable failure—with Latvia's first-ever referendum at the beginning of September. Calls from opponents of the referendum not to vote in fact helped secure a majority for the German draft law, but the overall figure fell far short of the 400,000 votes needed for acceptance. The state president subsequently rejected the German proposal, paving the way for the Papal Legate, Monsignor Zecchini, to celebrate the Jakobkirche as Latvia's cathedral church the following May.[36] In also agreeing to joint worship in the Domkirche with Latvians, the Baltic German body politic now lived with the virus of anxiety about the ultimate fate of their magnificent cathedral.

In other ways 1923 turned out better than Schiemann had reason to hope when he marked its opening with a gloomy editorial on Lithuania seizing Memel and the French occupation of the Ruhr. The latter he equated with inviting Bolshevism into Europe.[37] Schiemann was an influential member of the Saiema's Commission for Foreign Relations till 1928, and his 1923 analysis, *Europe's problems,* shows how prescient he could be. Assuming that Germany's fall would also be Europe's, 'removing' East Central Europe from the world economy, he reasoned: 'The salvation of Europe lies in solving three problems above all, which in their tragic seriousness have become world problems. The German-French problem, which is the problem of a European economic union. The Russian problem, which is the problem of a revision of capitalism. The minorities problem, which is the problem of solving national antagonisms.' Interestingly, Schiemann argued that only a European economic union, whose first task had to be the creation of a common currency, could transform the lethal Franco-German disputes over ore and coal into binding ties.[38] Gustav Stresemann's appointment as German Chancellor in August improved the year as far as Schiemann was concerned, not least because he saw it leading to better prospects for Franco-German reconciliation.[39]

That, on his own analysis, was vital for European minority issues. In this field, too, Schiemann's personal star continued to rise during 1923. His earliest post-war forays into Europe were often on behalf of all Latvia's minorities, as in 1921 and again in October 1922 in Vienna, but he quickly became prominent among the German communities scattered throughout Central and Eastern Europe. In the process he was re-united on a more regular basis with his former benefactor from Tallinn, the boisterous Ewald Ammende. Ammende's restless information-gathering journeys in East Central Europe had generated material for his doctorate for Kiel University in 1922, 'Die deutsche Minderheiten in Europa. Ihr Entstehen, ihre Organisation und ihre Zusammenschlussbestrebungen', and left him a large network of personal contacts in the field. As a result of his travels he became depressed by the defeatism and petulance among the *Auslandsdeutschen* and quickly saw the advantage of uniting them. Together with the Hungarian German Rudolf Brandsch, Paul Schiemann, Carl Georg Bruns and others at the October 1922 conference in Vienna, Ammende took part in the initial planning of what became in 1923 the Verband der deutschen Minderheiten in Europa.[40]

Apart from regular meetings of German minorities a standing committee of the Verband, comprising one member from each of the eleven countries involved, was to meet three or four times a year. Paul Schiemann represented the Latvian Germans on this committee. Through discussion of League and minority questions and the provision of legal advice the Verband aimed to bring greater solidarity to the post-war struggle of the different German groups and lobby for internationally recognised minority rights legislation.[41] However, as another element in the already labyrinthine collection of private and semi-official bodies springing up after the war to care for German minorities, the Verband attracted hostility from those viewing German minorities primarily as agents of German 'revisionism'.[42] In fact Germany's völkisch nationalists in particular were increasingly prone to conceive of 'Germany' not just as the country itself but in terms of the German '*Volk*'—thereby aspiring to bring into the fold the 6 million Germans left outside the motherland as a result of the detested peace settlement. The mindset was prevalent among the personnel of the major umbrella organization distributing secret government aid to the *Auslandsdeutschen*, the ostensibly private Deutsche Stiftung für Kulturbodenforschung.[43]

It originated in fact in the so-called Eastern Committee, set up in 1919 to protect Germans in lands lost to Poland. The Deutsche Stiftung's influential chief executive, Erich Krahmer-Möllenberg, had in fact been the liaison between the Eastern Committee and the Prussian Ministry of the Interior. Nationalist voices predominated on the all-party body (minus communists and national socialists) providing parliamentary cover for the Stiftung's work. Former nationalist Ostmark agitators in Arthur Moeller van den Bruck's right wing circle—provocatively calling themselves on signature of the detested Versailles treaty the 'June Club'—found key positions in the Berlin bureaucracy overseeing *Auslandsdeutsche* issues. For present purposes it is noteworthy that 'the spiritual centre of the *Volksdeutsche* movement', the enormously influential and revisionist Deutsche Schutzbund, itself an umbrella for 120 associations, particularly engaged Baltic German émigrés. These included Max Hildebert Boehm, originally from Estonia, fellow founder and active June Club member and later director of the Institut für Grenz und Auslandsstudien in Berlin.[44]

For Schiemann such figures were above all practitioners of '*Grenzlandpolitik*'—driven by concern for the Germans in the contested border regions (*Grenzlanddeutsche*). By inclination they focused dislike against the foreign element, whereas '*Minderheitenpolitik*' was necessarily premised on an ideal of national reconciliation. To him it was a matter of regret, if understandable, that the 'border politicians' in Berlin came to monopolise the Reich central offices concerned with the welfare of Germans abroad.[45] In such circles the initiative leading to the setting-up of the Verband der deutschen Minderheiten was not entirely welcome. Typically Ammende's hope of becoming the central liaison between the Verband and the Reich authorities was dashed. Instead the Berlin office of the Verband's legal adviser, the well-connected Carl Georg Bruns, became the conduit for Reich subsidies to the German groups in the Verband. Ammende's failure to secure the post was another indication too of the Auswärtiges Amt's determination to keep the activities of German minorities broadly in line with the priorities of Reich foreign policy.[46]

Intriguingly, then, the experience of Europe's mixed border regions, which spawned Nazis like Alfred Rosenberg, Max Scheubner-Richter and pan-German *völkisch* academics with nationalist *Grenzland* mentalities, by contrast nurtured in Paul Schiemann a profound and lasting commitment to multi-nationhood. Schiemann and others in the Verband der deutschen Minderheiten explicitly disavowed irredentism, the more effectively to focus their campaign for European minority rights.[47] The interplay between such *völkisch* figures as Boehm and dedicated liberals like Schiemann exemplified the intense struggle being waged after 1918 for the soul of the *Auslandsdeutsche*, and therefore also for the repositioning of Germany in the new Europe.

To ask whether Germany should not have subsidised the welfare and cultural needs of its hard-pressed minorities abroad is to see the question as rhetorical. By concealing the extent, if not always the fact, of such support, the covert funding mechanism centring on Berlin aimed to offset the stringent fiscal constraints imposed on the Reich by the Treaty of Versailles. On the other hand, secrecy also helped to prevent still more anti-German sentiment in post-war Europe. Nevertheless, the limited subsidies were premised on the German minorities ultimately supporting themselves, a goal best achieved through their cooperation with host-countries. That in turn was to promote the overriding priority of the Auswärtiges Amt during the 1920s: the peaceful restoration of the Reich's economic and political standing in Europe.[48]

The relevance of Schiemann's efforts to this aim is obvious, and 1923 brought him another ally in the form of the new Reich representative in Latvia, the social democrat writer and politician Adolf Köster who arrived in Riga in April. His was one more eloquent voice raised against the June Club and its values, if long since drowned, like that of Schiemann himself, by the clamour of historians hot on the trail of National Socialists and their mentors.

Born in 1883 near Hanover and trained in philosophy at Erlangen University, Köster taught at the Technical High School in Munich between 1911 and 1913, when he published a study of Kant as well as a novel, *An Anxious Night*. Subsequently, as war correspondent for the socialist newspaper, *Vorwärts*, Köster decisively rejected—like Schiemann—preserving the Baltic German 'colonial' ruling caste; he too saw an independent Courland under their control as an impossibility.[49] After a spell in the Reich Chancellery in 1918 and as plebiscite commissioner for Schleswig in May 1919, he was Foreign Minister for three months in 1920 and later, in Josef Wirth's second administration, Interior Minister (October 1921 to November 1922). He had already worried as Foreign Minister that the organisations for Germandom were 'to some extent making policy, the bill for which we will later have to bear. It is essential that they are brought firmly into line.'[50] Köster also tried to involve left-wing organizations in the Deutsche Stiftung. Anxious not to alarm the new states in East Central Europe, he tried in vain as Interior Minister to resist the combining of work for the *Auslandsdeutsche* and *Grenzlandsdeutsche*.[51]

It was as if preordained that Adolf Köster would form a close bond with Paul Schiemann. They shared the experience of being journalists and authors, as well as having a common interest in drama and a profound commitment to parliamentary systems. Wilhelm von Rüdiger described Köster as 'Outwardly a brutal strong-man of exceptional vitality, intellectually lively, an amusing talker' whose demeanour 'had nothing in common with received ideas of a skilled diplomat of the old school'.[52] Köster, like Schiemann, preferred the company of artists and novelists, although Baltic Germans who had read his one novel with a view to currying favour were discountenanced by a stringent ban on discussing it. His residence soon became a congenial social centre and his 'beer evenings' an essential part of his diplomatic armoury.[53] Shortly after Köster's arrival in Riga Schiemann wrote in a letter to Alfred Ruetz: 'Generally I go on a spree once a week with ambassador Köster, who attaches great value to this.'[54] At a later date, when Rüdiger accompanied Schiemann and Köster to Berlin to talk in the Auswärtiges Amt about additional financial support for the Baltic German community, he was shocked to find that his two companions embarked first on a three-day round of late night eating and drinking.[55]

In truth such informal personal ties between minority leaders and officialdom—often now untraceable—were crucially important in policy-making. The appointment of a man of Köster's stature to the Riga post was a further signal to Schiemann of the Reich's acceptance of independent Baltic states and the importance attached to them. One cannot exaggerate the moral support he derived from such a convinced republican, who strongly resisted the nationalist tendencies among Reich Germans resident in Riga. 'The more firmly and convincingly the belief in republican thoughts is expressed in Germany itself', Köster argued, 'the quicker will the *Auslandsdeutsche* understand that they will get no further with eternal complaints about the present state of Germany and the sooner will they reconcile themselves to the present form of the German Reich.'[56] Köster's appointment to the Riga post also signalled an overall rationalisation of previously *ad hoc* subsidies from the Reich for schooling and cultural purposes. As ambassador his influence was decisive for Schiemann's political strategy in Latvia. Important in this respect was the formation in Riga in November 1923 of the Zentrale deutschbaltischer Arbeit.

The final decision to set up the Zentrale was taken during a discussion of *Auslandsdeutsche* issues on 7 May 1923. Eventually, the new organization was affiliated to the Verband der deutschen Minderheiten and represented on this by Schiemann till 1933.[57] When formally constituted on 7 November 1923 the Zentrale was presided over by Wilhelm von Rüdiger, with Karl Stavenhagen as its general secretary. It aimed to coordinate the work of the many Baltic German non-political associations engaged with social, welfare and cultural issues. The point was stressed at a key meeting between Schiemann, Schoeler, Keller and some forty Riga welfare organisations on 22 November 1922.[58] For Schiemann assigning primary responsibility for 'non-political' issues to the Zentrale served several purposes. One was to counteract an unjustified feeling among broad sectors of the German community that funds raised for education and welfare might be diverted to purely political ends. Henceforth the CGBP could focus on parliamentary work, leaving the Zentrale responsible for 'non-political' activities.

Far from wishing to encourage the simplistic idea of a separation of politics and culture, however, Schiemann was bent on heightening the political awareness of his community. Thus initially the Zentrale was constituted as a section of the CGBP.[59] In his annual report for the *Jahrbuch des baltischen Deutschtums* Schiemann specifically criticised the 'senseless proposition' that improving welfare could ever be apolitical. 'If politics means handling an issue with a larger community in mind—and there can be no doubt of this—then it must be clear that any cultural, any economic and any social activity within our nationhood must be unwelcome, indeed wholly damaging, unless it serves the interests of the whole. The naive suggestion of politics as an unnecessary preoccupation, distinct from proper work in other fields, really ought no longer to be voiced by educated people.' The German community's 'entire public work' had to be given all possible 'inner coherence' and oriented according to a 'common criterion'.[60]

In pursuit of this goal Schiemann was perfectly prepared to override the objections to the Zentrale from within his own party. Its discussion of the Zentrale showed clearly enough that it suspected 'conservative German circles' of deliberately trying to undermine the CGBP by supporting a new centre of influence. 'The secret aim of the "Arbeitszentrale" is'—the German Balt Democratic Party's committee cautioned Schiemann on 19 October 1923—'the displacement of Dr Paul Schiemann as the current leader of German Balt politics and the restoration of those conservative politics so injurious to Germandom in Latvia. Dr Schiemann's expectation—that in the [new] Zentrale he can openly confront those opponents hitherto covertly working against him, instruct them through acquaintance with the actual practice of politics, and through reasoning bring them to a better understanding—will not be realised.' To Schiemann the risk had to be taken in pursuit of solidarity for the Baltic German community as a whole. As he reminded his party on 18 November 1923, the Zentrale could take no political decisions without the approval of the CGBP.[61]

The sympathetic Köster's presence in Riga was crucial to his project, since it became customary for the Zentrale to present a budget to the embassy at the start of each financial year, detailing what the community could raise through its own efforts and how the shortfall might be met from Reich subsidies for schooling and other cultural needs. Köster's personality made it virtually impossible to get round him on matters concerning the allocation of Reich funds. How important these became during Köster's five-year term of office is clear from Rüdiger's calculations. He mentioned cover for a quarter of the school budget and a third of the costs of the Herder Institute, as well as backing for the German theatre and the running costs of the Zentrale.[62]

The *Rigasche Rundschau* also benefited through the German government—funded Concordia Literarische Anstalt GmbH. This was set up in 1920 under a cross-party board to help the German minority press abroad and placed under Max Winkler, a key figure in the apparatus for distributing Reich subsidies. Ruetz finally managed to secure the *Rigasche Rundschau*'s long-term viability when Concordia took 40 per cent of share capital in 1921, a move leading to full control in 1924.[63] Thereafter Ruetz & Co. remained owners in name alone and a five-man board in Riga, including Schiemann, Fircks and Rüdiger, took over the day-to-day management. The paper was to continue speaking for the fraction as a whole, and Schiemann's new contract specified that he could dictate the paper's political line as well as deciding on appointments and dismissals. Although the Auswärtiges Amt now effectively owned the *Rigasche Rundschau*, Schiemann's editorial voice was emphatically not silenced. To his relief, however, he finally secured a pension for himself and his wife, with the new 'shareholders' agreeing to pay the premiums on his life insurance policies.[64]

Within the parliamentary arena he was now preoccupied by the struggle for a German autonomy law, a text for which was placed before the Saiema's public law commission on 15 December 1923, during the relatively favourable political situation at the time. Till then Schiemann had seen 'not the remotest chance' of the project passing under the great coalition. In spite of the working compromise on school inspection and language tests, it seemed advisable to secure additional safeguards for schooling practices. The reworked and greatly simplified 'Legislative project concerning the national cultural autonomy of the German national community and the use of the German language in Latvia' therefore included the draft of a general German school law, alongside the demands for compulsory enrolment, the right to raise taxes and a language law sanctioning the use of German. Schiemann doubted whether Baltic Germans could match the influence of the Jews and Russians in Zamuels' cabinet, but from January 1924 he chaired the sub-committee of the public law commission, where a sympathetic social democrat, Andrejs Petrevics, was overseeing the German project.[65]

The balance was not disturbed by the success of the social democrats on 3 April 1924 in finally persuading the Saeima to reject compensation for dispossessed estate-holders. Baltic German deputies could hardly endorse this, but the parliamentary arithmetic made their votes irrelevant. Schiemann led his fraction from the chamber before the final count, indirectly criticising the 'semblance of compensation' implicit in the risible sums bandied about by the Farmers' Union, but in doing so reserving an attack on non-compensation at a later date as a possible violation of minority rights.[66] The Farmers' Union was less than pleased by the German fraction's tactics. However, in the course of overtures by Schiemann, Fircks and Keller in the preceding weeks, Meierovics implied that electoral considerations were primarily fuelling his party's 'German hatred', which should abate in due course.[67] He could offer little more than his party's neutrality on the German autonomy project, and perhaps Farmers' Union deputies absenting themselves from a parliamentary vote. Still, within the German fraction cautious optimism prevailed.[68] At this juncture the situation was adversely influenced by the re-emergence of opposition to the project from within the Baltic German community.

From its left wing came a thrust from Robert Riedel, second chairman of the Progressive Party, who attacked the scheme as the product of an exclusive circle. Fircks was deeply annoyed that no such objection had been voiced when the Progressives first endorsed the German project. However, Riedel was already drifting away from his party, soon to found his own German Workers' Party of Latvia. (26.4.1924).[69] He also edited the Latvian—subsidised *Rigasche Nachrichten*, close to the Farmers' Union. Riedel, together with his successor Edgar Franz and Wilhelm Schreiner, a former member of the Latvian National Council and briefly Latvian diplomatic representative in Berlin and Prague, claimed to be defending the 'little man' against 'reactionaries' dominating the CGBP. Schiemann, writing in the previous autumn to a namesake of his who acted as the *Rigasche Rundschau's* Moscow correspondent, observed of Riedel: 'It has to be said that this man is an utter swine, who damages the German cause where he can. He masquerades as a good national "progressive" German.'[70]

Schiemann nonetheless recognised the threat to his own political leadership. While he considered Riedel to be ultimately 'too foolish to achieve anything', he took Edgar Franz more seriously. When Schiemann defended autonomy before an 800-strong Industry Association meeting in Riga in March 1924, Franz also repeatedly charged the CGBP with threatening the 'little man's interests' by insisting that all should 'join' Germandom. He was shouted down, but Schiemann and Fircks acknowledged the success of this 'refined demagogue' in exploiting the fact that leading positions in Baltic German organisations were often held by the 'eldest so-and-so'. 'Never a day passes', Fircks commented, 'without Mr Franz making a little bomb from the explosives at hand.'[71] Schiemann had long deplored the capacity of 'our intellectual élite' for acknowledging as German 'only someone who has read Kant and knows a dozen quotes from Goethe' and whose simplest thoughts were cloaked in scientific terminology and citations, forcing the average reader to put the pages down 'with a sigh' after thirty lines.[72] One such figure, the self-important Professor Sokolowsky, added to the fraction's difficulties by intimating in the course of a meal with Gailits in a Riga restaurant that autonomy would erect a 'dividing wall' between Latvians and Germans. Fircks observed scathingly: 'The stab in the back seems once more to be part of the iron tradition of German political realities.'[73]

Clearly Riedel, Franz, Sokolowski and others provided ammunition for Latvian politicians to argue that German autonomy would create 'a state within a state', thus indirectly encouraging the public law commission to whittle away at the German draft during 1924. By April, partly under the impact of similar arrangements imposed on Estonian Germans, Schiemann had to accept that the commission would agree to neither compulsory registration nor the right of taxation.[74] It was also evident that commission members would not sanction any investment of public law rights in the national council proposed under the German autonomy scheme. However, what Schiemann saw as the crucial right of nationality to be determined by free choice was accepted by the commission. So too was the notion of a language law. Schiemann's sub-committee managed to deal with most of the objections raised in the plenary commission by November 1924. He believed that the basis for compromise still existed, deftly using the occasion of Oswald Spengler's lecture in Riga in November to promote the idea of cultural autonomy as a 'third way' for Europe to escape its prophesied decline.[75]

Within days, on 1 December, an abortive communist coup in Tallinn conveniently demonstrated the advantages of national solidarity. Estonian politicians hastily dropped previous objections to a cultural autonomy law and it was duly passed on 5 February 1925. In Latvia an anxious new government under Farmers' Union member Celmiņš (19.12.24–23.12.25) proposed new legislation for the defence of the republic.

Faced with an uncertain foreign policy situation, Celmiņš readily accepted Schiemann's offer of support from the German fraction in return for government backing of cultural autonomy for the large minorities. The arrangement promised to deflect joint Jewish-social democrat moves against separate projects in favour of a general minorities law.[76] Schiemann's personal intervention was crucial to the public law commission's endorsement of the now heavily-amended German project on 19 February 1925. It then immediately met with resistance from the education commission, chaired by the Latvian nationalist poet and Democratic Centre deputy, Karl Skalbe. Pilloried by Schiemann as 'a reactionary of the purest kind', Skalbe used his commission's remit to review that part of the German scheme devoted to schooling provision in order to arouse hostility against the whole project.[77] Schiemann was forced to concede, after reviewing the concessions his fraction had made in the past year, that it was no longer a matter of a specific law, but rather a test of whether 'informed Latvians' even wanted compromise.[78] Prospects in the existing parliament were sufficiently bleak for the CGBP to hold back on its autonomy scheme until after the autumn elections for the second Saeima. Schiemann gave formal notification to this effect on 28 April 1925.[79]

Ironically, the Riga municipal polls in March suggested that the German fraction's commitment to above-party policies was slowly winning over sections of the Latvian public. Results in Riga had been expected to mirror the poor rate of return by Baltic German émigrés in comparison with Latvians coming home.[80] The CGBP also faced for the first time a separate German list, that of the German Workers' Party. Schiemann suffered no anxiety over counter-attacking Riedel, Franz and company. Schreiner, whose appointment to Latvia's Berlin embassy Schiemann once helped through his contacts in the Auswärtiges Amt, was now subjected to a blistering editorial in the *Rundschau*.[81] Were Schreiner's sudden aspirations to become a politician, Schiemann asked, 'Because as an engineer he bankrupted a factory a year? Because he presided over the decline of a flourishing party to a wretched rump? Or because he made himself the least indispensable in two diplomatic posts?'[82] In the event, demographic trends rather than Schreiner's efforts were the cause of some German seats being lost. Schiemann's person attracted significant Latvian support. Nevertheless, in order to concentrate his energies in parliament he almost immediately resigned from the City Council, where he was succeeded as leader of the German group by Waldemar Pussull.[83]

In the second Saeima convened in the autumn, however, Baltic German seats dropped to four. This was ascribed at least partly to the relative inexperience of the new German electoral association taking over the running of the campaign in the five electoral districts from the separate Baltic German political parties. However, the most important lesson the German political leaders drew from 1925 was that in future they should not target Latvian voters but instead find new ways of maximising the German vote. For the moment Paul Schiemann's growing apprehension that a special German autonomy law would never find acceptance deepened to conviction.

The other minorities had deliberately modelled their own schemes closely on the German draft to ensure that Baltic Germans received no preferential treatment; similar considerations now informed the Jewish and social democratic initiative for a general law. Schiemann also became convinced that the Farmers' Union—particularly after the influential Meierovics' death in a car accident in August 1925—would renege on its earlier promises.[84] The conclusion seemed inescapable; priority had to be given to passing a general law—the most, Schiemann now believed, that the Latvian left would accept. It promised at least to secure the important principle of nationality being determined by free choice, as well as a language law allowing the continued use of German in the public sector.

When Schiemann finally explained his thinking to a tense CGBP meeting on 20 November 1925, matters immediately came to a head. Fircks expressed distaste at the idea of receiving autonomy 'as the gift of those [left] Latvian groups with whom we are unable to work in the long run'. He rejected a general law 'as detrimental to our historic position in the country and our influence among the population'. The reference by Fircks to the 'odium' of inclusion with the Russians and Jews echoed the opinion of Karl Keller, who wanted three separate laws—even if they had identical wording. 'Otherwise we would be tossed in the same barrel with the others.'[85]

When the Democratic Party committee met to discuss the matter ten days later, Keller was still resolute on the need for a special autonomy law for Baltic Germans 'as a landholding element'. Schiemann's strictures against conjuring up the past, and a reminder that 'the democratic principle demands equal right for all and rejects privilege', obviously stung Keller. He not only contended that 'our future in Latvia depends on our past, on the work of our fathers'—a privilege 'he could not give up'—but also levelled the outrageous charge that Schiemann was using the democratic principle as a chess-piece to play at will. This outburst reflected deep frustration. Baron Paul von Kleist, who likened current events to having a cold shower, shared it: 'Instead of the special autonomy, the need for which has always been stressed hitherto, we are supposed to share a general law with the Russians and Jews at the whim of the social democrats.' However, comments generally critical of Keller after he had left the room showed that the majority of those present accepted the sense of a general law. Baltic Germandom's affairs, Heinrich Bosse noted in his concluding remarks, were 'in the good hands of Dr Paul Schiemann'. Nonetheless, the sharp differences within the German fraction as a whole meant yet again postponing the parliamentary battle for German autonomy.[86]

For the time being Schiemann at least had the satisfaction of keeping the option of a general law on the table without compelling advocates of a separate German project to climb down publicly. There were other important considerations behind the postponement. Karl Keller, for example, recorded the advantages of awaiting the final outcome for minority schooling of the general education bill being formulated in the Saeima's Education Commission (no one knew that there would in fact be no such bill before Latvia's parliamentary era ended). Secondly, the existing 1919 schooling law itself provided a relatively good basis for the time being for securing the most important minority cultural concerns. Finally the Saiema's Public Law Commission had amended the German autonomy law to the point where it could provide at most for a national association at *private* law, scarcely different from the body the CGBP had already created in the Zentrale. Conversely the Zentrale, intent on compiling its own register of Baltic Germandom, now assumed enormous importance as a forum for accumulating the invaluable practical experience of self-management—rare among European minorities but vital to any future autonomy.[87]

'Surely', Schiemann had asked Fircks at the 20 November meeting, 'nobody can seriously desire that we abandon the minority rights platform and proceed with a new construct on the basis of our historic position?' At the Democratic Party meeting on 1 December 1925 he again justified a general law in terms of the principles of 'modern minorities' policy. It was in fact in wider European developments, as much as in his frustration in the Saeima, that the major clues could be found to Schiemann's resolute advocacy of a general cultural autonomy law for Latvia from the summer of 1925. The struggle to show that cultural autonomy did not necessarily lead to the creation of a 'state within a state' could not be conducted in Latvia alone, while the insights he had gained from the specific struggle for minority rights in Latvia informed his growing engagement on the international scene on behalf of all European minorities. It was a process also committing him to a lasting struggle against the *völkisch* nationalists who challenged the Weimar Republic in the second half of the 1920s.

6. The Geneva Connection

For all his exasperation with Latvian public life Schiemann would not unreservedly have endorsed the German author who in 1926 described the Baltic Germans as 'a barely tolerated minority'.[1] Undeniably, Schiemann was exercised by the material conditions of life for his community as a whole and not just by the loss of its land. 'This economic war of attrition', he wrote at the time, 'increasingly important in the semi-intelligent chauvinist circles ganging around the centre, is the greatest worry for our people.'[2] However, in his view this was also a major factor in motivating Baltic Germans to lead Latvia's nationality groups in the quest for minority protection.[3] In other respects too he did not see the situation for Latvian Germans as unremittingly gloomy by the mid-1920s.

For one thing the absence of any immediate prospect of winning the autonomy argument in the Saeima was offset by the development of the Zentrale. It benefited indirectly from the fraction's concerted push after the 1925 elections to heighten the awareness of its work among Germans living outside Riga. Having 'woken up' the provinces with this initiative, the parliamentary deputies urged the case for maintaining contact, using the data collected as the basis of an extensive card index of Baltic Germandom. It had obvious value in enhancing the Zentrale's efficiency. Indeed, a major purpose of the exercise appears to have been to prepare for a system of self-taxation. According to a formal resolution of the annual meeting of the Verband der deutschen Minderheiten, chaired by Paul Schiemann in Vienna in August 1924, that remained an essential element of national autonomy.[4] Again, his community pioneered developments. Karl Keller drew up a memorandum on the subject as early as November 1925.

The collections, lotteries and other fund-raising events hitherto organised within the German community had been eminently successful in helping to meet the escalating costs of schooling and welfare.[5] Keller's memorandum confirmed, however, that 'the big collections have had their day.' He proposed instead a tax on all Baltic Germans aged twenty-one or over, which he hoped would yield around 16 million roubles per annum.[6] After prolonged discussion within the Zentrale, self-taxation was introduced for the German communities in Riga and Jelgava in 1926. Collections continued for the time being in the small towns. Contributors to the tax—those earning a living or with independent incomes—were asked to fill in forms saying how much they could afford to pay. They were given the option of monthly instalments if so desired. Commitment to self-taxation carried with it exemption from any future collections. The proposed tax scale envisaged contributions of 0.5 per cent of monthly income at the bottom end and between 1.5 and 3 per cent at the top. Though voluntary, the system was presented as a manifestation of the demand for cultural autonomy. There was considerable moral pressure to take part.[7]

The director of the Zentrale, Wilhelm von Rüdiger, well regarded and conservative by political inclination, belonged to no political party. Before becoming director he had not been much involved in active politics—not that he was without political ambition: in the Zentrale he found the perfect vehicle for it. His memoir praised Schiemann's vision and generosity in diverting social, economic and cultural tasks to a separate body, but he also admitted that matters went far beyond what the German fraction might have intended.[8] Alfred Ruetz told Schiemann in October 1925 that Rüdiger was already claiming 5 per cent of the *Rigasche Rundschau*'s annual profit for the Zentrale, as well as preparing to join the paper's enlarged management board. Rüdiger later confirmed that he tried to influence the *Rigasche Rundschau* through his office.[9] Ruetz assured Schiemann that the contract then being drawn up for him would pre-empt possible future moves in this direction. Rüdiger was even reported by Ruetz to have shown animosity towards Lotte Schiemann. He urged Paul Schiemann not to disclose his new pension arrangements to his brother-in-law.[10]

There is little doubt that Rüdiger's drive to forge a true apex of Germandom in Latvia heightened the dualism inherent in re-allocating tasks from the CGBP to the Zentrale in 1923. When it ceased to be a section of the CGBP and registered itself in the Riga District Court on 24 June 1926, the Zentrale developed into a powerful player in its own right. Self-taxation, overseen initially by a three-man committee elected by the Zentrale, accelerated the process. It changed the organisation from an association of various societies, clubs and other bodies into an association of taxpayers, formed into a network of 'working groups' throughout Latvia. From 1926 they elected officers to the delegate assembly, that replaced the existing plenary as the supreme organ, on the basis of occupation and profession. The delegate assembly then elected a management board, taking into account the three main areas of the Zentrale's work—cultural, social, economic.

The Zentrale displayed its same outward form on tactical grounds, but the significance of its reorganisation comes out clearly in an assessment of 1926. 'From a loose grouping, which had to find shared principles and watchwords, a close association has developed in the course of time, whose immediate practical goals have arisen from cooperation between the German institutions and grown ever clearer: an organic integration of Germandom as a whole through local groups, the enlistment of all our people [*Volksgenossen*] through self-taxation, setting up and executing an agreed budget.'[11]

The political implications are even clearer in Rüdiger's retrospective two years later. 'Forming the new "working groups", combining them to mutual effect, are steps on the way to a living national community, which we hope for in the future.'[12] The Zentrale certainly promised to sensitise Baltic Germandom to the political realities underlying welfare and culture, as Schiemann had argued in 1923, but perhaps not quite in the manner he had then envisaged. Even so, daily working relations between the CGBP and the Zentrale were never seriously disrupted. There also remained some overlap in terms of personnel in the management of the two bodies, so that there were constraints on the duality of the organisational set-up, at least for most of Schiemann's active public life.

That he brooked no challenge to editorial policy at the *Rigasche Rundschau* can be gleaned from surviving documents from the 1920s. On one occasion Schiemann is glimpsed berating a hapless colleague for 'capital stupidity' in trying to influence policy by a direct approach to Ruetz.[13] Elsewhere he compared himself to a 'gun-dog' in having to sniff out passive resistance from some reactionary and anti-Semitic staff on the *Rundschau*.[14] When a member of the Baltic German establishment insisted on the publication of an article he submitted, Schiemann took pleasure in replying that his normal practice in such cases was to consign the item immediately to the wastepaper basket. Such confidence derived also from his extensive working links with many major papers, including the *Frankfurter Zeitung* and the *Deutsche Allgmeine Zeitung*, while his smoke-filled office became an essential point of call for foreign journalists passing through Riga.[15] In discussing the new financial arrangements for the *Rigasche Rundschau* from 1925 Schiemann's own party committee could truthfully record that the editor 'would continue to follow the existing political line of the paper'.[16]

That line-practical and pragmatic support for above-party interests on the Riga city council and in parliament, particularly on its many commissions—was winning grudging respect, despite the loss of a deputy in the 1925 poll, under an electoral system which Schiemann was still anxious to make fairer. 'Accommodation breaks through' here and there, he reported in September 1925, and the fraction 'is listened to' because of its reliability, even though promises from the other parties mostly 'come when they need us'.[17] During a stalemate between the Latvian politicians in early December 1925 President Čakste even sounded out Schiemann on the prospects of forming a minorities' coalition. Schiemann was forced to admit that political differences between the nationality groups prevented them agreeing a common programme in time.[18] However, it was undeniable that the 'horrendous situation' of six years earlier had improved. Testimony to this were the 103 German educational establishments functioning by the mid-1920s, teaching almost 12,000 pupils.[19]

It is difficult to argue that anything but chance brought Schiemann to the parliamentary limits of what could be done for cultural autonomy in Latvia just as major shifts occurred in post-war Europe. They were marked by a slow restoration of economic order with the rescheduling of reparations (Dawes plan), the Locarno treaties signed in October 1925 between Germany and the Allied Powers, and finally German preparations to join the League of Nations. As a result pressure on the Reich government to clarify its own position on minority issues increased. Germandom's experts and lobbyists jumped at the opportunity.

As early as 1920 Carl Georg Bruns had noted the moral leverage to be gained from allowing autonomous schooling for the relatively small number of foreign minorities in the Reich. Ammende made a similar point when the Verband der deutschen Minderheiten was set up.[20] Once the Czech Germans finally made up their mind to join in July 1924 the Verband plausibly represented itself as having all German minorities behind its quest for cultural autonomy on the basis of the territorial status quo.[21] Something like an *Auslandsdeutsche* offensive on the German government built up in the second half of the year, culminating in a dinner held for the Verband in Berlin on 3 November 1924. Apart from Bruns, Paul Schiemann was there, as well as other leading minority politicians like Kurt Graebe from Poland and Werner von Hasselblatt. While trying to persuade the relevant experts from the Prussian and Reich ministries of the advantages of allowing cultural autonomy for Germany's national minorities, the Verband also launched a public debate on the subject.[22]

Such was the context of Stresemann's initiative to sound out opinion in the various German embassies in October 1924, yielding generally positive responses in the ensuing weeks. The replies, together with resolutions from the Berlin conference of German minorities in November, provided the mainspring for Stresemann's memorandum of 13 January 1925, 'The foreign policy imperative for a regulation of minorities' rights within the Reich corresponding to the needs of German minorities in Europe'.[23] Addressed to Reich and Prussian ministries, it was the beginning of Stresemann's hard and ultimately unsuccessful struggle to win over Prussia and other *Land* governments to the necessary internal reforms. His action also served immediate domestic political needs. It helped to offset the German right's fierce resistance to the Dawes plan by acceding to nationalist demands that the Reich be more active on minority protection issues. Germany's entry to the League of Nations was expected to help change its procedures, widely held to seek the assimilation of minorities. Stresemann emphasised instead the 'self-evident' political, cultural and economic value to Germany of helping the *Auslandsdeutsche* to preserve their national identity.

Major arguments have arisen over the final paragraph of this document, with its reference to Germany's search for 'step-by-step revision' of frontier provisions for the Polish Corridor and Upper Silesia, as well as to the 'distant goal' of 'creating a state whose political borders embrace all German groups inhabiting the compact German settlement areas in Mitteleuropa who wish to be part of the Reich'. In isolation the words have been taken as proof of Stresemann's minorities policy as the link between Weimar revisionism and national socialist expansionism. The argument does not even survive the restoration of the quote to its context: Stresemann's extended plea for cultural autonomy and his insistence that winning the moral argument was the only way to preserve the *Auslandsdeutsche*'s identity. His rationale was simple. Although the geographical location of German settlements that he identified as most important—those adjacent to Germany, along the Baltic coast and in the Danube basin—'coincided with areas of Europe where political and economic issues vital to Germany must be decided', the prevailing European balance of power precluded the Reich's intervention.

Equally, a financially constrained Germany could not provide adequate material support. At best it might help German minorities lucky enough actually to have cultural rights to use them; it could do nothing to redress their absence. Stresemann drew comfort from the fact that petitions to the League of Nations had already shown European governments the need for fair solutions to minority problems in the interests of lasting peace. The Reich's 'great task' was therefore to reinforce this perception and to engage world opinion in the fate of German minorities to a point where their host states succumbed to international pressure and allowed full cultural freedom. To be credible and effective, Germany had to campaign within the League of Nations and to provide cultural autonomy for national minorities in the Reich. With some justice Stresemann's memorandum has been called 'the birth certificate of the Weimar Republic's minorities policy'.[24]

Aside from the question of his ultimate goals, Stresemann's explicit rejection of force and his primary commitment to Germany's economic re-integration into Western Europe had a beneficial impact on the Baltic countries. Their long-standing resistance to being economically tied to Germany weakened in the course of 1925 to the extent that both Latvia and Lithuania signed full-scale economic treaties with the Reich the following year.[25] The strengthening of Germany's leading position in Baltic trade further reduced the likelihood of combined German-Soviet action against the border states. Stresemann had even seriously explored Köster's confidential proposal of 24 April 1925 for a joint German-Russian guarantee of the Baltic countries. The plan eventually foundered on the difficulty of finding a formula not sanctioning Lithuania's permanent control of Memel. If the desire to check Poland's influence in the region informed the flurry of memorandums, Stresemann's reminder to Moscow of the importance of not threatening the Baltic countries remains significant.[26]

The rejection of force underlying Gustav Stresemann's foreign policy—and therefore his minorities initiative—greatly encouraged Paul Schiemann. He recorded the German Foreign Minister's public commitment to cultural autonomy at the opening of the House of Germandom in Stuttgart on 21 May 1925, by stressing its profound importance for Europe as a whole. To Schiemann cultural autonomy offered 'the only clear and unambivalent release from irredentism'.[27] His response in this instance was naturally coloured by the fact that he lived in a state unburdened by territorial disputes. Equally, when reflecting on European relations at this critical juncture, he argued that the creation of non-revisionist, independent Baltic states respecting ethnic minorities automatically made them 'bearers of a new right'. They were dependent, like all 'small' countries, on promoting peace and thus had the potential to counter the dangerous bias within the League of Nations towards the great powers, whose fixation on national sovereignty had made Versailles 'no peace but war prolonged'.[28]

These functions of small statehood were even more vital in the case of the Baltic states, Schiemann argued, because they existed at the point where rival ideological systems met. The idea so imbued his work for the Nationalities Congress at Geneva from 1925 that it should be briefly examined here. His assessment was based on what he saw as the West's 'risibly low awareness' of the importance of maintaining the Baltic as a European border area—a notion echoed today as Baltic governments prepare for inclusion within the European Union and NATO.[29] Instead the Western powers 'danced around' the 'golden calf' of Russian friendship, chasing illusory profits and neglecting the Baltic countries as a bulwark. By 1925, Schiemann insisted, serious economic circles no longer expected huge profits from Russia.[30] Still the West failed to grasp that 1917 was an Asiatic revolution against the legacy of Peter the Great; thus a revolution decisively rejected by the Western peoples of the old Russian empire—Finns, Estonians, Lithuanians, Latvians and Poles. In that sense 'the establishment of the Baltic states as a new political factor in East Europe is perhaps the most significant event following the World War, demanding a rethink of European policy as a whole.'[31]

He had made a similar point in response to Leon Trotsky's threat in June 1924 to raise the Soviet flag over Latvia. Schiemann interpreted the remark as a reflection of Russian domestic considerations—'a dictatorship of the minority needs the sympathy of the majority'—before explaining why he discounted a Russian attack: 'Latvia is a member of a larger constellation whose toppling would force half of Europe to take up arms.'[32] In January 1925 he observed more explicitly: 'Maintaining the *status quo* in the Baltic is vital to Europe. Therefore the powers and the League in the long run will be unable to avoid offering the border states international security, which is security for themselves.'[33] The Tallinn putsch in December 1924 was a reminder that defensive wars waged by the Baltic states, Finland and Poland for their independence were fought in Europe's interest too.

Conversely, Schiemann took a development like the 1923 Estonian-Latvian defence agreement as evidence that a Baltic bloc could become 'the combination for the future, where we will by no means be just takers but givers'.[34] 'The supreme task of any joint Baltic states policy', he wrote of the Helsinki arbitration treaty between Finland, Latvia, Estonia and Poland in January 1925, 'must be to give the international community a proper recognition of their significance for world peace.'[35] His remarks eerily foreshadow latter-day comments about security for the Baltic being the 'litmus test' of the post-Cold War order.

Many would now accept Schiemann's explanation for Anglo-French reluctance after 1919 to intercede for the security of Europe's eastern borders; they did not understand 'that a threat to the security of the border states is a threat to their own security.'[36] Just as alarming to Schiemann was the West's inability to understand the full significance of the Baltic solution to nationality issues: cultural autonomy. Instead a 'Balkan model' of expelling minorities threatened to take hold, as in the case of Greece and Bulgaria, Yugoslavia and Italy.[37] For Schiemann here was fresh evidence of the promise of new solutions arising from the calamity of 1914–18 being eroded by the 'victor mentality'. New ideals like the League of Nations were in danger of subversion by 'winners' too weak to renounce the familiar temptations of the dance for power. Independent Baltic states could bring to the equation something new, earned from a difficult past: the spirit of national tolerance: 'It is a spirit which the whole of Europe desperately needs.'[38]

Schiemann hoped that Stresemann's endorsement of cultural autonomy would improve prospects for promoting the 'Baltic dimension' more widely, particularly since Baltic German parliamentarians were among the handful of European politicians with direct experience of building autonomy. Of these Ewald Ammende had been especially active in trying to internationalise the work of the Verband der deutschen Minderheiten for minority rights legislation by planning a new organisation that would bring in the other European minorities too. The 'fat doctor' was a tireless habitué of international conferences on minority issues and the epicentre of a swirling network of personal contacts. Perhaps for this reason he had as many detractors as supporters during his lifetime.

Ammende's 'unrestrained verbal torrent' and absence of diplomacy was attracting attention within the Auswärtiges Amt bureaucracy in 1923.[39] Even a co-founder of the Verband der deutschen Minderheiten, Rudolf Brandsch, categorised his colleague as a bankrupt adventurer looking for ways to boost his finances.[40] The view was shared by the German ambassador in Tallinn, Weyrauch, dismissive of Ammende as 'a busy but irresponsible Pärnu burger'.[41] Carl Georg Bruns was not enthusiastic either.[42] Other workers in the minorities field were to see Ammende as 'far too erratic' and showing 'a lack of tact'.[43] Ironically, his self-promotion brought greater dividends after his sudden death in Peking in 1936, to the extent at least that an Ammende-centric view of the birth of the Geneva based Nationalities Congress came to hold sway in the post-Second World War literature.[44]

The most recent work on the Nationalities Congress questions this by setting it against other international ventures, particularly the congresses organised in 1916 and 1917 by Juosas Gabrys for the Liga der Fremdvölker, whose Berlin organisation and press office, Neutral Correspondence, Schiemann headed at one point. Ammende's own contacts with the Auswärtiges Amt also date from that time. Like Schiemann, he had close ties with the head of the Liga, Baron Friedrich von Ropp.[45] Also in doubt is the idea that Europe's minorities all readily agreed to the decision of the Nationalities Congress to pursue a route similar to that resulting in Estonia's law on cultural autonomy. The background and priorities of, say, German, Hungarian and Polish national minorities coloured their perceptions of the planned new organisation. Even the German minority groups differed. Brandsch was initially against the venture, fearing that the Baltic German Ammende would disadvantage Southeastern Europe's interests. In fact Ammende's fellow Estonian Germans, and Schiemann's countrymen in Latvia, did not initially offer much support.[46]

Yet the more the differences within the minorities' camp are exposed—let alone the opposition of European governments to minorities seizing the initiative—the more understandable does Ammende's self-aggrandisement appear. Even critics of his ego centricity admit that he forced the idea of a new international congress on to the agenda.[47] Max Hildebert Boehm's depiction of Ammende as 'the essentially unifying and at the same time directive force' of the congress clearly goes too far. However, there is good reason to accept the post-1945 Baltic German historiographical assessment of Ammende as the organisational motor behind the Nationalities Congress, for all his propensity to gloss over the work of others in starting the process in 1925. One of those was Paul Schiemann, whose intervention in Berlin turned out to be absolutely critical. Schiemann had his differences with Ammende, particularly in the 1930s, but typically he capitalised on his co-worker's strengths rather than wasting energy exposing character defects. These were only obliquely hinted at in the obituary he wrote in 1936 for Ammende, whom he seemed to have few reservations about crediting with initiating the Nationalities Congress.[48]

Shortly after the passage on 5 February 1925 of the Estonian law on cultural autonomy, in which he had been involved, Ammende drafted his 'Reasons, principles and programme for a conference of representatives of all national minorities in Europe'. This became the basis for exploratory talks with other nationality groups in the ensuing months, notably in Warsaw on 8 July 1925. There he secured the agreement of representatives of the Catalans, Hungarians from Czechoslovakia, Ukrainians and White Russians from Poland, and Germans from Poland and the South Tyrol to convene the so-called 'Invitation Conference' in Dresden in August.[49]

Schiemann reported to his Democratic Party meeting on 13 August that the idea was to secure resolutions at a congress in September in the name of some 25 million Europeans and to present them to the League of Nations. Schiemann was to attend the Dresden meeting as an elected representative on behalf of German minorities in Europe (i.e. the Verband der deutschen Minderheiten) for talks with Slavic and Magyar delegates. It is interesting that in view of what transpired Schiemann thought the congress would probably not take place till 1926.[50] At Dresden Ammende was entrusted with the organisational preparations. In the face of considerable odds, the 'First conference of the organised national groups of the states of Europe' formally opened on 16 October 1925 in the place chosen, Geneva. Fifty delegates representing thirty-four national groups from fourteen states and belonging to seventeen different nations attended it.[51] This was obviously more than a 'Baltic German affair'.

Nevertheless, formative influence was exerted by among others Ewald Ammende, elected general secretary; Paul Schiemann, one of the four vice presidents in the new organisation—a post he only formally relinquished in 1935; Ferdinand von Uexküll, editor of the journal *Nation und Staat*; and Werner von Hasselblatt.[52] Alongside this Baltic German contingent on the management body sat Josip Wilfan, deputy of the Slovenes and Croats in the Italian parliament, now chosen as permanent president of the Nationalities Congress, and the Jewish spokesman and congress vice president, Isaack Grünbaum, as well as Hungarian and Polish figures. Baltic German input into the strategy of the Nationalities Congress was equally obvious. It promoted itself—as the Verband had in 1922—as a cause for 'genuine' minorities attached to their homelands and loyal to them. Admission criteria, which were disputed well into the 1930s ostensibly took into account not so much a minority's size as its level of cultural and organisational development and, above all, clear evidence of the majority of the group defining itself as a national minority.

Pointedly excluded from congress meetings were any discussion of border disputes and the airing of specific complaints against governments. The defined purpose was not irredentism, but a wide-ranging overhaul of the League of Nations' minority procedures and the implementation of European wide minority rights through cultural autonomy, a goal unanimously endorsed by the Nationalities Congress at its first meeting.[53]

It became normal practice for the delegates to meet in Geneva shortly after the annual meeting of the League Assembly, to discuss and assess developments in minority protection. The presence of many foreign journalists in Geneva at that time ensured publicity for the Nationalities Congress. But the new European nationalities movement drew life not only from that annual jamboree: during the months between congresses a number of delegates were engaged in related work through other international organisations. This partly reflected the fact that about half of the congress delegates were also parliamentarians in their home countries. A high proportion of them also had legal training and many others worked in journalism, if not all at Schiemann's level. Ammende was one of the very few gainfully employed by the Nationalities Congress, although his permanent secretariat was only fully set up and properly funded from 1927. From this he launched himself between times on travels to keep abreast of developments and to maintain contacts with leading personalities and organisations.[54]

Two distinct but interconnected questions arise, the one concerning the relationship between the new organisation and the League of Nations, and the second relating to German foreign policy. As for the first, Ewald Ammende had made careful preparations to allay uneasiness in League circles about his planned organisation, approaching the general secretary Sir Eric Drummond and the head of the minorities section of the League secretariat, Erik Colban, at the end of November 1922. They were unable to give an official position but Ammende plainly felt sufficiently encouraged to proceed with his frantic efforts 'to convince a wider public that the striving for cultural autonomy was a constructive contribution to the cause of world peace'.[55] When the great day arrived, an official League observer confessed to Schiemann that the League Council's initial distrust of the new Nationalities Congress had been dispelled by the obvious determination of the speakers to exclude border issues.[56] He might have been less sanguine had he read Schiemann's report, which suggested that since the recent Locarno agreements forced a re-think of the postwar European order, so the Nationalities Congress would compel a reconsideration of European minority issues. A journalist at the congress privately told Schiemann of his hopes for a fresh minority solution 'coming from your small states up there'.[57]

The plain truth was that the congress grew from a spreading disillusionment with League attitudes and procedures, and its *raison d'être* was to change them. Minority leaders were particularly irked by the fact that not all countries had been made to sign minority treaties as a condition of League membership, but only the states in Eastern Central Europe which had newly arisen (or been enlarged) as a result of the Peace Conference: Poland, Czechoslovakia, Romania, Yugoslavia and Greece, as well as the defeated powers of Austria, Hungary, Bulgaria and, later, Turkey. The Baltic states saw themselves outside these categories since they had won their own independence. Nevertheless, they were put under pressure to sign agreements on the assumption that former areas of the Russian Empire might inherit traditions injurious to minorities.

Lithuania's minorities declaration of 12 May 1922 was almost identical to the Polish minority protection treaty. It contained a 'guarantee clause' defining obligations to minorities as of 'international concern' and under League protection; they were not to be altered by the signatory state.[58] Latvia and Estonia, however, viewed this provision as an invasion of their sovereignty, arguing that their progressive legislation exempted them—like Finland—from the need to conclude guarantee treaties. Instead, after protracted wrangling, Latvia signed a declaration on 7 July 1923, merely agreeing to respect the principles of the League minority treaties. Estonia followed suit on 17 September. It has been said of the two states that 'they were willing to assure minority rights and protection but without having to assume *international* obligations in that regard.'[59]

Schiemann still felt the declarations to be helpful, particularly in the case of Latvia, where the second part of the constitution enumerating basic rights had yet to become law.[60] As with other 'minorities states', Latvia's declaration committed it to accepting the right of minorities to petition the League. However, it was in procedural practice that the Nationalities Congress found a potent source of resentment. Bluntly, the League's mechanism lacked transparency. Petitioners had no direct access to the League Council, which invariably referred such written complaints as were deemed valid within the terms of the treaty to an *ad hoc* committee of three. In other words only states and not minorities had standing in international law. The Minority Committee's subsequent discussions with those governments that became subject to a petition were confidential, excluding the complainant's representative.

The complaints process could also be protracted. One petition submitted by Fircks and Wegesack in 1925 regarding Latvia's recent decision not to compensate dispossessed landowners contained 138 pages, and Latvia's response to the League was three times as long. There is no record of Latvia's answer to subsequent League advice to explore compensation. Even so, the Minority Committee's review was concluded without any specific action being recommended to the League Council.[61] Such partial information and defective response proved the rule rather than the exception. Schiemann joined many critics in relating such flaws directly to the League's origin, not as a union of free and equal *peoples* but as one of the new and existing *states*, whose rights and duties were, as before, unequal.

Of fifty-five member states in 1924 only fifteen had formal obligations to the League in the realm of minority protection. Instead of coming under binding supra-national law, nationality conflicts were governed by the obligations of one state to another. 'Statutory international minority law remained as before particular inter-state law.'[62] Schiemann emphasised in addition that because League mechanisms focused on regulating relations *between* states, there were severe limits to what it could achieve *inside* them.[63] In this he rejected the League's equation of 'nation' with 'state' and sought to persuade the Nationalities Congress that its starting point should be the absence of any necessary identity between the two. He could see no durable solution to the minority problem in Europe's multi-ethnic border areas, while a nation could only express itself in territorial terms. In 1925, through the pages of the *Zeitschrift für Politik*, he contrasted for a wider audience the poor situation in most of Europe with the effort in his own country to secure, alongside a nation's right to form a state, the right of minorities to their own national identity within that state.[64]

Difficulties in accommodating this approach with League priorities became only too apparent in the course of December 1925. Colban understandably counselled his colleagues to be cautious in responding to the combined challenge of the Nationalities Congress, Stresemann's advocacy of cultural autonomy, and the prospect of Germany's imminent entry to the League of Nations. Afranio de Mello-Franco, the Brazilian ambassador in Rome and League *rapporteur* on minority questions, chose to ignore the advice. Furthermore, his address to the League Council on 9 December undoubtedly captured its mood. He reaffirmed the League's intention to forge complete national unity. Any lingering doubts as to what the 'Mello-Franco declaration' meant were removed by the comment of the British Foreign Secretary, Austen Chamberlain: 'The object of the Minority Treaties was to secure for the minorities that measure of protection and justice which would gradually prepare them to be *merged* [author's italics] in the national community to which they belonged.'[65] Colban—'architect of the minority treaties'—frankly admitted on another occasion that 'the political purpose of the [minorities] treaties was not humanitarian' but rather to keep the peace.[66] The emphasis remained as before on assimilation.[67]

It is clear from Schiemann's work in Latvia that he was not against *inclusion* in labelling the Mello-Franco declaration an attempt to prevent the right to nationality developing from the League minority treaties.[68] His criticism was directed not only at the incomplete application of the treaties but at solutions being imposed from outside. The resentment this aroused in the government of his homeland was echoed in other minority states. Equally, minorities subject to such outside rulings could not escape the fear that 'rights' imposed in such a way could be seen by obligated governments as concessions to be withdrawn at a future date. This fact of life reinforced the inclination of nationality groups towards self-help, through direct negotiations with host governments. The paradox for Schiemann and his colleagues in the Nationalities Congress was that internationally recognised statutory law for minorities could only arise from within the individual European states.[69]

The primary task of congress members was therefore to lobby tirelessly, exploiting contacts with the media, government, parliamentary assemblies, non-governmental organisations and powerful public figures, to win over public opinion to their cause in every European country. The members of what Boehm dubbed Ammende's 'curious nationalities circus' struggled to realise their vision on the fringes of the League of Nations. In sum, they could no more abandon that imperfect organisation while nothing better existed than the League could wholly ignore a Nationalities Congress claiming to speak for 40 million people.[70]

As to the second question, the uneasy dance on which Nationalities Congress and League embarked in Geneva in 1925 was inevitably complicated by the presence of the partner waiting to be invited on to the floor—Germany. Its brethren abroad, the *Auslandsdeutsche*, far outnumbered those of other national minorities in post-Versailles Europe. Poland especially feared the impact on minority issues of the Reich's entry to the League of Nations, notwithstanding the decision in June 1925 to exclude from the League's Minorities Committee 'delegates from either host or kin states relevant to a minority petition'.[71] This, like the Mello-Franco declaration, aimed to dampen inflated hopes for change, particularly among German nationalists, who saw preserving the separateness of German groups abroad in terms of preparation for a future pan-Germany.[72] Max-Hildebert Boehm's *Europa Irredenta* (1923) went so far as to refute any automatic right of small states to an independent existence. It was a view which another Baltic German émigré, Baron Schilling, did not hesitate to voice in the *Deutsche Zeitung* at the time of the attempted Bolshevik coup in Tallinn in December 1924: 'These small, completely insignificant border states are only reaping what they have sown.'[73]

The opinion undoubtedly appealed to Baltic German émigré circles, already resentful of Schiemann for 'betraying' Baltic German tradition in his advocacy of a Latvian state. Schilling's remarks also exemplify the growing assertiveness in the *völkisch*-nationalist camp following its electoral breakthrough in Germany in 1924. To such mentalities the prospect of prominent *Auslandsdeutsche* parliamentarians engaging with a multinational congress committed to universal minority protection was not welcome. It portended to Germandom's lobbyists in the Reich a weakening of purpose and control, as was evident from a flurry of articles in the *Rigasche Rundschau* in early autumn 1925 challenging the influential Max Hildebert

Boehm. The exchange originated in Schiemann's defence of an essay by his Berlin correspondent, Axel de Vries, on the pro-republican defence organisation in Germany, the *Reichsbanner*.

Schiemann used both Boehm's book and the *völkisch* agitation for a greater Germany to refute his adversary's claim to speak on behalf of the *Auslandsdeutschen* as a whole. Boehm and his cronies were furious at this public display of disunity within the Verband der deutschen Minderheiten but Schiemann was unrepentant.[74] To his fellow fraction members at home he justified his unusual personal intervention in Germany's politics as 'unavoidable, since *völkisch* agitation was increasingly spilling over on to us.'[75] The *völkisch* movement in the Reich, he argued, was a bigger threat to Baltic German unity than Latvian chauvinism. He predicted that if it ever had real success, then the days of Germans in Latvia would be numbered. 'Fighting against propaganda which threatens us with destruction is the first duty of self-preservation.'[76] Spann and Boehm even travelled to Riga for a secret meeting to call Schiemann to account. They failed, according to Köster, because of 'the superior way in which Schiemann defended himself and in turn attacked Spann and Boehm'.[77]

The tone of Köster's report suggests that sympathy within the Auswärtiges Amt was with Schiemann rather than the irate Germandom leaders at home. None the less, the office itself was uneasy about the Nationalities Congress. It arose, like the Verband der deutschen Minderheiten, from minority leaders outside the Reich seizing the initiative. The Verband's autonomy was not significantly curtailed at that time by German government subsidies it received through the Berlin office of its legal adviser, Carl Bruns, a man of strongly independent mind.[78] There was concern too about the fact that in planning for the Nationalities Congress Ammende had not even bothered to consult the German embassy in Tallinn, much to the chagrin of its incumbent, Weyrauch.[79] In Berlin Max Winkler later confessed privately to Ruetz: 'We are not at all pleased about what Schiemann and Ammende have set up there [in Geneva]. But Schiemann won't be persuaded to give up the idea. Luckily Locarno has put the Geneva minorities congress completely in the shade.' Ruetz passed the comment on to Schiemann along with the decidedly ill-chosen advice that he should distance himself from Ammende and allow him to set up a harmless organisation.[80]

The Wilhelmstrasse's chief concern was that uncertainty surrounding the affair might harm the Locarno initiative. The moderate revisionist policy line slowly being spun by Stresemann was not to be jeopardised by the slightest suspicion of the Reich sanctioning minorities' action against the League of Nations. The Verband der deutschen Minderheiten's pivotal role in the genesis and conduct of the Nationalities Congress made Germany vulnerable to this charge, promoted above all by Poland. The Auswärtiges Amt also feared that admission to the Nationalities Congress of German minorities in areas lost to Poland might be construed as indirect acceptance of the Versailles borders. It could also draw attention to the fact that Berlin, unlike Warsaw, had signed no minorities' protection treaty.[81] Finally, responses from German diplomatic missions in East Central Europe expressed concern for the Nationalities Congress not to undermine the Deutsche Stiftung's subsidies policy. It was left to Adolf Köster to emphasise the relevance of the planned congress for the protection of *all* minorities in Europe. He suggested that a meeting be arranged between Paul Schiemann and Gustav Stresemann to correct any false impressions.[82]

The Verband der deutschen Minderheiten had already authorised Schiemann to go to Berlin in the summer of 1925 to explain the thinking behind the Nationalities Congress.[83] He had been told at a meeting in the Auswärtiges Amt on 25 August, en route to Ammende's preliminary Dresden conference, 'that it would have been more desirable had the German minorities first been in touch with the Reich government before the affair had reached such an advanced stage.' His promise to procure a postponement of the congress at Dresden if possible was probably made without any great conviction to judge from Max Winkler's earlier comment. Indeed, Schiemann's account of the struggle in reaching the current stage with non-German minorities implied that it was already too late to halt the arrangements.[84]

No record of Schiemann's subsequent meeting with Stresemann has been found, but it ended with the Chancellor actually approving the convening of the Nationalities Congress. The proposition that Schiemann elaborated on his ideas on the 'anational state' (p. 133) is highly plausible. Stresemann could not have failed to appreciate the relevance of Schiemann's ideas for his own conception of Reich policy.[85] At any rate, Schiemann's involvement was decisive in defusing the reaction in Berlin against Ammende's high-handedness. The Wilhelmstrasse, as well as Germandom organisations in the Reich, now adopted a waiting attitude towards Ammende's venture.[86]

All of this indicated that the Nationalities Congress was not conceived by the Reich government at the outset as an organ of German revisionism.[87] Unlike Hungary, another major revisionist power, Germany provided no financial support for the inaugural meeting of the congress.[88] German delegates made up over one-third of congress membership but for most of the 1920s they were less inclined to see themselves as agents of Berlin than as misunderstood and not valued at their proper worth there. Nor can the integrity of influential *Auslandsdeutsche* leaders involved with the Nationalities Congress—especially Schiemann—be underestimated, let alone that of some of the non-Germans involved; within the membership ranks there was a profound concern to find new solutions to minority problems within existing European frontiers. Finally, the doctrine of cultural autonomy that the congress committed itself to promoting had deep intellectual roots. Its theoretical rationale—where Schiemann's role was central—opposed the aggrandisement of *any* nation (chapter 7).

Back in Riga, Schiemann already had the sense by this stage that his own Democratic Party was becoming politically more isolated within the Baltic German community.[89] Even his sympathetic obituary of the Latvian Foreign Minister Zīgfrids Meierovics on 26 August 1925 upset his political enemies.[90] Meierovics, whose slow-moving car mysteriously overturned on a narrow bridge, crushing him to death while his family escaped, was a man Schiemann came uniquely to admire among Latvian politicians as 'too clear headed to be a chauvinist'.[91] Schiemann's compliments prompted the Association of German Balt Christian Voters to demand his immediate removal from the electoral list. Woldemar Wulffius told Schiemann that his telegram of condolence had caused wide resentment among Riga's Germans by claiming that 'Germandom views the loss [of Meierovics] as its own.' Wulffius—who once urged Schiemann to show a 'certain reserve' towards the Jews, only to be rebuffed with the categorical 'We are not in a position to abandon a minority'—had no more success now.[92]

Ultimately Schiemann justified his action by reference to the fact that any autonomy law would be Meierovics' legacy and to the need to show solidarity with the Latvians.[93] He forcefully underlined the point in response to Hartwig Baron Bistram's letter to the *Rigasche Rundschau* on 3 October 1925. Bistram condemned the posting of anonymous notes calling for the fraction leader to be struck from the electoral list but also made clear that he was 'no friend of the political views of our Dr Paul Schiemann. I especially condemn in the strongest terms his almost pathologically false reportage of all domestic policy developments in Germany.'[94] Schiemann readily admitted that the unity of the Baltic German electoral list did not signify agreed political opinions; that many sympathised with the right in Germany, whereas he favoured the middle and democratic line, condemned the legend of the stab in the back, and deplored putting party interests first. In showing affinity with the *völkisch* right, Schiemann concluded, old Balt circles were, as ever, clinging to illusions of being the sole manifestation of Germandom in Latvia and dreaming of recovering control of the country.[95]

Schiemann rightly argued instead that conservative Baltic Germans' pretensions to parity with the Latvians as the second pillar of the state were against the constitution, which vested sovereignty in 'the *people* of Latvia'. To assign the other minorities a reduced role would mean abandoning the principle of equality of citizenship for which the German fraction stood in parliament. 'Can the free', Schiemann asked, 'in the hope of remaining free, opt for slavery?'[96] As we saw earlier, insurmountable domestic resistance at home partly explained Schiemann's insistence from the second half of 1925 that Latvian Germans should abandon demands for special German autonomy in favour of a general cultural autonomy law. In spite of disappointment at the wrangling that preceded the installation of Latvia's tenth cabinet in December 1925, he reiterated that Baltic German wishes were more likely to be achieved not as the price of bargaining 'but as the fruit of a spiritual disarmament, if I might venture, of an inner Locarno of the spirit'.[97]

All of this becomes more intelligible in the light of his leading role in the Nationalities Congress from 1925, with its call for European-wide minority rights legislation. That his political work for minority rights in Latvia could only be properly secured by comparable developments throughout Europe made the Nationalities Congress particularly enticing for him. Given the formidable obstacles to its birth, the very existence of the organisation—like the flight of the bumblebee—almost defied belief. However, the personal attacks on Schiemann confirm that his enthusiasm for the cause of European minorities was shared neither by nationalist minority activists in the Reich nor by old Balt forces, at home or in exile. It is time to examine more systematically Paul Schiemann's theoretical rationale for the Geneva connection.

Herder Square, Riga, with the *Rigasche Rundschau* building in the centre.

Café Otto Schwarz, Riga, frequented by Paul Schiemann and his circle.

Latvia's first Saeima in 1925. Schiemann is second from the left in the third row.

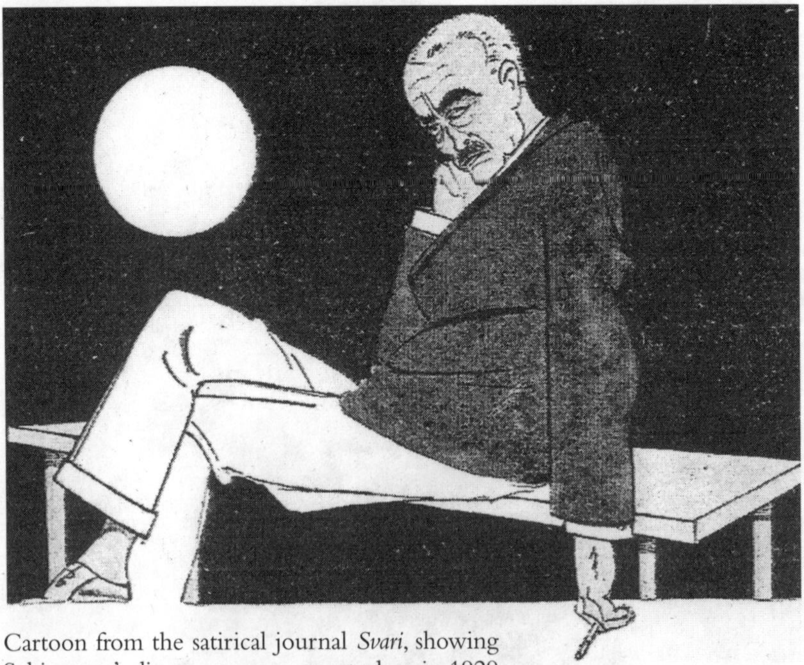

Cartoon from the satirical journal *Svari*, showing Schiemann's dismay at government plans in 1929 to exclude Landeswehr members from the category of freedom fighters who were allocated land.

Cartoon depicting Schiemann's efforts to mobilise Baltic German voters in 1928 parliamentary elections.

Schiemann in the 1920s.

The house in Atgazenes where Schiemann lived from 1940 till his death in 1944.

7. Thinker of the Minorities Movement

Components of Schiemann's ideas system could naturally be identified from his earliest *Rigasche Rundschau* editorials onwards, but he engaged more systematically with theory with the convening of the Nationalities Congress and the publication from 1927 of *Nation und Staat*. In these years above all he established a reputation—in the words of the President of the Nationalities Congress, Josip Wilfan—as the 'thinker of the minorities movement'.[1] His ideas expressed first and foremost bitter disappointment that the ordeals of 1914–18 had failed to unite friend and foe in a quest for new solutions and ideals. 'Already', he wrote shortly before the opening of the first Nationalities Congress, 'one can say that there are no longer victors and defeated in Europe, but only defeated—an economically, politically and morally broken Europe. World War has thus come to nothing.'[2] He was not so unrealistic as to think that minor powers could be decisive in warding off new threats, but he fervently believed that small states need not be inactive in the crucial area of nationality disputes, from which they arose in the first place.

Had Schiemann's ideas been too closely tied to his own *milieu* they would not have had the wider resonance encapsulated in Wilfan's description.[3] It helped, as we saw, that Schiemann built on foundations mapped out by the pre-war Austrian social democrats Karl Renner and Otto Bauer. For Schiemann they started the quest to escape from the confines of 'territoriality' towards a new conception of state based on considerations of ethnicity rather than on political, social and other party interests.[4] Unlike the Austrian thinkers, Schiemann had the advantage of entering active politics after the upheavals of world war, when minority issues were no longer treated largely as a state's internal concern. The agenda of the League of Nations held the minority problem to be 'in international life above all the problem of peace'.[5] It seemed a good moment to resume the quest for cultural autonomy, and Schiemann had exceptionally favourable opportunities to find *practical* expression for the doctrine in Latvia. As he insisted in 1925 it already had the preconditions for showing the world how to build 'a synthesis between nationality and state'.[6]

An answer to what he meant by this begins with his profound dislike of the nation state. It derived, in theoretical terms at least, from his interest in history, particularly—as a lawyer by training—constitutional history. Examining the development of the state idea in the Germanic world Schiemann proposed as a starting-point the independent disposition of a community with its own law (*Volksrecht*). Alongside this common law grew the law of rulers (*Königsrecht*), at first limited to the right of defence and military command. In so far as the functions of government—public order, transport and currency—also accrued to the ruler, it was from *Königsrecht* that the state idea ultimately came.

What struck Schiemann was the co-existence through the Middle Ages between common law and royal law. That is to say, he was impressed by the people retaining common law rights above those of the central authorities, as well as numerous functions of public and economic authority exercised through corporations.[7] This also suggested to him that the mixed nature of societies created from early migratory movements established in itself the rights of different national communities within the state. He inferred from this evidence that 'the dynastic state as such was in fact a-national.'[8] What had changed the situation?

He found part of the answer in the absolutism arriving from the seventeenth century onwards. It promoted the centralisation of all functions of organised government, expanding what began as a spatial community to an association gradually incorporating all human interests. All the same, the French Revolution played the decisive role by replacing dynasts with the people as state-bearers. By emphasising the unity of its people, Schiemann reasoned, France not only placed the national idea to the fore, but also carried it over into the concept of state.[9] This proved contagious. In 1848 the Frankfurt Parliament opened by embracing all those living in a state's territory, yet ended by referring to the union of members of a 'nation' in the sense of a specific people. As the British historian Alfred Cobban wrote of 1789, the state ceased to be 'a juristic and territorial concept'. It became 'embodied in the theory of nationalism, which posited as an ideal the identification of cultural and political communities in a universal system of nation states'.[10]

Schiemann particularly disliked two aspects of this development in nineteenth-century Europe. Firstly, the veneration of the state as the highest and ultimate human community made 'state egoism' the sole content of politics. Secondly, fusion of the idea of 'nation' or '*Volk*' with that of territory bred an insistence that belonging to a specific place (*Raum*) also demanded belonging to a specific people. 'It can hardly be doubted,' Schiemann decided, 'that the World War was ignited by these two principles.'[11] He was disturbed that the very forces of democracy displacing despotism aggravated such unwelcome characteristics.[12] As well as absorbing the powers of the crown, the state took over many functions of other national organs—notably the church. The state became so full of the functions of public life as to be unmanageable by any political system.

He made the point bluntly in 1926 when surveying responses from forty-two prominent European intellectuals to the *Prager Presse*'s debating theme: 'Democracy and parliamentarianism, difficulties and their solution.' Most correspondents suggested practical reforms—limits to the number of political parties, the creation of new vehicles of popular will and so on. In Schiemann's lofty view only the Frankfurt Professor Franz Oppenheimer found the key by insisting: 'The centralisation of the state must cease.' Schiemann agreed, that Europe's politicians had to realise that they were not facing 'a crisis in the technique of government but of the state form.'[13]

Since he believed that overloading the state endangered parliamentary democracy he logically wished to reduce its functions. It was the argument that he deployed in the immediate postwar months in Latvia to break down central power into various activities and spheres, to be managed by appropriate associations. An independent judiciary was a modest contribution to that end, as would be, he insisted, cultural autonomy for minorities. The watchword for economic, social and cultural conflicts had to be 'dethroning the absolutist state'.[14] Its accretion of authority was 'the sickness of our time'. It crippled democratic systems and reduced politics to toppling governments and breeding an aversion to parliament on which political extremism was feeding. While he perceived the clash between socialists and the middle classes as hardly worse than earlier historic conflicts between liberalism and conservatism, parties had become 'not communities for state work but communities for the struggle for power'. The cure lay 'in dismantling the central power of the state, in sharing out the areas of state authority to different self-regulating authorities'.[15] The new 'state absolutism' could be contained only by liberalism, which 'will be forced to make a critical distinction between itself and that of the mass dictatorship endangering personal freedom and human rights.'[16]

Those rights were also at risk from what Schiemann saw as the second defect of the nation-state tradition—its drive to identify specific territory with one nationality. Here he emphasised the differences between the historical course of Western Europe, where the ideology of the nation-state took hold fully, and that of the ethnically mixed Eastern Central Europe, only now belatedly trying to weld together nation-states by denationalising large minorities. Indeed, he presented the conflict between belonging to a nation and belonging to a state essentially as a product of this region.[17] Unfortunately, the chance of building on old Austria's experimental legal solution to nationality issues was not grasped when war ended. Instead, Western assumptions of the compact nation-state as the norm dictated the application of 'self-determination' at the Paris Peace Conference. Yet how, he asked, if there were to be only territorial expressions of national will, could smaller and weaker minorities realise *their* national identity? The pervasive disillusionment, particularly in Europe's multi-ethnic regions, generated an intolerable sense of injustice among weaker minorities, causing what Schiemann described as an 'open wound' that infected the striving for peace.[18]

However, there was hope. Since history showed how such an impasse was reached, it surely held the key somewhere to redressing the situation. Schiemann returned to the indisputable historical fact of different nationalities co-existing together for a common purpose, and used it to deny any necessary equivalence between 'nation' and 'state'. The point was obscured, he suggested, by the widespread use of the term 'nation' to describe both ethnic and territorial communities. He tried to avoid ambiguity by referring to minorities sharing the same language and culture as a *Volksgemeinschaft* (national community)—a term later thoroughly subverted by National Socialism.

For the collectivity of the different national communities sharing a given territorial space Schiemann favoured the expression *Staatsgemeinschaft* (state community). The meaning and purpose of this construct could not in his view derive only from its territoriality, although that could be an important factor. But he reasoned that if occupancy were the sole condition of belonging, then there could be no objection to a Napoleon slicing up regions like lumps of cheese to create 'states'.[19] Instead Schiemann followed precepts of constitutional law. He stressed that the ordering of a community—in other words the sphere of state authority—rested on a collective assessment of its best interests. This position made it feasible to expose the illegality of supposed 'interests of state' which did not derive in reality from the overall purpose.[20]

At first glance redefining the concepts of nation (as a national community—*Volksgemeinschaft*) and state (as the collective embracing all the different national communities—*Staatsgemeinschaft*) does not immediately clarify Schiemann's proposed 'synthesis between nation and state'. In fact the deconstruction of the elements concealed by the label 'nation' was an essential step towards determining 'the spheres of authority [respectively] of the state and national community'. To Schiemann the merging of the two was the 'essence of Europe's minorities problem.'[21] The harsh fact confronting the new Nationalities Congress was that there was still no legally defined sphere of influence for a national community in the European states system. Cultural autonomy could redress this deficit and facilitate conflict-free work for the state. This 'essential task of the minority movement' had taken 'by far the most positive forms in Latvia and Estonia'.[22] Yet what persuaded Schiemann that the fragile nation/state 'synthesis' implicit in the Baltic model held out hope for other European minorities? Why would defining the spheres of responsibility of the *Volksgemeinschaft* and the *Staatsgemeinschaft* reduce rather than promote a clash of loyalty?

However persuasive the case might be for overloaded state authorities not interfering in the cultural affairs of national minorities, some sort of clash between two sets of obligations—to the national community and to the state as a whole-seemed likely. Schiemann frankly admitted the risk but also the challenge. 'Resolving the conflict between belonging to a state and belonging to a nation is the duty and purpose of the nationalities movement: it is the very meaning of the minority problem.'[23] He was encouraged by his feeling that there did not have to be a conflict. That perception arose in turn from his contention that the two sets of obligations indicated were located in different spheres. To appreciate the point fully, we must bring into play Schiemann's views on the parallels between minority rights and religious rights.

Almost as if in passing he made a comparison of cultural affiliation with religious confession before the war but was increasingly preoccupied by it. When preparing the draft law for German autonomy in Latvia in December 1923, he defined cultural autonomy as 'the transfer of freedom of conscience from the religious to the cultural realm'.[24] Two years later came his first major public exposition of the idea during a keynote address to the Nationalities Congress. On the basis of the religious wars that broke out in the sixteenth century he reflected on how much blood was spilled to achieve freedom of conscience; thirty years of brutal fighting to oppose the principle that rulers determined religion (*Cujus regio, ejus religio*). Yet the wars finished with the founding of legal norms allowing mutual tolerance. These duly became universal as states in the civilised world relinquished the choice of confession to their citizens, dramatically reducing the likelihood of religious wars engulfing Europe. Instead, Schiemann focused on a new menace, arising from the abuse of another 'sacred right' of the individual—the choice of nationality. Peace was at risk not from religious but from nationalist zeal, from the very principle *Cujus regio, ejus natio.* The experience of the early fighters for religious freedom was therefore relevant for Europe's minority leaders in the 1920s.[25]

Schiemann's inference that choosing to belong to a national cultural community was akin to confessing a religion arose from his understanding of both as essentially matters of emotional conviction. National awareness, like religious belief, was integral to being a person and therefore not appropriate as a determinant of citizenship.[26] He was thoroughly sceptical of the idea of 'objective' determinants of nationality. In September 1925, for example, he ridiculed his government's use of such 'indicators' of national identity as Latvian-sounding names of grandparents as 'police enforcement of genealogical studies'.[27] He was persuaded in sum that the very nature of religious and national communities made them a matter of innate right and individual choice. In practice electing to belong might indeed have the character of fulfilling a deeply-felt need. At the heart of it nonetheless remained the individual act of will. 'From this reality, that it is purely a private human matter, stems the right to demand that the state does not interfere.'[28]

This condition provided no international guarantee as such—although the Catholic Church's universality afforded a high order of protection for its believers. Unlike Boehm, who insisted that Christian values were innate to the modern state, Schiemann recognised the exercise of religious freedom as ultimately dependent on state authority, in the sense that it could in theory be revoked. Even in a Christian state, therefore, religious minorities were in a similar position to national minorities, in so far as the essential interests of both were subject to a state community with expressly different concerns to represent. But the actual withdrawal of religious freedom was unlikely because of the supranational support arising from all civilised states accepting the principle. History had shown the unproductiveness of efforts by a state to control religion. Thus it came to occupy its own sphere in relation to the *Staatsgemeinschaft*, escaping in *practice* the fate of most national minorities.

The task Schiemann set himself and the Nationalities Congress was to create conditions for Europe's national minorities comparable to those enjoyed by religious communities—including the international security derived from nationality rights, like religious rights, being accepted—in all civilised states. 'The nationality movement must become part of a bigger movement which quite simply sets out to preserve individuality in the various spheres of public life.'[29] In other words, just as the a-religious nature of the modern state paradoxically offered the final guarantee of freedom of conscience, so the anational state would provide the necessary freedom to practice one's culture.[30] With this we return to the central purpose of Schiemann's comparison between religious and national confession; namely to show how obligations to both could be reconciled with duties towards the *Staatsgemeinschaft* because they lay in different spheres.

Schiemann used his speech at the second Nationalities Congress in August 1926 to go further, beginning first with a review of why existing mechanisms were proving incapable of resolving the disturbing tension between national identity and statehood. Efforts to create statutory minority law on the basis of the League of Nations were 'illusory' since it was able to create legal ties only between states, not between a state and its members. On the other hand, for a nation to establish itself as a fully *independent* entity within a state required territorial as well as cultural expression. This was feasible only rarely in the form of federations, and impossible where—as in Eastern Central Europe—many nationalities shared the same space. While implementation of minority protection treaties *could* provide full cultural freedom and equal rights, it was not happening. Schiemann concluded that nationality had to proclaim culture its domain. The 'national' interest must be scrupulously confined to the cultural sphere, and the state interest released from the cultural. He could see no solution to existing nationality conflicts other than the 'separation of the state from the nation' and 'eliminating the concept of "nation-state"'.[31]

The sophistication and novelty of Schiemann's arguments for cultural autonomy and his demand for what he called the 'a-national' state instantly struck foreign press observers at the Congress. Basle's *National-Zeitung* observed: 'Schiemann's address provoked a storm of applause from all sides, although the implication of his ideas seemed too new and too revolutionary to many members of the congress.' The *Frankfurter Zeitung* was unsure about how far the parallels drawn with religious freedom could extend. Even so, it used Schiemann's phrase about the paramount need to resolve the struggle between belonging to a state and belonging to a nation to end its report.[32] The Dutch newspaper *Het Vaderland* had no doubt that Schiemann was the leading thinker of the congress, and published lengthy extracts from his speech under the heading 'Dr Schiemann's Programme'. Summarising his views on the state invasion of culture and the clashes it provoked, the paper perceptively dismissed the oversimplification that Schiemann and his supporters believed that 'one fine day all states will resolve to liquidate the idea of the nation-state'. It also disagreed with those categorising Schiemann's thought as revolutionary. 'It is on the contrary in the nature of an evolutionary idea. Schiemann apparently hopes for a lengthy development, whereby theory will become a more active factor in the reform movement.'[33]

This was indeed crucial for Schiemann. He held clearly articulated theoretical foundations to be the only way to provide a focus for effective and directed action, lifting the nationalities movement above local anomalies and the temptations of short-term compromise. He was therefore delighted by the unanimous congress resolutions in favour of cultural autonomy (p. 117). The media coverage of this event—not only in countries with significant national minorities but also in Britain, France, Germany and Switzerland—Schiemann took as evidence that one of the main goals of congress leaders was already in sight, namely 'to create a European atmosphere which no longer allows the minority problem to be ignored'.[34] An interview he gave in a Geneva coffee-house after the 1926 congress tended to confirm *Het Vaderland*'s insight. Having dismissed as 'senseless' Mello Franco's remark, at the previous year's League Council, that the nationalities gathering was a transitional phase towards full national assimilation with majority peoples, Schiemann was pressed by his Geneva interviewer on the feasibility of his call for separating national cultural organs from the state—for realising the a-national state. Schiemann readily agreed that it was an ideology whose practical consequences lay in the distant future.[35]

The problem, as Schiemann also stressed at the close of his speech, was that without a lessening of distrust between the major European powers it would be hard to eliminate clashes of loyalty between national and state duties entirely. Only a united Europe, he told delegates, could fully preclude the possibility of such conflicts. 'However, it seems to me that it is precisely for such a united Europe that the uncoupling of state and nation prepares the way.' In short, the 40 million people for whom the Nationalities Congress claimed to speak could provide the foundations for a peaceful Europe.[36] Unlike the League—functioning not as a union of nations but of nation states—the Nationalities Congress offered proof that international organisations did not have to be fixated on state sovereignty. Equally, Wilfan imagined the Congress developing into a League of Peoples.[37] Schiemann reminded his interviewer at Geneva that the concept of supranational cultural communities—integral to his thinking on the *Volksgemeinschaft*—was already being realised by the very existence of the Nationalities Congress.[38] The notion prompts the question of where borders fitted into Schiemann's overall thinking.

European conflicts over borders exemplified his arguments about the danger of preoccupation with national sovereignty. Even so, excluding minorities demanding frontier rectifications from the Nationalities Congress altogether, thereby confining it to 'genuine' minorities who nursed no revisionist ambitions, was never a serious option. It would have hopelessly limited the scope of the new movement, depriving it of international weight. Irredentist minorities admitted to the Nationalities Congress even retained their theoretical right to demand border changes. Yet they also had to pledge themselves to help bring about a situation in international law (cultural autonomy) that could, in effect, allow them in time to forgo their original goal. While the Nationalities Congress accepted no responsibility for maintaining the postwar territorial settlement, it therefore eschewed formal protests against it and up till 1934 its rules banned the debate of specific complaints against governments. Schiemann could fairly claim to be trying 'to remove the nationality question from state conflicts over borders'.[39]

His emphasis on space shared over time also attacked the folly of trying to resolve nationality conflicts through defining borders. Because of Europe's history it was 'impossible to have a European country where belonging to a state and nation were necessarily the same thing, so the only alternative to destroying or expelling the "foreign" element was to separate the concept of belonging to a state from belonging to a nation.' No matter how carefully physical boundaries were drawn, there would always be minorities left within states. The actuality of postwar irredentism was itself proof of that.[40]

The parallel between religion and culture further challenged conventional views on borders. As the idea of religious freedom conveyed the right to links with fellow—believers across physical boundaries, so the doctrine of cultural autonomy must allow national minorities communion with their brethren—in Schiemann's terminology, 'co-nationals.' The idea was integral to his personal vision of Europe's future. He conceived European unity in terms of networks of co-nationals—if not physically removing borders, then making them less relevant. Agreeing with contemporary pan-Europeanists that economic forces pushed in the same direction, he differed fundamentally in his belief that a solution to minority conflicts was the *precondition* for lasting European union (p. 173).[41]

Schiemann's awareness by 1925 that further progress inside Latvia on cultural autonomy was unlikely without movement outside helped to fuel his growing engagement in Europe, where the challenge to his powers of exposition was heightened by Germany's entry to the League of Nations in September 1926. It compounded international unease about the ultimate purpose of Berlin's endorsement of cultural autonomy. Was the doctrine, given the prominence of German minority leaders in the Nationalities Congress, more than a means to reform existing minority protection procedures? Was it not also a device to create 'states within states' in the interests of revising the peace settlement? For example, to the *Gazette de Lausanne*, reporting in 1926, the Nationalities Congress was little more than 'a pan-German Trojan horse.'[42] The idea was reinforced by *Kulturwehr*, the journal edited by Jan Skala, of the Polish-dominated Association of National Minorities in Germany, which among others included Friesians. Skala argued that only well-off and well-organised minorities could attain cultural autonomy; that it advanced the interests of the 'strong' minorities at the cost of the 'weak' ones.

The inference was clear and, given the attitudes of German *völkisch* nationalists at least, not wholly unjustified—namely, that through cultural autonomy the German minorities were primarily pursuing national advancement. Those less fortunate, less organised and less wealthy faced the risk of splitting, assimilation and decline.[43] Schiemann's response to Skala thus undoubtedly also contained an implicit warning against German nationalists when he reminded the 1927 congress that the German groups in the Nationalities Congress supported, 'unconditionally and without reservations', absolute parity between national minorities; that there were also weak German minorities; that cultural autonomy was predicated on the state bearing the administrative costs; and that the Germans had refused the presidency of the Nationalities Congress.[44] Nevertheless, the charge of German self-interest gained substance with the decision of the Congress in August 1927 not to admit the Friesians in Germany, on the technical grounds that they did not conform to congress statutes as to what constituted a minority. In protest the Polish-dominated Association of National Minorities in Germany withdrew from the congress.

The rationale for refusing entry to the Friesians was that admitting any group having the slightest difference with the totality would discredit the Nationalities Congress and promote the atomisation of peoples.[45] It followed the so-called Dresden resolution, evolved by the German group, to the effect that where history and practice had not clearly established the existence of a minority, then a positive and unambiguous expression of national will was required as a condition of congress membership. The provision glossed over the inherently problematic nature of admission criteria, but undeniably most Friesians in Germany did not express any will to be a national minority.[46] In Schiemann's reasoning a minority was 'on the one hand a community which, through historic development and present will, is united in its conviction that its moral and spiritual well-being is possible only in the context of a specific national culture, and on the other hand, is tied through historic development and present will to a specific space and a specific state.' One implication was that the culture arising for example from Baltic Germandom's shared experience with Latvians and Estonians was as important as that shared with the German people.[47]

Not surprisingly, Schiemann's thinking on this score elicited heavy criticism from *völkisch* German minority representatives, with Boehm and Werner von Hasselblatt among others also attacking the notion of the a-national state as detrimental to national sovereignty.[48] In reality, Schiemann was trying to re-define the concept by distinguishing between a state's external sovereignty and its powers in relation to its inhabitants. Another reason why a cultural community did not have to impinge on state sovereignty any more than a religious one was that it had no need of the power of a territorial entity. Admittedly, because cultural development 'can only occur with the will of the individual, but not against it', the state's inner peace demanded that it protect the culture of its nationalities. However, this action had to be confined to cases where indisputable evidence existed of the will to belong to a nation ('*Rechtsschutz wird nur einem Rechte gewährt hinter dem ein Wille steht*').

By contrast 'state protection against desertion [from the national community] wholly contradicts the fundamentals of confessional freedom.' This is what Schiemann meant by stating that the state's general good 'is founded exclusively on the will to belong to a specific nationality, but not on the maintenance of this or that nationality.'[49] In cases where state community and national community were not identical, removing matters specific to the ethnic minority from the competence of the state—far from creating a 'state within a state'—offered all inhabitants a stake in the state's wellbeing.[50]

However, basing policy on the negative principle of attacking 'foreign' culture offered only cultural decline; a state forcing minorities to conduct a separate policy was a sick state, also likely to suffer economically. Only spatial constructs sustaining living communities were viable. 'In this solution of the *Staatsgemeinschaft* and *Volksgemeinschaft*', Schiemann proposed, 'I believe not to have encroached further on the concept of [state] sovereignty and to have made possible the implementation of all the freedoms for which we [the nationalities movement] are striving.'[51] Furthermore, while those freedoms pre-empted assimilation—as understood by the likes of Mello Franco—they emphatically did not rule out inclusion or indeed political integration.

That should have been beyond doubt from Schiemann's intensive and committed day-to-day political work in Latvia. 'I have always said', he had written of his country in 1925, 'that the minority movement in our state is limited to achieving the specific goal of unimpeded inclusion in the state idea, with guaranteed cultural freedom.'[52] The Nationalities Congress, as he argued in 1927, was 'striving basically for the inclusion of minorities in normal state life. A minority that is more concerned with its own interests than with the general good acts against public interest and violates the fundamental idea of our Nationalities Congress, which seeks not to set minorities apart from the state but to engage them in its life. We want indeed to show the world that granting rights to minorities does not threaten the state but strengthens it. We can only win this trust by taking an honourable political line in all matters concerning the generality.'[53] Schiemann did not naïvely believe that cultural autonomy would remove all tensions between nationalities. He fully accepted that the doctrine could threaten rifts in the cultural life of the state. For this reason he also expressed hopes for a future study of the possible consequences of complete implementation of national cultural autonomy, as well as the risks of distinct cultural entities leading to undesired mutual isolation.[54] He believed that such divisions were unavoidable at primary school level, but envisaged the different nationality groups being more united through their middle schooling and beyond. In fact he held common schooling at this level to be vital for the social and national solidarity of citizens. However, it had to be the outcome of organic growth, and not imposed by central government. It was his conviction, in other words, that the majority—not just minorities—would benefit from cultural autonomy through the release of the state's dead hand. 'The final goal of the minorities policy', he suggested, 'cannot be to free national schools from the state but to free schools in general from the state. … Only then will the concept of a national minority vanish from public life and be replaced by a free association of citizens.'[55]

Schiemann was equally firm in deflecting the argument of Hasselblatt and Boehm that the term 'minority' (*Minderheit*) connoted something of 'lesser value' (*Minderwertig*). Among other things this again betrayed conservative Baltic Germandom's aspirations to equal state-bearing status with Latvians and Estonians.[56] Schiemann dismissed Boehm's reference in this context to the example of Finland as the product of ignorance of the actual situation. He treated demands for state construction on the basis of several state-bearing nationalities as unrealistic-outside rare opportunities for federation. Again he resorted to paradox: in order to control its cultural life (to abandon *in effect* the existence of a minority, since it already necessarily shared majority concerns for the general good of the common territorial space), the nationality group first had to embrace *being* a minority. All those unwilling 'to bury their heads in the sand', he insisted, must use the term 'minority' when referring to the national community. The retention of the term was essential to the work of the Nationalities Congress precisely because it had gained widespread usage and acceptance in the international arena.[57]

More seriously, the clash of definitions exposed differing views on the meaning and purpose of any supranational national community arising from Europe-wide cultural autonomy. The fierce debate that Schiemann provoked in 1927 with his highly public exposition of the a-national state also explains the appearance of his most substantial essay on the subject up to that time. It appeared in the first edition of *Nation und Staat* in the autumn, called simply 'Volksgemeinschaft und Staatsgemeinschaft'.

His belief that the title's two components lay behind the blanket term 'nation' has been examined. It remains only to consider more closely his vision of the *Volksgemeinschaft*, and which of the traits commonly ascribed to the 'nation' as a whole (territory, language, customs, character, culture, history, origin, power, economy and religion) he ascribed to the *Volksgemeinschaft*. His insistence that religion was a trait inherent in neither state nor national community should not by now come as a surprise. Of the *Volksgemeinschaft*'s claim to remaining traits he took origin and history to be non-essential. The innate right of individuals to voice the will to belong to it exempted them from the need to have been part of it ethnically or historically. He admitted the force of the myth of common origin for the nation as *Volksgemeinschaft*, as for example when Baltic Germans in Estonia and Latvia referred to their 700-year history, although most families had in fact first come no more than 200 years earlier. The only justification for such myths, in Schiemann's opinion, was the obligations they imposed for the environment and the assumption of historic responsibilities.

As to language, Schiemann found remarkable that not all recognised it, along with the act of will to belong, as an 'unavoidable and obligatory characteristic for the nation in the sense of a national community'. He naturally acknowledged instances where different traditions and history separated users of the same language, as for example the English and Americans. Nevertheless, he held language to be vital to the sense of belonging together, from which the national community, with its shared customs and culture, first arose. Protection of the language was imperative for the *Volksgemeinschaft*; a community not bound by common language could not be seen in the European sense as a *Kulturnation*.[58] The importance Schiemann attached to language is particularly clear in his response to contemporary suggestions that the Jews were not a nation because they had no territory.

Instead Schiemann focused on the intense feeling of commonalty that existed between Jews—a phenomenon appearing to the European understanding as a religious community. In this respect he could see no obstacle to Jews with appropriate language and culture forming a *Volksgemeinschaft* with other races. In his view the significance of Zionists as nation-builders derived less from their demand for a homeland (which non-Zionist Jews could support) than from their insistence on a common language. However, the existence of two languages, Hebrew and Yiddish, made the Zionist goal problematic, but it was perfectly feasible in Schiemann's reasoning for Jewry to become a nation in the European sense, if Zionist *linguistic* goals were attained. Indirectly, the point reinforced his argument that, in contrast to language, territory was not a necessary trait of the nation as *Volksgemeinschaft*.[59]

His arguments on the nature of the *Volksgemeinschaft* were elaborated in his critique of the work of Elijah Ben-Zion Sadinsky, who also conceived 'national societies' existing alongside the state, but in addition wanted a supreme world court of justice above nations and states—a 'great council of the nations'. Schiemann had not read this work when making his own plea for the a-national state at Geneva in 1926, but soon indicated where Sadinsky diverged from his own thinking. As a member of the German Pro-Palestine Committee, Schiemann sympathised with Sadinsky's work for a state in Palestine and could understand why the Zionist committee appealed to the nationalities movement for support. At the same time he asked how German, Polish, Magyar, Slavic and Romanian minorities could make the founding of a Palestinian *state* an aim of their own. The Nationalities Congress was predicated on minorities' demands deriving from the overall needs of the community in which they existed.

Schiemann also differed sharply with Sadinsky over the allocation of responsibilities between the state and national community.[60] The demand for the national community to have its own force—specifically in this instance a million-strong army of workers to build and prepare Palestine—flatly contradicted the core of Schiemann's thinking on the proper concerns respectively of the nation as *Volksgemeinschaft* and the nation as *Staatsgemeinschaft*. Schiemann categorically affirmed the state authority's role in promoting the physical and economic wellbeing of the territorial space shared by minority and majority peoples alike. Nothing made this clearer than his insistence on minorities' duty to share the military defence of their host-states; as an actual entity (*Tatsachengemeinschaft*) the state could juridically have only one executive.[61] Schiemann also rejected Sadinsky's case for transferring some civil or criminal punishment rights to the *Volksgemeinschaft* on the grounds that democracies (as opposed to fascist or communist states) already acknowledged the equality of all citizens.

He also objected to Sadinsky removing social welfare functions from the state. Schiemann treated the exceptions in the Estonian cultural autonomy law and the German draft autonomy law in Latvia as apparent rather than real, in that specific arrangements were intended only to supplement state care and to offset the sudden and massive poverty of Baltic Germandom after 1918. However, he conceived social welfare generally in terms of a moral imperative arising from the relationship of the state to all its inhabitants. To transfer social welfare generally to the *Volksgemeinschaft* would be 'to abandon the dictates of love of humanity and replace them merely with love of one's own kin-quite clearly the inspiration of a nationalism injurious to ethics.'[62]

Schiemann's treatment of Sadinsky also belies any attempt to see his theoretical work as reducing the state—in classic liberal mode—to the mere function of a night-watchman.[63] His purpose in clarifying the obligations incumbent on the *Staatsgemeinschaft* was the better to establish, in the non-territorial realm of education and culture, that the rights allocated to the *Volksgemeinschaft* were absolute. Territory as such, if not a necessary trait of the *Volksgemeinschaft*, could nevertheless be formative, as Schiemann's own experience confirmed. 'Without doubt, a community based wholly on the settlement of a specific area defined by actual borders is not a living community. It is no nation. But different nationalities who look back together on a shared past on the same territory, these also have an element of culture in common. Therein lies their strength.'[64]

So it was that Schiemann arrived at the heart of his reflections on nation and state. 'We can see then, how alongside the nation as *Volksgemeinschaft* a second form of nation can evolve from the *Staatsgemeinschaft*, containing important elements of a feeling of belonging together.'[65] If the nation as *Staatsgemeinschaft* was an actual community (*Tatsachengemeinschaft*), then the nation as *Volksgemeinschaft* was 'essentially an emotional community (*Gefühlsgemeinschaft*)'. The image of something floating above the corporeal state is deepened by Schiemann's insistence that the *Volksgemeinschaft* involved 'a universal tie between all those having common national cultural interests' and that it extended 'throughout the world'.[66] It was thus not merely the nationally mixed states of Eastern Central Europe that had to be interested in building supranational networks, since all European states had co-nationals living outside their borders.

Schiemann's thinking was undoubtedly subversive of prevailing nation-state preoccupation with absolute sovereignty, but not of the state form as such, precisely because he emphasised the collective interest of *Volksgemeinschaft* and *Staatsgemeinschaft*. Far more than Renner, Schiemann stressed the dangers of hindering the territorial state in its integrative functions. Thus, emphatically, his understanding of individuals as members of both national and state communities pre-empted claims advanced on the basis of ethnicity that conflicted with the overall good. For Schiemann politics entailed 'work for the good of the place one inhabits. Any diversion to other ends is suicide.'[67] He therefore asked that ethnic minorities creating a cultural community across borders accept non-involvement in the *political* life of their mother-country; they could not answer any call to 'betray the state for the sake of the nation'. Groups unable to identify with the policy of the state in which they lived 'must forgo any sort of political activity in an international sense'.[68]

This central tenet of Schiemann's thinking made him particularly sensitive to Polish attempts to exploit the Friesian affair to brand the Nationalities Congress as a vehicle for German foreign policy, and so discredit it. In the face of this implication that all German minorities were indeed fifth-columnists[69] it seemed to Schiemann all the more important to counter Polish pressure by improving the situation of national minorities in Germany—in keeping with Stresemann's public commitment He claimed to have had assurances in Berlin to this effect, but everything still depended on the attitude of the *Land* authorities, those of Prussia above all.[70] At the same time he mounted a damage-limitation exercise against Jan Skala's *Kulturwehr* by developing a comparison between 'Germanic' and 'Slavic' conceptions of minority rights within the European nationalities movement.

As a German he identified a commitment to reconciling the conflict between ethnic identity and citizenship, the defining of minority rights in terms of managing one's own culture, and above all stress on individual will as the sole determinant of membership of a national minority ('*Zur Minderheit gehört wer will*'). By contrast, the Slavic position was the belief that the nationality movement was primarily to protect the weak (the more groups joining the Congress the better), rather than to develop positive minority rights legislation; that the state had the duty to meet the cultural needs of a minority; and that membership of a nationality was to be determined by the state according to objective criteria. To Schiemann these conditions amounted to minorities being robbed of the most fundamental of rights, that freely to profess one's own culture. 'A cultural life received through the mediation of a different nationality can never ever constitute a national existence of one's own.'[71] He had in mind the demands of the Polish minority in Prussia for objective determinants of nationality in allocating schooling by the Land authorities. 'A minority made up of members involuntarily thrust into it by the state is, without any doubt, an absurdity.'[72]

Schiemann also responded sharply to an edition of *Kulturwehr* in September 1927, which criticised the Nationalities Congress on behalf of the Association of Minorities in Germany and insisted that only minorities 'loyal' to the existing territorial order merited rights—or indeed admission to the Nationalities Congress. To Schiemann this error, again, stemmed from prewar conceptions of minority issues as primarily a matter of drawing boundaries—an illusion long since exposed by the reality of postwar Europe, where interpreting self-determination in purely territorial terms had elevated irredentism 'to a principle of law'. He emphasised that far from seeking solutions outside the states system, as Skala suggested, the Nationalities Congress sought instead to implicate *all* European minorities in a project transcending frontiers: cultural autonomy. Schiemann countered Skala's insistence on the loyalty test by asking how, for example, it could be passed by the Polish minority in East Prussia to the satisfaction of the majority. By contrast the Nationalities Congress promoted the maintenance of a minority's culture as an *absolute* right. Loyal cooperation was not a condition but rather an outcome of granting such rights.[73]

Schiemann could justly deflect suggestions that his own ideas were the centre of an ideological system for Germandom as a whole by referring to the powerful critics within the German minorities' movement of his thinking on the 'a-national' state. The 'heart of the matter' remained the *Kulturwehr*'s accusation that, unlike the altruistic Slavic community, German minorities were exploiting the minority movement they had called into being simply to pursue the aims of German power politics. Where, Schiemann asked, was the evidence for such a policy on the part of the Nationalities Congress?

The German groups wanted to exclude the political issue of borders from the congress; to include in the nationalities movement all organised minorities with their own culture; and to create internationally acknowledged laws guaranteeing minorities their cultural development, irrespective of the state in which they lived. By contrast, the Association of National Minorities in Germany wanted to tie the Nationalities Congress to the maintenance of peace treaties; to exclude from it minorities perceived as threatening to European peace; to make the state the guardian of the culture of national minorities. This, Schiemann concluded, would remove any international significance from the European nationalities movement and perpetuate conflict.[74]

In Paris and Warsaw, however, the pointed avoidance of border issues by the Nationalities Congress was itself construed as an indirect attempt to undermine the Versailles peace settlement. Certainly the *Kulturwehr* offensive from 1927 made the Auswärtiges Amt more aware than hitherto of the potential value of the Congress for German foreign policy. It is also in this context that—in Schiemann's words—Skala's 'single-minded rule' must be seen.[75] From 1927, as well as the expenses of German congress delegates, the Auswärtiges Amt bore the costs of Ewald Ammende's permanent secretariat in Vienna, where his brother Erich was office manager. In addition, what publicly proclaimed itself the organ of the Nationalities Congress, *Nation und Staat*, was set up under Max Winkler's Consortia, following a decision of Reich and Prussian officials in March 1927. The new journal's publication costs, together with those of its editorial office in Vienna, were estimated at 57,000 Reich Marks annually. Additional subsidies were set aside for the key German minority leaders on the editorial board: Rudolf Brandsch, Johannes Schmidt-Wodder, Jakob Bleyer, Paul Schiemann and one other.[76]

With some justice *Nation und Staat* has recently been described as 'an outlet for minority leaders under the "control" of the Reich' and 1927 as the year when the Auswärtiges Amt secured its influence over the international work of German minorities.[77] How this might benefit Germany was already evident from the Friesian crisis. This relieved Berlin of pressure: if the Friesians had been admitted to the Nationalities Congress, they would officially have become a fifth national minority in the Reich—alongside the Poles, Danes, Sorbs and Lithuanians—on whose behalf Stresemann was committed to promoting cultural autonomy before his country joined the League of Nations. The departure from the Congress of the Polish-dominated Association of National Minorities in Germany also made it difficult for other Polish groups to join, automatically tilting the agenda of the Nationalities Congress towards that of the German groups. It is not without irony, therefore, that Schiemann—himself a leading figure in the Verband der deutschen Minderheiten and a key presence on the intellectually weighty *Nation and Staat*—described Jan Skala as the leader-writer of a journal that was a tool in foreign hands.[78]

Although Schiemann was strictly correct in stressing that the minorities themselves initiated the Nationalities Congress, he was well aware of its increasing recourse to and need for Reich aid, and often apprehensive about it. Indeed he argued for this in an influential memorandum, delivered personally to Stresemann in Berlin on 26 March 1928. Stresemann's support was crucial in overcoming resistance within the Auswärtiges Amt and Schiemann's memorandum appears to have been a preliminary stage to a significant increase in Reich funding for the Nationalities Congress—to the point where this ultimately kept the organisation afloat. Schiemann made his case by reviewing the previous three years: 'The main demands and principles of the German minorities [i.e. the Verband der deutschen Minderheiten Europas] became the official arguments and aspirations of the various European minority groups, irrespective of nationality. They thereby had greater impact. The view of the minority problem, hitherto dismissed as a matter for the plaintiffs, was transformed in Europe.'[79]

However, it can scarcely be emphasised too strongly that for the Auswärtiges Amt a major purpose of the exercise was to reduce the chances of the Nationalities Congress impacting adversely on German foreign policy. The dominance within the Congress of the German groups slowly but surely introduced into it the clash within the *Auslandsdeutsche* community; between democratic/republican and *völkisch*/nationalist values; between those for whom cultural autonomy might help towards a future pan-German order, and those for whom the doctrine held the key to domestic and European harmony. However, that conflict had yet to be resolved and Reich government subsidies for the Nationalities Congress—flowing indirectly through the Verband der deutschen Minderheiten—were predicated for the time being on the likes of Schiemann, Kurt Graebe and Carl Georg Bruns being closely involved in the process.[80] Schiemann's democratic credentials were perhaps exceptional, but Max Hildebert Boehm would later record with contempt that support for the *Auslandsdeutschen* during the life of the Weimar Republic was monopolised by those embracing 'the dominant liberal jargon'.[81]

8. The Return of the Right

Although Schiemann contrasted Nazi manipulation of the *Auslandsdeutschen* with the autonomy enjoyed by German minority leaders in the 1920s, his heavy personal engagement in the conflicts swirling through the Nationalities Congress in 1927 seems at odds with his insistence on keeping politics out of the relationship between minority and mother-state. What reduced any attacks of conscience he might have had was his belief in, and identification with, Gustav Stresemann's ambition to reintegrate the Reich peacefully into the post-war European order. When Stresemann also committed himself from 1925 to the goal of cultural autonomy in Europe, the symmetry between his diplomacy and Schiemann's work in Latvia and Europe was complete. The worst enemies of both men were on the far right. As far as Schiemann was concerned, checking these forces more than justified what contribution he was able to make to the success of the Weimar Republic's foreign policy. His support for the Latvian-Soviet trade treaty of 1927 illustrates the general point.

Schiemann naturally had close links with the Berlin bureaucracy as a leading figure in the Verband der deutschen Minderheiten in Europa. His involvement in Germany's 'new' *Ostpolitik* from 1918 also left him a lasting constituency among Auswärtiges Amt personnel, notably the head of the Eastern Department, Maltzan, as well as other officials working on the genesis and implementation of the Rapallo treaty.[1] They included the economist Eric Wallroth, Köster's forerunner in Riga and successor to Maltzan when the latter became State Secretary in late 1922. As to Köster, Schiemann credited him with first alerting the Auswärtiges Amt to the new realities in the East, to the 'profound significance of the Baltic problem' and to the need to abandon old preoccupations with Russia.[2] Accordingly, Rapallo was presented by the German government not as a threat to the border states but as an inducement for similar German-Baltic treaties. Schiemann supported this concept, using the *Rigasche Rundschau* to promote Köster's idea of a Russo-German guarantee of the Baltic states in 1925.[3] It failed to materialise, but some progress was made through a conjunction of separate pacts in 1926: the German-Soviet Treaty of Berlin, the German-Latvian trade agreement and the Soviet-Lithuanian non-aggression pact.[4] Understandably, Berlin wished for a positive outcome to the new Latvian government's negotiations with Soviet Russia in 1927.

It happened that the German fraction became of crucial importance to the electoral arithmetic behind social democrat Mārğeris Skujenieks' cabinet (19.12.26–23.1.28). It closed a crisis-ridden interregnum on the fall of Alberinq's bourgeois coalition—likened by Schiemann to a toy car with a broken spring being pushed by hand. He had been critical of the poverty of Alberinq's social policy and deplored the cabinet's failure to tackle corruption or produce a sound fiscal strategy because of its dependence on different interest groups.[5] Skujenieks, on the other hand, had a reputation—at that time—for being moderate. He was committed to cleaning up the bureaucracy and looking after the economy.[6] The German fraction felt it had little to lose by giving such a government of the left a chance, and adopted a benevolent neutrality towards it. Fircks expressed some of the uneasiness of Baltic German conservatives in particular by underlining the German fraction's 'purely bourgeois' platform in his welcoming address on 17 December 1926. Forced to acknowledge the unlikelihood for the moment of a solid bourgeois government, he contented himself with warning against social and economic experiments typical of the radical left.[7]

Schiemann's assessment—that it was less a question of 'what course?' than 'we have *a* course'—referred also to Latvia's diplomacy.[8] His strictures against Soviet attempts to undermine Locarno and the League did not alter his opinion that the Baltic states should not allow their inclusion in the West's sphere of interest to make them anti-Russian. He saw one solution to the dilemma as being a joint acceptance of Moscow's offers of non-aggression treaties to the Baltic countries in 1926, commending the Treaty of Berlin as a model. This allowed the Reich specific exemptions from obligations as a League member that were likely to bring it into conflict with Russia.[9] Köster himself explained Riga's calm reaction to the Berlin agreement in terms of Latvia searching, like Germany, for a formula 'combining the maximum of neutrality towards Russia with full loyalty to the League'.[10] Echoing the Auswärtiges Amt's view of the Berlin treaty—'only conceivable on the basis created by Locarno and entry to the League'—Schiemann editorialised it as an extension of peace to the East.[11] When Lithuania concluded a separate non-aggression pact with Russia he was even more concerned that Latvia should follow the same path.[12] Skujenieks' willingness to do so was a major incentive for the German fraction to stifle its reservations about a left-wing cabinet.

Schiemann's vote on the Saiema's foreign affairs committee was crucial in empowering the Foreign Minister Felix Cielēns to resume talks with Moscow. These eventually led to the initialling of the Latvian-Soviet non-aggression pact on 9 March 1927.[13] Economic negotiations with Russia followed hard on the March agreement and culminated in the signing of a trade treaty in June. Schiemann was also concerned that the severance of Anglo-Soviet relations in May 1927 would prompt Britain to take a more active interest than previously in creating a barrier of border-states, thus indirectly encouraging the aspirations of Poland and its mentor France.[14] He remained solidly behind Cielēns in backing the Soviet-Latvian agreement.[15] 'If the Latvian government resigns', he insisted in a CGBP meeting in early October, 'the whole *Ostpolitik* will be reconfigured. In Berlin the situation is seen as serious.'[16]

He floated a 'trial balloon' in the shape of an article for the *Frankfurter Zeitung* in mid-October, also outlining the gist of it to German minority leaders from all three Baltic states during a meeting in Tallinn. Essentially, he restated the case for a joint German-Russian interest sphere in the Baltic. 'Opposed to this is the Polish plan for a five-state bloc operating in common against Russia. The unanimity Poland is striving for will become illusory with the making of the treaty between Russia and Latvia. If the Latvian-Russian treaty is concluded, then there is no longer any point in Estonia postponing its trade agreement with Russia.' Werner von Hasselblatt conceded that Poland would be checked, but agreed with Fircks in stating that, Bolshevik or otherwise, 'the main enemy is not Poland, but Russia.' Hasselblatt saw the treaty as 'the beginning of a slide into a Russian federation'. Schiemann did not dispute the potential threat from the East but drew from it the opposite conclusion: 'We must create conditions which show the border-states to be feasible in the event of Russia growing strong, indeed they could even be advantageous to it. Logically, then, Cielēns' goal is the guarantee of the *status quo* by Germany and Russia. Precisely by accommodating ourselves [Baltic countries] to both these states we deflect the threat of being a lasting obstacle to them.'[17]

In an effort to make the public debate more balanced, Schiemann had the historian Hans von Rimscha analyse for the *Rigasche Rundschau* what was happening to the Russian people. Yet Baltic Germans distrusted Russia under *any* regime.[18] For Fircks the price of ratifying the trade treaty—continuing collaboration with the Latvian left—was too high. In the June issue of the *Baltische Monatsschrift*, refounded by Woldemar Wulffius in 1927, he urged German Baltdom to orient itself definitively to the Latvian right, unleashing a debate that made it even more difficult for Schiemann to keep the fraction on its existing course.[19] Since the German deputies were indispensable to the ratification of the Russian treaty they came under 'unexampled pressure' from all sides. 'All of us in Riga', Köster reported, 'are used to having garlands of thorns wound round our foreheads or other parts of our bodies. But this time it has really gone too far.' While the right spread rumours that the Bolsheviks were financing Schiemann, the left accused 'poor Keller' of having 'immoral relations with a schoolgirl, the Procurator being ready to drop the matter only if he [Keller] votes for the treaty.'[20]

Schiemann's editorial—two days before the CGBP met on 24 October to review its stand on ratification—was addressed as much to his own community as to Latvian opposition parties. For the Baltic to shun its 'mission' as an economic and commercial bridge would be to pander to those who saw 'our independence' only for the duration of Bolshevik Russia, and would then make their own direct contacts. For Latvia to follow Estonia and regulate relations with Russia on the basis of agreement with Warsaw would encourage the enlargement of Russian and Polish influence to the Baltic—rather than the maintenance of independent coastal states—as well as the encirclement of Central Europe by France. The Baltic states had therefore to reach an understanding, on the one hand with a Russia diverted by countering Britain in Asia, and on the other with a Germany favouring Baltic independence. This was neither pro-Reich nor anti-Entente 'but in our own political interests, making our independence central to any Baltic foreign policy'.[21]

In correctly assuming that a bloc *à trois* was the only combination acceptable to Moscow on its Baltic front, Schiemann arrived at the paradoxical conclusion that a joint German-Russian sphere of interest would actually promote neutrality for the Baltic states, which was 'above all working to become free of the net of great power cliques'.[22] His analysis was diametrically opposed to the arguments of conservative Baltic Germans that Latvian social democracy's 'flirtation' with Moscow would prove fatal for 'a bourgeois, European Latvia'.[23]

Although Keller had reservations, Fircks was the only Baltic German deputy in the free parliamentary vote allowed by the CGBP on 26 October to come out against the Russian treaty.[24] Once this was ratified by a small majority in the Saeima, however, Schiemann could no longer resist conservative pressure for the early dethronement of Skujenieks.[25] He insisted on agreement being reached on principles first with an alternative administration, and was concerned to avoid charges that his fraction had acted only on orders from Berlin.[26] 'There could be no clearer proof of this', Köster wryly observed 'than if eight days after the [Russian] treaty's acceptance the [German] fraction took the first possible opportunity to topple the government.'[27] Schiemann even privately asked Berlin, through Köster, to encourage the fraction to support the existing cabinet for the time being. Wallroth's response was a private letter to his ambassador. 'If—as in the case of the Latvian-Russian trade treaty—the properly understood interests of German Balts and Latvians conform so completely with the foreign policy aims of the Reich, it is—exceptionally—both possible and necessary to exert from here, as happened, influence beyond that exercised purely locally and personally. But to make available to the German deputies a telegram from the Auswärtiges Amt bringing Reich policy interests to bear on their stance towards a given cabinet is quite another matter.'[28]

The exchange well illustrates the rigorous constraints within which Stresemann's strategy of peaceful revisionism came to operate. Although unwelcome to Poland, particularly when taken in conjunction with the way the Nationalities Congress was developing, Weimar *Ostpolitik* did leave space for a *modus vivendi* to be worked out over time. This was noteworthy enough in an era when nationalism was manifestly not confined to the Reich. Looking back on the episode of the Russian treaty in the autumn of 1932, with a very different Germany set to emerge, Schiemann specifically related his actions in 1927 to the Weimar Republic's commitment to peaceful change in Europe through diplomacy and discussion. He cautioned Cielēns in the autumn of 1932 not to abandon the earlier policy of cooperation with the Reich until there was a clearer picture of the likely new regime in Berlin. The implication was clear: that the *nature* of German foreign policy would be the decisive test of Schiemann's readiness to promote its ends—as a German minority leader—in Latvia and the Baltic region.[29]

Schiemann's reluctance to let Skujenieks fall without specific cause also showed distaste for the way the German fraction had jettisoned the responsible behaviour he persistently claimed for it.[30] According to Köster, it was 'mainly due to Schiemann' that the cabinet was spared an abrupt end in early November 1927.[31] The Latvian President, Gustavs Zemgals, suggested to Schiemann at one point that he should form an administration. Schiemann eventually refused on the grounds that the 51 or 52 votes he could expect to muster were insufficient for a stable government. It is apparent that Schiemann had only agreed to an early regime change after Keller came out in support of Fircks. However, when a majority was eventually put together in the Saeima for a new administration, it was feasible only with the inclusion of the German deputies. Magnus became Minister of Justice in the new coalition of the right under P. Juraševskis. (24.1.–30.11.1928).[32]

The episode confirmed that in spite of his reservations about the Latvian left Schiemann was still inclined to work with the social democrats when circumstances dictated. He was almost certainly influenced by his great regard for Adolf Köster. Both men opposed Fircks' call to have no relations with the left *on principle.*[33] Köster's gloss on the whole affair is apposite: 'The actions of Herr Cielēns compared with his predecessors, except for Meierovics, are acclaimed by all. And we are the ones in the last resort who have benefited most from this activity.' As to the new government slowly being assembled, 'the heavens are kind to us, in so far as we are also deeply involved through Schiemann.'[34]

The German fraction's influence in 1927 and 1928 was undeniable. Magnus's appointment marked the return of a Baltic German to the cabinet after ten years. The new government promised to continue the foreign policy of its predecessor, to fight corruption and to be less interventionist in the economy—all issues close to the German community's heart. Legislation on autonomy remained in abeyance pending the completion of a Latvian school law, still at the commission stage, but a steady recovery of German education was apparent. There were now 110 German schools, ten of them at secondary level. These, like primary schools with fewer than thirty pupils, had to supplement the grants from state and communal authorities from private sources. Still, all private minority schools enjoyed the same rights as state schools, including secondary school examinations (*Abitur*) in the mother-tongue. Teaching programmes had to be comparable to those in the public sector but were devised by the minorities. They also had the right to train their own teachers, if again to public sector standards. Critical in this respect was the Saiema's legalisation of the Herder Institute as a German private higher education institution in May 1927. These advances were recorded in Karl Keller's review of his ten years at the head of the German education authority, penned after he handed over the post to Wolfgang Wachtsmuth in November 1928.[35]

Keller could not deny the ferocity of the struggle for those engaged in Latvia's unique experiment, with petty bureaucratic obstructions early on and varying degrees of chauvinism from Latvian political parties throughout. Yet he believed the *principle* of school autonomy had become accepted in official circles—by some, no doubt, as a necessary evil. Nor was there widespread public resistance, beyond intermittent concern that privately supported schools might enjoy advantages denied to public institutions. 'So even making allowance for variations, according to the political situation or the attitude of specific minorities, does not change the overall picture, namely that the right of the national minorities to their own cultural life is recognised as being to the general good.' Schiemann's annual political survey agreed.[36] Keller, like his successor, also highlighted cultural cohesion and identity in his overall balance-sheet. In spite of severe economic and other setbacks, he concluded, things would have been worse without Schiemann's leadership.[37] Wilhelm von Rüdiger had to agree: 'The successes of the political leadership—forging the Germans [in Latvia] into a resilient community ready to rebuild, securing the education of our young in German schools and maintaining the sparse [Baltic German] farming sector would be enough in themselves to justify the parliamentary work of Paul Schiemann and Baron Fircks.'[38]

Nevertheless, the ideological flare-up over the Russian treaty had severely strained the common parliamentary line fashioned between Baltic German parties since 1920. Once the new government was in place, Schiemann returned to the tussle between 'right' and 'left'.[39] The likelihood of a coherent Baltic German voice emerging on the left was not strong, and his task was more irksome than difficult. True, Robert Riedel and his followers in the short-lived Workers' Party pricked the fraction's bubble by defending the 'little man' against the 'literary cliques' dominating the CGBP. This explained, among other things, Schiemann's efforts to prevent tension between German landlords and tenants in Riga escalating into open conflict.[40]

After the closure of the *Rigasche Nachrichten* in 1925, Riedel continued to inflict discomfort through the pages of the *Riga am Sonntag*. It too started as a paper of the left, polemicising on behalf of the little man against self-taxation and ridiculing the Baltic German political leaders.[41] When Schiemann eventually responded 'once and for all' to the *Riga am Sonntag*'s incessant attacks, he had an easy target. He reviewed Riedel's career—first on the left at the *Rigasche Nachrichten*, then on the right as editor of *Neue Tageblatt*, and finally as an a-political patriot when editing the *Woche im Bild*—parodying Riedel's 'Damascus conversion' from democrat to monarchist.[42] Riedel's journalism increasingly sounded the note of national renewal as, from 1928, the *Riga am Sonntag* shifted towards the *völkisch* camp.[43]

Rosenberg was even less of a potent force on the left, although he re-emerged in 1928 with a memoir containing a vituperative attack on the CGBP. 'This disastrous system of uncritically subordinating all vital forces to a small, absolute ruling leadership group I make responsible in the first instance for Germandom's carriage being today so deeply and helplessly mired in the swamp.'[44] His words contradicted what the fraction had manifestly achieved, confirming his days as a politician over.[45] However, in so far as Rosenberg's stance frustrated Schiemann's wish to incorporate a 'more leftist line' into his own party, it heralded a further erosion of democratic values among Riga's Germandom. To Schiemann's mind this reflected not just the decline of the little man's interest in politics but also a drift among German Balt youth towards *völkisch* ideals.[46] It is clear from discussions within the German Balt Democratic Party in early 1928, that Schiemann was unwilling to describe Riedel and his kind as an 'opposition'. He preferred to confine the term to those within the Baltic German community frontally attacking the fraction's common line, like Schreiner on the left and, above all, Woldemar Wulffius on the right.[47]

Schiemann's three defiant editorials on 'Right and Left' in the first two weeks of 1928 were prefaced by a reminder on New Year's Eve of what solidarity had so far achieved for the German community in Latvia—something even the conservative 'opposition' acknowledged of the previous twelve months.[48] He left no doubt as to where the main threat lay. The old ruling élites—who had 'failed in the hour of decision'—were cynically using the moment the cart was finally 'dragged from the mud' and their *existence* secured in order to regain their pre-eminence and re-impose 'traditional' *baltisch* values.[49]

Heated discussion of the issue broke out in 1927, fanned by new publications on the right, notably the *Baltische Monatsschrift, Baltische Stimmen* and *Baltische Heimatblätter.* Wulffius and other reactionary elements also profoundly distrusted the urban values they associated with Schiemann's leadership and their impact on Baltic German tradition.[50] When Bernard von Schrenk sent to Rüdiger a copy of *Baltische Heimatblätter,* focusing on 'The essence of Baltdom', he bitterly complained of how difficult it was for old Balt voices to be heard.[51] More disturbing to Schiemann was the distaste being displayed by young Baltic Germans for parliamentary politics and their express admiration for the 'Young German Order' (*Jungdo*) in the Reich, with its call for 'national renewal'.[52]

Schiemann's first editorial on 'Right and Left' justified the CGBP's pursuit of solidarity in specifically rebutting Rosenberg's calumny.[53] His second took a wider perspective, using the Reich's participation in Europe's democratisation during the nineteenth century to discredit any talk of 'German' and 'Western' as opposites. He could see only psychological grounds for such an idea appealing to the Young German Order, in that its members had endured four years of hatred and then defeat from the Western democracies. Young Baltic Germans had no such excuse. They embraced Young German terminology but their struggle took them back in time to the ideas of their fathers and a rejection of consensus. He attributed their hostility to the fact that the democracy they knew had yet to mature, but reminded them tartly that even princely electors had voted. 'The dumb and the clever, the good and bad were also randomly scattered through the old corporations of birth and profession.'[54] In only the third editorial of the series Schiemann specifically tackled the argument raised by Fircks in the summer of 1927 on the respective merits of 'right' and 'left' for the Baltic German fraction in the Latvian parliament.

He strongly rejected Fircks' call for a permanent alliance with bourgeois parties in the Saeima, as well as his argument that social democracy would undermine German Balt existence by taking Latvia eastwards. Schiemann did not deny the inherently conservative nature of Baltic Germandom—how could he?—but labelled attempts to divide people between 'bourgeois' and 'socialist' as a relic of prewar thinking; the distinction had become less relevant, both as a result of social democracy's central state-bearing role in post-war parliamentary systems and because the prospects for Marxism being widely applied were dim. Nor would Schiemann accept Fircks's image of the pendulum to portray the German fraction's strategy in the Saeima. The German community certainly profited from the left's support for freedom of expression, minority culture and the separation of church and state, but this was not a matter of exclusive self-interest. Rather, it served the good of the country. Conversely, Schiemann insisted that the promotion of Latvia's wellbeing, never mere preference, must remain the criterion of the fraction's willingness to work with any bourgeois government.

Schiemann claimed that in deepening the debate he sought to safeguard the fraction's common line and not 'victory' for either side. Yet he specifically cited Fircks' 1927 article in the *Baltische Monatsschrift* ('Latvian domestic policy and us'), as well as one for the *Libausche Zeitung*, as the most resolute expression of the right's standpoint, '*which we cannot accept*'.[55] Frustration with Schiemann's robustly liberal tone and the monopoly of the fraction's newspaper by its editor's values were what the *Baltische Monatsschrift* tried to counter: it reviewed young conservative and national revolutionary literature appearing in the Reich, openly admired pan-German sentiments, and aspired to reunite Baltic Germandom in Estonia and Latvia with the émigré community in the Reich. It rejected the European minorities policy of Paul Schiemann and joined others in accusing him of being '*unbaltisch*'. Schiemann's attitude is exemplified by his riposte to the Riga correspondent of the *Dorpater Zeitung*, who described Schiemann as *unbaltisch* for calling for European peace at Easter 1928. Schiemann cited Henry Ford—'Mankind has become so intelligent and the prestige of the statesman so low that no new war can arise'—then suggested that the dictum was now disproved by the said Riga correspondent, 'admittedly no statesman, although it is true that he does not exactly belong to the category of the intelligent.'[56]

Beyond pronounced old Balt elements, whose ruffled feathers Schiemann enjoyed not smoothing, acknowledgement of his abilities in conservative circles was never free of anxiety about his hold as an outspoken democrat over Baltic Germandom.[57] Erich Wallroth neatly encapsulated the general dilemma for Schiemann's critics in a memorandum of 9 January 1928, when he rejected a request from P. S. von Kügelgen that the Auswärtiges Amt buy up the *Rigasche Rundschau* and found a new paper, where Schiemann would merely be a member of the editorial board. Wallroth referred specifically to Schiemann's 'strong and distinctive personality'; he 'would certainly not adapt to a new editorial board under von Kügelgen's leadership'. Secondly, while freely admitting that Schiemann's democratic line was not approved by significant sectors of Baltic Germandom, Wallroth insisted that such differences were outweighed by the recognition 'of Schiemann's impressive leadership quality in uniting the German fraction, Schiemann's important success in minority politics there [in Latvia]…and the great influence of Schiemann in the European minorities' movement.'[58] Clearly, the architects of the 'new' *Ostpolitik* after 1918 were holding their own, and the spirit of Locarno still lingered.

However, the community of interest between *Vernunftrepublikaner* and an exceptional *Auslandsdeutsche* leader like Schiemann was undeniably more at risk from 1928. Along with young Baltic Germans returning from study visits and holidays in the Reich, the *Baltische Monatsschrift* was spreading awareness at home of Germany's movement for 'national renewal', thereby indirectly preparing the ground for the later spread of National Socialist thinking through the so-called

'*Bewegung*'. That could also be said of the Baltische Bruderschaft—emerging into daylight eight years after its formation.[59] One of its founders, Harald Berens von Rautenfeld, whom Schiemann had already criticised for praising Bermondt and who was the Reich correspondent for the *Baltische Monatsschrift*—called for Baltic Germans in the Reich and the Baltic states to be guided, through shared ancestry, love of the homeland and battle-hardened readiness for sacrifice, towards 'inner renewal'.[60] The *Baltische Monatsschrift* and its supporters were incensed by Schiemann's stubborn refusal to devote more space in the *Rigasche Rundschau* to describing events in Germany. He allotted a mere paragraph to the NSDAP winning twelve seats in the May 1928 elections to the Reichstag.[61]

Schiemann did not respond at length to his critics for a while, being preoccupied with planning for the Latvian elections to the third Saeima in October and with his work for the European minorities' movement. Then on 15 November he delivered a lecture, 'The cultural tasks of the German Balt press'.[62] It was given in a tense atmosphere to the Euphony Society in Riga and opened with a deft sketch of the tribulations of all daily newspapers, including pressure of time and the need to educate as well as inform. Schiemann then essayed the specific problems of producing a viable German-language daily in Riga, where less affluent Germans often bought Latvian papers; their bigger circulations kept their price at something like half that of the *Rigasche Rundschau*. Assuming the survival of the national community to be the basis of all Baltic German political work in Latvia, Schiemann inferred that the first cultural duty of a German-language press was to win over a majority of ordinary Baltic Germans as readers. This need, he found painful to record as a journalist of twenty-five years' standing, had still to be met—a failing that made the burden on the *Rigasche Rundschau* all the heavier.

He flatly rejected the argument of those who clamoured to be heard in 'lengthy articles', on the grounds that there was only one German-language daily in Latvia. Precisely because there was one paper, Schiemann retorted, it could not afford the 'luxury' of favouring specific interests. 'Excessive regard for the particular concerns of a small sector of our society and individual persons significantly constrains the German Balt press from fulfilling the tasks dictated by the overall interest of the national community.' Having rejected preoccupation with Baltic Germandom's components who were highly educated and therefore culturally secure, Schiemann approached their affinity with the radical right in Germany by first asking what principles *should* govern the final choice from the available mass of cultural and political data.

'I believe the correct answer must be as follows. In politics: far-reaching and conscientious coverage of domestic issues, and brief treatment of the problems of Germany and the rest of the outside world, focusing on essentials. In cultural reportage: conscientious and deliberately varied coverage of issues in Germany, perhaps also elsewhere abroad, and brief treatment of domestic aspects, focusing on those that are really significant.' Politically the Baltic German community should not merely pay lip-service to Latvia but inwardly identify with it in order to survive and develop. 'Political work, to which all are called in some way, entails first a degree of awareness and thereafter the most conscientious immersion in the particular circumstances of the country in which a person is called to be a politician. Only with conviction thus formed can one take the further step towards doctrine and by studying the politics of other states, eventually reach a more principled standpoint. With us it is the other way round. People derive their world view emotionally from the political life of Germany, embrace a party even though it is also a party attacking political parties, and armed with this wisdom feel ready to solve a political problem arising even in their own homeland.'

To those who accused him and the *Rigasche Rundschau* of betraying Balt traditions he gave no quarter. 'We belong to the German culture and there is no more a *baltisch* culture than there is a Bavarian, Saxon or East Prussian culture.' What made a German a 'Balt' was the daily interaction with different peoples in specific political, social and even climatic conditions; any attempt to construct a '*baltisch*' culture would have to embrace all inhabitants of the Baltic states. The 'increasingly obvious effort' to ascribe special qualities to Baltdom was tactically ill advised, in that by no means all Germans in the Baltic subscribed to notions of uniqueness hallowed by tradition. 'This lesson derives exclusively from a small circle of the intellectual élite and perhaps also a sector of our business community and associations, steeped in the tradition of our *ständisch* organisations, whereas broader circles of endangered Germans view it with complete incomprehension, perceiving it as nothing less than a dividing line within the national community.' Furthermore, 'this cultivation of the balt individual generates a delight in self-aggrandisement, an arrogance that threatens to make us laughable in the eyes of the whole world.' One of Schiemann's fiercest critics, Reinhard Wittram, unintentionally vindicated his judgement by responding to the lecture: 'Logical thought alone can never reveal the meaning of history, the meaning of balt history.'[63]

Schiemann's justification of his political strategy and his disdain for those élites who dismissed parliamentary work as sordid reflected the fraction's confident performance in the previous month's Saeima elections. Extensive debates in the preceding weeks within the Saeima's electoral commission—of which Schiemann was a member—had failed to reform Latvia's fivefold electoral division. Open lists tempted even the most hopeless to try their luck—in spite of new arrangements for lost deposits—and no fewer than forty-four parties battled for the million votes on offer in 1928. There were fifteen lists for the national minorities, six socialist lists and twenty-four bourgeois lists. Schiemann exempted only Arvēds Bergs' National Association from the 'complete political helplessness' of the bourgeoisie, split 'in really grotesque fashion'.[64]

The CGBP, on the other hand, profited from abandoning its previous targeting of non-German voters—held partly responsible for the return of only four German deputies in the 1925 elections. Instead the focus was now firmly on mobilising and maximising the German community's vote. Elaborate plans were made to transport surplus German voters from the Courland and Riga electoral districts to less favoured Semgalle and Livonia—a task commendably facilitated by the Latvian authorities.[65] Schiemann explained the strategy to the German Trade Association in Riga on 27 September 1928, in a lecture entitled 'Why we need six deputies'. His impassioned plea for every individual to vote and for every vote to count met 'with thunderous applause'.[66] He was able to record after the election that probably only the German fraction had achieved the targets it set for itself.

Schiemann especially regretted the divisions within the Jewish camp and the failure of Paul Mintz to make Riga Jewry a stronger force through a combined Jewish list. The splintering of the Latvian left continued, with the loss by the social democrats of seven seats to candidates who were communists in all but name. Schiemann believed that this disarray, rather than a significant increase in its own support, strengthened the Latvian right. Without the votes of the German fraction, however, there could now be a coalition of neither the right nor the left. Schiemann anticipated an even stronger Baltic German presence on the parliamentary commissions.[67] The German fraction held on to the Ministry of Justice post during negotiations to form a new government, and pressed its concerns for sound economic management, further retrenchment in the public sector and the fight against corruption. While Schiemann continued to regret that the Latvian bourgeois parties lacked 'the big unifying idea', he was inclined to see the Celmins government (1.12.28–26.3.31) as the strongest bourgeois front yet achieved.[68]

His message on the eve of 1929 was that the past year had witnessed a significant shift in Baltic Germandom's relationship to Latvians—now at last 'calling us to common work for our state'. He naturally did not believe that the problems of building a mixed-nationality state were resolved. There were still deep wounds below the surface on both sides. The lack of understanding among Baltic German youth and demands for more '*baltisch*' and 'aristocratic' leadership for the German community particularly irked him;[69] among other things it played into the hands of the Latvian socialists, anxious to claw back supporters from the far left and to undermine the German fraction's good relationship to the government.

From April 1929 Cielēns of all people unleashed 'the sort of agitation not seen for a long time' by trying to overturn an earlier agreement that *Landeswehr* members could also acquire land for their part in Latvia's defence. To make matters worse, the Baltic German memorial celebrating 22 May 1919 was blown up in June 1929.[70] When Cielēns finally got his way in November 1929, Schiemann had no option but to recall the Baltic German Minister of Justice—Baron Düsterlohe—from the cabinet. Nevertheless, the fraction continued to give general support to the government—Hahn unofficially joined meetings of the cabinet as it grappled with the impact of the world slump on Latvia[71]—and among the advantages of this course were comparatively generous budgetary allocations for Baltic German cultural purposes.[72]

None of this prevented the declining interest of Latvian Germans in their parliamentary representatives in the second half of the 1920s. The trend was marked by falling party membership and above all by the Zentrale becoming the focus of the network of personal, financial and educational links developing between the Reich and the German community in Latvia from 1923. Its prominent and growing role in bringing the community together was pointedly emphasised by its further reconstruction in May 1928 as the Deutschbaltische Volksgemeinschaft, which Baltic German conservatives clearly regarded as in some sense restorative. It had corporate traits, its delegates were chosen by local associations and branches of the professions, and non-elected members were also co-opted on to the managing board. Rüdiger emphasised these points in his report, as well as the right of every individual taxpayer to have a say in all matters affecting the national community through the delegate conference. 'On this basis we have united all sectors of our people and all those sources of strength left to us. We have created an organisation which is adapted to the changed political and social realities, which no longer permit some of our people to avoid working for the generality.'[73]

Schiemann and his fellow fraction members continued in spite of this to be paramount in the public political arena, even though their painstaking work in the Saeima escaped the attention of most Baltic Germans, for whom political parties had a 'shadow existence'.[74] Schiemann was astonished by the refusal of so many members of his own community to take part in debates concerning their very future, although he was never short of letters 'telling me what a pitiful fellow I am and that no decent German Balt wants to have anything more to do with me'.[75] His call to all those interested in politics to become active party members increasingly fell on deaf ears and his own party found it difficult to attract new blood.

With the drop in membership dues the German Balt Democratic Party faced a deficit of 106.55 Lats at the close of 1929. By April 1930 poor attendance at party committee meetings forced Schiemann to propose changes to the statutes, so that a third rather than a half of the committee could make a quorum.[76] It is difficult not to apply to his own predicament the analysis he offered the Association of National Minorities in Germany after its support slumped in the 1928 Reichstag elections: the national struggle 'is 75 per cent not a struggle against hostile surrounding forces but against the sloth and indifference in one's own camp'.[77] Matters promised to go beyond that in the case of Schiemann's conservative opponents in Latvia; their antipathy to his liberal values was reinforced by the clamour of *völkisch* elements in the Reich.

Since this impacted adversely on Latvian opinion as well as on the *Auslandsdeutschen* and therefore the European Nationalities Congress, demands on Schiemann's inner reserves grew apace. Far from his conviction weakening under the pressure, it became stronger, the link between his work at home and in the European nationalities movement becoming ever more pronounced. The a-national state, inherently democratic and founded on free cultural choice, offered the only hope before the 'collectivist menace' facing Europe on all sides. 'Whereas Russia's collectivism is born of the idea of social power', he argued, 'collectivist ideas in Europe arise from the idea of national power.'[78] Returning to the wider post-war clash between right and left, he warned: 'Nationalism, as the sole ideology of the middle classes, leads to wars of states, and socialism's ideology of class war leads to civil wars. Behind every urge to power there also stands a demand for servitude. Thus neither nationalism nor socialism can be achieved other than through oppression.'[79]

Schiemann continued to be thankful above all for Stresemann's support for cultural autonomy and reform of the League of Nations minorities procedures. He saw the German Foreign Minister as one of the few major statesmen to understand the importance of differentiating between the concepts of statehood and nationhood.[80] Here, however, the work of both politicians continued to be dogged by German-Polish differences. These were again highlighted by the ruling of the Hague International Court in March 1928 on the 1922 German-Polish schooling convention in Upper Silesia. The Court found the Polish authorities at fault in having imposed language tests to determine nationality for the purposes of schooling. However, it failed at the same time to endorse the German case that the 1922 convention sanctioned subjectivity of choice.

The judgement was aptly described as 'Delphic'. It was unlikely to stem the flow of appeals to the League coming from German groups in Upper Silesia.[81] Reviewing developments for the Nationalities Congress in August Schiemann once more criticised the absence of a standing committee on minorities, which allowed the committee of three to 'swallow' minority petitions. He found the reduction of the will to peace to mere lip-service a 'shocking manifestation'.[82]

In the event the Hague judgement unexpectedly rekindled interest in minority protection procedures. The Dutch Foreign Minister, Beelaerts von Blokland, the Swiss President Motta and the Austrian Chancellor Seipel all made speeches touching on reforms during the ninth League Assembly meeting in Geneva in September 1928. Gustav Stresemann, still recovering at home from the stroke he suffered during the Reichstag elections, glimpsed possibilities for a fresh minorities initiative by the Reich at the next meeting of the League Council. When it duly convened in Lugano in December, events fortuitously played into his hands, after an intemperate and badly-judged speech by the Polish Foreign Minister Zaleski had lost the audience's sympathy. The German Foreign Minister was stung into banging his fist on the table in the course of an impassioned reply stressing the profound hopes that Europe's minorities attached to the League. His call for a proper debate of the whole minority question at the next League Assembly prompted Aristide Briand to reassure the 'deathly white' Stresemann of the respect of all League Council members for the 'sacred rights' of minorities.[83]

Briand's phrase was promptly taken up by Paul Schiemann's editorial on the 'exceptional importance' of Stresemann's outburst. The German foreign minister—like the Nationalities Congress—stood for combating the inertia of state governments on the minority question; Zalewski recalled the likes of Mello Franco and the Greek international law specialist Nicolas Politis, who subverted the essential nature of minority treaties 'in making the ultimate purpose of those treaties not the free cultural development of a people but its assimilation with the majority'. Zalewski equated nationality issues with threats to peace and wanted the League to bury them; Stresemann's stance implicitly recognised the minority movement as 'a peace movement of purest provenance'. He had reminded the League of its duty—which, if unfulfilled, would make the organisation's existence illusory. Minorities' rights were once more at the centre of international concern, as Briand's closing words acknowledged. 'That', Schiemann concluded, 'is the great and inestimable importance of the "incident at Lugano". The minorities question has been activated.'

Tellingly Schiemann expressed the hope that the Germans were fully behind their Foreign Minister.[84] One disappointment was the long-awaited Prussian decree on minority schooling a week later (31.12.28). On the grounds of not creating second-class citizens, the Prussian authorities opted against cultural autonomy and for retaining responsibility for the education and cultural development of *all* citizens in its realm.[85]

Although nationalist German minority lobbyists were pleased by Lugano Schiemann was privately sceptical as 1929 dawned,—the so-called 'Year of the Minorities'.[86] His offensive brought a small advance at the meeting of the League Council in March, when the British foreign secretary Austen Chamberlain admitted that he took the verb 'merge' in the Mello Franco declaration of 1925 to mean political integration, not cultural assimilation, but in other ways the Auswärtiges Amt's meticulously prepared legal case for reinterpreting the guarantee clause found little resonance. Council members had no enthusiasm for Stresemann's contention that the guarantee covered the *cultural* integrity of minorities, not just the territorial integrity of the states concerned. Also unwelcome was the argument that the League's supervisory obligations necessarily extended beyond hearing petitions to examining their *causes*, thereby justifying the setting-up a permanent standing committee of experts. The first suggestion would have made nationalities in East Central Europe subjects at international law—an essential step in achieving cultural autonomy; the second would have sanctioned a permanent minorities commission, undermining the League's Minority Department and ending the confidentiality insisted on by the committee of three.[87]

While Stresemann's offensive prompted the League Council to produce the so-called London report of May 1929, this finally rejected the German case and reaffirmed the responsibility of governments of the Eastern Central European states to the Allied powers in the matter of minority protection. Furthermore, it emphasised that refusing national minorities or their associations direct access to the Council had been intended to forestall the development of states within states. Minorities thus had no status in international law. According to the report, confidential and informal collaboration between the League secretariat and the governments of the states in East Central Europe was the only way to make the system work.

Stresemann had hoped for a prolonged public debate, not only drawing on experience accumulated from the petitioning process but also taking into account the views of 'private' European minority associations, leading in time to widespread recognition of the inevitability of reform.

This expectation ended at the Madrid meeting of the League Council in June, when Stresemann failed to persuade members to reject the London report or even to ask the Hague Court to rule on the guarantee clause. Eventually, the German Foreign Minister yielded to peer pressure, allowing the Council on 13 June unanimously to endorse a shortened report, concentrating on promised improvements to existing petitioning procedures. Stresemann at least managed to have the Council debates made public so that he could convince the German minority associations of his own personal effort to implement their wishes. Nevertheless, his strong emphasis on collective League responsibility at the same time signalled to Germandom's leaders and their associations that they could not be over dependent on the Reich.

It has justly been said that German diplomacy under Stresemann saw the limits of the campaign against the League's minorities' policy at the moment when *Verständigungspolitik* was at risk, threatening to undermine foreign confidence in Germany's peaceful intentions. It was notable that Stresemann justified Madrid before the Reichstag in terms of the need to allay fears of Reich expansionism in East Central Europe, by means of a 'tolerant cultural policy' that acknowledged the freedom of all peoples of the region. 'Anyone', he wrote in August 1929, 'insisting that the human rights of language, race and religion be respected and valued irrespective of state borders is interceding on behalf of peace and against conflict through force. Peace between peoples will be the more securely founded the less often the public hears the cry of minorities whose culture is threatened. That naturally presupposes that the leaders of the minorities' states increasingly become aware that it is in the most essential interests of a state to strive in its own realm for a positive constitutional solution to the minorities question.'[88]

His words betray a striking affinity with the idea of the a-national state, of which the leading proponent remained Paul Schiemann. He had already cautioned the Nationalities Congress in August 1929 against expecting too much from the renewed flurry of interest by the League Assembly in the minority question. He felt that most of its members continued to see nationality issues in terms of territorial disputes, whereas a 'wholly different question preoccupies us: that within *prevailing* borders minorities are assured the possibility to exist.'[89] Schiemann remained sceptical about the outcome of improvements to existing League procedures promised at Madrid. His 'Geneva Impressions' castigated the League as 'the attempt to realise a modern idea looking to the future in a spirit inherited from the past'. He had to admit that despite the faults in the League's parts, the whole 'had somehow become a force', but he was influenced in this assessment less by the League machinery and bureaucracy than by the stature of the key figures on the Geneva stage at the time: Ramsay MacDonald, Aristide Briand and, of course, Stresemann.

In spite of personal disappointment, Schiemann understood why the German government, distracted by its preparations for the evacuation of the Rhineland, agreed at Geneva in September 1929 to postpone discussion of the minority question. However, Schiemann's praise for the German statesman who had become central to his own life's work was unqualified. 'From the very outset of the League session', Schiemann recalled, 'the question heard everywhere was: When is Stresemann coming, when will he speak? The excitement grew from day to day and after he finally arrived on the Friday, his speech again postponed on Sunday, his appearance on the stage on Monday was one of the truly great events. If MacDonald impressed as a powerful ideologue and Briand as a refined orator, then with Stresemann the immediate human impact was strongest. People felt that this man was probably standing on this platform for the last time...that everything he said about peace and the duties of the League of Nations was honourably meant.'

Schiemann's description of the impression made by Stresemann in private personal contacts at Geneva went beyond mere respect. 'One saw a sick man,' Schiemann wrote, 'but it was not pity one felt so much as admiration—love. He always grasped the main line of an issue; one saw here always that high ideals were married to the thinking of *Realpolitik*. One saw a man who believed in himself and his work, and precisely because of this he was so deeply upset by the hateful misrepresentation from which his enemies [National Socialists] in his own nation profited.'[90] In the course of his interesting and problematic engagement with the *Auslandsdeutsche* issue and its leaders and lobbyists, Stresemann ultimately sided with those, like Paul Schiemann, who were committed to work loyally within and for their host country. They were far removed from the strident nationalist individuals and groups originating directly or indirectly in the 'June Club' and gathered under the umbrella of the Deutsche Schutzbund at its headquarters in 22 Motzstrasse, Berlin. Here, in the 'hateful' *völkisch* camp, the passing of 'Weimar's greatest statesman' occasioned few regrets.[91] Stresemann's untimely death therefore also marked a turning-point in Schiemann's life. Only a short time earlier he had predicted at the Nationalities Congress that minorities would 'have to wait until the passing of time gives the peoples statesmen who feel answerable not only to their parties but to Europe, and not only to Europe but to the whole world.'[92]

9. The New Nationalist Wave

The intensity of Schiemann's engagement in day-to-day politics, the demands on him as an editor and his commitment to the European minorities movement virtually turned his private life into an extension of his public one. Even after the Zentrale took on more of the burden of care for the Baltic German community, the CGBP remained at the very heart of all-important initiatives. Its members, together with various willing helpers, made up a broad and demanding circle, ultimately centering on Paul Schiemann. It became customary for them to call in at his office at the *Rigasche Rundschau* between mid-day and 2 o'clock in the afternoon.

From noon, with the most pressing of his daily tasks as editor behind him, Schiemann and his visitors held informal discussions of current problems. From time to time he called individuals together over the telephone, perhaps to run through a leading article or to express an opinion on a specific theme. Often exchanges ran on till late in the evening over beer. Even these social occasions took on the 'character of a sitting'—where clashes between very different individuals could be fierce, even if usually resolved fairly quickly in the common interest.[1]

For Schiemann in addition there were the formal CGBP sessions to preside over, as well as his major contributions to parliamentary business and his international work for minorities. He also chaired the almost daily meetings of the German deputies, either in their fraction office at the Saeima or in the parliamentary corridors. According to Valentina Freimane, Lotte Schiemann later confessed during chats in her kitchen to having left the absent 'great man' in the course of the 1920s. Ultimately she found that, whatever the attractions of other partners, Paul Schiemann was the only person she could actually live with.[2] She was with him in the summer of 1930, when constant work and lifestyle habits—not least the incessant smoking—

began to undermine his constitution. After tuberculosis was diagnosed, Schiemann left Riga with Lotte in August for treatment and convalescence at Davos in Switzerland. No sooner had he settled there than news came of Adolf Hitler's dramatic electoral breakthrough in the Reich.

The omens for 1930 had been poor as the year broke. Shock waves from the Wall Street Crash in 1929 were slowly working their way through Europe, radicalising politics *en route*. Schiemann the theatregoer found some comfort in George Bernard Shaw's *The Apple Cart*—first performed late in the 'tired year' of 1929. He interpreted the play not as an abandonment of democracy but as an attack on the lack of ideas and relevance of politicians.[3] He saw other indications of 'Europe's fatigue' in the approach of the League of Nations to Russia becoming a member; Geneva was more concerned about Russia's debt than its bloodshed. As to suggestions that Russia was practising cultural autonomy by tolerating other languages in its realm, Schiemann retorted that German-speakers were allowed to read Marx but not Goethe. Communism's response to the crisis displayed, like the 'solutions' offered by National Socialists and Fascists, a collectivism inimical to European culture. 'To damage this foundation, to replace individual existence with that of the herd, is to destroy Europe.'[4]

The twin threat to the continent from doctrines of class and national exclusivity reinforced Schiemann's arguments for strengthening the 'European idea'. He urged this again on the eve of Aristide Briand's proposals for European Union in May 1930, already signalled at Geneva in the winter of 1929. Organisations and individuals had propagated various pan European projects since the First World War, but the intervention of a major statesman like Briand energised the debate. However, Schiemann was less than enthusiastic about Briand's specific proposal for a new organisation of European states. He viewed it—as he had the August 1928 Kellogg-Briand multilateral pact to outlaw war—as a political manoeuvre rather than a genuine bid for peace. The Baltic states could not afford to be left out of such arrangements, but a project seeking to be acceptable to the 'Moscow class dictatorship' and 'West European imperialism' was 'a gesture, not an act'.[5]

In responding to Briand, Schiemann first considered how the idea of empire helped bring about war in 1914. He felt that in the pursuit of the imperial ideal only North America, Britain and Russia had met the essential test; namely, the ability to provide all needs within their realm. Nevertheless, the impulse behind empire to enlarge the state sphere persisted in Western Europe. So too did aspirations to economic self-sufficiency, although even France had inadequate resources of its own. Worse, the new states became infected. As a result, governments perpetrating the fiction of being economic master in their own house threatened Europe's economic order. Dreams of autarchy encouraged thoughts of 'expansion, borders and sea ports'. Yet in now proposing a new 'European Imperium' as the only alternative to a war putting one of the European powers in a position to destroy the old system, Briand placed state sovereignty at the heart of his schemes.[6] He had failed to escape the mindset that led to 1914.

In Schiemann's words, 'Pan Europe has been made respectable by Briand, integrated into the dialectical armoury of post-war diplomacy, itself increasingly difficult to distinguish from pre-war diplomacy.'[7] Ultimately, he inferred, Briand desired pan-Europe only on the basis of French hegemony, thereby underpinning the peace settlement of 1919. In this spirit Schiemann dubbed Briand 'the Metternich of the twentieth century'.[8] Like Briand, Coudenhove-Kalergi also envisaged his pan-European association as a collection of sovereign states. Inevitably, Schiemann argued, it would be one more arena, alongside the League of Nations, 'for the swordplay of narrow diplomacy, with words of peace as the slogan'. He could not imagine the states reaching consensus over an enlarged Europe while their own territorial claims were unsettled; primarily political projects encompassing the maximum territorial space would focus more, not less, attention on borders. That negated what was for Schiemann the central purpose: to foster untrammeled European economic cooperation. In prioritising political and security issues Briand and Coudenhove-Kalergi were forcing the treatment of Europe's economic ills back into 'the narrow cauldron of state territories'.[9]

They not only failed to acknowledge as a precondition of European unity 'the regulation of the European economy as a whole'. They also behaved as if unity were feasible before reaching a solution to the nationalities' question.[10] To Schiemann this lay at the heart of Europe's reformation. Karl Anton Prinz Rohan in the *Europäische*

Revue acknowledged something of that in June 1930.[11] In proposing a union of Central and Eastern Europe on economic grounds, Rohan in addition drafted a minorities' statute to secure the cultural life of the different nationalities involved. He conceived his statute as the basis for a multilateral international treaty, to come into force when any three states joined and to remain open to all. Schiemann was not fully persuaded by Rohan's scheme either. He could not see international statutory law on minority rights developing from such treaties, since they were to be of finite duration and concluded between governments. Nationality issues would still be displaced to the realm of inter-state bargaining and the work of the Nationalities Congress made more difficult rather than less so.[12]

Schiemann's engagement with pan-Europeanists manifestly reinforced his commitment to the a-national state. It alone promised a future where the Europe of nation-states gradually transmuted to one of 'co-nationals'—respecting one another's culture within a framework of Europe-wide minority rights legislation. Unlike Briand and others seeking to impose schemes from the top down, Schiemann believed that a more peaceful and therefore more united Europe could only evolve from below. Admittedly, he did not doubt that economic factors would be paramount in prompting the creation of a common European space, in determining which states joined and when. At any stage, however, unresolved nationality disputes could disrupt the process. For Schiemann therefore a prior solution to the European minorities' problem seemed as indispensable to lasting European union as transnational regulation of economic life. That is quite clear from his response to a contemporary work by Giselher Wirsing, a Young German member of the *Tatkreis*. In *Zwischeneuropa und die deutsche Zukunft* he contended that the German people's anti-Western mood and the anti-capitalism of the peasant populations of Central Eastern Europe created the psychological grounds for a large new federation.

Echoing his earlier argument with young Baltic Germans in Latvia, Schiemann insisted that Germany's influence in the East was related to its own character as a prototype of Western culture. 'If the German were to cast this robe aside and suddenly appear as primitive Eastern man, then his influence in all of these countries would be at an end.' Schiemann was not against the idea of federation, as opposed to 'integration'—'a dreadful and thoroughly confusing term' with no place in the mixed nationality areas of the East. Yet, 'As long as Wirsing is unable to opt for the a-national state, he fails to redress Coudenhove's shortcoming. But if Wirsing were to understand by federalism not merely a federation of state territories retaining their administrative sovereign functions, but also a federation of *peoples* inhabiting the large economic space into supranational communities, exercising the new function of cultural administration, then he would stand with us and our proposition of the a-national state.' Schiemann deflected charges that his vision was impractical by ridiculing in turn those misguided enough to believe that the creation of a new economic space would itself reduce nationality conflicts.[13]

Not that Schiemann saw early prospects of European union. Franco-German relations cooled rapidly after the collapse of Germany's SPD-led coalition on 28 March 1930. While the foreign minister Julius Curtius broadly continued Stresemann's policy, Heinrich Brüning's government marked a shift to the right. The mood encouraged Schiemann's *völkisch* opponents in the German minorities' camp. Their dislike of his insistent use of the term 'minority' in international discourse was plain from the re-launching of the Verband der deutschen Minderheiten in Europa in 1928 as the Verband der deutschen *Volksgruppen* in Europa. 'Greater German' undertones were also evident in proposals for Reich German and Austrian delegates to be invited to future Verband conferences. As for the Deutsche Schutzbund, it avidly promoted a new all-German forum in 1929 as a way of ultimately controlling the Verband der deutschen Volksgruppen and through this the Nationalities Congress. The challenge to Schiemann's efforts on behalf of all European minorities, independently of any one state, was clear.[14] For the moment he was able to resist the manoeuvres with the help of others in the Verband, including Carl Bruns, a close ally.[15]

Bruns' role in the distribution of Reich funds to the Verband der deutschen Volksgruppen, and thus indirectly to German delegates in the Nationalities Congress, was vital to Schiemann's operational autonomy. Both men were becoming aware of the creeping sympathy among Verband members, including Ammende and von Hasselblatt, with the Greater German mindset. Bruns was much respected in conservative *Deutschtum* circles and had personal reservations about the Weimar political system, but he scrupulously avoided open disavowal of it.[16] Nor, in the interests of his office, did he have difficulty working closely with fully-fledged republicans such as Adolf Köster. Bruns shared Schiemann's gratitude for the ambassador's strong personal commitment to the German minorities' movement.[17] Like Schiemann, he also viewed Köster's sudden death in Belgrade in January 1930 as a major setback. This followed acute appendicitis, aggravated by several wild nights of heavy drinking.[18] Köster's earlier cabinet career had ensured that he remained one of the 'biggest guns' in Auswärtiges Amt circles during the 1920s. 'What we are losing for our purposes', Bruns wrote to Schiemann, 'apart from everything human, is unforeseeable. Whether we would always have agreed with him I rather doubt, but he was almost the only diplomat who treated our problems seriously and took them to heart.'[19]

The loss was particularly hard for Schiemann—a cause of 'bitter grief'. Köster once confided to Wallroth that 'work here [in Riga] is beginning to be exceptionally pleasing to me and I detect no longing to be in Berlin, or indeed any other battleground.' The good impression he made on Latvian opinion had been a reflection of this commitment to the Riga post, as well as his dislike of old Balt values and a refusal to pander to nationalists in the large Reich colony in Riga.[20] Köster's death robbed Schiemann of a charismatic and close supporter just as the arrival of economic crisis worsened the relationship between Germans and Latvians.

In spite of this deterioration Schiemann tried to exploit what influence his fraction retained with Celmiņš after withdrawing formally from his cabinet in November. In particular he tried to focus parliamentary debate on the economic crisis, finding the major source of corruption in the politicisation of economic life. He specifically targeted the Bank of Latvia, which rejected credit applications from non-Latvians but was ready to prop up even failing Latvian enterprise, creating businesses 'which cannot live but cannot die'.[21] In fact average income levels of Baltic Germans remained higher than those of most Latvians, but Schiemann's general point was valid.[22] Partisanship of this order was an abrogation of the central authority's responsibility for the overall economic health of the territorial space that majority and minority peoples shared.

Certainly, prominent Latvian authors like Ernests Blanks, Arturs Kroders, Janis Lapins, Arveds Bergs and Adolfs Klive supported Latvianising the economy. Credit policy and governmental decrees were seen as breaking the alleged domination of Germans and Jews. The stereotyping dismayed Schiemann. A slogan such as 'Down with the Barons' had been progressive when they had ruled the roost, but with their power broken the call had become anachronistic. Unfortunately 'political anachronism is the foundation and precondition of political reaction.' Economic discrimination against minorities, depriving them of their share of a budget to which all the peoples of Latvia contributed, and treating their rights as a tiresome and thankless task, was dangerously misconceived. 'It is rather a question of policy in the direct interests of the state, and all those working against it are contriving to dismantle the state.'[23] For their part many Baltic Germans were also culpable in contending, wrongly, that Latvia's economic progress was due only to what it took from Germany and Russia and to wealth 'stolen' from Baltic Germans.[24]

When Schiemann warned the latter that the future depended on their participation in the 'Latvian state idea' he referred to the shared 'Latvian' identity arising—alongside the other national identities—from centuries of cohabitation.[25] To old Balt conservatism such thinking had always been anathema, and Schiemann's strictures had even less resonance with them now. Their mood was more accurately reflected in Wittram's 1930 article for the *Baltische Monatsschrift*, comparing Baltic German 'liberal' and 'conservative' responses to Estonian and Latvian efforts to build nation states. In it Wittram again attacked liberal acceptance of the term 'minority', as well as calls for greater affinity between Germans on the one side, and Latvians and Estonians on the other. He categorically rejected Schiemann's insistence on Baltic Germandom's participation in Latvian (or Estonian) state sentiment. Wittram wished instead to look for new concepts of state, taking the German community's historic position more seriously into account. 'We cannot view the state as the ultimate fount of law because we have experienced the origin of our own laws from older sources.' As to the quest for a new role for Baltic Germans: 'If we wish to remain capable of expanding culturally, then we can perhaps best do so in relation to the new all-German cause. The work within the German *Volk* on the idea of a supranational ordering of the European East is such a task, where we need lose nothing of our own.'[26] The remark well illustrates how Wittram and young urban Baltic Germans in his circle indirectly contributed to the take-up within their community of National Socialist thinking.[27]

Strangely, he was to ask after the Second World War how Baltic Germandom came so completely under the spell of National Socialism *in spite of* its rich tradition.[28] The outcome may rather have been partly at least *because of* key elements in that tradition. Those identified in recent work include the historic emphasis on a strong corporate identity, both in the *Ritterschaften* and in the Great and Small Guilds of Riga. Views and attitudes associated with such institutions survived their demotion or demise after 1918, as did many of the social relationships and hierarchies involved. These even dictated the specific forms of Baltic German self-help after 1918, with its 'frenzy' of association building and its basic distrust of political parties and parliaments. Add to the mixture an inherited sense of mission reinforced by pronounced anti-Bolshevism, and Baltic German susceptibility to the strident call of Hitler's movement for an all-German renewal becomes more intelligible. The step from being a cultural to a national outpost seems to have been unexpectedly small.[29]

It was aided by such 'precursors of Nazism' as the forty-one members of the Baltische Bruderschaft working illicitly in Latvia during the 1920s, as well as the developing network of ties between Reich German and Baltic German organisations before the founding of the first Nazi *Ortsgruppe* in Riga in 1931 under Ernst Munzinger.[30] Suggestions that Latvian Germans 'mistook' the NSDAP for a variant of the nationalist/romantic movement for renewal in Germany, or even that many were hardly aware of Hitler's party before 1933, are unconvincing.[31] It is useful to recall briefly Schiemann's own prediction in 1924, that the victory of the *völkisch* movement in Germany would signal the end for Germans in Latvia. In May 1930 he again charged National Socialism with being 'ready to participate in any action undermining Europe'.[32] Moreover, in the winter of 1930 Schiemann essayed the Nazi movement in depth for the *Rigasche Rundschau*. It brought to a head the conflict between the paper and the *Baltische Monatsschrift*, making it even harder to credit Baltic German society with ignorance of what the NSDAP portended.

By this time Schiemann had settled into the sanatorium at Davos, leaving his editorial functions for the time being to Karl Keller. The *Rundschau*'s staff initially responded favourably to Keller, judging from Otto Grosberg's note in September, conveying regret at Schiemann's enforced stay at the 'Magic Mountain'.[33] Keller made a 'long speech' to the German Balt Democratic Party committee meeting on 25 September, dismissing press rumours of Schiemann having suffered a stroke. The committee decided unanimously against Schiemann resigning his parliamentary seat, a decision which an enlarged CGBP meeting upheld a few days later. Fircks told those present that Schiemann was expected to be fit to return to work the following May.[34]

Thus it was at Davos that Schiemann received the depressing news of Hitler's party capturing 107 seats in the Reichstag elections on 14 September. Hans von Rimscha, recently made foreign leader writer at the *Rigasche Rundschau*, wrote almost at once to tell Schiemann that 'our so-called good society' was convinced that all decent men must be National Socialists.[35] Friedrich Stieve, Köster's successor at the Riga post, confirmed that the National Socialist wave in Germany had seized certain circles in Latvia, that the *Völkische Beobachter* was being avidly read, and that *Riga am Sonntag* was now a veritable Hitler organ.[36]

The first three of the five articles which Schiemann felt compelled to write on National Socialism focused largely on economics. He agreed that the prolonged nature of the world economic crisis seemed to vindicate Karl Marx before insisting that the Moscow model offered no solution. He cited the hatred with which bolshevism persecuted its opponents, the 'loveless' nature of its work for the oppressed and 'the folly of pedantic bureaucracy' doggedly pursuing a programme. In words recalling his earlier days with the 'solidarists' and Eduard Stadtler's Anti-Bolshevik League, Schiemann then postulated the alternative of a genuinely 'national' socialism—that was to say springing from the people. Such a phenomenon, Schiemann suggested, ought to appeal neither to crass equality nor to the depersonalisation of work through nationalisation. It would not be trapped by dogma and could attract the best elements to it; it would empirically tackle perceived social evils, keeping the general good in mind.[37] How, he asked, did German nationalism measure up to this?

He did not reject outright the idea of breaking interest bondage, or of putting common before individual use, but behind these Nazi slogans he found no new economic order. Instead he foresaw a displacement of the modern economic apparatus and a reversion to the state controls of the mercantilist era. The Nazi emphasis on common bonds of blood as the key to economic strength would give priority to establishing and checking on race. 'Germany for the Germans!' Schiemann noted. 'What a familiar sound for every politician in the East! Latvia for the Latvians! Poland for the Poles!'[38] The third article examined how Hitler modified policy as he approached power. Using Goethe's comment about dilettantism as the underestimation of difficulties, Schiemann charged the NSDAP with having 'no principles whatsoever in the social and economic sphere'. The party called for support in the name of attacking Marxism but, 'If such a [National Socialist] revolution succeeds, the communist with firm plans could take it over at once.' He added: 'The one un-ambivalent programmatic point of National Socialism is anti-Semitism. It is possible to wreck a state with pogroms but certainly not to construct one.'[39]

Before the publication of the fourth article Fircks reported to the CGBP about his recent meeting with National Socialist leaders in Berlin and of their general assurances of support for Germandom abroad. The CGBP now resolved 'that the current treatment of the national socialist movement in the *Rigasche Rundschau*, taken in Germany to be the fraction's voice, was inappropriate, and steps should therefore be taken to change this hostile attitude to a more objective one.'[40] Schiemann's answer was a searing indictment of the hatred released by Hitler's racial propaganda.

It threatened political life, science and the arts with the hooliganism of the streets. 'Domestically, National Socialism is aggressive nationalism of a brutality and bias as yet unknown in history.' He specifically deplored the idea of Baltic Germandom—opposed to extreme nationalism for half a century—drinking from a poisoned cup just because fellow Germans proffered it.[41] Finally, in considering Hitler's 'foreign policy' Schiemann denied that Italy would risk war for Germany's eastern frontiers and argued that any 'alliance' with Britain would have to be within the framework of the League of Nations and the parameters set by Stresemann. Schiemann refrained from calling Hitler a traitor only because the man had no convictions to betray.[42]

The anger in conservative Baltic German circles with the *Rigasche Rundschau* is easy to imagine. Because of Schiemann's illness his regular editorials did not resume till June the following year, and the paper was distinctly more vulnerable to pressure under Keller's temporary guidance. It quickly became apparent that he was less able—perhaps less inclined—to deal with it effectively. Most of the editorial staff were sufficiently worried a week before Christmas to back foreign editor Hans von Rimscha's brusque questioning of Keller, as to whether the *Rundschau*'s political line had suddenly changed. Assurances from the management board member and lawyer, Erich Pabst, that this was not the case spared Keller immediate loss of face. Very shortly, however, his reaction to renewed attacks on the paper from circles close to the *Baltische Monatsschrift* pitched him into the middle of another staff conflict. It originated in the *Rigasche Rundschau*'s warm review on 17 December, by the editor Baron Sass, of Ernst Penzoldt's *Die Powenzbande*. Sass found it 'a life-affirming tale', rare 'in an age that has forgotten humour'.[43]

On the basis of the review Hugo Wittrock—later Mayor of Riga under the Nazi occupation from 1941—bought the volume thinking it an ideal gift for 'a German family at Christmas'. After reading thirty pages, however, he was 'so filled with rage' that he ripped out the flyleaf on which he had already inscribed 'To my dear wife'. Nothing 'more common, dirty and perverse'—he wrote to Keller on 27 December—had ever come his way. Wittrock 'felt obliged' to inform Pastor Schabert, the man responsible within the Baltic German community for overall care and welfare of German families. Wittrock helpfully marked the book's offending passages for Schabert's benefit and demanded 'the most energetic measures' from all the German organisations. Schabert associated himself with Wittrock's diatribe and asked Keller to prevent 'further poisoning of our homes through the press' and so remedy the present injustice. Others had already whispered to Keller and Pabst, who in fact both sided with critics of Sass. It was after Sass had caught sight of some of the written protests on Keller's desk that a furious altercation took place between the two men. Sass immediately lodged a formal grievance complaint.

Since Sass demanded formal arbitration, Keller pronounced himself unable to work with the editor until the honour affair was settled. On the grounds that the paper's business would suffer, the managing board decided on 30 December to dismiss Sass. He was given notice that afternoon, but thanks to Keller's worry about being seen to be too harsh the action was watered down. Pabst implied to Sass the next morning that the notice of dismissal was not necessarily the publisher's last word, although he advised keeping clear of the editorial offices until the complaint had been heard. Plainly the intention was to give a salutary shock, but editors Oskar and Werner Grosberg, G. H. Eckardt, Hans von Rimscha and C. Klassohn protested in writing that Keller had engineered the dismissal on account of the honour affair, thereby breaking the *Rundschau* tradition of allowing editors to defend the integrity of their work even against superiors. Keller was stung into submitting his own resignation, leaving Otto Grosberg to run the paper pending the hearing. In the event this quickly cleared up misunderstandings. After appropriate concessions from all sides, Sass was back at his desk by 10 January 1931.

Behind the Lilliputian clash there were nevertheless serious issues. At one point Schiemann wrote an open letter (now missing) to the staff and business managers of the paper. It is by no means certain that he fully endorsed Sass's behaviour, but under the terms of his contract with the *Rundschau* Schiemann retained the last word over staff dismissals.[44] Rimscha and his colleagues were manifestly affronted at the idea of one of their number being sacked over Schiemann's head. Their letters kept him well informed in Davos and show that Keller's inexperience and management style compounded the quarrel. 'That he [Keller] strikes us old saddle-worn cavaliers as a Sunday rider is obvious,' Otto Grosberg wrote to Schiemann, 'but he has no need to advertise his inability.' To the independent-minded editors—'unaccustomed to standing to attention'—Keller's '*mania grandiosa*' was 'unspeakably funny'. 'Dear Paul', Otto Grosberg wrote, 'come back and rule us again!' He labeled Keller 'a born resigner'.[45]

Far more seriously, the Penzoldt affair confirmed von Rimscha's feeling of growing pressure on Keller from 'National Socialist quarters' to abandon the 'Schiemann line'.[46] In this connection the conditions set by Keller for resuming his post are revealing. They included not being placed in a position of having to disavow the newspaper by articles 'flouting Christian principles'. Still more interesting: 'The treatment of foreign issues must be on the basis of full and objective reporting. Any subjective analysis of critical current events must be reserved to the chief editor, Dr Paul Schiemann.'[47] The ultimate dependence of the *Rigasche Rundschau*'s liberal political line on Schiemann's personality and standing was never clearer.

If Keller's trimming over the Penzoldt affair in Schiemann's absence exposed the latent fragility of a liberal daily paper receiving significant Reich subsidies, a similar point can be made about the vulnerability of the Nationalities Congress, also more reliant on Reich subsidies from 1930 onwards. 'Behind Geneva', wrote the Director of the Deutsches Auslands Institut, Dr Wertheimer, 'stand the elected and responsible political leaders of the *Auslandsdeutschen*, perhaps more sceptical than the passionate internationalists, but all the same resolute because they see in Geneva a means of campaigning.'[48] However, he had to mount this defence against an angry circular to various Reich officials in March 1930 from Percy Bleyer, headed '"Nationalities studies" as pseudo-science and source of political unrest'. It viewed equal rights for all minorities as 'nonsense', specifically criticised Schiemann, and dismissed the Geneva congress as 'part swindle, part hopeless cause'.[49]

These words were yet another reminder of the aspiration of those close to the Deutsche Schutzbund leader Karl von Loesch to control the European minorities movement. Few more depressing items of news could thus have reached Schiemann at Davos than that of the death on 27 February 1931 of Carl Georg Bruns. A letter from Kurt Graebe, spokesman for the German minority in Poland on the committee of the Verband der deutschen Volksgruppen, indicates that even during Bruns's illness before Christmas there were intrigues in Schutzbund circles to have his office merged 'with some other agency'. One of Bruns's last notes to Schiemann on 1 December 1930 mentioned 'fantastic skulduggery' that he hoped to put a stop to.[50]

Graebe, chairman of the Nationalities Congress organising committee and thus the channel for subsidies coming in via the Verband, was as anxious as Schiemann to preserve the independence of Bruns's office after his death against pressure from the Schutzbund.[51] Graebe and Schiemann both tried to postpone a decision on a successor, but illness kept Schiemann from Carl Bruns's funeral in Berlin, as well as from the Verband committee meeting that immediately followed it. It was in the course of that session that Werner von Hasselblatt emerged as favourite to succeed Bruns. Ominously Max Hildebert Boehm and Karl von Loesch among others soon signalled their approval of Hasselblatt.[52] His most active advocate, Ewald Ammende, then mounted a characteristically emotional assault on Schiemann's fierce resistance to the appointment with a series of letters to Davos.[53]

He conceded to Schiemann that Hasselblatt had 'many failings' and that 'you have long had your doubts' about him. Ammende's main justification for Hasselblatt nevertheless centred on the need for a strong leader and 'creative jurist' to replace Bruns at a critical stage for the minorities movement. Ammende argued that in a Europe of rising nationalism only a decisive, resolute figure, well respected and able to hold his own with the Auswärtiges Amt bureaucracy, could hope to consolidate what the Verband had already achieved in Berlin. These were similar to points immodestly made by Hasselblatt himself, in responding to Schiemann urging him to refuse the post.[54] Ammende's wish for a fixer flatly contradicted Schiemann's idea of replacing Bruns with two appointees. One would be a general manager looking after office routine and links with officialdom; the second, versed in legal theory, would advise on preparing League petitions and developing minority rights. That Schiemann aspired to this position has been inferred from his close liaison with the Verband's lobbyists on League-related issues in Paris and London, Nicolai von Berg and George Popoff.[55] Ammende curtly reminded Schiemann that he had been engaged in journalism for the last twenty or thirty years, whereas all that time Hasselblatt had continued to practise and study law.

Schiemann's cause was made no easier by the fall from grace of the chairman of the Verband der deutschen Volksgruppen, Rudolf Brandsch, as a result of a conflict with the Hungarians. The absence from key meetings of both Brandsch and Schiemann gave Hasselblatt, Ammende and company more room to manoeuvre for a quick decision. It even seemed likely for a time that Hasselblatt would also occupy Brandsch's post. That Ammende and Hasselblatt attached more importance to concentrating all work for Germandom than on the Verband's autonomy is confirmed by Hasselblatt's summary of why his supporters wanted him to relocate to Berlin.[56] They placed particular emphasis, he told Schiemann, on 'the necessity of forging a close inner and organic link between Germandom abroad and at home'. That required the full authority of the Verband der deutschen Volksgruppen to be invested in Hasselblatt so that he might 'work day and night in the Reich capital, whether on the creation of the [*Gesamtdeutsch*] forum or on preparation for the first ethnic German conference and the organism to be formed through this for the entire German *Volk*.'[57]

This confirmed Schiemann's personal doubts. He had already told Kurt Graebe on 10 March 1931: 'I regard Hasselblatt's candidacy as a very unfortunate event.' His public reasons for this, addressed as we have seen by Ammende and Hasselblatt, included concern that the election would appear to be an 'Estonian affair' to others in the Verband der deutschen Volksgruppen. Schiemann then added privately for Graebe's benefit: 'H. would quite definitely not put up the proper resistance to the persistent attempts of the Motzstrasse to bring the German minorities movement within their sphere of competence. The consequence of that could only be ceaseless friction within the Verband. Nor am I discouraged from this opinion by a letter from Ammende, who sees Hasselblatt's election as the ideal solution and regards it as self-evident that I will support him.'[58] Schiemann did not doubt that the difficulties European minorities faced in 1931 from extremist and totalitarian elements were unprecedented, but drew the opposite conclusion from Hasselblatt—namely, that the Verband der deutschen Volksgruppen must at all costs be kept on a strictly democratic path. Hasselblatt's election was a political decision to abandon the more independent course taken by the Verband under Bruns.[59]

Shifting priorities within the Auswärtiges Amt were evident from its delayed and routinely worded response to Schiemann's objections. It urged him to support the new appointee, knowing full well that Schiemann would indeed try to continue working with Ammende and Hasselblatt as far as possible. All the same, the latter's 'victory' signalled Schiemann's star beginning to fall, within both the German minorities' camp and the Nationalities Congress. From 1931 its Reich subsidies came exclusively through the international account of the Verband der deutschen Volksgruppen, under newly regularised procedures.[60] Ironically it meant that Ammende—also in poor health due to the diabetes diagnosed the previous summer—became more dependent on his protégé Hasselblatt.[61] Generational changes among congress delegates were also militating against Schiemann's liberal line, as were the frequent absences of Jewish delegates, who from 1929 were finding the costs of attending meetings harder to meet.[62] Other indications of Schiemann being edged from centre stage included the marginalisation of his friend Nicolai von Berg by Ammende. It must be said that Berg heartily reciprocated Ammende's distrust.[63]

While Schiemann struggled from Davos to check German nationalist influence over the Verband der deutschen Volksgruppen, his parliamentary colleagues in Riga faced sharper hostility from Latvian nationalists during the deepening international economic crisis. Latvia suffered from a severe drop in its exports, particularly agricultural ones, as well as the withdrawal of foreign capital and rising unemployment, worsened by the collapse of German banks in 1931. The Democratic Centre, the new Progressive Union (under Skujenieks), the party of New Settlers and others fumed against anything that smacked of concessions to the country's minorities.[64]

Such was the environment in which early in 1931 the Latvian Democratic Centre and Progressive Union launched a campaign to dispossess the German community of its Dom. The probability of a close vote prompted Schiemann to let the next man on the German list, W. Sadowsky, take over his mandate. On 9 March the *Rigasche Rundschau* announced: 'The leader of the German fraction, Dr P. Schiemann, resigns his seat, since through illness he is unable to come to Riga to take part personally in the battle for the Dom.'[65] The fraction's intention was that Schiemann would resume his place in time for the elections to the IV Saeima in the autumn.

The 'battle' was to rage till September. It brought forth unprecedented acrimony against the German community, uniting against it Latvian radical nationalist groups and the congregation of the Riga military garrison. The campaign undermined the German fraction's working relationship with the Celmiņš cabinet, which fell over the affair in March, as well as with the subsequent Ulmanis administration. Advocates of dispossession failed to reach their goal through normal parliamentary legislative channels and even lost a referendum. So with renewed determination they resorted finally to an emergency decree on 29 September 1931 whereby a council comprising eight Latvians and three Germans was appointed to regulate the use and administration of the Dom and all its possessions and real estate.[66] The law, duly accepted by the IV Saeima in November, ended the historic reign of the German Lutheran congregation over the magnificent Dom.

Although declared 'tuber free' in March, Schiemann did not return to Riga until 8 June, half-way through the conflict. A crowd of supporters and friends met him and Lotte at the railway station. For the time being he lodged with Dr Hach at the sanatorium in the town's Waldpark, but this did not prevent him from immediately resuming responsibility for the *Rigasche Rundschau*, to the relief of a chastened Keller. Schiemann also re-joined the CGBP meetings. Not by chance, new guidelines were adopted tightening fraction discipline, including clearing press interviews first, especially in Latvian papers.[67] Even so it is doubtful if Otto Grosberg was right—given the political temperature—to suggest that the Dom affair might not have so divided Germans and Latvians had Schiemann been in post.[68] Certainly his return injected a more pragmatic note into the affair, keeping the focus on the legality issue but showing flexibility over the Dom's day-to-day management.[69]

More important, Schiemann immediately made a connection between the church/state conflict on the one hand and, on the other, Latvia's existence and the European crisis. 'That at such a grave time our political circles feel justified in devoting themselves for an entire year almost exclusively to nationalist squabbles and vanities is a fact which alienates—and shocks—anyone long absent.'[70] Yet both sides were to blame for the rapid deepening of the rift between German Balt and Latvian in the course of 1931. Ruetz had told Schiemann that the National Socialist 'pest' was already affecting the Dom quarrel. One Hans-Joachim Voss was not untypical in asking Schiemann of Hitler: 'Do you really believe yourself that a time-server and cretin could have unleashed a movement of such power and stayed at the head of it?' He went on, 'Has your policy, my good Doctor—this policy of "restraining oneself nationally"—succeeded in bringing Latvians and Balts one hair's breadth closer? The Dom quarrel gives you your answer.'[71] Indeed Skujenieks, the man who four years earlier praised the German community's contribution to Latvia, now formed a 'national government' committed to a new course—deliberately preferring and strengthening Latvians in all areas of state life.[72]

Skujenieks' government (6.12.31–23.3.33) benefited directly from the outcome of the elections of 3/4 October for the fourth and final Saeima of interwar Latvia. Employing the tactics used to good effect in the 1928 elections, the German fraction again had six seats, but for the first time the Latvian bourgeois parties had a majority on their own. Schiemann, who viewed the increase in political groupings itself as a manifestation of extreme nationalism, argued that Skujenieks' call to reduce the parties through electoral reform addressed the symptom, not the 'illness'.[73]

With the German fraction in opposition, Schiemann's domestic political strategy focused on three areas: 'firming up' a minorities front; securing support for minority rights from the social democrat opponents of the government in return for concessions on social policy; and discussions with our 'old Farmers Union allies', who felt the coalition would not last. Schiemann was too adept a tactician—apart from his fraction's commitment to helping develop sound economic policy—to exclude direct discussions with the government of the day, since it was still vulnerable to foreign opinion. When Schiemann approached the prime minister initially by way of an evening drink, Skujenieks was careful to play down minority fears about the new education minister Atis Ķeniņš.[74]

Schiemann's distaste for the new 'national' government remained. He compared it adversely with the 'National Government' recently formed in Britain, which had a genuinely national agenda whereas Latvia had simply cobbled together the different party programmes. Far from being national it was united by hostility towards people of foreign origin.[75] This manifested itself in immediate government pressure for budgetary cuts in the minorities' school inspectorate, raising the spectre of all inspections being conducted by the Latvian education ministry and, as Schiemann argued, effectively ending autonomous schooling.[76] Atis Ķeniņš threatened what had hitherto been a fundamental of peaceful coexistence between German fraction and governments; namely, an understanding that the long-projected general education act would allow matters concerning minority schooling to be incorporated into a separate law. A German draft for this was tabled early in 1931. For the moment the German fraction had to rely on exploiting Lothar Schoeler's influence in the Saiema's education commission to delay the final draft of the education act, in the hope of a better political climate sooner or later.[77]

'Today', Schiemann had warned on returning from Davos, 'we confront the following remarkable phenomenon; nationalism is acknowledged throughout bourgeois Europe as virtuous and fundamentally moral, but with the caveat in practice that every people and every state approves only its own nationalism and denies that of the foreigner.'[78] The 'local' crisis bore witness to this maxim and matters worsened in the course of 1932. Schiemann pulled no punches in accusing Skujenieks of having an affinity with Hitler in his readiness to reduce basic legal rights at the behest of the majority people. Faced with Latvian press cries to use the financial crisis to break 'foreign' dominance, Schiemann observed that it had historically rested on *class*—German admittedly, but depriving German as well as Latvian peasants of property and rights. 'This new theory of national oppression… has been invented lately by those who in their youth fought furiously against national coercion.' Depriving 'foreigners'—who paid 25 per cent of the tax—of access to the state's wealth would bring decline for Latvia.[79]

The same point applied to the Latvianisation of education, although it has to be said that Baltic German anxieties on this score were matched by suspicions of even minority-friendly Latvian politicians that National Socialism was now infecting German schools.[80] Certainly it was above all in the ongoing school conflict that Schiemann found further confirmation of what he had come to visualise as a 'wave' of nationalism, lapping across the multi-national states of Central Eastern Europe from the old nation states in the West. He was not so much troubled by thoughts of physical danger to Latvia, but rather by the possibility of its middle parties being infected by 'the *new nationalism* [author's italics] of states without space' like Germany and Italy. On the eve of 1932 he sensed the wave that was about to 'break' his life's work for national harmony in Latvia. It was characteristic that he doggedly urged the rebuilding of the dike.[81]

However, the wave metaphor surely implied that conflict between German and Latvian during the life of the IV Saeima derived as much from Adolf Hitler as Mārĝeris Skujenieks. Responding to a hostile open letter from Ernst Munzinger, Schiemann described

National Socialism as 'above all the movement forging for all states and all peoples the ideological weapon to make rights in the state dependent on belonging to a specific people. That', he predicted, 'signifies the eradication of German nationality beyond the borders of German states. Hitler's battle-cry "Germany for Germans"—which has little practical political significance for Germany itself—must imbue corresponding calls from the eastern and southeastern states with new force ...Not to oppose this would be to go against my duties as a responsible leader of my people. To ask such disloyalty of me you have no right.'[82] That it *was* increasingly being demanded of him partly explained the 'deep anxiety' with which he contemplated New Year 1932.[83]

Intemperate remarks by such as Ķeniņš, describing Latvia as an 'Eldorado' of the minorities, whose industry and trade exploited Latvian peasants and workers, convinced many in the German community finally to abandon political cooperation.[84] That was impossible for Schiemann although, as well as subjecting Ķeniņš' actions to an extensive critique in the *Rigasche Rundschau*, he directly attacked the education minister in the Saeima for the legislative attrition against minority schooling.[85] Contemplating in February 1932 a proposal to make Latvian the state language and to tighten up on its usage by public authorities, Schiemann ridiculed Ķeniņš for creating a situation where passengers not understanding Latvian would have to take a translator with them on the trams.[86] In June, after a self-regarding speech by Ķeniņš, Schiemann promptly suggested that he had done more for Latvia's standing abroad than Ķeniņš, who had behind him a mediocre career as teacher, Russian censor and unsuccessful diplomat and minister. Schiemann's subsequent proposal for a vote of no confidence in Ķeniņš only narrowly failed, securing thirty-eight votes against forty.[87]

As the conflict between German and Latvian escalated sharply in the course of 1932 Schiemann was the first to admit that 'unnecessary provocation' came from both sides. His commitment to parliamentary democracy and his outspoken opposition to National Socialism exposed him to ever more intense criticism from fellow Baltic Germans, at home and in the Reich. Early in 1932 Felix von Uexküll-Güldenband, soon to take over editing *Nation und Staat*, warned Schiemann that since his opinion might be taken as representative of the journal he should bear in mind that National Socialists would sooner or later have decisive influence on German nationalities policy.[88] Schiemann's reaction to such advice is best gauged by a letter he wrote to the Auswärtiges Amt a few weeks later, critical of German acquiescence in the League of Nations' dismissal of the Ukraine petition against Soviet attacks on its autonomy. 'The moral position which Germany has won for itself in the minorities' question since Stresemann will be lost on the day it becomes apparent that it represents only the interests of its own minorities, but not even the most elementary legal claims of [other] minorities, irrespective of their nationality.'[89]

Nor would Schiemann allow himself to be deterred by the shift in *Auslandsdeutsche* priorities that Hasselblatt's appointment marked. Subsequently both Ammende and Hasselblatt made efforts to mend fences, although what Schiemann made of the patronising approval of his latest articles for the *Rigasche Rundschau* is anybody's guess. 'In my opinion', Hasselblatt wrote, 'you have been more successful than hitherto in adapting your doctrine to current political practice.'[90] Schiemann's correspondence with Nicolai von Berg reveals a continuing distrust of both Ammende and Hasselblatt—the latter dubbed by Berg as '*bei uns in Estland*'. Schiemann and Berg shared the suspicion that Hasselblatt was primarily interested in the European minorities movement as a vehicle to promote Germandom's cause.[91] The extent of the gap opening between Schiemann on the one hand and Hasselblatt and Ammende on the other became all too evident in the run-up to the meeting of the Verband der deutschen Volksgruppen in June 1932, as ever before the annual meeting of the Nationalities Congress.

According to Schiemann, pessimism about the League of Nations convinced many delegates that the 1932 congress should be held in Vienna rather than in Geneva.[92] By now Josip Wilfan, the Slovene deputy in the Italian parliament and chairman of the executive committee of the Nationalities Congress, had joined the ranks of those hostile to Ammende. Wilfan complained bitterly to Schiemann of Ammende giving the impression of being the sole author of the huge 1932 situation report, *Die Nationalitäten in den Staaten Europas*, rather than the collator and editor of the work of contributors, Wilfan among them.[93] As to Ammende, his and Hasselblatt's immediate anxiety was what Schiemann might say in his addresses in Vienna.

They knew the general topic was to be the new nationalist wave. 'To what extent we wish to arrive at a general consideration of the problem of national socialism', Hasselblatt wrote to Schiemann at the end of March, 'we can probably most expediently discuss in the board meeting beforehand.'[94] It was Hasselblatt's understanding that the discussion of nationalism scheduled for the first day of the meeting would not highlight National Socialism.[95]

Before Schiemann left for Vienna with Lotte he sent a concept of his congress speech for Ammende to look over. Ammende could hardly have endeared himself by mentioning in passing in his reply that he had forgotten the name of Schiemann's wife. More to the point, he was unwise enough to ask Schiemann to tone down the part of the speech that talked of opponents being possessed by the spirit of war, on the grounds that it might be construed as meaning that nationalists were actually trying to bring about another war. Ammende professed himself merely to be thinking of Schiemann making the best impression, since the speech was to be broadcast on the radio, not just in Vienna but also in Stuttgart and Königsberg. His real concern was the risk that Schiemann's voice might be taken as representative of the Verband der deutschen Volksgruppen.[96] Schiemann's withering response is best printed in full.

> The best of thanks for your friendly letter, alas with which, however, I cannot in fact agree in any way. The central theme of my speech is that the present aggressive nationalism originates in the ideas of the war, and specifically that the new and purely negative attitude towards the idea of [international] cooperation derives from this. Were I to abandon these views, or modify them to the point where they became unrecognisable, I would be left with a collection of platitudes that I am not disposed to associate abroad with my name. Besides, I shall also be expressing similar opinions at the German [*Verband*] conference about the nationalist wave, and if our committee chooses not to approve then I am willing to resign my present position. For the conclusion would follow from this that the [German] groups had deviated so radically from the fundamental principle of our movement that there would no longer be a place for me within such a community. My fraction agrees with my statement completely, as do those with whom I work. I must ask you therefore to leave all as it is, for as long as I hold my present office.[97]

He had his way and opened his address to the Verband der deutschen Volksgruppen in Baden near Vienna on 26 June 1932 with the words: 'The spirit of peace is in deficit.' He referred not to actual conflicts but to the fact that the mentalities causing the World War were thriving: 'It is the *spirit* of war, seeing peace only as a continuation of war by other means, that holds sway today.' It meant losing the individual in the masses, who demand an enemy, and equating the concepts of 'national community' and 'state community' even in peacetime. In attacking the current trend of treating national sentiment as a virtue of the masses he again resorted to comparisons with religion. Just as religious piety was not a virtue if practised not for its own sake but for reward, so national sentiment ceased to be a virtue if it were not the basis for human activity in public life. It could not be a virtue if detached from serving its own community and used as a basis for aggrandisement in another community. For how could national sentiment—'an inner spiritual emotion'—be applied to *external* goals? 'Only if it manifests itself not as love of one's own people but as hatred against another.' Service to one's people 'can never be placed above morality if we don't wish entirely to destroy the moral order'.

As for the National Socialists, their concept of nation was so tied to that of the state that they could only envisage supporting the *Auslandsdeutschen* by their inclusion in German territory or by the application of force. Although Soviet Russia, for its part, treated nationality as a private affair, it nevertheless made atheism the basis of its concept of state power. The soviet concept of state thus entailed 'mental compulsion' in the matter of its citizen's attitude towards God. The nation states of Europe had similar aspirations concerning their citizens' attitude to nationhood. 'That', Schiemann argued, 'is the nationalism of present-day Europe, which had its greatest boost from the undisguised victory of the nationalist idea in the World War. The postwar espousal of national self-determination merely provided 'new theoretical grounds for the idea of forging an identity between belonging to a nation and belonging to a state.' He went on: 'The struggle for nationality rights that we are called to lead has no other aim than to destroy this enforced identify in mankind's consciousness.'

Reviewing earlier efforts in this direction by Renner and others, up to and including the Baltic peoples, Schiemann deplored the fact that 'a new nationalist wave has gradually washed over these ideological impulses and has now brought the nation state concept of power to our [eastern central European] territories.' He placed some of the blame for that on the practice of the League's minorities' committee, for allowing modest concessions to nationality rights to be seen not as an obligation but as a favour. Economic crisis had also contributed, tempting politicians powerless to cope with it to find scapegoats among those of foreign origin. The most important cause, however, was the ceaseless advance of the nationalist ideology. It undermined the sense of justice in majority peoples and made the idea of equality laughable. Without directly attacking the Hitler movement, Schiemann left nobody in doubt of his main target in the final part of his address.

'Our' youth was being infected with the idea that only racially pure members of a people have unrestricted citizenship rights. Even more provocatively, he claimed that talk of conquest and settlement from the Reich made the Germans in the East the menace they claimed to see in the Jews of Central Europe. How, he asked, could German minorities fight for law and freedom when daily fellow Germans contested those rights? He had no scruples in insisting that German minority leaders oppose not just the nationalism of majority peoples they lived among, but also the nationalism of the German people. Whereas the *Auslandsdeutschen* could not interfere in the internal politics of the Reich, Schiemann made the case for their right and duty to oppose principles damaging to their work. He ended with a ringing declaration in favour of building, besides a federation of state authorities in Europe, a federation of peoples transcending borders with their own rights and spheres of interests. Thereby states would finally be 'denationed' and the different national communities given their due. He ended: 'I believe that such must be the aim of our struggle for rights in this time of hopelessness.'[98]

The bleak message was essentially repeated at the European Nationalities Congress immediately after the meeting of the Verband der deutschen Volksgruppen, when Schiemann in addition drew a parallel between the European crisis and a medical emergency, where sick and healthy forces also competed within the body, but where at least the doctor was outside events and able objectively to promote the healthy elements. However, the political 'doctor'—the statesman—was part of, and might even be the cause of, the 'illness' now threatening the world and its 'central organ', Europe, in the battle between the spirit of war and the spirit of peace. He found 'instead of reconciliation between peoples, an ever more unbearable tension in international relations; instead of an economic community—an increase of tariff barriers around the smallest state, instead of minority rights—the repression of minorities.'[99]

The 1932 Vienna meetings were to mark a decisive shift in the attitude of the Verband der deutschen Volksgruppen towards a greater German policy, providing additional evidence for the view that 1932 was a cut-off point in the history of the *Auslandsdeutsche.* Thereafter 'loyalty' and 'co-operation', so characteristic of Stresemann's tenure of office, ceased to be key terms in the political dialogue. Schiemann received the bronze shield of the Verein für das Deutschtum im Ausland in 1932 but attended no further meetings of the Verband der deutschen Volksgruppen.[100] His fierce opposition to Hasselblatt had undoubtedly helped to edge him finally into the role of an outsider, albeit an honourable one. When he was also given the Goethe Medal in August 1932 the Auswärtiges Amt hoped that he would long reign over the *Rigasche Rundschau* and continue to enjoy being 'emperor of minorities', while the Reichstag president Paul Löbe called him 'the pioneer of German minority rights'. Yet in the thick folder of congratulatory messages one of the few going beyond conventional forms was from a Dr Nanette Goldberger, who in passing urged: 'Give up your atrocious cigarettes.'[101]

Schiemann's unshakable conviction of the rightness of the a-national state in a Europe of unrepentant nationalism made it easy for contemporaries to dismiss him as utopian. However, to citizens of the European Union his ideas must now appear ahead of their time. His final address to the Verband der deutschen Volksgruppen in 1932, as well as being politically courageous,.was strikingly prescient. On that score the reaction of Thomas Mann on reading the Vienna address in *Nation und Staat* unintentionally settles any doubts. Writing to Schiemann, Mann cited the passage from *Die neue nationalistische Welle* bitterly regretting that the very freedoms for which German minorities fought were increasingly contested in the Reich. 'It looks bad in Germany at the moment,' Mann conceded. 'But what does that help? We must let this wave of wretched reaction pass over our head—whereby, I believe, the German sense of freedom will prove itself tougher and more tenacious than the stupid and cocky victors of the hour.'[102]

10. Passage to Exile

The nationalist imperatives driving the Skujenieks government between 1931 and 1933 offered no obvious prospect of the German fraction restoring the basis of its political influence in the Saeima—namely, good working relations with Latvia's bourgeois parties. Schiemann's determination in spite of this to defend parliamentary rights did not weaken. It committed him—as bitterly hostile to communism as ever—to attack the Saeima for not condemning the arrest of a communist deputy in the winter of 1932. Although accused of distributing illegal propaganda, the deputy in question, Ruhtinsch, was not caught *in flagrante*—the only ground for Parliament agreeing to the detention of one of its members. To Schiemann party-political considerations had therefore overridden justice and given communists just the ammunition they wanted. 'The western idea of law', he concluded, 'has been severely damaged.'[1] A month later he recorded dismay at a bourgeois government accepting a social democrat motion to have the appointment of judges confirmed by Parliament, threatening the judiciary's independence.[2]

It all seemed depressingly consistent with the widespread resurgence after 1931 of extreme right-wing calls for a more powerful executive, first heard in Latvia in the mid-1920s. The demand was coupled in the case of overtly fascist organizations, notably the *Pērkonkrusts* (Thunder Cross), led by Gustav Celmiņš, with anti-Semitic, anti-minority and above all anti-German attitudes. It is not without irony that the journal of *Pērkonkrusts*—itself inspired by Hitler's successes—would comment: 'Your time, you German people, is over. In Latvia of the Latvians there is no room for you.'[3] Other nationalist and conservative forces, including the agrarian right around Kārlis Ulmanis, were increasingly frustrated at being unable to implement policy in the faction-ridden Saeima. They too contemplated authoritarian rule.[4] Schiemann's response to the clamour for change was that a strong personality could function equally well in a democracy.

'Propaganda for a dictatorship does not signify a solution to the parliamentary crisis, but rather legitimises those very forces that generated the crisis.'[5]

Not all Latvian parties and newspapers were ill-disposed towards the German community. It goes without saying that Schiemann steadfastly refused to give up hope of compromise during what were to be his final months in the Saeima. Of the clash between Schoeler and Ķeniņš on the Saeima's education commission in November 1932, for example, he advised that the minister might actually prefer to reach agreement: 'Harsh quarrels with him might not have a favourable effect. In future we must be more discreet and try to handle Ķeniņš psychologically in the right way.' At the same time he cautioned fellow Baltic Germans against expecting a full restoration of lost positions in education or business as a condition of negotiating with government.[6] As far as many Baltic Germans were concerned, Schiemann and his fellow deputies offered them little more in Latvia than a future of diminishing returns and further retrenchment. Not for the first time in history the messengers were targeted.

Arguments over 'leadership' within the Baltic German community had not really abated from the inception of independent Latvia. For conservative Baltic German circles a grudging acceptance of harsh necessity after 1919 never signified any real liking for parliamentary politics. This, as we saw, partly explained their aspiration to integrate the CGBP more effectively into the Zentrale/Deutschbaltischer Volksgemeinschaft. The idea gained fresh impetus from Reinhard Wittram's article 'Political leadership', published in the *Baltische Monatshefte* in 1933. Describing the separate Baltic German parties as 'talking shops', Wittram could hardly not admit in parenthesis the CGBP's importance in providing parliamentary unity for his community. However, he believed that the leader of the parliamentary fraction, 'irrespective of personality', should no longer chair it. Instead he suggested that a non-parliamentarian, remote from the political battlefield, would facilitate calm continuity. Such a figure could also—here was the key point—better integrate politics into the work of the Deutschbaltische Volksgemeinschaft, recovering the trust that Wittram claimed the CGBP had lost among Baltic Germans. His notion of personality being irrelevant to the proposed change deceived no informed observer.[7]

Wolfgang Wachtsmuth later wrote of the Committee of German Balt Parties: 'At its head stood a politician of the most outspoken and idiosyncratic character. Clearly, it was unavoidable that he had political opponents.'[8] These had persistently failed to overcome the challenge of their political leader's personality. Wittram's bid in 1933 seemed unlikely to fare any better, for in truth the question of the individual could not be divorced from the issue. Precisely because Paul Schiemann was 'the strongest, most intellectually fertile and thoroughly independent entity (which even his enemies fully acknowledged), it would have been impossible in practice to "subordinate" him to a higher office.' Wachtsmuth added pointedly: 'There was nobody of substance prepared to take this on.'[9] For Wittram and other Baltic German conservatives the preferred replacement for Schiemann would probably have been Fircks. However, even some of his close supporters had to concede that Fircks was 'an outstanding ambassador but no foreign minister'.[10]

On the other hand, because Schiemann enjoyed good standing in many Latvian political circles, to withdraw him as a parliamentarian, either to chair a reformed CGBP or to replace Rüdiger over the Deutschbaltische Volksgemeinschaft, would have damaged the German cause in general. Conversely, as relations between German and Latvian worsened after 1930, leading elements in the Deutschbaltische Volksgemeinschaft saw less to lose from a more overt and robust challenge to the German fraction's political line. Their mood was coloured, as even Wittram's comparatively restrained critique showed, by admiration, particularly among young Baltic Germans, for the 'national renewal' gathering pace inside Germany. 'Whoever was pessimistic', Wittram recalled, 'was easily persuaded to place hope no longer on the eventual triumph of legality but on the resurgence of one's own people.'[11]

Not only youthful Baltic Germans found immensely attractive the concept of a resolute and united German '*Volk*'. The idea accorded well with conservative resentment at Schiemann basing political strategy on Baltic Germans being a minority instead of capitalising on their historic position to secure special status.[12] It is not always easy to distinguish clearly between such attitudes on the one hand and, on the other, the sentiments prevalent among Erhard Kroeger and his followers, who in the late 1920s set out to forge their own brand of national renewal. What came to be known as the Baltic German *Bewegung* received a warm welcome from the delegate assembly of the Deutschbaltische Volksgemeinschaft in 1931. Admittedly Fircks recorded that Baltic German reactions to Kroeger and company covered every nuance of opinion between two opposite extremes; on one side, unqualified enthusiasm and, on the other, apprehension about the *Bewegung* usurping the leadership of the community. The latter concern was purportedly more noticeable among the older generation of Baltic Germans,[13] some of whom recorded strong reservations at the spread of National Socialist ideas; remarkably few of them endorsed Schiemann's strong opposition.

Schiemann reaffirmed his stance in late January 1933, amid increasingly acrimonious arguments over leadership. He accepted that Baltic Germandom in Latvia was not a community of *political* opinion; that its political front arose specifically to promote the general defence of the Baltic German community. Complete agreement on every political issue was therefore not required. Nor was there justification for branding individuals 'good' or 'bad' Germans in terms of their patriotism. What *was* needed was trust in the elected leaders to respect the interests of different sectors of Baltic Germandom while working for the overall good of the state. Schiemann referred yet again to earlier religious wars and to the subsequent spread of peaceful coexistence between confessions across borders, free of aspirations to wield power in the state. 'To achieve such an outcome for all human communities is the task of the hour. Two strong movements are against this, claiming an exclusivity backed by all the state's power. The one demands one people, one ideology and one way of life. The other demands one sociological class, one ideology, one way of life. To me both claims seem equally intolerable.'[14] Two days after the editorial appeared Hitler was in power in Berlin.

The event immediately placed a question-mark over Schiemann's future on the *Rigasche Rundschau*. His refusal, in an Auswärtiges Amt—subsidised newspaper, to devote more than minimal space to political events in Germany after 1928 infuriated Baltic German critics, at home and in Berlin. Never mind that the *Rigasche Rundschau* was now the best-known German minority paper in northern Europe, or that Schiemann's 1,500 articles had been crucial to this achievement.[15] Not surprisingly, he had discussed the possibility of a

Nazi victory in Germany with colleagues, notably his political editor Hans von Rimscha. According to Rimscha, Schiemann initially expected the NSDAP to be constrained by its coalition partners. He also placed some reliance on his contract, giving him control of the newspaper's general political line as well as a veto over engagements and dismissals. Finally there was hope that the representative of the Reich 'shareholders'—Max Winkler—could continue to shield the *Rigasche Rundschau* from direct pressure.[16] However, it is highly unlikely that Schiemann envisaged more than a holding operation in the light of his well-known views on Hitlerism.

According to one unkind rumour that Rimscha heard from a Berlin news correspondent Richard Bahr, Winkler had a 'crying fit' on the day of Hitler's seizure of power and became a Nazi the next morning. Certainly Winkler wrote to Schiemann on 4 February 1933 urging him to draw the 'appropriate conclusion' from the changing times and to dismiss Rimscha. There was displeasure in Berlin at Rimscha's prediction of conflict within Hitler's coalition. The struggle would be won, Rimscha had written, either 'by von Papen, behind whom stand Hindenburg and big business, or by Hitler, behind whom stand the millions'. The event was not, Rimscha added, something a responsible politician would wish to celebrate. Schiemann's reply to Winkler on 9 February 1933 also leaves no doubt that he expected intrigues, because the daily *Rundschau* was a 'red rag' to Reich German and Baltic German party fanatics in Latvia. Yet Schiemann refused to replace Rimscha 'with a brown-hued party man' and reiterated his view that the paper's and the fraction's democratic line offered the best chance for the German minority to influence Latvian policy. For the *Rigasche Rundschau* suddenly to peddle National Socialist ideas would be 'wholly intolerable'.[17]

This, as well as his reluctance to accept Winkler's invitation to Berlin because it would be 'noticed' by the Latvians, suggests that he also calculated on political considerations weighing against open interference in Riga by the Reich government. Indeed, while the newspaper's detractors smeared it publicly the real pressure to 'coordinate' went on behind the scenes. Auswärtiges Amt policy of non-interference in the *Rigasche Rundschau*'s editorial line was clearly over. As Schiemann informed fellow fraction members on 8 March 1933, Winkler was initially told that if he wished to keep his own shares in the paper both Schiemann and Rimscha had to go. Berlin eventually acknowledged that Schiemann might remain, but only if Rimscha went. The German fraction agreed there was nothing to be gained by Schiemann's resignation. With Schiemann as chairman abstaining, they recommended Rimscha having three months' paid leave, followed by three months' notice. Tellingly Lothar Schoeler was anxious to inform Berlin that the fraction was not against Rimscha's dismissal as such, but only against the way it had been engineered. Magnus unkindly implied that the sacking would make little impact on Latvians. Schiemann evidently did not share Westermann's optimism that the paper could at least keep its chief editor.[18]

Rimscha's account of these days cites a confidential note by Martius, the German ambassador, of an informal meeting of Baltic German deputies three days later, 11 March 1933. This time Schiemann was not present, although Rüdiger was—on behalf of the Deutschbaltische Volksgemeinschaft. The upshot was unanimous agreement that Rimscha should be asked to leave at once. Subsequently Schoeler, Pussull and Westermann took him to lunch and told him of the fraction's conviction that editorial staff changes were unavoidable in the light of events in Germany. The *Rigasche Rundschau*'s lawyer Erich Pabst made plain—to a perfectly healthy Rimscha—that the offer of sick leave until his notice expired on 1 October 1933 was not one he should refuse.[19] Rimscha was particularly upset that in order to conceal Berlin's role in the affair the impression was being given that he was leaving over differences with Paul Schiemann. His suspicion that Wachtsmuth, Keller and von Rüdiger were happy to see him go was well founded. His cause was not helped by his earlier conflict with Keller at the *Rigasche Rundschau*. The Reich press chief and future economics minister Walther Funk was also making known his opposition to Rimscha—a foretaste of how Hitler's Enabling Act would extend his government's controls in all spheres.

As well as having to live with the growing uncertainty at the *Rigasche Rundschau* offices in February and March, Schiemann was also preoccupied with the sustained political crisis in Latvia after the fall of Skujenieks on 3 February 1933, when a majority of sixty-five threw out proposals for further drastic cutbacks in support for minority school buildings and cultural institutes. Schiemann hailed this as a vote against open warfare between government and minorities. It was in no small part the outcome of intensive political activity by the German deputies in the previous months, among other things revitalising cooperation between Latvia's minorities.[20] Thereafter the German fraction was better able to focus against Ķeniņš himself, who eventually also had to resign as education minister in June. Ķeniņš had inflicted serious financial blows but somehow the Baltic German leadership managed to defend both the national identity and standards of their schools, frustrating Ķeniņš' proclaimed goal of creating 'a single Latvian culture.' What Schiemann saw as a predominantly nationalist mood in Latvia still made it impossible for him to accept the invitation of President Kviesis to take part in forming a new government. However, the offer surely vindicated Schiemann's political strategy.[21]

That was not how his detractors viewed matters. Emboldened among other things by Hitler's seizure of power, the *Baltische Monatshefte* in February 1933 opted to publish Erhard Kroeger's crude polemic 'On political inversion'. Without actually naming names, Kroeger categorically rejected the re-statement of the German fraction's line in the *Rigasche Rundschau* article of 28 January 1933. History had shown Kroeger the need to oppose enemies with resolution. Instead, he went on, 'political inverts place the intercession for the interests they represent behind the wish to avoid conflicts with the enemy as far as possible, and look for voluntary compromise on the basis of honourable cooperation.' Political discussion, Kroeger argued, 'is determined by the precocious, the cautious, the aesthetes'. Protesting that 'the invert recoils from the will to power', he deplored the fact that 'for many years we have lived in the shadow of an inverted political ideology'—which, he demanded, should be subjected to a thorough revision. Implicit in his argument was the suggestion that if Baltic Germans resisted Latvian nationalism they would not stand alone.[22]

In one of the last articles he wrote for the *Rigasche Rundschau* Schiemann dismissed accusations that he had pursued compromise with Latvians at *any* cost as a gross over-simplification, a product of resentment not worthy of serious discussion. Instead he reviewed the decision of organised Baltic Germandom in 1919 to work for equality of treatment in an independent Latvia, on the basis of the National Council's platform. There had been no illusions about the coming struggle to implement rights, but it was accepted that it had to be fought on the basis of a democratic constitutional order. Differing party-political values therefore ensured that even if it was sometimes a simple matter of Latvians ranged against non-Latvians, it was not always so. 'In the varied shifting of the parliamentary play of forces there was at least success in deflecting decisive attacks on the free cultural development of our people.' Schiemann underlined his point by contrasting the situation of German schools in Latvia, which was favourable, with that of German institutions in other mixed states. Admitting serious setbacks in the process, he again cited the fate of Ķeniņš's proposals as proof of responsible Latvian political circles being wary of the dangers of a divided state: 'In such a moment certain circles of our [Baltic German] community feel justified in branding a policy based on moral and legal considerations as risibly utopian; in treating nationality conflict as the only problem of state; and in commending even to the weaker the illusion of future power as the only real basis of policy. Such an attitude to our political problems results first in giving to those [Latvian] nationalist elements currently in power a moral foundation for their acts of force.' In effect Schiemann placed Kroeger and his ilk on a par with Ķeniņš himself. Even worse, they were 'shifting responsibility for the fate of our people from our own strength and work to the uncertain successes of forces active outside our own sphere of influence. A community no longer building its future on its own sense of purpose has no future.' The article ended by reaffirming the fraction's duty with the phrase 'Our own effort; our own responsibility'.[23]

The difficulty in getting the message across is clear from Schiemann's editorial of 18 March 1933. It addressed the previous day's turbulent Saeima discussion of terror reports from Germany. He naturally shared Latvia's dismay. However, his immediate purpose was to counter 'false conclusions' inimical to his fraction's entire strategy. The first misconception was that the terror arising from the revolutionary change in Germany would be prolonged. The second was that the terror signified the end of German *culture*; France's revolutionary terror had not ended French culture. The third was the belief that those Baltic Germans in Latvia who sympathised with the new German movement approved of its excesses. Rather—like those Latvian politicians simultaneously wondering how best to counter a

'German menace'—they were impressed by the prospect of Germany and its people resuming their place in Europe. Whether or not the Nazi regime survived, Schiemann argued, there would sooner or later be a stronger Germany. With this he arrived at the last of the 'wrong conclusions' that Latvians should not draw. The analysis merits extensive quotation, not least for its continuing relevance:

'A strong Germany does not itself mean a threat to the independence of the Baltic states. It *can* be the firm basis for a lasting guarantee of that independence. There is no sense in conjuring up a spectre from past literary tales and speechifying. Europe's policy will unfold according to the inner laws of the economic and cultural structure of its states. As will German policy. However unlikely it may seem today, circumstances are impelling towards a lasting combination in central Europe on the basis of shared interests. The focal point and foundation of any such central European economic area can only be a strong Germany. Everything depends on the Baltic countries securing their position in the economic combination of those European states that are dependent on one another. Just as the Germans in Latvia must carve out their own fate in the country, so Latvia's place in a future central European economic zone will depend on its political astuteness and its economic capacity. It is therefore right that the three Baltic states, precisely at this point in their existence, urgently pursue the path towards a close alliance between them—not to protect themselves by military means against external dangers, but to become a more unified and stronger economic entity, that can pull its weight and be ready to assume its role in a larger organisation.'[24]

By now the additional strain on Schiemann was taking its toll on his heart and lungs. Illness and the need for recovery in a better climate provided the public explanation of his sudden departure for Mödling in Vienna at the end of March.[25] Riga's journalists were not fully convinced by what they took as a cover for his removal, and Russian papers depicted him as the 'first sacrifice' of the new order.[26] Indeed, physical ill-health alone—he needed a procedure to treat his tuberculosis—might not in itself have prompted his departure at that moment. Other members of the German fraction and key members of the Deutschbaltische Volksgemeinschaft played a part in his decision by strongly urging him to take a break abroad. Undoubtedly they breathed a collective sigh of relief when he left the firing line, sparing them some embarrassing dilemmas as the pressures increased on the *Rigasche Rundschau.* Outwardly the impression was maintained that Schiemann would return to the newspaper later, and resume his seat in the autumn session of parliament. In reality he had already embarked on the painful inward journey towards accepting that he would not be returning to the newspaper he loved.

Support for this idea comes from a report of the Latvian ambassador to Berlin, Roberts Liepins, who briefly met Schiemann in transit in Berlin around 20 June 1933. Liepins could see for himself that Schiemann was not in good health, although he talked of his plans to resume his seat in the Saeima. On the other hand Liepins was told in passing of Schiemann's resolve to break completely with the *Rigasche Rundschau.* Lotte Schiemann, who happened to travel with Liepins on her brief return to Riga at the time, was more forthcoming; she told Liepins how hard it had been for her husband to leave the *Rigasche Rundschau* because of his long and close association with it. But his mind was made up by the newspaper's new (National Socialist) orientation. Paul Schiemann, his wife reminded Liepins, was a man of strong character who would not sacrifice his political opinions. She said that he showed no concern about who would be the next editor; he 'was not interested in that any more'. Liepins added for the benefit of the Latvian foreign minister Munters that the now overwhelmingly pro-National Socialist German press in Riga would certainly campaign to keep Schiemann's name off the lists of German candidates, thus also putting an end to his parliamentary career.[27]

The mood behind Schiemann's dispirited reaction to the future of the *Rigasche Rundschau* is easily accounted for by the dismal news reaching him in the weeks after he left Riga. One of his sources was Rimscha, who used his period of 'sick leave' from March to find out more about his own predicament from his Berlin contacts—including relatives in the 'Brotherhood'—and explore the possibility of setting up another paper. He found that political moves against him originated with Winkler himself, 'whose nerves had gone' and who refused to see him in Berlin.[28] Rimscha's correspondence with Schiemann also had a sly dig at Sass—'who seems comfortable on the powder keg and obviously hopes to exploit his old (physical?) relations with Funk. Well, needs must.'[29] Mostly his spleen was directed at Keller who, immediately after Schiemann's departure, allowed the

Rigasche Rundschau to publish an article on the 'Jewish war'—'crassly different' from the paper's normal tone. Rimscha assured Schiemann that Keller had wanted to replace him ever since 'your first illness. If he really does resign his job and leaves, as he threatens to do three times a day, it will only be because he has not become Chief Editor himself.'[30]

Apart from the gloomy tidings of the *Rigasche Rundschau*, Schiemann knew how the rump German fraction's dilemma had worsened since May 1933, when Kroeger, with a group of young Baltic Germans drawn largely from the old leadership caste, announced the formation of the National Party. Its political credo—'What we want'—bitterly attacked the Baltic German leaders. It also made clear that the new 'party', which was never in fact formally registered by the Latvian authorities, had no intention of being a party in the conventional sense. Insisting that Baltic Germans were divided and weak, Kroeger and his followers affirmed: 'We want to be the cell of a new community.... Our *movement* should embrace all classes of our people, particularly its youth, and give it inner vitality.' From his determination to forge a united national community Kroeger derived his rejection of the minority concept. 'The word minority is a meaningless mathematical term, from which follow certain useful public law conclusions, no more, certainly not the basis for an existence in our country. The national community must consist of Germans, who are proud to be German and ready to make any sacrifice for this. The national idea must regain completely its original purpose in unity and defence, and not be reduced to the concepts of "language" and "culture".'[31]

The inversion of Schiemann's thinking on the 'national community' could not have been more pointed. In his absence it fell to Fircks in June 1933 to publish a defence of the German parliamentary fraction against Kroeger's accusations. He argued with some justice that since 1919 the Baltic German community had been more united than before. He roundly disputed that younger Baltic Germans were as politically disengaged as Kroeger suggested. However, Fircks also claimed that *all* Baltic German political leaders recognised the distinction between the minority rights concept needed to make an impact on the international stage and, on the other hand, Baltic German historic right in Latvia. That was not Schiemann's position. His argument with Fircks over autonomy in Latvia in 1925 had made that all too apparent. Nor is it conceivable to imagine Schiemann agreeing with Fircks's closing expression of readiness to work with the new movement, or sharing the Baron's perception 'that a new initiative has arisen among us, seemingly able, with the right guidance, to give new strength in the battle for our national existence and our rights in our home.'[32]

Kroeger's memoir is at pains to give credit for setting up the *Bewegung* to his own efforts and those of other local Nazi leaders, without prompting from the Reich. Yet the propensity for accommodation with the *Bewegung* was more typical of the traditional élites and older political leaders than is apparent from Baltic German historiography, which emphasises the quarrels between the leaders of the *Bewegung* and the Volksgemeinschaft in Latvia. Admittedly, discord within the Latvian German community was fuelled by a degree of weariness with what to many seemed meagre results from their parliamentary fraction's defensive line. Opting for national socialism was not always necessarily involved.

Symptomatically the Baltische Landespartei, founded in June 1933 by Helmuth Stegmann, a vocal opponent of Schiemann's 'leftist politics', affirmed that its desire for renewal expressed loyalty to the Baltic homeland; and that it was not comparable with developments inside Hitler's Germany. Yet Stegmann, a longstanding member of the Riga city council, also observed: 'Democracy was a problematic political form, a necessary evil.' His short memoir of political life in Latvia omitted the names of Baltic German National Socialists because 'many of them would behave very differently today from then.'[33] Perhaps the general situation is most charitably described by the observation that the *Bewegung* won many more sympathisers to its cause than actual members. Even more of course admired the Third Reich and Adolf Hitler. Only a small number were known opponents of the new German government.[34]

June 1933 was therefore not a good month for Schiemann, as he reflected on the news coming from Riga and made final preparations for another spell in the sanatorium; this was scheduled to last till September, confirming the seriousness of his physical condition. Whether he had any detailed knowledge of what was going on inside the CGBP, or indeed inside his own party, is unclear. He might in any case have concurred by then with his fellow party member Beshardt, who on 7 June 1933 suggested that the German Balt Democrat Party needed a new chairman: 'Dr Schiemann, who spends the whole time convalescing abroad, is not the man to represent the party today.'[35] When Rimscha got back to Riga in June he reported to Schiemann 'indecision and panic' in the rump fraction, as well as great uncertainty at the *Rigasche Rundschau*. Rimscha desperately wanted to know if Schiemann, who was technically still chief editor, had yet reached a decision about returning. 'Or do you really intend to throw in the towel and never come back, as is frequently (probably with specific purpose) reported here?'[36] Rimscha's anxiety for Schiemann to 'save' matters manifestly reflected his own 'hopeless' situation. Keller, he reported gloomily on 4 July 1933, was 'still advancing' in the *Rigasche Rundschau*.[37]

As we saw, however, Schiemann had already decided to resign from the paper and his formal departure was announced in its pages on 8 July 1933. The intermittent exchanges between Rimscha and Schiemann about founding another and more independent publication also ran into the sand at this point.[38] From Berlin it was indicated to the fifty-five-year-old Schiemann that the continuation of pension arrangements made for him and Lotte in 1925 depended on his not publishing further articles in the German press in Riga. Felix von Uexküll-Güldenband took over from Keller as editor of the *Rigasche Rundschau* in July, only to be replaced by Ernst von Mensenkampf when the paper was 'co-ordinated' in November 1933. In Berlin Winkler was pushed aside for Heyde.

Schiemann's dismay at the trimming within Riga's Baltic Germandom could only have deepened when he heard subsequently that Rimscha had at one time written as '*Germanicus*' in Riedel's *Riga am Sonntag*, the *Rigasche Rundschau*'s bitter rival. Referring to Rimscha's capacity to 'play on two violins', Otto Grosberg lost no time in dispelling Schiemann's ignorance on this point, or in assuring him that Rimscha was buttering up Kroeger like many others.[39] Rimscha later protested that 'there were never any differences of opinion' between him and Schiemann. Even so, his letters to Schiemann in 1933 betray evident discomfort over his own actions.[40]

The interdependence between Schiemann's powerful and influential journalism and his success as a parliamentary politician had been obvious to all. Few therefore could have expected him to return as leader of the Baltic German parliamentary fraction once he abandoned the *Rigasche Rundschau*. There were continuing expressions of regard for him within the rump fraction, but in his absence, under Lothar Schoeler's leadership, it remained largely quiescent before Kroeger's onslaught. Undoubtedly this reflected a growing readiness for accommodation with the *Bewegung* and for the resolution of differences within the Latvian German community. That was likely to involve the replacement of separate Baltic German political parties by a general German Electoral Association, whose committee would supplant the CGBP. Both Rüdiger and Kroeger supported proposals along these lines at the Delegate Conference of the Deutschbaltische Volksgemeinschaft on 24 September 1933, bringing closer the day when this became the political as well as the socio-economic apex of Latvia's Germandom. To this Schiemann's return would have presented an insurmountable obstacle.[41]

When the Saeima re-convened in the autumn of 1933, the fraction therefore agreed unanimously that Schiemann remain abroad and his mandate be handed over to somebody else. It was left to Karl Hahn to insist that the CGBP send Schiemann a telegram on 16 October, reading 'Friday extremely important Saeima session. Presence or authenticated telegram of resignation essential.' Schiemann complied by relinquishing all offices and from 17 October his parliamentary career was at an end.[42] Plans for Fircks to take over the fraction's leadership were thwarted by his own illness and resignation the day after Schiemann's, leaving Karl Keller and Hellmuth Stegman respectively as replacements for the two former leaders of the parliamentary fraction.[43] Wilhelm von Fircks died on 10 December 1933. In spite of his own bitterness at the encroachment of National Socialism, his 'final testament'—in the form of two letters written from hospital to his own party—betrays the differences between him and Schiemann that had often made their working partnership fraught.

Fircks had clearly shared Schiemann's recognition of an independent Latvia as being the basis for Baltic German existence after 1919. But unlike Schiemann, who repeatedly urged that rights could not derive from past privilege alone, Fircks believed in the idea of a 'special' position for Baltic Germans 'because without us our homeland would have long descended into the swamp of slavery.' He also endorsed Schiemann's attachment to the rule of law and cautioned against copying events in the Reich. Unlike Schiemann he argued at the same time: 'We should never lose sight of the fact that right not backed by might can be thwarted by anybody who does have such power. Thus all our hope is directed also to a strengthening of the prestige of the entire German people.'[44] Schiemann's otherwise generous obituary of his former co-worker nevertheless made passing references to 'an incredible mixture of opinions and ideas, as well as some personal animosities'. Of his original decision to make common cause with the Latvians Schiemann noted: 'When I espoused such a policy immediately after the Russian Revolution, on the basis of the October manifesto in opposition to those circles where Fircks felt at home, then agreement with him signified nothing less than an intellectual sacrifice.'[45]

The ideological gap between Schiemann and Fircks is also clear from another obituary of Fircks, published in the *Baltische Monatshefte* by Woldemar Wulffius. Arguing that more had been lost than gained by the German fraction's work in the Saeima, it looked back to when the Baltic German National Committee, chaired by Fircks, was still important. 'The disastrous mixing of German Balt policy with general minorities policy, an unfortunate doctrine later implemented for our sake, did not exist in 1919.' Fircks 'never thought the common "minorities barrel" a goal worth pursuing.' Citing a description from 1927 of the 'heartfelt' collaboration between Fircks and Schiemann, the article asked: 'Heartfelt? The Fircks-Schiemann dualism remained a constant on which so much *baltisch* hope would be dashed.' Attributing much of Schiemann's political success to Fircks bringing with him the loyalty of Latvia's Balts, Wulffius regretted that Fircks had never insisted on heading the German electoral list, or gone into opposition in 1931. Under Schiemann's leadership there was no prospect of 'inner unity' for Latvia's Baltic Germans. Under Fircks 'this would always have been possible.'[46]

What the Latvian majority would have made of that sort of unity is easy to guess from the *Jauankas Sinas* quote from Schiemann: 'If one puts Germany's interests above those of Latvia, then there can be no talk of Latvian cooperation.' It is not in the least surprising that—apart from ill-health—Schiemann now saw no prospect of continuing his political work in Latvia. His departure from Riga and Fircks's, death removed any serious obstacle to dissolving the different Baltic German parties in favour of a German Electoral Association, integrated into the Deutschbaltische Volksgemeinschaft. Depressingly, there was little resistance even within Schiemann's own party—only concern lest merging parties inflame Latvian opinion, and that the 'little man' would be under represented. Karl Keller even claimed never to have felt tied to the German Balt Democratic Party. He maintained that for Baltic Germans political parties had never played a prominent role, so their demise was no misfortune. He wanted to emphasise that 'new ideals abounded here and abroad' and 'new forces' were breaking through.[47]

Keller had not of course had in mind Kārlis Ulmanis and his supporters, whose *coup d'état* on 15 May 1934 finally banned the activities of *all* political parties. The Deutschbaltische Volksgemeinschaft became by default the centre of all Baltic German work. The leadership dualism that Schiemann's enemies claimed was caused by his dominance in the political field was ostensibly over. In fact there would be another and ultimately unsuccessful struggle against the slow but relentless accretion of influence to Kroeger's supporters. Although forced to take different forms of association after the party ban of 15 May 1934 the *Bewegung* undeniably capitalised on state laws that in practice hit Baltic Germans hardest. The measures included the dissolution of the minority school authorities (12.7.1934), a language law in effect excluding German from public life (5.1.35), cuts in the number of German lawyers allowed to practice (31.1.35) and a law making it virtually impossible for Germans to buy real estate. Other banking and commercial legislation damaged German trade and industry.[48]

The reversal of what had been won under his leadership pained Schiemann but he no longer had direct influence in Latvia. Nor did he derive satisfaction from proof of his prediction of a Nazi victory dividing German minorities abroad. Here there *was* still work for him to complete, even if the prospect of doing so through the European Nationalities Congress was increasingly dim. By 1933 it was well on the way to becoming an extension of the Verband der deutschen Volksgruppen, which in turn quickly lost what autonomy it still had. Rüdiger soon found what the new Reich regime portended at the Verband's 1933 Berlin conference, listening to the newly appointed leader of the *Verein für das Deutschtum im Ausland* (VDA), Hans Steinacher. Steinacher's speech pointedly emphasised 'the great German *Volksgemeinschaft*, at the head of which stood the German Chancellor' and indicated that beyond the purely caritative nature of its work the VDA might need 'to interfere directly' in the German groups abroad.[49]

Germany's right to do this had of course long been preached in *völkisch* and far right circles, but from 1931 the idea also made much greater headway inside the Verband der deutschen Volksgruppen. A major conference of German jurists at Lübeck in 1931 urged the use of the term '*Reich deutsch*' in future citizenship legislation, the better to demonstrate that only a fraction of Germandom lived in Germany; that ethnic Germans abroad were not only subjects of foreign powers—as they had been before 1914—but integral parts of a supra-national *Volksgemeinschaft*.[50] Such an entity, in Max Hildebert Boehm's *Das Eigenständige Volk* (1932), became the 'living' alternative to the post-war settlement 'imposed' in 1919; the territorial ordering being simply one aspect of the people's aspirations to pan-national integration.

Only in the most superficial sense did this idea resemble Schiemann's vision of borders being less important in a future Europe of 'nations'. Contrary to Schiemann, Boehm insisted on the centrality of the state's role in promoting the process, and ridiculed the concept of an a-national state and the notion of 'state-free culture'.[51] Boehm, Schiemann responded, naively confused laws governing territory with those governing intellectual life. 'The [territorial] realm comprises a community of like interests of all its inhabitants in upholding law and order and in the economic wellbeing of the land. From this community of interests naturally grow the particular tasks of the ruling authority, which will be damaged once the sense of individuality, *proper to the intellectual community*, impinges on such tasks and atomises them.' Schiemann warned Boehm: 'The inner laws of these two communities [territorial and intellectual] are by their nature different from each other, and must always be in conflict with each other.'[52]

Das eigenständige Volk was needless to say unhelpful to Schiemann's mission to clarify the concepts of 'nation' and 'state' in order to win European-wide acceptance for cultural autonomy. Instead *völkisch* and national conservative circles inexorably promoted the idea of cross-border national communities as *political* entities.[53] In Schiemann's thinking, however, a viable supra-national *Volksgemeinschaft* was necessarily premised on the absolute political loyalty of its members to the host-state, not to the motherland. He conceded in responding to Boehm's book that the struggle to differentiate the national community's sphere of authority from that of the territorial community would be virtually hopeless, but for one thing: the prospect of economic forces eventually militating against the continuation of sovereign, omnipotent nation states. 'The necessity for a large European economic space must sooner or later limit the sphere of authority of states, impelling the territorial state on organizing its economic life within the larger community and focusing it on the purely administrative functions within its realm.'[54]

Although Schiemann ceased to attend joint meetings of the Verband der deutschen Volksgruppen after 1932, he retained for a while longer his functions within the Nationalities Congress. In this his last major involvement was with the controversy over 'dissimilation' arising at the September 1933 congress meeting in Berne.

The idea found strong support from Hasselblatt and others in the Verband der deutschen Volksgruppen, therefore within the Nationalities Congress.[55] 'Dissimilation' extolled the value of excluding foreign elements from the *Volksgemeinschaft*, ostensibly for their own good and purportedly in keeping with the Nationalities Congress' campaign from 1925 against cultural assimilation. In practice, as propounded by Max Hildebert Boehm, the doctrine foreshadowed Nazi plans to forge a national community based on race as distinct from culture. While dissimilation allowed opting for one nationality alone, this element of choice effectively vanished in 1933. Hitler's maltreatment of Jews in the Reich indicated compulsory 'exclusions' from the German *Volksgemeinschaft* as the order of the day. Following a call from the Second Jewish World Congress, Leo Motzkin, executive chairman of the committee of Jewish delegates in the Nationalities Congress, therefore made the participation of Jewish groups at the coming Berne congress dependent on the congress explicitly condemning Germany's actions as being against human rights and against the minority movement. Motzkin also asked for a full debate and a clear resolution on 'dissimilation and nationality rights'—the subject of Schiemann's proposed lecture at the congress.

Depressingly, the presidium of the Nationalities Congress refused Motzkin's demand, arguing that rules prohibiting discussion at the annual conference of specific complaints against governments still stood. That was strictly the case. However, when the congress opened on 16 September it quickly became clear just how far the organisation was now in thrall to Reich policy. In the absence of the Jews—and, as it happened, of Paul Schiemann—the German delegates pushed through a resolution favouring the 'dissimilation from the body of the nation of those of different nationality and especially of different race'. Admittedly the meeting acknowledged at the same time that those made into minorities through dissimilation were entitled to strive for the rights endorsed by the Nationalities Congress, but this offered no immediate comfort to Jewish groups.[56] Leo Motzkin resigned his seat on the congress presidium on 26 September 1933, while the plenary body's failure to condemn what was happening in the Reich made it virtually impossible in practice for Jewish groups to continue working in the Nationalities Congress.

This bleak situation ultimately frustrated Schiemann and Josip Wilfan in their personal attempt from the autumn of 1933 to patch up a compromise with the Jewish minority leaders for the sake of the Nationalities Congress. Ewald Ammende's explanation for the continuing impasse with the Jewish delegates in 1934 merely reinforced the disreputable reasoning behind the 1933 resolution on dissimilation. Jewish delegates, Ammende told Schiemann in a letter from London on 16 June 1934, were fighting not for the Jewish *people* in the Reich but for Jews assimilated to the German majority. '"German nationals of Jewish religion" who come here [to Britain] have but one wish, Ammende opined', 'which is to assimilate themselves in England as quickly as possible. Most don't think of preserving or fighting for their people's rights.'[57]

For Jewish minority leaders to be kept from the congress flatly contradicted Paul Schiemann's long-standing effort to integrate Jews into the work of the Nationalities Congress. He had tried earlier without success to persuade Jewish bankers in the Reich to help with the membership costs of Jewish minority delegates. However, he was not uncritical of Jewish strategy, in spite of his outright opposition to the line taken since 1933 by Hasselblatt and others in the Verband der deutschen Volksgruppen. Though supportive of the

Zionist cause, and indeed the sole voice on the Verband in 1927 favouring the admission of Zionists to the Nationalities Congress, Schiemann also censured Zionists—as we saw—for asking the minorities movement for support in setting up a *state*. On similar grounds, and 'precisely as a resolute opponent of anti-Semitism', he cautioned Zionists in 1932 against insisting on Old Hebrew as the language of instruction in Latvia's Jewish schools, where in fact Yiddish was mostly spoken. Such actions, like nationalism, aspired to control and so would be incompatible with the minorities ideal 'which is a defensive ideal'.[58]

The issue of dissimilation was made more problematic in that Zionist leaders themselves treated the assimilation of German Jews to Germany as a betrayal of Jewishness, making it tactically easier for the Verband der deutschen Volksgruppen to refuse to condemn anti-Semitism in the Reich. Hasselblatt buttressed this position by arguing: 'The Jews of eastern Europe are expressly minorities, those in western Europe in no sense a minority.'[59] Schiemann, who in February 1933 in the *Allgemeines Jüdischer Familienblatt* branded anti-Semitism 'the most unhappy manifestation of national propaganda', also recognised a general distinction between the situation of Jewish populations in the east on the one hand and those in western Europe on the other. Unlike Hasselblatt he argued that anti-Semitism might persuade German Jews to take the same route as Jews in eastern Europe by becoming a national minority. The editor of this Jewish paper happily underlined the importance of Schiemann's analysis of the perversions of democracy but expressed misgivings 'about his [Schiemann's] conclusions for Germany's Jews and their self-emancipation.'[60]

However, Schiemann's initial thinking on this issue hardened into certainty as matters grew worse for Jews in Germany. In 'Minorities and Jewish Question', published in April 1936, he tried first to develop the case for Jews *as a minority*. The description was already true, as all agreed, of Jews in eastern Europe, but Schiemann observed that it also applied to Zionists who, adapting to Western concepts, wanted the Jewish community also to be a language community. Equally, the term 'minority' fitted Orthodox Jews, for whom traditionally 'national community' and 'religious community' coincided. Yet what of German Jews? Schiemann branded Germany's anti-

Semitic laws a 'catastrophe' precisely because Reich Jews had become members of the state that embodied the national culture. How, then, could they be a minority? First, because although Western Jews had joined the German or Polish or Russian culture, Schiemann insisted that they saw themselves in the first instance as Jews. Only baptism or initiation in another religion constituted the definitive act of leaving the Jewish community. Secondly, the consciousness of being Jews was heightened by Germany's persecution.

Had central European Jewry not been a national minority, Schiemann inferred, it had become one through having to deflect hatred and contempt. In spite of that, 'the closer one moves from eastern Europe to the West, the more obviously is the Jewish question separated from the minority question.' Schiemann's desire to change that reality gives the key to his treatment of dissimilation. By arguing that forced dissimilation of the *already* assimilated amounted in effect to renewed and violent assimilation, he tried to bring what was happening to German Jews within the remit of the Nationalities Congress. He called for Jewish leaders to admit that atomised Jewish parties and groups could not solve the problem and encourage German Jews to declare themselves a national minority. 'If the majority of Jews belong to a national minority, then they also have the right to complete equality with all other citizens.' Schiemann's point was that it would be problematic for Reich governments to dispute minority rights as such, given the millions of *Auslandsdeutschen*.[61]

To Schiemann's intense regret, Germany was spared far greater embarrassment and difficulty in the international arena than might otherwise have been the case if Jewish leaders had not reaffirmed the non-minority character of German Jewry. For example, Hasselblatt, in his quest to prevent discussions of the Jews in Germany at the Nationalities Congress planned for London in 1937, blatantly exploited the cynical logic behind the 1933 congress resolution. He stressed that 'the rejection of assimilation by the congress justified accepting the admissibility of dissimilation, that is to say an exclusion of the foreign national element from the body of a people possessing a nation-state'.[62]

Hasselblatt matched the effort Schiemann expended in trying to link the Jewish and minorities questions in keeping the two issues apart. Few things could have saddened Schiemann more than to witness the organisation to which he had once attached such hope helping Hitler's regime to isolate the German Jews from the European minorities' movement. Not surprisingly, by the time he published his 'Minorities movement and the Jewish question' Schiemann had already abandoned the Nationalities Congress. What he refused to give up was his quest to shame the enemies of minority rights.

11. Full Circle

The fraught political circumstances attending Schiemann's re-settlement in Austria were highlighted by the abortive coup of the Austrian Nazis on 25 July 1934, resulting in the murder of the Chancellor Engelbert Dollfuss. To Schiemann's relief the restoration of order came quickly under the new Chancellor Kurt von Schuschnigg. In the calmer political atmosphere that ensued he slowly battled towards better health, but his financial circumstances were constrained. The pension from the *Rigasche Rundschau* hardly compensated for his lost income as editor, while the support he once had for subsistence and travel on behalf of the European minorities' movement had also vanished.

On 1 March 1934, from his apartment at 6 Bergstrasse in Mödling near Vienna, he had written to Nicolai von Berg: 'I am living here with my wife, very quietly and pleasantly but extremely short of money. I no longer get anything from the Verband [der deutschen Volksgruppen] and would not wish to ask for it, although must still occupy myself more, especially if Ammende leaves me out. What I would like would be regular press reporting. But where is there anything for me today? Can you help me in any way in this respect?'[1]

For Schiemann work as a journalist remained hard to find. The writ of Hitler's regime ran widely in Europe. Even so, the reaction in Austria against the murder of Dollfuss made Vienna a suitable place for Schiemann to campaign against the relentless 'coordination' of the *Auslandsdeutsche.* He was able to write articles for the *Christliche Ständestaat,* albeit to his irritation subject to some censorship by the paper.[2] His writings mostly appeared in the anti-Nazi newspaper *Der Deutsche in Polen,* published by Eduard Pant. Until 1935 a deputy in the Silesian assembly and a member of the Polish Senate, Pant spoke for the Christian, Catholic opposition to National Socialism among Germans in Upper Silesia. Schiemann's articles promised to give the publication a wider impact than it enjoyed inside Poland.[3] Whether Schiemann derived significant monetary reward from his association with this extraordinary newspaper—inexplicably overlooked by historians of National Socialism—is doubtful.

The course the two men charted against the 'coordination' of German minorities put them on a final collision course with the Verband der deutschen Volksgruppen after a further shift of influence towards Nazi elements at its conference in Gablonz in 1935. It was presaged in a memorandum of September 1934 from the chief executive of the Deutsche Stiftung, Erich Krahmer-Möllenberg, to the foreign minister Joachim Ribbentrop. Krahmer-Möllenberg urged, apart from cultural and economic support, 'a systematic integration of the Volksgruppe in foreign policy'.[4] In the course of the conference at Gablonz (26–29.8.1936) Konrad Henlein, actively encouraged by Ewald Ammende and Werner von Hasselblatt, became the Verband's new leader. Paul Schiemann, who had not been invited to Gablonz, opposed the change with Eduard Pant from afar.[5] For the first time Schiemann was not elected to the management committee. As a result he also sent Josip Wilfan a formal letter of resignation from his vice presidency of the Nationalities Congress.

In the letter, published in *Der Deutsche in Polen*, Schiemann excused his absence through illness from the last two congresses and expressed sorrow at giving up work so close to his heart and parting from friends with whom he had campaigned for ten years. Though leaving at an unfavourable moment for 'our movement', he believed in the ultimate victory of 'our ideals'—imbued with 'inner truth and ethical imperative.' Commenting on the 'utterly transparent manoeuvres' at Gablonz, Pant's paper recalled how at Geneva Schiemann once had the ear of Europe and its statesmen. 'He has often been called the thinker of the minorities movement. And rightly.' Schiemann 'created the ideology of this movement' and was 'a sacrifice of National Socialist intolerance. To say that is our duty today.'[6] Schiemann, as his letter of resignation made plain, had no intention of ceasing to work for the cause of European minorities in whatever capacity he could.

Nevertheless, his departure from the Verband der deutschen Volksgruppen in 1935, like that of Pant and Nicolai von Berg, poignantly underlined the generational and ideological shifts that had overtaken the European minorities movement since its inception in the early 1920s. At Gablonz the Verband finally turned its back on the principle of solidarity with other minorities. Given the dominance of the German groups, it also ended hopes of the Nationalities Congress functioning independently of Nazi foreign policy.[7] Eckhard von Schack, German ambassador to Latvia, provides one example among many of the push to control German minorities in 1935. He met Rüdiger's reluctance to involve the Bewegung in the work of the Deutschbaltische Volksgemeinschaft with the threat of withdrawing Reich subsidies.[8] When Rüdiger decided he had had enough and resigned from his position later in 1935, Schack lost no time in reminding the successor, Erich Mündel, what was expected of him.[9] The pressure on the *Auslandsdeutschen* to conform to Berlin's priorities increased with the setting up in 1936 of the Volksdeutsche Mittelstelle (VOMI). It incorporated the Deutsche Stiftung the following year.

'World history would have lost its sense', *Der Deutsche in Polen* proclaimed on 10 June 1934, 'if Paul Schiemann's chapter in the annals of the German minorities were to be closed.' Indeed, his publications after 1933 continued to display verve under the most adverse conditions. His immediate and urgent task was to analyse and publicise the disastrous impact of National Socialism on *Auslandsdeutschen*, with the hope of persuading them to return to the internationalist ideals first prompting the creation of the Verband der deutschen Minderheiten in 1922. On the face of it the cause was already lost, in so far as Henlein's leadership of the Verband favoured German groups pushing for complete separation from the host-state. However, Schiemann took heart for a while from the fact that in spite of Nazi triumphs among Germans in former Reich areas, the old leaders were hanging on in other regions, including the Baltic.[10]

Thrust from the centre stage of the Verband der deutschen Volksgruppen, now appropriated by his enemies, Schiemann planned a new organisation for German minorities. He took the first steps towards forming the Deutsche Verband zur nationalen Befriedigung Europas (hereafter Deutsche Verband) at a meeting of German groups in Vienna in February 1936. Other key figures included Eduard Pant from Poland and Carl Kostka from Czechoslovakia. All hoped if possible to attract private funding to avoid dependence on any government. 'I was pleased with my conference,' Schiemann wrote to Nicolai von Berg later in the month, shortly before turning sixty. 'Do you believe that Berlin will do something against me via the *Rundschau*?'[11]

He celebrated his sixtieth birthday in Vienna on 29 March. *Der Deutsche in Polen* reported the event and was 'filled with joy' at this 'pioneer and herald of morally-founded minority rights' recovering from severe illness to resume his work on behalf of Germans abroad.[12] Wolfgang Wachtsmuth, who had missed signing a birthday greeting sent by Schiemann's old colleagues on the CGBP, wrote privately, regretting the end of the 'the Schiemann era' in Latvia. What that meant 'is becoming ever clearer even to your opponents, as we watch what you won demolished bit by bit.' According to Wachtsmuth, even Wittram—'your greatest political enemy'—said: 'Over the past century German Baltdom has produced only two really significant politicians, two politicians on the grand scale: Fölkersahm and Schiemann.'[13] What Schiemann made of the comment can only be guessed. A few years later Wittram still insisted that the *Rigasche Rundschau* had 'completely reneged on the task of *völkisch* education for the national group'.[14]

It was clearly not without sadness that Schiemann found himself, within a month of his birthday, writing the obituary of Ewald Ammende, who died from diabetes at the age of forty-four on a visit to Peking. Schiemann's past exasperation with the problematic Ammende is only barely hinted at. There was a note of reproach in his recording of his co-founder's particular closeness to the German groups in the Nationalities Congress, but he described Ammende as a 'preacher in the wilderness' at Geneva. 'He accomplished much through the force of his personality, sometimes with abruptness and a heavy hand, but the memory remains of a genuine, idealistic personality wholly committed to his cause.'[15] From a very different angle Boehm confessed to a sneaking regard and even genuine love for Ammende, 'in spite of the annoyance he could also cause us', before describing, no doubt with pleasure, how the 'wheel of high policy' had finally rolled over Ammende's 'strange nationalities circus'.[16] Boehm certainly would not have welcomed Schiemann's new initiative to revive the values promoted by the Nationalities Congress in its early years.

When Schiemann's and Pant's Deutsche Verband unveiled itself before a wider public in April 1937 it launched at the same time a regional sub-group for Germans in Poland. The gathering was disappointingly small.[17] It was significant that of the key figures who joined Schiemann on the presidium of the new association only Kostka had also been a delegate to the Nationalities Congress. Most German minority groups failed to send delegates, doubtless fearing the loss of material support from the Reich or worse. Contrary to Schiemann's intentions a conspiratorial air thus hung over his venture.[18] The Deutsche Verband endured constant attacks from the Nazi-dominated *Auslandsdeutsche* press, more often than not resorting to the personal. 'The new national catechism', Schiemann tartly observed, 'has even excluded balanced debate from German intellectual life.'[19] He met his critics with the claim that only his association—comprising old 'non-coordinated' fighters of the minorities' movement—remained true to the original ideal—now abandoned by the Verband der deutschen Volksgruppen; that the *Auslandsdeutschen* must determine their own fate, rather than live at the whim of prevailing international conditions.[20]

Conditions had undoubtedly worsened for German minorities. Apart from Germany's departure from the League of Nations and the German-Polish non-aggression pact, Poland abrogated its international obligations towards minorities in September 1934. Schiemann freely acknowledged the predicament for the *Auslandsdeutschen.* Nevertheless, he argued that 'rightly seen' the biggest threat arose from the ideological battle *inside* national groups. That of course had been the gist of his final speech to the Verband der deutschen Volksgruppen in 1932. Yet now, five years later, 'the idea that in each state only the racially pure representative of a people has unrestricted citizenship rights has been elevated to a national axiom.'[21] Rather than blaming events, Schiemann argued, politicians forced to watch their life's work subverted must critically examine their own part in the process. 'That certainly applies to the *Auslandsdeutsche* leaders.' Many of them, having made the minorities' ideology of nationality rights 'a moral force founded in international acceptance of law', only undermined their cause by embracing National Socialism. 'How could this happen?' Schiemann asked; 'how could the defence of the right to national existence lead to nationalism, which by its nature is the true enemy of this defensive struggle?'[22]

The question was a focal point of a collection of his articles in a short book, *Ein Europäisches Problem*, published in 1937 and partly serving as a programme for the Deutsche Verband zur Befriedigung Europas. True to his own maxim, Schiemann admitted his responsibility, with that of other older *Auslandsdeutsche* leaders, for promoting the concept of a supra-national *Volksgemeinschaft* embracing all Germans. He did not, of course, regard the *idea* as misconceived; it continued to provide a key to his vision of Europe. Moreover, most of his generation had not let their desire for a supranational community stop them from serving the states they lived in. The trouble was that he and other minority leaders failed to foresee the mood of a post-war generation who rejected the idea that 'a special fate imposes a special obligation too' and for whom the *Volk* ideal 'displaced thoughts of the homeland'. The development threatened to subvert the concept of the supranational *Volksgemeinschaft* advocated by the nationalities movement by transforming it to one of *race.* 'It is the task of the nationalities movement', Schiemann warned, 'to make absolutely clear the confinement of the *Volksgemeinschaft* to a *cultural* community, thereby once more making room for genuine minorities work.'[23]

That was the immediate priority of the 'new work' of re-education on which he and his fellow veteran fighters in the Deutsche Verband embarked in 1937. He reasoned that a minority allied with National Socialism forfeited the moral right to protest against similar doctrines used in its host state. For Germans abroad to agree to a state's or a people's right to take away citizenship on the grounds of race would provoke others to treat them in the same way. Schiemann was particularly troubled by the support for anti-Semitism in the 'coordinated' minority German press outside the Reich. It served only the interests of the Hitler state.[24] Anti-Semitism 'cannot from its very essence be reconciled with the minority rights position'.[25] In sum, tempting as it might be for Germans abroad to profit from their co-national state's resurgent power, there *could* be no guarantee that such favourable circumstances would last. Nationalist subversion of the supranational *Volksgemeinschaft* was forcing *Auslandsdeutschen* to abandon the principles on which their very existence as a minority rested: loyalty to the homelands they inhabited and non-involvement in the politics of the motherland.

The problem was not of course unique to Germany. Schiemann admitted in 1937: 'National minorities have ceased to be, or to want to be, in charge of their own policy, and have become objects of European states policy. With this the European nationalities movement has lost its most valuable quality, and today the nationalities question more than ever threatens the peace of Europe.'[26] The valuable quality to which he referred was precisely the dual allegiance—on the one side to a homeland and on the other to a different national culture. This was what was meant by being a national minority. In launching the Deutsche Verband he defiantly reaffirmed: 'The problem of the national minority is the problem of a legal demarcation between the tasks and spheres of authority of state community and national community.'[27] In these later writings, however, there is more pronounced stress on the minority's duties and obligations to the host state, including military service, as well as more explicit recognition of the importance of preserving the stability and integrity of the state.[28] Nevertheless, supranational cultural communities—which could not vanish while minorities existed—still offered to Schiemann the only real hope for lasting reconciliation in Europe.

With the deepening of the European crisis through 1937, ideas of restraining the creeping Nazification of the *Auslandsdeutschen* were harder to sustain. As the likelihood of war became impossible to ignore, the second major theme of Schiemann's later journalism came to the fore: this was the connection between the turmoil in the minorities movement and the disorder in Europe. It disturbed Schiemann that minorities were still seen, even by well-disposed states, as a special problem, somehow distinct from world events. To him it was self-evident that any ordering of Europe that ignored the problem of national minorities inside states contained the seeds of its own downfall. In urging that 'the minority problem is a European problem' he meant literally that it affected every state, even those without nationality groups or only with small ones within them—'for there is no European state whose fate could be independent of Europe's fate as a whole.'[29] He elaborated on the idea, analysing what he saw as the ongoing battle between nationalist and 'European' trends in the 1930s. The 'trend' favouring what Schiemann described as world revolution on the ruin of separate states and western culture he curtly branded as alien to Europe and not rooted in Western humanity.

While the nationalist trend exalted the state, 'the European trend does not contest the value and importance of the individual state, or deny that the ties in the state sphere offer the necessary preconditions for preserving law, morality and freedom. But it indicates at the same time that the rightful and therefore lasting success of the individual state can only be achieved when Europe as a whole is thriving in the spirit of the laws of Christian-western morality.' It was not that Schiemann considered the nationalist trend to be consciously *anti*-European. Rather, its fanatical belief in its uniqueness made it equate Europe's wellbeing with its own success. Since nationalists in every state shared this conviction, the peace of Europe was increasingly at risk. 'Nationalism proclaims the maxim: "state or national interest before that of the individual". The European adds to this the phrase: "the common good of Europe before that of the individual state or individual nation".'[30]

Schiemann's point was that the nationalities movement had espoused the 'European tendency' from the outset. It alone gave hope of a solution to the task allotted by fate to minorities, of reconciling good citizenship *vis-à-vis* their host-states with commitment to their own culture. In this context he also favoured terms like '*Lettländer*' or '*Estländer*' rather than 'Latvians' or 'Estonians'. This helped, like the expressions 'Britons' or 'Swiss', to revive the concept of community. Much sensitivity might disappear, he thought, if an Upper Silesian were asked not to be 'a good Pole' but a 'good citizen of Poland' (*Polenländer*).[31] Equally, he felt that there would be a greater likelihood of mutual tolerance if people were persuaded that all work for national culture in Europe was also work on behalf of European culture; and that political collaboration would be easier if it was assumed that every state had an obligation to preserve and strengthen Europe. Nobody, Schiemann argued passionately, was more committed than minorities to the duty of Europe's statesmen and peoples to eliminate war from the continent. 'The national minorities are good Europeans because of their fate.'[32]

The thought that many Russians now living in Estonia and Latvia have yet to pass Schiemann's test for good citizenship is a reminder that he specifically excluded from the category 'national minority' those who merely lived as members of their nation in 'foreign countries.' 'Only when they perceive the country in which they live as their country, that they are bound to their homeland by the roots of their historical being, that they share responsibility for the well being of the territory in which they were born, do they become a genuine minority.' Amidst the growing unrest he reminded readers that far from being a union of repressed peoples, the congress had been a community of ideas arising from a shared fate, setting out to convince the world that a synthesis *was* possible between the ideas of 'state' and 'nation'.[33] Its original agenda 'asked of the ethnic community its confinement to cultural purposes and the renunciation of political goals outside the given realm of state. It demanded of the state the renunciation of cultural and national totality.'

The very fierceness of the economic rivalry of the 1930s deepened Schiemann's feeling that economic forces would ultimately work to promote the synthesis of state and nation. He kept returning to the fact that 'viable economic space' in Europe did not coincide with the territory of the individual states. The selfish state fixated on national sovereignty—'the irrational state'—portended material ruin for Europe by perpetuating the fiction that it could control its own economy.[34] Schiemann tackled the theme in two linked essays for the *Oesterreichische Volkswirt* early in 1938. Assuming the economic development of a territory to be subject to its own laws, and the object of rational economic policy to be to recognise and adapt to them, he posited first an inherent conflict between 'ideology' and 'economy'. It applied both in democracies, where the pursuit of power produced economic 'programmes' directed at the interests of those giving support to the party in question, and dictatorships, where the opposition between 'ideology' and 'economy' was 'raised to an axiom, and the attempt was made to resolve the tasks of state according to ideological tenets, irrespective of considerations of the pace and laws of the economy'. It went without saying that in excluding national minorities from working for the overall good the 'irrational state' was further damaging itself.[35]

If the acceptance of national diversity within the state was a precondition of its economic viability, so Europe's strength ultimately depended on the same diversity. Schiemann's maxim—'joint work by different nationalities can only derive from their difference'—applied to the state and to Europe as a whole. It followed that 'small states' had a vital role to play. 'The multiplicity of states is itself no burden but an enrichment of Europe.'[36] The bleak alternative that Schiemann envisaged to a common European economic space, revelling in the multiplicity of cultures that made up the whole of western culture, was the inevitable creation by force of a grossly enlarged nationalist economic realm, at the expense of the small nations.[37] 'The removal of national minorities and their uniqueness from the life of a state', he warned, 'must bring with it cultural deprivation for that state. The elimination of small peoples from the life of the European states must lead ultimately to the arrest and paralysis of European cultural life.'[38]

The threat to Europe's variegated culture in the 1930s turned Schiemann's thoughts again and again to his comparison between religion and culture and to the fanatical European wars of religion three centuries earlier. In 1936 he wrote: 'Just as a modern state, whose majority holds to a specific religious belief, is willing for the sake of freedom of conscience to declare itself a-confessional, so the nation state, which arose from the need for national tolerance, will very probably be able to declare itself a-national as soon as the independent cultural development of the majority is secured through founding of the state. From this moment the economic and political tasks, which derive above all from the geographical location of the state, come to the fore and constitute the common bond for all citizens, irrespective of nationality. In all areas of public life, with the exception of national culture, all citizens are directly and equally interested in the further progress of the state, and that will depend on whether all citizens are given equal possibilities in free competition for work and development.'[39]

Schiemann admitted sadly that 'the political control of nationality endangers the existence of Europe in the same way as the politicisation of confession centuries ago. At that time religious wars threatened the destruction of Europe. Only the separation of confession and state averted this menace. Will it be possible now, at this time of gravest danger, to achieve the separation of state and nationality?'[40]

The build-up to the German occupation of Austria in March 1938 provided an answer. For Schiemann to remain any longer in Vienna would almost certainly have resulted in arrest and imprisonment by the invaders as a reward for his public and unrelenting anti-Nazi line.[41] As in 1903, returning fresh from his studies in Germany, as in the summer of 1919 when he became a full time politician, and as in the summer of 1932, coming back from an enforced absence caused by illness, so now Schiemann, with his wife, returned to his home country. He would not leave it again. That he acted wisely is confirmed by a confidential report on Schiemann for the German government, dated 13 April 1938:

'In his political conception he parted from the leading Balts. He was not conservative as they were, but had liberal ideas. Rejection of all nationalist tendencies. For him the state was no more than the idea of a territorial community.' Later, referring to the Nationalities Congress, the report noted: 'Ever closer link with Geneva and to the governments in Berlin. Slide to the left wing of the Democrats.' It continued: 'National circles among German Balt *Volksgruppen* against him. Strongest protest when he was awarded the Goethe medal of the German Reich at the end of 1932.' The writer doubted illness as the reason for Schiemann's move to Vienna in July 1933, though acknowledging that he had been ill. 'In Vienna nothing was heard of him at first.' Then came the publication of *Ein Europäisches Problem* and the setting up of the Deutsche Verband. 'This seeks to restore, inside and outside the state, the legal order threatened by National Socialism. Europe must free itself from grip of National Socialism; a European culture must be created.' 'Schiemann is dangerous', the report concluded, 'because he is politically shrewd and intellectually exceptionally fertile. He can also be dangerous from Riga—where he returned after the seizure of power in Austria.'[42]

However, it has rightly been said that in leaving Austria for Riga Schiemann 'took the road to isolation, to an exile in his homeland'.[43] Among the influential Baltic Germans in Riga his critics easily outnumbered those who had affectionate feelings towards him. 'Look at the "German" Schiemann', ran the taunt, 'who has to run from the "Germans".'[44] Living modestly with his wife from 1938 onwards in their small house in the Riga suburb of Hagensberg, Schiemann was now politically neutralised by the shifts in power that had taken place within the Baltic German community since his departure in 1933. Rüdiger's successors at the head of the Deutschbaltische Volksgemeinschaft in Latvia—first Erich Mündel and then, from 26 November 1938, Alfred Intelmann who was not a member of the Bewegung but a confessed admirer of nazi Germany—progressively involved Kroeger and his henchmen in their work. Indeed, Kroeger's followers celebrated the date of Intelmann's appointment at the Delegate Assembly of the Deutschbaltische Volksgemeinschaft on 26 November as the 'Day of the *Machtergreifung*'.[45]

That Schiemann remained defiant is clear from the obituary he wrote for Eduard Pant on 13 November 1938 in *Der Deutsche in Polen*. Pant, incidentally, had been, like Schiemann, the subject of a Reich risk assessment from a similar source the previous year. 'Dr Pant has variously preoccupied us. Unfortunately, never in a happy way.'[46] Schiemann's headed his recollection of Pant 'A leader dies'. It allowed him to look at the current vogue for the charismatic 'leader'—behind whom stood the jubilant masses whom he commanded—only to ask if a 'leader' might not also be somebody apart from the masses—without power and popularity, struggling against the tide and 'blessed only with a firm belief in the good in the world'. 'Such a path is martyrdom, the narrow path it treads one of suffering, rich in disappointment and pain, far from the noise of victory. Eduard Pant was such a leader.'[47] This passionate eulogy for a man who died without even seeing a 'glimmer of light' on the horizon, 'but with the firm belief that the battle he has had to fight must eventually lead to victory', also graphically expressed Schiemann's own non-surrender.

That much is evident from one of his last articles for *Der Deutsche in Polen* in April 1939, 'End of the Nationalities Movement?' In it he conceded that minority rights campaigners would be deceiving themselves if they denied that the objective grounds for achieving their goals had vanished. It pained him to admit that the aim of creating a legal basis for peaceful coexistence between different nationality groups in the territory of any given state for the overall good of the common home had been for some groups in the Nationalities Congress, notably the Sudeten Germans, no more than a cloak to cover their drive for dominance. Nevertheless, the main thrust of his article was to restate categorically the values and aims on which the congress had been founded. His reasoning? 'The nationalities movement, which has already made its way in the face of nationalism from the pre-war era, will do so again in the future against similar resistance.' The imminence of war was itself proof that a forceful solution to nationality conflicts—that is to say a solution based purely on the prevailing power balance—could never be lasting.[48]

That balance soon impacted in the most dramatic way on Baltic Germans. Other than criticism in the German press about their treatment by the Ulmanis government, Baltic Germandom had found little reflection in nazi foreign policy before 1939. For his part, Ulmanis combined initial admiration for Hitler's achievements with anxiety about the intentions of Latvia's Baltic Germans. That had been clear from the brief imprisonment of Kroeger and some of his followers in 1936. Even so, the absence of any overt pressure from the Reich on Latvia facilitated outwardly normal relations between Riga and Berlin. With the Austrian *Anschluss*, the ensuing crisis over the Sudeten Germans and the transparent weakness of Britain and France at the Munich meeting in September 1938, Latvian press treatment of Baltic Germans also became less hostile. Prospects seemed fair for a more 'realistic' stance by the Latvian government towards the Baltic German community, even to the extent that the autonomy project was again revived in the wake of Munich.[49]

The notion aroused enough interest in Berlin for a special discussion on 6 February 1939 between relevant Auswärtiges Amt officials, including the German ambassador to Riga, Ulrich von Kotze, as well as VOMI representatives. Even so, Intelmann found it difficult to get beyond Ulmanis' intermediary, Friedrich Keyser. By the time a formal reception was at last arranged to discuss the project face to face with Ulmanis, his attitude had once more hardened. The rape of Prague, together with mounting evidence that Britain would after all resist German demands against Poland, was decisive for Ulmanis. He concluded that there was no longer a need to prioritise better treatment of Baltic Germans living in Latvia in order to improve Latvian-German relations. Jürgen von Hehn, who lived through the events, wrote: 'Instead of the hoped—for consolidation of the *Volksgruppe's* existence in its homeland through autonomy, it came in the autumn of 1939 to resettlement and, with it, the end of Baltic Germandom in Latvia, as in Estonia.'[50]

The chain of events leading to this began with the Nazi-Soviet Non-Aggression Pact of 23 August 1939. Baltic German leaders were at first relieved when they learned about the pact, unaware of the secret protocol assigning Latvia and Estonia to the Soviet sphere of influence (later extended to Lithuania and half of Poland by a supplementary pact of 28 September). However, the outbreak of war in

Europe and the Soviet advance into eastern Poland, coupled with rumours of partition, quickly spread anxiety through the Baltic German community.[51] Kroeger's worst fears were realised when he heard in strict confidence from Himmler at the Führer HQ in Zoppot, on 25 September 1939, of the secret protocol to the German-Soviet pact. The Reichsführer SS, Kroeger recalled, was surprised to hear his impassioned plea that Baltic Germans could be seriously at risk in the event of a Bolshevik takeover of the Baltic countries, in spite of any German-Soviet agreement, but promised to talk the matter over with Hitler.[52]

For both Himmler and Hitler humanitarian considerations were not paramount, and several factors fed into the Führer's decision on 26 September to evacuate Baltic Germandom *en masse*. The Reich had an interest in resettling the newly-retaken West Prussia and Warthegau with solid German elements, while younger Baltic Germans promised more recruits for the Waffen-SS; foreign policy concerns played a part, in that any action against Baltic Germans during a Soviet occupation of the Baltic countries could impact negatively on German-Soviet relations. Finally, Himmler undoubtedly relished the expansion of his own domain, in so far as VOMI, an agency of the SS, would carry out the resettlement. On Hitler's instructions, his foreign minister Ribbentrop quickly secured Molotov's agreement that no difficulties would be put in the way of those of German origin wishing to go to the Reich or resettle in the German sphere of interest.[53] Even as Hitler made his Reichstag speech on 6 October, proclaiming his regime's general intention to re-settle in the Reich the German groups from outside, hasty preparations for the *Umsiedlung* were already under way.

The sheer pace of events surprised Stalin and his colleagues in Moscow. Even the leaders of Baltic Germandom in Latvia and Estonia were not told officially of the resettlement through VOMI till 2 October 1939. The German ambassadors to the Baltic countries were no better informed. They had assumed that mutual assistance pacts negotiated by Russia with Estonia (28 September) and Latvia (5 October) postponed the immediate threat of full occupation. On 6 October they were told to prepare for resettlement irrespective of domestic considerations in the Baltic states and that the first transportation ships were already at sea. When Intelmann informed the presidium of the *Volksgemeinschaft* in Latvia of the action on the evening of 6 October he made no mention that Hitler had allocated the Baltic countries to the Soviet sphere. Instead he resorted to the Führer's Reichstag speech calling Germans home for new duties in the Reich. All present, apparently, saw the real reason for haste as the imminent arrival of the Bolsheviks. It could hardly be admitted officially under the circumstances of the Nazi-Soviet non-aggression treaty.[54]

Paul Schiemann knew no more than most Baltic Germans of these preparations until the news burst upon the community. It was barely a month before the first boatload of settlers left Riga on 7 November, following the German-Latvian agreement of 30 October on the details of the resettlement. By 15 December 1939 it is likely that 87 % of the Baltic Germans in Latvia had been resettled, showing the remarkable solidarity among the group as a whole when it came to the crunch. Remaining were the elderly and ill; those related to Latvians; ones who could not give up employment or professional duties; individual priests in Latvian parishes; the many Germans married to Jews; and finally principled opponents of National Socialism. Almost all leading personalities and all the big German institutions—especially the church leaders, notably and fulsomely Bishop Harald Poelchau—supported re-settlement after the initial shock had passed. There was almost no organised resistance, and of the few individuals who spoke out against what was happening Paul Schiemann was by far the best known.[55]

His attempts to wage counter—propaganda were severely hampered by his personal circumstances, but other newspapers, notably the *Neue Zürcher Zeitung*, took up his interview for the Swedish paper *Sydsvenska Dagbladet* on 10 November 1939. The Swedish paper reported first the bitterness of those choosing to stay in Latvia at the huge panic propaganda in favour of mass evacuation. 'As Germans, said Dr Schiemann, as decent beings and Christians we need not obey any orders or heed any directives from outside. Many people are allowing themselves to be swayed by panic propaganda and the spectre of the Bolshevik menace, with the slogan "Whoever stays behind is no German!" Those of us who have decided not to exercise the right of option are influenced by the following considerations: We believe it an injustice, at such a critical time, to desert our home and inflict severe economic hardship through the flight of capital linked to the evacuation. We have no wish to travel to a country on whose citizens an ideology has been imposed that is contrary to our idea of religion, of the conduct of life and justice.'[56]

Not surprisingly, Schiemann was sharply critical of the German bishops. The article referred to his letter to them, attacking their stand on the question of evacuation and accusing the spiritual community of using religion to exert political influence on Latvian Germans; that is to say, to persuade them to leave and acquire German citizenship. The *Sydsvenska Dagbladet* interview also recorded the damage to the friendship between Germans and Latvians caused by the hasty evacuation and the option to become German. Already, the interviewer reported, anybody heard speaking German in the more modest restaurants was asked 'politely but vigorously' to use Latvian or Russian. According to one source, Schiemann had also sent a telegram to Kārlis Ulmanis in early October, taking up a point that the Latvian president had made in a speech published in 1937. Referring to the Latvian nation, Ulmanis had expressly included all citizens, irrespective of nationality. Schiemann wanted to voice the loyalty of 'German citizens of Latvia' who, unlike most of the 'Latvian citizens of German nationality', were not breaking with their home.[57]

Schiemann's efforts had little impact on the majority of the Baltic Germans rushing to take up the 'dictated option' of resettlement with German nationality. However, the notion that Schiemann's argument in the *Sydsvenska Dagbladet* was unconvincing to those aware of the real situation implies, against all reason, that Schiemann was no more able than Estonians and Latvians to deduce the true cause of the extraordinarily hasty evacuation.[58] The diary of Alfred Intelmann indicates that the decision was taken not to make an official complaint in Berlin about Schiemann's public stand against resettlement. In the patronising but dismissive tone characteristic of many of Schiemann's former opponents now that his career was over, Intelmann cited as his reason respect for an old man who had tried in the past to help Baltic Germans build a new life. His insinuation that Schiemann himself might have been persuaded to leave Latvia would not have convinced even his worst enemies, let alone former co-workers like Hans von Rimscha, who poured scorn on the idea.[59] To Schiemann's thinking the *Umsiedlung*—irrespective of why it happened when it did—was the logical outcome of National Socialist coordination of the *Auslandsdeutschen*.

Hitler's Reichstag speech of 6 October had expressly identified 'a reordering of ethnographic relations' as the most important task in the wake of Poland's collapse.' The idea that the 'intolerable scattering' of the German nation throughout eastern and south-eastern Europe could best be dealt with by creating 'better demarcation lines' was diametrically opposed to Schiemann's conviction that no redrawing of borders could in itself remove minority conflicts. In an unpublished manuscript dating from the spring of 1940 he again contrasted the non-interference of pre-1933 German governments in the affairs of German minorities with the interventionism of the nazi regime. Although Schiemann's own actions in 1927 indicate that he was not above requesting political support from Berlin for his fraction's position, he was broadly correct in arguing that even if enjoying help from the Reich when needed the minorities made minority policy. After 1933, however, the focus of policy shifted irrevocably towards the German government. That, in Schiemann's view, transformed the supra-state *Volksgemeinschaft*, confined to language and culture, to a 'total' community, making the German minorities a foreign policy tool of their co-national state.[60]

The logic of this development, Schiemann maintained, suggested either conquest of the host-state by the co-national, or enforced resettlement of the minority from the host-state—more exactly, conquest and resettlement. Nothing in his examination of the Reich resettlement treaties concerning Poland and the Germans in Estonia, Latvia and Italy convinced him otherwise. He found it deplorable enough that through resettlement the Reich effectively washed its hands of the future of its minority in Latvia, which in itself was likely to lead to an exodus of capital. Worse, the Reich was in effect accepting that a German minority would cease to exist there; that there would be no German parishes, no German schools and associations—in other words, no minority rights for Latvian citizens of German origin who rejected membership of the Reich through non-option. The precondition of minority rights was after all the *existence* of a minority. 'Whether a minority exists is a question not of law but of actuality, and from this alone comes what we call minority rights.'[61]

The Ulmanis government's use of resettlement to reduce German influence in a Latvia for Latvians confirmed Schiemann's analysis. According to the Latvian interior minister, Veitmanis, the 4–5,000 people hitherto counted as Germans who had not taken up the option for German citizenship by the cut-off date of 15 December 1939 'were Germans neither by inclination nor blood, for then they would not have remained here.' After 15 December, he insisted, there would be neither a German national group nor Germans in Latvia. Those choosing not to leave 'can no longer call themselves Germans'. The paper close to President Ulmanis, *Brīva zeme*, urged: 'Not everything is accomplished with the departure of the Germans. Let this event move us at the same time to free our country and people from the traces of German culture.'[62]

Who then can gainsay Schiemann's view of the *Umsiedlung* as the 'death sentence' of Baltic Germandom? He refused to accept suggestions that deprivation forced the community to leave, pointing to its 'very solid' economic position in 1939, its share of agriculture and urban business. All this, as well as the fellow-feeling with Estonians and Latvians arising from their joint community of fate in difficult times, was thrown away because of artificially induced panic and 'wrong perceptions' of national identity. What affronted his sense of moral rectitude above all was the fact that so many Baltic Germans had been prepared, despite their own past, to resettle on land confiscated from Polish landowners. In one of his later manuscripts he then used the resettlement issue to demonstrate why the Nazi approach to nationality issues must lead to all states becoming nation states, through conquest or resettlement.

He began by emphasising from his own observations in Latvia that voluntary resettlement by option, in spite of the application of huge 'moral' pressure, would not automatically produce the desired result. A significant percentage, he believed, would always wish to remain through love of *Heimat*. Therefore force would ultimately have to be deployed to lead them into a new state community. 'All the unspeakable human suffering that the Jewish laws have caused must be increased tenfold throughout Europe. And apart from the Jews there are other nationality groups with no nation-state behind them. Are they to be treated in accordance with the example of German Jewish policy and German Czech policy?' Eventually, Schiemann decided, all nation-states would prefer conquest to resettlement, since every resettlement reduces living space in the motherland. That in turn would ultimately lead to fewer but larger states, in which the smaller would have to join, willingly or not. Yet large states, with the only community being that of nationality, would also hate and envy one another, impelled by the nationalist imperative to increase the population and to find new living space.

Implicitly indicting Germany, Schiemann thus concluded that a solution seemingly to the benefit of one European state, but which at the same time damaged Europe as a whole, would finally also threaten that same state. However, in his overall assessment the damage to Europe's culture still, in spite of everything, outweighed the political dangers. For all the current calls for a 'dynamic attitude' to life, he pointed out, the only dynamism in the realm of culture and, of intellectual and artistic life was 'multi-coloured'—whereas the monochrome and uniform 'signified stagnation and torpor'. Thus he arrived at the profoundly depressing conclusion that the Nazi solution to minority problems could have only one outcome. 'The astonishingly rich-sounding orchestra of western intellectual life will be deprived of one instrument after another until finally one piercing and dissonant trumpet of war shrieks through a gigantic barracks.'[63]

By a heavy irony Schiemann, who had fiercely criticised the 'collectivism' of both nationalism and communism, was forced to spend his last few years living under both variants. What might be considered as the companion piece to his analysis of the *Umsiedlung* was an incomplete manuscript he prepared on his impressions of Bolshevik rule in Latvia between the summers of 1940 and 1941.

Latvia experienced something like its own 'phoney war' after the German invasion of Poland although, in accordance with the Soviet-Latvian mutual assistance pact of 5 October, 30,000 Soviet troops were based in the country by the end of 1939. The Soviet occupation that many in Latvia dreaded, but half hoped would not follow because of initial protestations of goodwill from Moscow, came on 17 June 1940. Not surprisingly it followed the unexpectedly rapid German victories in the west. Two days later a 'people's government' in Riga under the left-wing academic and microbiologist Augusts Kirchenšteins displaced the Ulmanis administration.[64] The new government, like those in Estonia and Lithuania, was confirmed in office by rigged elections between 14 and 15 July. In their wake 'demonstrators' in the main Baltic cities called on 18 July for the incorporation of the Baltic states in the Soviet Union. Within three days the Baltic parliaments declared their countries Soviet republics and applied for membership. Latvia was formally incorporated into the Soviet Union on 5 August 1940, bringing the end for Ulmanis. He was arrested and deported, later to die in a Soviet prison on 20 September 1942.[65]

Schiemann confessed that before the pseudo-elections he had been momentarily optimistic enough to write to the 'completely unpolitical' Kirchenšteins, known to him as president of the PEN Club, hoping that he would succeed in defending Latvia's independence during the most difficult time it had ever experienced. He also appears to have sounded out Kirchenšteins on prospects for setting up a German list, but was advised against it, given the public feeling that Germans left in Latvia were a fifth column.[66] Schiemann was advised to attach himself to a democratic Latvian list, headed by Atis Keninš, who in fact chose not to include a German candidate for reasons of international diplomacy. Schiemann put the initial Soviet hesitancy down to the supposition that since they believed themselves called to assume a position of European power, they felt obliged 'to prove that hunger and terror were not the automatic concomitants of their regime'. It had all been a charade. 'Two days before the elections police declared the list illegal; barely two weeks later most of the candidates on the list were imprisoned and never again released.'[67]

With the German-Soviet 'friendship' formally still in play the immediate targets of Soviet repression were the native Latvian intelligentsia and political strata. Although unable to secure meaningful employment as a journalist under Soviet occupation, Schiemann quietly recorded his personal impressions of the first western countries exposed to life under communism. With biting sarcasm he catalogued the constant duplicity and broken pledges to all sectors of society, not least the workers and peasants who were ostensibly the ideological darlings of the regime. The only exception to the rule in this 'true democracy' was 'the artificially sheltered cast of party comrades'. Everybody, in the shortest possible time, lost all faith in Bolshevik assurances. 'Every denial was treated as confirmation of the rumour denied.'[68] As in his 1918 pamphlets, however, he remained preoccupied above all with analysing the reasons for the 'utter failure of the bolshevist order'. He found its source in a combination of the conditions created by the nature of the Russian people, the methods derived from the October revolution, and finally Marxist theory itself.

As in 1918, he remarked on the dearth of organisational ability—the precondition for constructing a state. Not that he viewed Russians as inherently unable to organise. Rather, he located the shortcoming in their historical development, making his point by comparisons with the experience of Germany, where private individuals had been deeply implicated from the beginning of the nineteenth century in communal and provincial self-government and in a long, evolutionary development of the economy. By contrast the Russian people, faced after their release from the Tatars with the task of governing an exceptionally large realm, endured an Asiatic despotism that resorted exclusively to a corrupt and narrow bureaucracy. No room was left for private initiative among Russians or the other peoples of the Empire. The stultifying impact of official bodies carrying out all administrative and economic duties deprived the people ultimately of the singleness of purpose needed for successful enterprise; officials and workers alike became accustomed instead to the appearance of success—in Schiemann's harsh words, 'to the construction of Potemkin villages'.[69]

When it came to assessing the qualities of Soviet Russian man, Schiemann tried to take into account the massive upheavals of the previous quarter of a century, including the elimination of the entire European educated upper class through emigration or physical destruction. As a result, the juxtaposition of a highly educated intelligentsia with the broad mass of the uneducated had given way to a general loss of culture, compensated for only partly by 'specialised semi-education'. 'That is the material with which communism wanted to construct a new world. Having failed to do that in the course of twenty-three years, or to feed and clothe its citizens in a realm blessed by all of nature's resources, it deems the time to have come to make its debut in the European cultural arena.'

The sarcasm of Schiemann's account of the impact this had on the flourishing Latvian economy is relentless. According to his testimony, the machinery of terror worked relatively unobtrusively at first, so that what struck the objective observer in Riga was 'the absolutely astounding incompetence' in every sphere of activity. His description must evoke a distant memory in older citizens of present-day Latvia. 'The factories, whose smallness the press ridiculed in the very first days as a sign of economic failure, were enlarged; the office personnel especially were significantly increased, so that the previous ratio between white-collar and blue-collar numbers was completely changed. And actually these officials are constantly busy. They labour into the night far beyond the prescribed hours, working on something quite novel, on something at which the backward West has yet to arrive: communist statistics. Despite the discernible paper shortage, such a mountain of written works and printed materials is produced daily that the individual clerk has permanently bated breath and nobody asks the question: what is all this for? The graphic account of every single act of production is a thing of wonder, that the true communist reveres with a near—religious fervour.'[70]

Clearly everything that Schiemann had feared in his first writings on the Bolshevik regime he saw or claimed to see actualised in the daily reality of life during his one year under communist rule. While humour and irony marked his assessment of the economic impact of bolshevism on his own country, his revulsion is tangible to the heightened terror on the eve of the Soviet retreat before the German army in the summer of 1941, and to the surge of deportations on 13/14 June of that year. By the time the Soviet forces pulled out, some 35,000 Latvians had been imprisoned and killed or deported.[71] Schiemann was struck not just by the random, brutal and senseless cruelty of the occupiers towards Latvians, Jews and Germans in this process, but to their own ranks. 'It is known that in the flight from Riga those communists leaving on foot knelt before the cars of their comrades driving by, to beg a lift. Anybody able to see the army's flight had to watch time and again how large lorries with three or four passengers cold-bloodedly drove on, pitilessly leaving behind in the dust exhausted comrades asking to be given a lift.' Those forging this 'twenty-five year permanent revolution' were 'really no longer human beings'.[72]

Tragically for Schiemann, much the same applied to many of the Germans who occupied Latvia on 5 July 1941, twenty-two years after the ending of the first German occupation of the Baltic states had launched his full-time career as a politician.

12. Epilogue and Epitaph

On 5 July 1941, just under a fortnight after Hitler launched the long-awaited assault on Russia, German troops entered Latvia, leaving Schiemann to live out the last three years of his life under German occupation. That he was able to do this owed as much to the special arrangements made for the Baltic region within the Nazi realm as to the state of his health.

Undoubtedly the Latvian population hoped for a less harsh regime than that endured under Soviet Russian command, its destructiveness marked by the description of 1940–1 as 'the year of horrors' and prompting many at the time to view the German army as liberators.[1] What was actually in store for the Baltic area in the long run was indicated in an earlier planning document prepared by Alfred Rosenberg: 'General Commissars in Estonia, Latvia and Lithuania will take measures to establish a German protectorate there, so that it will be possible in the future to annex these territories to the German Reich. The suitable elements among the population must be assimilated and the undesirable elements exterminated. The Baltic Sea must become an inland German lake, under the protection of Greater Germany.'[2] The arrangement was unique in the occupied east.

Latvia was included with Estonia, Lithuania and Belorussia in the Reichskommissariat Ostland, one of four administrative units created in 1941 for the newly-occupied territories. Alfred Rosenberg, a Baltic German himself, whom Hitler appointed Reich Minister for the Occupied Eastern Territories (Reichsminister für die besetzten Ostgebiete—RfBO) on 16 July 1941, ruled over all four units.[3] Hinrich Lohse, the unsavoury Gauleiter of Schleswig-Holstein, served under Rosenberg as head of Reichskommissariat Ostland. Immediately subordinate to him was a General Commissioner for Latvia, Otto-Heinrich Drechsler, who in turn supervised Latvia's six regional commissariats.[4] A meeting on the Führer's special train the day before Rosenberg's appointment—between Hitler, Goering, Keitel, Bormann, Lammers and Rosenberg—agreed not to provoke resistance by revealing Germany's intentions. Aside from 'essential tasks' like 'shooting and resettlement', Germany was to act as though it had a temporary mandate to keep peace and order.[5]

The Reich therefore sanctioned the formation of Latvian—led 'directorates' with limited responsibility in agriculture, social welfare, finances, education and transport, under the overall command of a former Latvian general, Oskars Dankers. Baltic Germans were also drafted in to help with self-administration (*Landeseigene Verwaltung*). One of these was an old adversary of Schiemann's, Hugo Wittrock, who had settled in Germany in 1936. Fortunate in knowing Alfred Rosenberg from their shared student days as members of the Rubonia Corporation, Wittrock found himself appointed mayor of Riga, as well as head of the regional commissariat for the city.[6] His job was to implement what proved to be severely circumscribed self-government for Riga and its environs; Baltic German and Latvian officials alike were soon sucked into the institutional Darwinism characteristic of Nazi rule. The SS and police authorities, military leaders, Reich economic authorities and labour organisations all vied with Rosenberg for control in the east.

Rivalry was all the more intense because Rosenberg vacillated between backing the aspirations of Baltic Germans, who glimpsed a distant restoration of their influence in a Germanised Baltic, and encouragement for the majority Baltic peoples, whose support the Reich intermittently had to cultivate for the war effort.[7] The uncertainty this created among Latvians engendered both resistance and collaboration. Notable instances of the first were the Latvian National Union between 1941 and 1942 and the underground Central Council of Latvia, formed in August 1943. Of collaboration, easily the most depressing aspect was the role played by Viktor Arājs' native unit, alongside German *Einsatzgruppen*, in the brutal execution of Latvia's Jews through to the autumn of 1941.[8] Among Jews liquidated in the Riga ghetto in November were the parents, grandparents, aunts and uncles—together with their families—of a nineteen-year-old girl, Valentina Freimane, soon to find concealment in Paul Schiemann's house.

The engagement of Baltic Germans and Latvians in the administrative limbo of nazi-occupied Latvia undoubtedly helps to account for Schiemann being left to die unobtrusively at home. Wittrock and other Baltic Germans working in the administration could tolerate Schiemann in his marginalised state, which indeed they helped to maintain by supervising the ban on his journalism.[9] Few of them visited him. A number of Latvian political figures also held Schiemann in high regard. Inevitably the Reich security services monitored Schiemann's correspondence and kept an eye on the comings and goings at his house, which stood sheltered behind a high fence in a suburb across the river from the main city. Schiemann told Valentina Freimane that his wife had a relative in the German occupation authority, whose anxiety to forestall problems in the ambit of his kin 'kept a protective hand like an umbrella over the house on Atgazenes Street'.[10] Schiemann's 'private resistance' was to exploit the circumstances as far as he could to involve himself in the fate of fellow-citizens of Jewish origin. He also collected information on the destruction of Jews on Latvian soil.[11]

Nonetheless, as Dr Freimane recorded, 'The Gestapo and the threat of death were real, and we had to be careful.' How wary of Schiemann the Nazi authorities were is shown by their over-reaction to his written greetings to Wilhelm von Rüdiger, read out on the occasion of his seventieth birthday in January 1944. Rüdiger was subsequently ordered to report to the Sicherheits Dienst offices in Berlin. A young officer informed him of the inference drawn from Schiemann's letter, together with Lothar Schoeler's subsequent communication to Schiemann (which of course was opened and read); namely 'that he [Schiemann] was still playing a political role, which could not be tolerated. He had been left in peace in Riga only on condition that he kept himself completely withdrawn.' Rüdiger conceded, depressingly, that Schiemann had played 'a very dubious role in Austria' before insisting that for Baltic Germans what mattered most was what Schiemann had earlier achieved for them in Latvia. 'Schiemann is now a seriously unwell old man and we Balts cannot be expected to be wretched enough to reject him today in his serious condition.'[12]

Poor health—added to his isolation—undoubtedly spared Schiemann a worse fate. At the time of the German occupation his condition had rapidly deteriorated under the twin assault of tuberculosis and diabetes. It speaks volumes that treatment had to be given in his own home. There was a Jewish doctor, Dr Idelsohn, who ministered to Schiemann's needs, especially on his worst days. This was risky too, since as a Jew Dr Idelsohn was forbidden to practise medicine. Idelsohn, had been rescued from the ghetto, but was later recaptured and killed as the Germans evacuated Riga.[13] Wilhelm von Rüdiger, whose commercial involvement with a cement works occasionally, took him back to Latvia, saw from his first wartime visit in May 1943 that 'He [Schiemann] has become an old man and is visibly seriously ill.' When Rüdiger returned to the house in August 1943 Schiemann gave the same impression of 'grave sickness'. On his final visit in May 1944, Rüdiger had no doubt that the ever more frequent bleeding in Schiemann's lungs would prevent his brother-in-law from finishing the memoir he was working on. 'We both knew', Rüdiger recorded of saying good-bye to Schiemann on 17 May 1944, 'that we would never see each other again.'[14]

Yet the outward impression given to those who made the effort to call on Schiemann was of calm acceptance, in spite of being virtually branded an outcast by the German authorities, hardly able to leave his house and garden, save for a rare car trip with friends. 'Those who visited him during the occupation years 1941 to 1944 in his Riga refuge heard not a word of complaint, no expression of bitterness from him.'[15] The inner conviction and moral force that marked Schiemann's political career and gave him the fearless quality observed by Fircks and others remained to the end. That is also evident from the recollection of Valentina Freimane. Today she regards the two years she spent hiding as a young girl with Schiemann and his wife as 'among the most precious memories in my turbulent life'. Currently a film historian, still working in Berlin and Riga, Dr Freimane recalls Schiemann not just as a remarkable politician, publicist, democrat, anti-fascist and anti-communist, but 'primarily as a unique individual, as a human being—as a person, without whom perhaps I would not be here today.'[16]

Quite apart from the deaths of her parents and all relatives, her young Latvian husband was imprisoned and killed for aiding her escape. Entering the shelter of the Schiemann house as a twenty-year-old widow around New Year 1942/3, after months of hiding in different places, including a home for old women, was 'like arriving in paradise'. She found an 'ethical microclimate'. Her belief was confirmed 'that it is possible to retain self-esteem, honour (in the chivalrous even "quixotic" sense) and inner freedom, even in the most extreme circumstances. A person such as Paul Schiemann could only be exterminated. It was not possible to take away his freedom, to make him a slave—a hypocritical compliant servant, or to get him to collaborate. This conviction of mind and this model of virtue I have adopted in my own later life. It was a gift of fate at a moment when everything else had been lost.' In truth Schiemann also benefited from her presence.

Her father, a lawyer and financial expert from a family of Germanised Baltic Jews, who left Berlin with his family in 1936 for the safety of Riga, had also worked for the UFA Film Studios in Berlin. His wife filled their Berlin home with actors and extras, banning her husband's 'boring' business friends from the house unless their wives were interesting. As a result the young Valentina Freimane grew up in a lively bohemian environment. She later found that Schiemann enjoyed hearing about the goings-on which at the time so upset her Calvinist French governess. Nor, from her background, did she find extraordinary the fact that the well-preserved Lotte—not regarded by the authorities as a 'political person'—had a full social life 'all over the town'. Nor that there was a good-looking younger man in attendance, who was also 'like a servant of the house. He had to do chores for Schiemann and she sent him here, there and everywhere.' Touchingly the man had enormous respect for Paul Schiemann, who naturally knew what was going on. 'Schiemann liked [his wife's] way of living lightly,' Dr Freimane believed. 'She never made a tragedy out of anything. There were no problems for her.'[17]

Paul Schiemann admitted to Valentina Freimane that it was comforting in his illness to have the attendance of a good-looking woman. 'He liked to look at a young face.'[18] She soon came to realise that her multicultural and intellectual milieu also made her a valued conversational companion to Schiemann, who digressed on the past and on his own work in between dictating his memoirs. He did this, when he felt well enough, from a reclining chair or sometimes even lying down on his bed. Valentina Freimane typed up the manuscript on the second floor, where she also withdrew during the rare visits from outside. Occasionally, she was forced to hide temporarily across the avenue with Maris Melnikov—widow of the director of the Latvian

Opera, Pyotr Invovitch Melnikov—who had brought her to the Schiemanns in the first place. Dr Freimane remembers Schiemann as usually indoors, often reading alone and withdrawn in his room. Sometimes he liked to walk in the garden. Her recollections of Schiemann's asides during their working hours confirm the evidence of the memoir itself, that he retained his conviction of the rightness of his life's work to the end.

Dr Freimane is, at the time of this writing, the last living witness of Schiemann's responses to the news of momentous events from outside that reached his shrunken world. Only seldom did the two of them discuss the Jews: 'Because of such a tragedy there was little to be said.' For her part she welcomed Schiemann's simple acceptance of her and of the reality of their situation—because she refused and still refuses to regard herself as a victim. 'Victims are the ones who are dead.'[19] However, of those Latvians involved in executing Jews she remembers Schiemann asking 'How will they explain this, that they have helped the Germans?' He went on: 'The Jews, in a way unknown to them, are the lambs they [Latvians] sacrificed to the Gods to get Latvia back.' He refused to believe that Germany under Hitler would allow Latvia its independence.

In the course of 1943 he also heard about Germany setting up a Latvian Legion in the growing struggle to contain the advancing Soviet armies. Like other non-German military units fighting for the Reich, it became part of the SS.[20] Some of Schiemann's guests at the time talked of the Legion in terms of patriots fighting against Stalin for a free Latvia. When they had gone he came to the second floor where Valentina was hiding and displayed outrage at 'incompetents who wanted to cure one evil with another' and at the betrayal of 'those boys' by the absurd hopes of their leaders.[21]

Shortly before his death in 1944 a small delegation of Latvian social democrats and former parliamentarians visited Schiemann. They included Paul Kalniņš, who had briefly been imprisoned after the Ulmanis coup. Schiemann had come to like and respect these men, he told Dr Freimane, but not their illusions. On this particular occasion they showed Schiemann a manifesto for Latvian autonomy, based on the assumption of support from Sweden and the west as Germany weakened. After their departure Schiemann 'curtly' informed both Lotte and Valentina that he had refused to put his name to such 'day-dreams'. She remembers him again being 'very angry' because 'the people would pay too high a price for the self-deception and illusions of politicians.'

This was the time, Dr Freimane recorded, with the Soviet troops advancing and the return of Soviet power to Latvia looking more likely, that he felt most profoundly depressed about the Latvian cause. He told her that she was in a better position 'because anything that comes for you will be preferable.'[22] For his own part, he remained adamant that he would never go to Germany while Hitler ruled. Equally he had no illusions about what to expect once the Soviet authorities came back.

'In his aloof, stoical manner, with a touch of sad irony, he said that even if there were no Soviets, just Russians, after what has happened nobody could expect them in those first weeks to reflect on who is a "good" German and who a "bad" one.' Valentina Freimane found it painful to watch Schiemann in his dilemma. It was more and more evident that he had not long to live. He became increasingly withdrawn. With the benefit of hindsight perhaps, Dr Freimane had the sensation that he was waiting for something. She confessed to a 'mystical feeling' that finally he decided simply to let himself die, saving his integrity and freeing his wife from the obligation to live in Latvia.[23] The day after his death on 23 June 1944, aged sixty-eight, Valentina Freimane left the house to shelter once more at the Melnikovs. Before she departed Lotte Schiemann gave her a photograph of Paul Schiemann and some of his books. The two women never met again.

Paul Schiemann was buried on 26 June 1944. On strict instructions from the occupying authorities the funeral gathering was small. Gestapo agents controlled the burial. The priest conducting the rites at the small United Evangelical Church in Riga, Max Stender, was warned not to refer to Schiemann's political work, but this seems not to have prevented a warm and 'not entirely careful' address from one of his old colleagues, Werner Westermann. Paul Kalniņš said goodbye to Schiemann as a friend of the Latvian people. Hugo Wittrock was also present; he reportedly had contacts with Schiemann in his final years, but regarded this 'highly controversial figure' as 'imprisoned to the end of his life' in his democratic politics. Along with the head of the press department of the mayor's office, Carl Klassohn,

Wittrock placed a wreath on the grave of a man 'highly deserving of our city's regard' as Riga's last goodbye.[24] The irony would not have been lost on Schiemann.

Scarcely a month after his death the relevant office of the Higher SS and Police Chiefs confirmed 'in accordance with the decree of the Reich Accommodation Commissar of 20 January 1944, III, 1, Nr 4001/4/1944—that Frau Lotte Schiemann has a private dwelling in Riga/Ostland that she had to vacate by order of the Reichsführer SS.'[25] The house was subsequently used by the Army. In another act of petty vindictiveness it seems from 1940 the Nazi regime reneged on the agreement made by the German government in 1924 to pay Schiemann's life insurance premiums until he died to the Berlin insurance company Viktoria. As a result Lotte Schiemann was forced to appeal for the missing sums from the Reparations Office in Berlin after the end of the war.[26]

When she left her Riga home almost immediately after her husband's burial, she transported what she could of his books and his papers. These might already have been 'cleaned' by Schiemann on his hasty departure from Austria in 1938, and even further depleted when the boat carrying his wife's belongings back to the Reich suffered bomb damage in Stettin harbour in 1944.[27] She eventually gave the papers and books that she kept for years in German Eggenfelden to the care of an energetic collector of Baltica, Otto Bong, in the summer of 1963. The new acquisitions were incorporated into the huge private collection—the so-called Baltische Zentrale Bibliothek—that he assembled at Lüneburg during the 1970s and later. The step appears to have been taken partly in reaction to his disappointment at not being supported by the Baltische Historische Kommission, set up in September 1951.

Certainly, Bong's private correspondence with Lotte Schiemann notes that there were forces on this Commission 'diametrically opposite to the liberal views of your husband'.[28] Others confirm that Reinhard Wittram's powerful chairmanship of the Commission in the 1950s 'sublimated' conflicts within its annual historical conferences.[29] Wolfgang Wachtsmuth, who spitefully wrote of Wittram the historian 'A Plato we comprehend, a Wittram we do not', also regretted, for example, that the discussion of the *Umsiedlung* in 1959 mirrored the weight of the '*Bewegung* group' on the Historical

Commission.[30] Wittram's successor Hans von Rimscha—'industrious and intelligent but tactless'—also did not do as much as younger members in particular would have wished at the Commission's annual historical conferences to foster the sort of self-critical Baltic German historiography that flourishes today.[31]

This is not the place to follow its evolution from the earlier soul-searching of Baltic Germans resident in the then Federal German Republic. All that need be said here is that interesting as the historiography of interwar Baltic Germandom is, the most intriguing aspect remains the absence of a book-length study of its most able, intelligent and humane political figure. Michael Garleff and Helmuth Kause, German and Baltic German respectively, are notable exceptions to the prevailing disinclination of most scholars of Baltic German history to write at any length about Paul Schiemann. Kause provocatively explained that the omission was due to Baltic Germans wiping out their existence as a minority in the exodus of 1939/40. 'With the ancestral realm Schiemann…also receded. Baltic German destiny hardly encouraged the memory of Schiemann the politician, even if in the aftermath his minority policy and theory were cheerfully reclaimed as a *baltisch* contribution to the problem of Europe.'[32]

Looking back after the Second World War, Wolfgang Wachtsmuth concluded that 'a heavy air of tragedy hangs over the fate of Schiemann, this life-affirming and life-embracing man. All that he built is broken; he never attained the broad European goals he set for himself. They were mostly not understood among wider circles of his national community, indeed mostly not even known of. What he first sketched out already over thirty years ago is only now beginning to materialise.'[33] In truth, however, Schiemann surely rose above tragedy by retaining the inner peace that came from a seemingly unshakable belief in his life's work on behalf of Europe's national minorities. Even Wachtsmuth's own final sentence indicates that Schiemann's ideas *did* survive the wretched era in which he had to live, when ultra-nationalism in the form of National Socialism and fascism raised the identification of 'nation' with 'state' to an extreme pitch.

More recent clashes in Europe, most obviously on the territories of the former Yugoslavia, attest graphically to the risks of setting aside fundamental cultural and linguistic rights of nationality groups. 'Of the thirty or so conflicts going on today', it has rightly been pointed out, 'virtually every one is taking place within a state and not across a border.'[34] These are precisely the conflicts that proved most difficult to resolve, first for the League of Nations in Schiemann's day, and now in the United Nations—organisations conceived primarily to regulate clashes between states. Even the European Framework Convention on National Minorities 'simply outlines good practice for minority policy; international actors and states may only provide an advocacy role for minorities in other states.'[35]

Under sovereignty norms, in short, state governments still decide how to deal with the demands and needs of minorities within their own borders. One recent challenge to this norm was the Hungarian Status Law of 19 June 2001, allowing ethnic Hungarians (as well as their spouses and families, irrespective of ethnic origin) who are citizens in the surrounding states to apply for certificates making them eligible for certain benefits from the Hungarian state. These include educational benefits inside and outside Hungary as long as study is in Hungarian. Interestingly, one review of the legislation closes with sentiments easily transferable to Schiemann's world: 'European agreements on the rights of minority populations first arose in the late seventeenth century as a way to quell wars over religious minorities. To prevent other states from intervening on behalf of their co-religionists, states accepted religious toleration and, in this way, enhanced their sovereignty. Minority-kin state laws such as the Hungarian status law inevitably whittle away at this notion of territorially bounded sovereignty. [...] The territorial principle of nation-states is indeed a problematic phenomenon for ethnic minorities with strong ties to cross-border ethnic kin.'[36]

The selfish nation-state that Schiemann targeted as the enemy of European unity and of European-wide national cultural autonomy has yet to pass into history. However, chipping away at its rationale continues and EU enlargement brings a growing awareness of regional diversity transcending individual states. Even a British politician, who some years ago welcomed in the British context the greater attention to regional diversity and acceptance of the value of devolving tasks of central government, felt it would be an added bonus if this process also 'began to convince the British people of a new truth. In the modern world the nation state is out of date. It is too small to exercise some of its present powers and too big properly to implement others. The future belongs to Europe and the regions.'[37] The protagonist of this study would have agreed with that sentiment.

Paul Schiemann was but one member, albeit an important one, of a generation of minority leaders who have disappeared from the general view under the weight of historical attention devoted to the breakdown of the European state system. His commitment and personal courage, like that of other 'forgotten Europeans' working alongside him, are worthy of celebration in their own right. Their biting critique of the European states' obsession with national sovereignty has much to interest present advocates of a genuinely integrated Europe, as does the case they argued for European borders becoming less relevant. Paul Schiemann's example is of direct interest to a Europe still falling short of the statutory and universally recognised minority protection to which he aspired. As for the Baltic countries, his views on language laws, citizenship and multinational tolerance are of value to these states as they reconstruct themselves today. That is already recognised above all by younger academics, who have become aware that 'the roots of liberty in the Baltic nations are inseparable from the former German community.'[38]

It is fitting that some years ago a plaque was erected on the old *Rigasche Rundschau* building in the Domplatz, hailing Paul Schiemann as an opponent of all totalitarianism. In September 2000 the Latvian Academy of Sciences held a conference on 'Paul Schiemann's historical contribution to equality and harmony between national minorities in Europe and Latvia'. Schiemann's portrait, projected large on a screen, looked down appropriately on an international and multi-cultural audience. It was there among other things to celebrate the honouring of him and his wife Charlotte by the Holocaust memorial Yad Vashem in Jerusalem for saving the life of Valentina Freimane from Nazi persecution.[39] In the late afternoon, after the formal recognition of Schiemann as 'Righteous among the Peoples' and various papers and tributes, speakers and other guests went to the church where he was buried in 1944. His grave, along with those of other Baltic Germans buried in the cemetery, can no longer be identified because the Soviet authorities bulldozed the site many years before. But in the small and intimate church a short memorial service was held, at last giving Schiemann the proper recognition—denied at his funeral—that his life's work merited. For this writer it was a privilege to be present.

Notes

Chapter 1 The Making of a Democrat

1. Paul Schiemann, *Zwischen zwei Zeitaltern. Erinnerungen 1903–1919*, Lüneburg, 1979. See the short account by Valentina Freimane, 'Remembering Paul Schiemann.' *Journal of Baltic Studies.*
2. See for example Eberhard von Vietsch, *Wilhelm Solf. Botschafter zwischen den Zeiten*, Tübingen, 1961; Edgar Stern-Rubath, *Graf Brockdorff-Rantzau. Wanderer zwischen zwei Welten*, Herford and Bonn, 1968.
3. Cf. W. Schlau, ed. *Die Deutschbalten*, Munich, 1995, pp. 55 ff.
4. A. Plakans, *The Latvians. A Short History*, Stanford, CA, 1995, pp. 81 ff.
5. On the *Literaten* see W. Lenz, *Der baltische Literatenstand*, Marburg, 1953.
6. Schiemann, *Erinnerungen*, pp. 92–3.
7. Cited E. C. Thaden, ed., *Russification in the Baltic Provinces and Finland, 1855–1914*, Princeton, NJ, 1981, p. 128.
8. Cf. G. von Pistohlkors, 'Russifizierung und die Grundlagen der deutschbaltischen Russophobie' in *Zeitschrift für Ostforschung*, 1976, pp. 618–31.
9. Schlau, ed., Deutschbalten, pp. 64 ff.; M. Haltzel, *Der Abbau der deutschen ständischen Selbstverwaltung in den Ostseeprovinzen Russlands*, Marburg/Lahn, 1977, p. 1.
10. Schiemann, *Erinnerungen*, p. 69.
11. Ibid., p. 93. Cf. G. Kroeger, 'Zur Situation der baltischen Deutschen um die Jahrhundertwende.' *Zeitschrift für Ostforschung*, 17, 1968, pp. 614–15.
12. C. Schirren, *Livländische Antwort an Herrn Juri Samarin*, Leipzig, 1869, p. 174
13. Schiemann, *Erinnerungen*, p. 13.
14. Cf. R. Wittram, 'Das Reich und die baltischen Deutschen. Beiträge zur Vorgeschichte der Umsiedlung' in *Das Reich. Idee und Gestalt. Festschrift für Johannes Haller*, Stuttgart, 1940, pp. 304–47; K. Meyer, *Theodor Schiemann als politischer Publizist*, Frankfurt am Main, 1956.
15. H. Bosse, A. Taube, *Baltische Köpfe. 24 Lebensbilder aus 8 Jahrhunderten deutschen Wirkens in den baltischen Ländern*, Bovenden, 1953, p. 153. Cf. remarks of H. Donath, who knew Schiemann, 'Paul Schiemann—ein deutsch-baltischer Politiker. Was er den Letten heute sagen würde.' Photcopy of July 1994 lecture in author's possession.
16. Schiemann, *Erinnerungen*, p. 14.
17. Ibid., p. 14.
18. H. Donath, ed., *Paul Schiemann. Leitartikel, Reden und Aufsätze in Auswahl*, vol. 1, Part 1, (1980), p. xvii. Donath's collection of Schiemann's editorials and articles

is in two volumes. vol. 1: 1907–1914, has four parts (Frankfurt am Main, 1980); vol. 2: 1920–1933 (Frankfurt am Main 1986–92) has twenty parts. Hereafter citations will be Donath, + vol + part + page. Articles cited from it are by Schiemann unless otherwise stated. For Schiemann's views on journalism see H. Kause, 'Die Jahre 1930 bis 1933 als Wende im Leben der deutschen Volksgruppen in Lettland' In *Jahrbuch des baltischen Deutschtums*, 1971, pp. 34–5.

19. On Naumann, L. E. Jones, *German Liberalism and the Dissolution of the Weimar Party System 1918–1933*, Chapel Hill, NC, 1988, p. 24.
20. Schiemann, *Erinnerungen*, pp. 15–16.
21. Ibid., p. 16.
22. Ibid., p. 31.
23. Memoir by Oskar Grosberg on occasion of Schiemann's 25th anniversary as editor of the *Rigasche Rundschau* in 1932. 'Begegnungen mit Paul Schiemann'. Donath, I, 1, pp. xi–xii.
24. U. Ģērmanis, 'Die Autonomie- und Unabhängkeitsbestrebungen der Letten' in J. Von Hehn, H. Rimscha, H. Weiss, eds, *Von den baltischen Provinzen zu den baltischen Staaten. Beiträge zur Entstehungsgeschichte der Republiken Estland und Lettland 1917–1918*, Marburg/Lahn, 1971, pp. 2–3. See also E. Benz, *Die Revolution von 1905 in den Ostseeprovinzen Russlands. Ursachen und Verlauf der lettischen und estnischen Arbeiter- und Bauernbewegung im Rahmen der ersten russischen Revolution*, Mainz, 1990; E. Anderson, 'The Baltic Region on the Eve of World War One' in A. Loit, ed., *The Baltic Countries 1900–1914*, Stockholm, 1990, pp. 31–3.
25. A. Plakans, *The Latvians*, p. 101; cf. G. von Pistohlkors, 'Die historischen Voraussetzungen für die Entstehung der drei baltischen Staaten' in B. Meissner, ed., *Die baltischen Nationen. Estland, Lettland, Litauen*, Cologne, 1990, p. 24.
26. Cf comments of D. Henning, 'Letten und Deutsche. Aspekte einer schwierigen Nachbarschaft', *Nordost-Archiv*, Neue Folge, Bd 5, Heft 2, 1996, p. 262.
27. Schiemann, *Erinnerungen*, p. 55.
28. Ibid., p. 47.
29. Ibid., p. 67.
30. Ibid., p. 64.
31. *Revalsche Zeitung*, 27.10.1905.
32. Cf. J. Hiden, P. Salmon, *The Baltic Nations and Europe*, London, New York, 1991, pp. 21–3.
33. Schiemann, *Erinnerungen*, p. 7.
34. Ibid., p. 75.
35. P. Schiemann, *Die Arbeiten des estländischen Provinzialrats. Ein Beitrag zur Zeitgeschichte der baltischen Landespolitik*, Tallinn, Leipzig, 1907, p. 4.
36. See 'Schlechte Waffen'. RR. Donath, I, 1, pp. 216–21. Donath does not always date the editorials. For the period 1920–33 more exact dating can be found in M. Garleff, M. Imhof, 'Paul Schiemanns Veröffentlichungen', *Jahrbuch des Bundesinstituts für Ostdeutsche Kultur und Geschichte*, vol. 6, 1988.
37. G. von Pistohlkors, *Ritterschaftliche Reformpolitik zwischen Russifizierung und Revolution. Historische Studien zum Problem der politischen Selbsteinschätzung der deutschen Oberschicht in den Ostseeprovinzen Russlands im Krisenjahr 1905*, Göttingen, 1978, p. 24.

38. G. Dehio, *Livland und Elsass*, Berlin, 1918, p. 14.
39. 'Wir und der Oktoberverband', RR Donath, I, 3, pp. 562–3.
40. 'Ein offenes Wort in ernster Zeit', RR, cited by Schiemann, *Erinnerungen*, p. 81.
41. Ibid., p. 81.
42. Bosse, *Baltische Köpfe*, p. 153.
43. Plakans, *The Latvians*, p. 108. Cf. Janis Krastins, *Riga: Art Nouveau Metropolis*, Riga, 1996.
44. Schiemann, *Erinnerungen*, p. 83.
45. 'Rasseninstinkt und nationales Bewusstsein', RR 17.11.1907. Donath, I, 1, pp. 209–12.
46. 'Über nationale Jugenderziehung', RR 4.8.1907. Donath, I, 1, pp. 200–4, and ibid. 24.8.1907.
47. 'Ein neues Jahr', RR Donath, I, 1, pp. 229–30.
48. Schiemann, *Erinnerungen*, pp. 92–3.
49. Ibid., p. 98.
50. Ibid., pp. 112 ff.
51. Ibid., p. 115.
52. Ibid., p. 116.
53. Ibid., p. 122.
54. Ibid., p. 126.
55. 'Unsere landische Sozialpolitik', RR Donath, I, 1, pp. 107–11.
56. 'Im Banne der Vergangenheit', RR 1913, Donath, I, 1, pp. 152–3.
57. G. von Rauch, *The Baltic States: Estonia. Latvia. Lithuania: The years of independence 1918–1940*, London, 1974, p. 17.
58. 'Der Nationalismus in der Kommunal-Politik', RR 1911, Donath, I, 1, pp. 92–5.
59. 'Der zweite baltische Journalistenkongress' RR 1910, Donath, I, 1, pp. 40–50.
60. Germanis, 'Autonomie und Unabhängigkeitsbestrebungen', p. 5.
61. In general, G. von Pistohlkors, *Ritterschaftliche Reformpolitik*, pp. 236 ff. Cf. C. L. Lundin, 'The Road from Tsar to Kaiser: The changing loyalties of the Baltic Germans, 1905–1914', *Journal of Central European Affairs*, vol. 10, 1950, pp. 223–55.

Chapter 2 Leaving Russia

1. Schiemann, *Erinnerungen*, p. 135; also his 'Eindrücke und Betrachtungen eines Reserveoffizieres', RR 1914. Donath I, 3, p. 745.
2. Schiemann, *Erinnerungen*, p. 130. See Lotte Schiemann, 'Meine Reise von Riga nach Krementschug. Der Liebe wegen'. A copy of this manuscript was kindly sent to me by Monika von Hirscheydt at the request of Ruth Gostic.
3. Schiemann, *Erinnerungen*, p. 131.
4. Cf. W. Lenz, 'Vom politischen Schicksal des baltischen Deutschtums: Welches Mass an Freiheit besassen die beiden letzten baltischen Generationen?' in *Jahrbuch des baltischen Deutschtums in Lettland und Estland*. (1959). 62–9.
5. Schiemann, *Erinnerungen*, p. 135.
6. Oskar Grosberg, 'Begegnungen mit Paul Schiemann', Donath, I, 1, xi–xiii.
7. Schiemann, *Erinnerungen*, p. 136.

8. Ibid., p. 137.
9. Cited in W. Conze, 'Nationalstaat oder Mitteleuropa? Die Deutschen des Reiches und die Nationalitätenfragen Ostmitteleuropas im ersten Weltkrieg' in W. Conze, ed., *Deutschland und Europa*, Düsseldorf, 1951, p. 205.
10. In general, see B. Mann, *Die baltischen Länder in der deutschen Kriegszielpublizistik 1914–1918*, Tübingen, 1965; J. Elvert, *Deutsche Pläne zur europäischen Neuordnung, 1918–1945*, Stuttgart,
11. See S. Zetterberg, *Die Liga der Fremdvölker Russlands 1916–1918*, Helsinki, 1978, pp. 69 ff.
12. Schiemann, *Erinnerungen*, pp. 138–40.
13. Protocol of DBRP meeting, opened by Schlachat. Latvian State Archives (hereafter LPSR) F[onda] 4985, Apr[aksta] 1, L[ieta] 3.
14. Cited in M. Garleff, *Deutschbaltische Politik zwischen den Weltkriegen*, Bonn-Bad Godesberg, 1976, pp. 30–1.
15. Schiemann, *Erinnerungen*, pp. 138–9.
16. Erinnerungen, p. 143.
17. P. Schiemann, *Massenelend. Russische Erfahrungen und deutsche Besorgnisse*, Berlin, 1918, p. 20.
18. Schiemann, *Erinnerungen*, p. 144.
19. Ibid., pp. 145–6.
20. P. Schiemann, *Das Fiasko der russischen Demokratie. Ein Beitrag zur Pyschologie der letzten Revolution*, Berlin, 1918, p. 77.
21. Plakans, *The Latvians*, p. 117.
22. R. Stupperich, 'Siedlungspläne im Gebiet des Oberbefehlshabers Ost.' *Jomsburg*, 5, 1941, pp. 348–67; H. -E. Volkmann, *Die deutsche Baltikumpolitik zwischen Brest-Litovsk und Compiegne*, Cologne, Vienna, 1970, pp. 92 ff. See also, K. -H. Janssen, 'Die baltische Okkupationspolitik des deutschen Reiches' in J. Von Hehn *et al.*, eds, *Von den baltischen Provinzen zu den baltischen Staaten*, Marburg, 1971, p. 220; G. von Rauch, *The Baltic States*, p. 48.
23. K. Epstein, *Matthias Erzberger and the Dilemma of German Democracy*, Princeton, NJ, 1959, p. 234.
24. Rolnik, *Die baltischen Staaten Litauen, Lettland und Estland und ihre Verffassungsrecht*, Leipzig, 1927, p. 21; W. Baumgart, *Deutsche Ostpolitik. Von Brest-Litovsk bis zum Ende des Ersten Weltkrieges*, Vienna-Munich, 1966, p. 370.
25. Schiemann, *Erinnerungen*, p. 160.
26. On Roemershof see G. von Pistohlkors, 'Führende Schicht oder nationale Minderheit.' *Zeitschrift für Ostforschung*, 21, 1972, pp. 601–18.
27. Schiemann, *Erinnerungen*, p. 148.
28. 'Bürgersinn', RR 23.2.24. Donath, 2, 7, pp. 1926–7.
29. Schiemann, *Erinnerungen*, p. 148; Baum to Schiemann, 17.8.1918. LPSR, F. 4011, Apr. 1, L.
30. Garleff, *Deutschbaltsiche Politik*, p. 56.
31. Schiemann, *Erinnerungen*, p. 151.
32. On Naumann, see L. E. Jones, *German Liberalism and the Dissolution of the Weimar Party System 1918–1933*, Chapel Hill, NC, 1988, pp. 17–21.

33. H. von Rimscha, 'Paul Schiemann als Minderheitenpolitiker.' *Vierteljahrshefte für Zeitgeschichte*, 4, 1956, pp. 44–5.
34. Ibid., pp. 68–76. Also, Schiemann, *Erinnerungen*, pp. 150–1.
35. On Maltzan and Baltic Germans, cf. J. Hiden, *The Baltic States and Weimar Ostpolitik*, Cambridge, 1987, p. 39.
36. W. Wrangell, 'Ausschnitte aus der estnischen Politik 1918–1920'. *Baltische Monatsschrift*, 1930, p. 529. Cf. in general, H. von Rimscha, *Die Staatswerdung Lettlands und das baltische Deutschtum*, Riga, 1939. Cf. B. Mann, *Die Baltischen Länder*, pp. 134–5.
37. Cf. Hiden, *Baltic States and Weimar Ostpolitik*, pp. 8–9.
38. Cf. *Baltische Zeitung* 20.4.1918: 'German policy is at the same time *Mitteleuropa* alliance policy'.
39. 'Ueber die Aussichten des baltischen Staates' in *Preussiche Jahrbücher*, Bd 173, 1918, pp. 305–19.
40. Cf. arguments of 'Grossbaltische Kulturpolitik', *Baltische Zeitung*, 20.4.1918, that the *Mitteleuropa* policy promised to end Baltic's inner contradiction between being in a 'foreign' Empire but belonging culturally to western Europe.
41. See also H. -E. Volkmann, *Die deutsche Baltikumpolitik*, p. 214.
42. 'Ueber die Aussichten des baltischen Staates', pp. 305–19.
43. Delbrück to Schiemann, 9.9.1918, LPSR, F. 4011, Apr. 1, L.
44. Cf. Rimscha, 'Paul Schiemann als Minderheitenpolitiker', pp. 46–7.
45. P. Schiemann, 'Deutschland und die Balten' in *Baltische Zeitung*, 10.8.1919.
46. The exchange of letters is printed in Schiemann, *Erinnerungen*, pp. 159–64 and originals can be found in the archive in Riga. LPSR, F. 4011, Apr. 1, L.
47. Cf. Baron Otto von Grotthuss to Schiemann, 14.9.1918. Ibid. Also for Schiemann's letter of 14 September 1918.
48. Ibid., Schiemann to Wilhelm Baum, 21.9.1918, on the importance of attending the forthcoming Sunday evening meeting with Reichstag members at Erzberger's house and on the advantages of meeting beforehand to coordinate tactics.
49. A. von Taube, 'Das Auswärtiges Amt und die estnische Frage.' *Jahrbücher für die Geschichte Osteuropas*, 17, 1969, pp. 542–80.
50. Schiemann, *Erinnerungen*, p. 152.
51. The letter is to be found in LPSR, F. 4011, Apr. 1, L.
52. Text in *Erinnerungen*, pp. 152–3.
53. Cf. H. -E. Volkmann, *Die deutsche Baltikumpolitik*, p. 214.
54. Cf. Hiden, *Baltic States and Weimar Ostpolitik*, pp. 11 ff.
55. Schiemann, *Erinnerungen*, p. 154.
56. Ibid., pp. 154–5.
57. S. Zetterberg, *Die Liga der Fremdvölker Russlands 1916–1918*, pp. 252–6.
58. Volkmann, *Deutsche Baltikumpolitik*, p. 216.
59. Schiemann, *Erinnerungen*, pp. 156–7.
60. Ibid., p. 156.
61. Ibid., p. 157; Volkmann, *Deutsche Baltikumpolitik*, p. 218.
62. See D. Unfug, 'The Baltic policy of Prince Max of Baden', *Journal of Central European Affairs*, 23, 1963, pp. 152–65.

63. Schiemann, *Erinnerungen*, p. 154.
64. *Korrespondenz Osteuropa*, 6 November 1918, Nr 19, quoted in Schiemann, *Erinnerungen*, pp. 157–8.
65. Ibid., p. 167. Cf. L. Dribins, 'Die Deutschbalten und die Idee vom nationallettischen Staat (1918–1934),' *Nordost-Archiv*, Neue Folge, V, 1996, pp. 277–99.
66. Schiemann, *Erinnerungen*, p. 166.
67. P. Schiemann, *Massenelend: Russische Erfahrungen und deutsche Besorgnisse*, Berlin, 1918, pp. 4–11.
68. Ibid., p. 19.
69. Ibid., p. 21.
70. P. Schiemann, *Die Asiatisierung Europas. Gedanken über Klassenkampf und Demokratie*, Berlin, 1918, p. 5.
71. Ibid., p. 14.
72. Ibid., p. 19.
73. Schiemann, *Erinnerungen*, p. 170.
74. Ibid., pp. 169–70.
75. Ibid., 176.
76. Ibid., p. 164.

Chapter 3 Joining Latvia

1. Schiemann, *Erinnerungen*, p. 171.
2. E. von Rosenberg, *Für Deutschtum und Fortschritt in Lettland. Erinnerungen und Betrachtungen*, Riga, 1928, p. 53.
3. *Nachlass Keller.* Undated memorandum: 'Die deutsche Parlamentsfraktion (Juli 1919–Mai 1934)'. Herder Institute, Marburg.
4. Schiemann, *Erinnerungen*, p. 173.
5. Speech by Wulffius to the National Liberal Party Congress, 29.11.1918 LPSR Fonda 2626, Apr. 1, L. 2.
6. See 'Richtlinien der Deutsch-Baltischen Fortschrittlichen Partei (Beschlossen December 1918 in Mitau)', LPSR, F. 2575, Apr. 20, L. 2.
7. Rosenberg, *Für Deutschtum und Fortschritt in Lettland*, pp. 54–5.
8. Garleff, *Deutschbaltische Politik*, pp. 22–3.
9. For the renaming of the old party as the German Balt Democratic Party see record of latter's General Assembly on 8 December 1918. LPSR F. 4985, Apr. 1, L. 3.
10. Schiemann, *Erinnerungen*, pp. 171 ff.
11. Herder Institute, Marburg. 100 Wachtsmuth, Wolfgang, 36: Briefwechsel Wolfgang Wachtsmuth (1876–1964) mit Wilhelm Schlau 1946–1964, letter of 4.7.1958. Cf. H. Dopkewitsch, 'Zur englischen Politik im Baltikum 1918–1919.' *Deutsche Archiv für Landes- und Volksforschung*, 6, 1942, p. 133.
12. Schiemann, *Erinnerungen*, pp. 180–1.
13. 'Resumé der Besprechung der Vertreter des lettländischen Volksrats und der Baltischen Deutschen Parteien' and 'Einigungsvorschläge des Generalbevollmächtigten des Deutschen Reichs für die Baltischen Lande'. Both are undated, the first is in LPSR, F. 2575, Apr. 20, L. 2 and the second in LPSR, F. 4060, Apr. 1. See also L. Dribins, 'Die Deutschbalten und die Idee vom nationalle-

ttischen Staat (1918–1934)', *Nordost-Archiv, Neue Folge*, vol. V, 1996, Part 2, p. 279.

14. Hiden, *Baltic States and Weimar Ostpolitik*, p. 15.
15. Schiemann, *Erinnerungen*, pp. 180–1.
16. Rosenberg, *Für Deutschtum und Fortschritt*, p. 63.
17. Protocol of German Balt Democratic Party meeting 8.12.1918. LPSR F. 4985, Apr. 1, L. 3; For general assessment of the impact of Rosenberg's actions, M. Garleff, *Deutschbaltische Politik*, pp. 22–3.
18. On the composition of the new committee, Garleff, *Deutschbaltische Politik*, 23–4.
19. Winng, *Heimkehr*, Hamburg, 1935, p. 178; on the lax control of events in the Baltic at this time, cf. J. D. Gregory, *On the edge of diplomacy*, London, 1928, p. 187.
20. On Winnig generally, W. Ribhegge, *August Winnig—eine historische Persönlichkeitsanalyse*, Bonn, 1973.
21. G. Noske, *Von Kiel bis Kapp. Zur Geschichte der deutschen Revolution*, Berlin, 1920, p. 178. 'What was not promised on recruitment posters was conveyed verbally by recruitment officers to the men.'
22. 'Baltische Demokratie', RR 21.7.1919. Donath, II, 1, pp. 7–13. On urban influences, K. Stavenhagen, *Das Deutschtum in Lettland. Taschenbuch des Grenz- und Auslandsdeutschtums*, Heft 20, Berlin, 1927, p. 4.
23. Schiemann, *Erinnerungen*, p. 176.
24. Ibid., p. 173.
25. M. Bischoff, *Die Letzte Front. Geschichte der eisernen Division im Baltikum 1919*, Berlin, 1935, p. 53.
26. Memorandum by von der Goltz, 2.10.1917, Bundesarchiv, Nachlass Reinhardt, Bdle 18 (HO 8/82 12–17); On the attitude of other military leades towards the Baltic campain, F. L. Carsten, *Reichswehr und Politik*, Cologne-Berlin, 1964, pp. 74 ff.
27. Hiden, *Baltic States and Weimar Ostpolitik*, pp. 19 ff.
28. Schiemann, *Erinnerungen*, p. 174.
29. First quotation from Wachtsmuth, *Wege, Umwege, Weggenossen*, Munich, 1954, p. 175, the second from G. von Rauch, *Aus der baltischen Geschichte. Vorträge, Untersuchungen, Skizzen aus sechs Jahrzehnten*. Hannover-Döhren, 1980, p. 601.
30. In general W. Lenz, 'Deutsche Machtpolitik in Lettland im Jahre 1919. Ausgewählte Dokumente des von General Rüdiger Graf von der Goltz geführten Generalkommandos des VI. Reserve Korps', *Zeitschrift für Ostforschung*, 36, 7, 1987, pp. 526–7, 541; Bernard von Nottbeck, *Vorgeschichte einer Schlacht von Libau nach Wenden*, Tallinn, 1992, pp. 36–7.
31. Dribins, 'Die Deutschbalten und die Idee vom nationallettischen Staat etc.', pp. 284–5.
32. Schiemann, *Erinnerungen*, p. 202.
33. Ibid., p. 174.
34. Ibid., p. 177.
35. D. Henning, 'Letten und Deutsche. Aspekte einer schwierigen Nachbarschaft', *Nordost-Archiv*, V, 2, 1996, p. 273.
36. Schiemann, *Erinnerungen*, Letters to his mother, 27 April and 29 May, p. 17.

37. Rauch, *Baltic States*, p. 61; W. Lenz, 'Zur britischen Politik gegenüber den baltischen Deutschen 1918/19' in R. Von Thaden *et al.*, eds., *Das Vergangene und die Geschichte*, Göttingen, 1973, p. 279; cf. Memorandum of 20.8.1919, Cabinet Records, Public Record Office (Hereafter PRO), London, CAB 24/88.
38. Plakans, *The Latvians*, p. 119.
39. Schiemann, *Erinnerungen*, pp. 178, 179.
40. Ibid., p. 179.
41. S. Tallents, *Man and boy*, London, 1943, p. 336; cf. dejection of Seeckt and others, Hiden, *Baltic States and Weimar Ostpolitik*, p. 24.
42. Garleff, *Deutschbaltische Politik*, pp. 25 ff.
43. Rosenberg, *Für Deutschtum und Fortschritt*, pp. 101 ff; for a favourable Allied assessment of Fircks, H. Niessel, *L'evacuation des Pays Baltiques par les Allemands*, Paris, 1935, pp. 209–10.
44. W. von Rüdiger, *Aus dem letzten Kapitel deutsch-baltischer Geschichte in Lettland, 1919–1939*, Hanover-Wülfel, 1955, p. 6.
45. W. Fircks, *Meine Reisedecke, Erinnerungen*, ed. K. Stavenhagen, Riga, 1934.
46. Bosse, *Baltische Köpfe*, p. 153.
47. Niessel, *L'evacuation des Pays Baltiques*, p. 210.
48. Schiemann, *Erinnerungen*, p. 182.
49. Bosse, *Baltische Köpfe*. 155.
50. W. Wachtsmuth, *Von deutscher Arbeit in Lettland*, vol. 3, Cologne, 1953, pp. 89 ff.
51. 'Alle Mann auf Deck' was published in *Baltische Heimat*, 5.7.1919. Printed in Rosenberg, *Für Deutschtum und Fortschritt*, p. 95.
52. Schiemann, *Erinnerungen*, p. 181; see also Garleff, *Deutschbaltische Politik*, p. 33.
53. 'Rechts und Links', RR 7.1.1928. Donath, II, 12, pp. 3487–9. For approval of Rosenberg by a Latvian commentator, A. Salts, *Die politische Parteien Lettlands*, Riga, 1926, pp. 39–40.
54. Schiemann, *Erinnerungen*, pp. 90–1, 181.
55. Ibid., p. 181.
56. Cited in H. Rimscha, 'Paul Schiemann als Minderheitenpolitiker', pp. 49–50.
57. Garleff, *Deutschbaltische Politik*, p. 59, implies Schiemann picked up his ideas on solidarity in Berlin.
58. Schiemann, letter of 9.2.1919, *Erinnerungen*, p. 176.
59. 'Wehe den Kleinmütigen', RR 22.7.1919. Donath, II, 1, pp. 14–17.
60. 'Mitarbeit', RR 28.7.1919. Donath, II, 1, pp. 32–5.
61. 'Die Abseits stehen', RR 23.8.1919. Donath, II, 1, pp. 72–5.
62. 'Baltische Outsider', RR 1920. Donath, II, 1, pp. 196–9.
63. 'Das Sozialisierungs problem', RR 24.7.1919. Donath, II, 1, pp. 18–22.
64. 'Johannes und Marx', RR 11.8.1919. Donath, II, 1, pp. 65–8.
65. 'Ueber den Klassen', RR 1920, Donath, II, 1, pp. 260–3.
66. 'Lettlands Staatsproblem', RR November 1919 Donath, II, 1, pp. 136–40.
67. 'Parteigruppierung des Baltischen Deutschtums in Lettland', RR n.d. Donath, II, 1, pp. 175–7.
68. 'Die Überwindung des nationalen Hasses', RR 26.7.1919. Donath, II, 1, pp. 27–31.
69. 'Eine Manifestation des Chauvinismus', RR 23.8.1919. Donath, II, 1, pp. 76–7.

70. Wachtsmuth, *Von deutscher Arbeit*, 2, Cologne, 1952, pp. 41 ff; R. Wittram, 'Die Schulautonomie in Lettland', *Zeitschrift für Ostforschung*, 1, 1952, pp. 256–1.
71. 'Rechts und Links', RR 7.1.1928. Donath, 12, pp. 3487–8; Dribins, 'Die Deutschbalten und die Idee vom nationallettischen Staat,' p. 289.
72. Cf. Garleff, *Deutschbaltische Politik*, p. 87.
73. Ibid., p. 87.
74. Bosse, *Baltische Köpfe*, p. 161; K. Kause, 'Paul Schiemann (1876–1944), die Balten und ihre Zeitgeschichte. Zu Schiemanns 100. Geburtstag am 29 März 1976', *Jahrbuch des Baltischen Deutschtums* 1976, p. 37.
75. Undated review (1929) of ten years of the law by Karl Keller. 'Schulen der Minoritäten in Lettland'. Nachlass K. Keller. Das deutsche Bildungswesen in Lettland 1919–1929. Herder Institut Baltikum Nr 285.
76. See also 'Die Schulautonomie der Minoritäten im Volksrate.' RR, December 1919. Donath, II, 1, pp. 155–6.; K. Stavenhagen, '*Das Deutschtum in Lettland.*' *Taschenbuch des Grenz- und Auslandsdeutschtum*, Heft 20, Berlin, 1927, p. 16.
77. Wachtsmuth, *Wege, Umwege, Weggenossen*, p. 179.
78. For a scathing picture of these forces see report of German Chargé d'Affaires in Estonia. Foreign Office Film (FO), Auswärtiges Amt, Akten betreffend politische Beziehungen Estland zu Russland, vol. 1, K249/K076313–4.
79. Wachtsmuth, *Von deutscher Arbeit*, 3, p. 103.
80. 'Ein neues Jahr', RR 31.12.1919. Donath, II, 1, pp. 170–1.
81. 'Parteigruppierung des baltischen Deutschtums in Lettland', RR 1920, Donath, II, 1, pp. 178–81.
82. 'Die Überwindung des nationalen Hasses', RR 26.7.1919. Donath, II, 1, pp. 27–31.
83. Source, note 84.
84. 'Eine Reifeprüfung', RR December 1919, Donath, II, 1, pp. 160–2.
85. Source, note 80.
86. Garleff, *Deutschbaltische Politik*, p. 34.
87. Text of guidelines printed in RR 12.1.1920, Donath, II, 1, pp. 185–9. 88.
88. 'Das proportionale Wahlrecht und die Minderheiten.' RR 2.8.1919. Donath, II, 1, pp. 46–8.
89. Cf. Wachtsmuth, *Von deutscher Arbeit*, 3, p. 134.
90. LPSR F. 2626, Apr. 1, L. 6.
91. Garleff, *Deutschbaltische Politik*, pp. 45–8.
92. 'Aufruf an unsere Landesleute im Auslande', RR 1920. Donath, II, 1, p. 222.
93. 'Ich warne', RR 1920. Donath, II, 1, pp. 235–8.

Chapter 4 Practising Democracy

1. Plakans, *The Latvians*, p. 120.
2. Cf. 'Der Antibolschewismus und die Randstaaten', RR 18.8.1920, Donath, II, 2, p. 465.
3. Schiemann, 'Russland und Wir', RR 1920. Donath, II, 2, pp. 495–7.
4. A. Blodnieks, *The Undefeated Nation*, New York, 1960, p. 183.

5. Note on recognition by J. D. Gregory, 9.4.1920, *Documents on British Foreign Policy* (DBFP), Series 1, vol. 11, pp. 352–5.
6. 'Lettlands aussenpolitische Lage zur Jahreswende', RR 3.1.1921. Donath, II, 3, pp. 713–4.
7. 'Am Scheidewege?', RR 10.8.1920. Donath, II, 2, p. 411.
8. 'Kulturkampf', RR 2.9.1920. Donath, II, 2, pp. 524–5; 'Das kleinere Übel', RR 17.9.1920. Donath, II, 2, pp. 543–4; 'Demokratie und Agrarreform', RR 23.12.1921. Donath, II, 4, pp. 1053–4.
9. J. von Hehn, *Die Umsiedlung der baltischen Deutschen—das letzte Kapitel baltischdeutscher Geschichte*, Marburg, 1982, p. 17.
10. Statistical data in K. Maydell, 'Die Baltendeutschen vor ihrer Umsiedlung. Ein statistischer Rückblick', *Jomsburg*, 4, 1940, pp. 59–90.
11. 'Vogel Strauss', RR 8.12.1920, Donath, II, 3, pp. 676–80.
12. Wachtsmuth, *Von deutscher Arbeit in Lettland*, 3, pp. 5–9; cf. W. von Knorre, 'Vom Wirtschaftsleben des baltischen Deutschtums' in M. H. Boehm, H. Weiss, eds, *Wir Balten*, Salzburg-Munich, 1951, pp. 112–16.
13. For discussion of the parties, Wachtsmuth, *Von deutscher Arbeit in Lettland*, 3, pp. 104 ff.
14. Radowitz to Auswärtiges Amt, 9.10.1920, *Auswärtiges Amt*, Akten betreffend Deutschtum im Ausland, Lettland. 1. Politik 25 Lettland, Political Archive, Bonn; on the split, W. von Rüdiger, *Aus dem letzten Kapitel* etc., p. 13.
15. Source, note 7.
16. R. Wittram, *Livland. Schicksal und Erbe der baltischen Deutschen*, 2nd edition, Berlin, 1941, p. 47.
17. M. Walters, *Baltengedanken und Baltenpolitik*, Paris, 1926, p. 259.
18. 'Parteien I', RR 1920, Donath, II, 1, pp. 215–17.
19. Ibid.
20. See bibliography for full details of all three volumes. Garleff's indispensable writings on Baltic German politics include his *Deutschbaltische Politik*.
21. H. von Rimscha, 'Paul Schiemann als Minderheitenpolitiker', pp. 49–50.
22. H. Kause, 'Paul Schiemann (1876–1944). Die Balten und ihre Zeitgeschichte', *Jahrbuch des baltischen Deutschtums*, 23, 1976, pp. 32–9.
23. M. Garleff, 'Deutschbaltische Publizisten. Ewald Ammende-Werner Hasselblatt-Paul Schiemann', *Berichte und Forschungen. Jahrbuch des Bundesintitut für ostdeutsche Kultur und Geschichte*, vol. 2, 1944, pp. 189–229.
24. Garleff, *Deutschbaltische Politik*, p. 79.
25. Salts, *Die politische Parteien Lettlands*, p. 38.
26. 'Moralischer Mut', RR 9.4.1921. Donath, II, 3, pp. 842–3.
27. These were thought to have been destroyed, with only a few remnants remaining in the papers of Wolfgang Wachtsmuth at Marburg. In fact there are surviving records in the Latvian State Archive. In the present study these are usually referred to as the source on the CGBP meetings.
28. 'Staatliches Denken', RR 1920. Donath, II, 1, pp. 264–6.
29. Rauch, *Baltic states*, pp. 92 f.
30. See J. von Hehn, *Lettland zwischen Demokratie und Diktatur*, Munich, 1957.

31. Wachtsmuth, *Von deutscher Arbeit*, 3, pp. 358 f. See also 'Projekt über die nationalen Rechte der Minderheiten ausgearbeitet von Dr Paul Schiemann' in LPSR, F. 575, Apr. 20, L. 2. Also CGBP protocol 22.4.20. LPSR F. 2626, Apr. 1, L. 6.
32. Cf. M. Garleff, 'Ethnic minorities in the Estonian and Latvian parliaments. The politics of coalition' in V. S. Vardys, R. J. Misiunas, eds, *The Baltic States in Peace and War, 1917–1945*, Philadelphia, London, 1978. p. 86.
33. P. Schiemann, 'Die nationalen Minderheiten in Lettland', *Zeitschrift f. Politik*, 14, 1925, p. 279.
34. Cf. Mendelsohn, *The Jews of East Central Europe between the world wars*, Bloomington, IN, 1987, pp. 241 ff.
35. Garleff, 'Ethnic minorities etc.', pp. 81–94. see also A. Plakans, *The Latvians*, pp. 126–30.
36. 'Minister und Autonomie', RR 3.9.22 Donath, II, 18, pp. 5315–16.
37. Cf. Schiemann's remarks to the CGBP, 16.12.20. LPSR F. 2626 Apr. 1, L. 6. Wachtsmuth, *Von deutscher Arbeit*, 3, pp. 361–7.
38. Protocol of 13.9.20. LPSR F. 2626, Apr. 1, L. 6.
39. Ibid., protocol of 5.8.1920.
40. Paul Schiemann, 'Innerpolitischer Jahresüberlick', *Jahrbuch des Deutschtums in Lettland*, 1927, pp. 24–5.
41. See 'Libau und Riga', RR 9.2.1921. Donath, II, 3, pp. 779–80; 'Reaktionär.' 3.8.1922. Donath, II, 6, pp. 1513–5.
42. For extensive discussion, Wachtsmuth, *Von deutscher Arbeit*, 3, pp. 297 ff.
43. Protokoll der Sitzung des Ausschusses der Deutsch Baltischen Parteien, 29.11.1920. LPSR. F. 2626 Apr. 1, L. 6.
44. See Schiemann's speech to the Constituent Assembly, 'Die Agrarreform als chaunvistisches Kampfmittel', RR 26.5.1921. Donath, II, 4, pp. 933–6.
45. See also Schiemann, 'Vom Tage', RR 22.0.1920. Donath, II, 3, pp. 606–7. Cf. Hiden, *Baltic states and Weimar Ostpolitik*, pp. 82 ff.
46. 'Lettlands wirtschaftliche Zukunft im Lichte der Wahlergebnis'. Donath, II, 1, pp. 277–80.
47. Cf. CGBP protocols of 14.11.21 and 28.11.21. LSPR F. 2626. Apr. 1, L. 6. See also 'Eine deutsche Wählerversammlung in Libau', RR 26.7.1922. Donath, II, 5, pp. 1293–4. Wachtsmuth, *Von deutscher Arbeit*, 3., pp. 387–8.
48. P. Schiemann, 'Die Tätigkeit des Ausschusses der deutsch-baltischen Parteien in Lettland', *Jahrbuch und Kalender des Deutschtums in Lettland*, Riga, 1924, p. 24.
49. 'Aus der Konstituante', RR 152/1920. Donath, II, 2, p. 334. See Plakans, *The Latvians*, p. 126.
50. 'Freiheit und Gleichheit', RR 18.1.1922, Donath, II, 5, pp. 129–20. Cf. K. Keller, 'Die deutsche Parlamentsfraktion (Juli 1919–Mai 1934)', n.d. Keller Nachlass, Marburg.
51. 'Staatssprache und Landessprache', RR 143/1920. Donath, II, 2, pp. 324–6.
52. 'Ein neues Heldenstück des Bildungsministers', RR 7.8.1920. Donath, II, 2, pp. 406–8.
53. Cf. 'Heimat und Emigration', RR 3.9.21. Donath, II, 4, pp. 981–3.
54. Source, later note of his 25 May 1921 speech.

55. Cf. Protocol of 23.5.1921 LSPR. F. 2626 Apr. 1, L. 6.
56. For detailed discussion, Hiden, *The Baltic States in Weimar Ostpolitik* and 'The significance of Latvia: A forgotten aspect of Weimar Ostpolitik', *Slavonic and East European Review*, 53, 132, 1977, pp. 295–317.
57. 'Am Ziel', RR 28.1.1921. Donath, II, 3, p. 732.
58. 'Zwischen West und Ost', RR 2.4.1921. Donath, II, 3, pp. 640–1.
59. Source note 57.
60. Cf. J. Hiden, 'Baltic gold and Latvian privatisation', *Journal of Baltic Studies*, 23, 1, 1992, pp. 63–72.
61. Protocol in LPSR F. 2626 Apr. 1, L. 6.
62. Cf. 'Moralischer Mut', RR 2.4.1921, Donath, II, 3, pp. 842–3.
63. Cf. Protocol of Minorities Committee, 13.4.1921. LPSR. Apr. 1, L. 6; Wachtsmuth, *Von deutscher Arbeit*, 3, pp. 364–6.
64. Garleff, *Deutschbaltische Politik*, p. 131.
65. P. Schiemann, 'Die Tätigkeit des Ausschusses der deutsch-baltischen Parteien in Lettland', *Jahrbuch und Kalender des Deutschtums in Lettland, 1924*, pp. 19–26; P. Schiemann, 'Molochopfer', RR 18.3.1922. Donath, II, 5. pp. 1251–2.
66. 'Die Tätigkeit des Ausschusses etc.', p. 19.
67. 'Der neue Kurs', RR 4.6.1921. Donath, II, 4, pp. 946–7.
68. 'Die Parteien zur Regierungsdeklaration', Report on Constituent Assembly session of 17 June 1921, RR 18.6.1921. Donath, II, 4, pp. 953–8.
69. 'Vor dem Sturz der Regierung Ulmanis', RR 1.6.1921. Donath, II, 4, pp. 940–1.
70. 'Ultimo', RR 11.6.21. Donath, II, 4, pp. 951–2.
71. 'Der richtige Weg', RR 2.7.21. Donath, II, 4, pp. 966–7.
72. C. Siegert, 'Deutschbalten in Deutschland in der Zwischenkriegszeit. Versuch einer politischen Einordnung', *Nordost-Archiv. Zeitschrift für Regionalgeschichte*, Neue Folge, vol. 5, Part 2, 1996, pp. 326–8.
73. Ibid., p. 329.
74. Schiemann to Berg, 14.1.1923, Schiemann Nachlass. Nikolai von Berg 1922–1936. Baltijas Centrala Biblioteka, Riga.
75. 'Nationalistische Torheiten', RR 15.3.1923. Donath, II, 7, p. 1819.
76. CGBP Protocol of 24.8.1921. LSPR. F. 2626, Apr. 1, L. 6; 'Heimat und Emigration', RR 3.9.1921. Donath, II, 4, pp. 981–3.
77. For general overview, J. Hiden, 'The Weimar Republic and the problem of the Auslandsdeutsche', *Journal of Contemporary History*, 12, 1977, pp. 273–89.
78. Protocol of 2.6.1921 LSPR F. 2626 Apr. 1, L. 6. See also M. Garleff, 'Autonomiemodelle in den baltischen Staaten zur Zeit ihrer Selbstständigkeit', *Jahrbuch des baltischen Deutschtums*, 1980, 150–6; Dribins, 'Die Deutschbalten und die Idee vom nationallettischen Staat', pp. 290–1.
79. Garleff, *Deutschbaltische Politik*, p. 115.
80. Cf. R. P. Peters, 'Baltic states diplomacy and the League of Nations Minorities System' in J. Hiden, A. Loit, eds, *The Baltic in International Relations between the Two World Wars*, Stockholm, 1988, pp. 281–302.
81. 'Im Völkerbund', RR 21.7.1921 Donath, II, 5, pp. 1193–5.
82. Protocol of meeting of Minorities Office, 16.9.1921. LPSR F. 2626 Apr. 1, L. 6.

83. 'Ein Interview mit Dr Paul Schiemann'. Originally published in Sevodnia and reprinted in the *Rigasche Rundschau* on 11.10.1921. Donath, II, 4, pp. 1018–9.
84. Cf. CGBP protocol of 3 June 1921. LSPR F. 2626. Apr. 1, L. 6.
85. Baron A. Heyking, *The Main Issues Confronting the Minorities of Latvia and Estonia*, London, 1922, pp. 5, 7, 17.
86. Cf. 'Minoritätenverband', RR 6.2.1922. Donath, II, 5, p. 1230.
87. 'Minoritätenrechte', RR 26.10.1921. Donath, II, 5, pp. 1196–1200.
88. Cf. Schiemann to Mintz, 4.1.1922, inviting him to a meeting on 7 January at the *Riga Rundschau* offices to discuss the draft of statutes for the planned Liga für den Völkerbund. Baltijas Central biblioteka, Schiemann Nachlass. Correspondence. Verband der deutschen Volksgruppen in Europa 1921–8.
89. 'Der Staat und die Minderheiten', RR 7.2.1922. Donath, II, 5, pp. 1231–3.
90. Ibid.
91. Cf. P. Schiemann, 'Die Minoritäten in den Lettländischen Völkerbundliga', RR 10.12.1923. Donath, II, 7, p. 1878.
92. Protokoll der Sitzung der erweiterten Ausschusses der Parteien, 29.10.1921. LSPR. F. 2626, Apr., 1 L. 6.
93. Cf. Garleff, 'Autonomiemodelle in den baltischen Staaten zur Zeit ihrer Selbstständigkeit', pp. 152 ff.
94. 'Ein Schritt zum Ausgleich', RR 8.2.1922. Donath, II, 5, p. 1234.
95. 'Der Herr Innenminister als Deutschbaltenfresser', RR 29.10.1921 Donath, II, 4, pp. 1025–8.
96. 'Die Balten in Lettland', RR 5.11.1921. Donath II, 4, p. 1031.
97. 'Das Echo', RR 25.1.1922. Donath, II, 5, pp. 1224–5.
98. CGBP protocol of 12.12.1921 LSPR F. 2626. Apr. 1, L. 6.
99. Cf. Garleff, *Deutschbaltische Politik*, p. 115.
100. 'Molochopfer', RR 18.3.1922. Donath, II, 5, pp. 1251–2.
101. Adolfs Silde, 'Die Entwicklung der Republik Lettland' in B. Meissner, ed. *Die baltischen Nationen. Estland, Lettland, Litauen*, Cologne, 1990, p. 65.
102. 'Osterwünsche', V 1258.

Chapter 5 A Place Within

1. 'Abendröte', RR 1.7.1922. Donath, II, 5, pp. 1284–5.
2. 'Reaktionär', RR 3.8.1922. Donath, II, 6, pp. 1513–6.
3. 'Der 7 November 1922', RR 7.11.1922. Donath, II, 6, pp. 1536–7.
4. Cited by H. Kause, '"Es ist eine Lust zu Leben". Einige Beobachtungen zur Stellung Paul Schiemanns (1876–1944) in der deutschbaltischen Oeffentlichkeit vor und nach dem Ersten Weltkrieg' in J. von Hehn, C. J. Kenez, eds, *Reval und die Baltischen Laender. Festschrift für Hellmuth Weiss zum 80 Geburtstag*, Marburg/Lahn, 1980, p. 112.
5. Cf. Schiemann's analysis 'Innerpolitischer Jahresüberblick', *Jahrbuch des Deutschtums in Lettland*, 1925, pp. 15–18.
6. P. Schiemann, 'Die Tätigkeit des Ausschusses der deutsch-baltischen Parteien in Lettland', *Jahrbuch und Kalender des Deutschtums in Lettland*, 1924, pp. 19–20.

7. Cf. CGBP protocols of 15.1.1923 and 23.1.1923. LSPR. F. 2626, Apr. 1, L. 7. 'Das neue Kabinett', RR 27.1.1923. Donath, II, 6, p. 1565.
8. 'Kabinettbildung und Minoritäten', RR 25.11.1922. Donath, II, 6, pp. 1544–6.
9. 'Ein gefährdetes System', RR 2.12.1922. Donath, ibid., pp. 1546–8.
10. 'Die Judenfrage II', RR 8.7.1922. Donath, II, 5, pp. 1286–7.
11. 'Lenins Ende', RR 17.6.1922. Donath, II, 5., pp. 1280–1.
12. 'Genua', RR 26.4.1922. Donath, II, 5, pp. 1261–2.
13. 'Um Russland', RR 6.5.1922. Donath, II, 5, pp. 1266–7.
14. 'Deutsche Osteinstellung', RR 22.8.1922. Donath, II, 5, pp. 1266–7.
15. 'Der ratifizierte Vierbund', RR 1.4.1922. Donath, II, 5, p. 1255.
16. 'Der baltische Staatenbund', RR 26.8.1922. Donath, II, 5, pp. 1299–1300.
17. 'Baltische Orientierung', RR 12.8.1922. Donath, II, 5, pp. 1295–6.
18. 'Lettland und die europäische Neugruppierung', RR 19.1.1924. Donath, II, 8, pp. 2144–5.
19. 'Liberalismus und Demokratie', RR 24.5.1924. Donath II, 8, pp. 2117–8.
20. 'Die nationalkulturelle Autonomie', RR 2.3.1922. Cf. Schiemann's emphasis on the importance of Renner on pre-war thinking in Russia too, *Nation und Staat*, 5, 1932, p. 806 f.
21. Garleff, *Deutschbaltische Politik*, pp. 104–5.
22. 'Die national-kulturelle Autonomie. Vortrag Dr. P. Schiemanns im Deutschen Elternverband', RR 2.2.1924. Donath, II, 5, pp. 1245–6.
23. CGBP Protocol 5.3.1922, cited Garleff, p. 115; 'Nationale Kataster', RR 25.1.1924. Donath, II, 7, pp. 1887–8.
24. In general, Wittram, 'Schulautonomie etc.', pp. 259–60.
25. 'Minoritätenschutz', RR 19.9.1922. Donath, II, 6, p. 1521.
26. Wachtsmuth, *Von deutscher Arbeit*, 2, pp. 67 ff.
27. Schiemann, 'Die Tätigkeit des Ausschusses der deutsch-baltischen Parteien in Lettland etc.', p. 21.
28. 'Zur Lage im Autonomiekonflik', RR 10.2.1923. Cf. Wachtsmuth, *Von deutscher Arbeit*, 3, pp. 354 ff., on the privileged position of the German education authority in comparison with the other minorities.
29. CGBP protocol 12.2.1923 LSPR F. 2626, Apr. 1, L. 7.
30. Schiemann, 'Die Tätigkeit des Ausschusses der deutsch-baltischen Parteien in Lettland etc.', p. 21.
31. Ibid.
32. Cf. accounts by Schiemann of talks with Meierovics on school issues at various points. CGBP protocols of 21.9.23, 15.10.1923, 16.11.1923. LSPR F. 2626, Apr. 1, L. 7.
33. Garleff, *Deutschbaltische Politik*, pp. 94–6.
34. Cited ibid., p. 96.
35. Cited ibid., p. 136.
36. See RR articles, 'Konkordat und Kirchenbesitz' 13.3.1923. Donath, II, 6, pp. 1571–2; 'Kirchenschutz.' 28.4.1923, ibid., pp. 1589–90; 'Parlament und Volk.' 25.8.1923, ibid., pp. 1607–11; 'Trennung von Kirche und Staat.' Schiemann's lecture to the Public Law Commission, 27.10.1924. Donath, II, 8, pp. 2245–6.

37. 'Europa's Niedergang', RR 13.1.1923. Donath, II, 6, pp. 1555–6, and 'Der Kommunismus als Retter', RR 16.1.1923. Ibid., p. 1557.
38. 'Die Probleme Europas', RR 4.8.1923. Donath, II, 7, pp. 1837–8.
39. 'Die neue Regierung in Deutschland', RR 16.8.1923. Donath, II, 7, pp. 1843–4.
40. Schot, *Nation oder Staat*, p. 103.
41. Rüdiger, *Aus dem letzten Kapitel*, p. 62.
42. See hostile view of the Verband in M. Rotbarth, 'Grenzrevision und Minderheitenfragen. Zur Funktion des Europäischen Minderheitenkongresses in der Ostpolitik des deutschen Imperialismus', *Studien zur Geschichte der deutsch-polnischen Beziehungen*, 6, pp. 5–30, Rostock, 1982.
43. In general, N. Krekeler, *Revisionsanspruch und geheime Ostpolitik. Die Subventionierung der deutschen Minderheit in Polen*, Stuttgart, 1973, pp. 133 ff.
44. Grundmann, *Deutschtumspolitik*, pp. 186 ff.
45. Cf. Hiden, 'The Weimar Republic and the problem of the Auslandsdeutsche', *Journal of Contemporary History*, 12, 1977, pp. 273–89.
46. In general, S. Bamberger-Stemmann, *Der Europäische Nationalitätenkongress 1925 bis 1938*, Munich, 2000.
47. Cf. J. W. Hiden, 'The Baltic Germans and German policy towards Latvia', *Historical Journal*, 13, 2 (1970), pp. 295–317.
48. 'Das nationale Problem', RR 19.8.1923. Donath, II, 7, pp. 1845–6.
49. A. Köster, 'Oestliche Zukunftsfrage', *Die Glöcke*, 3.2.1918, p. 136. Cited in B. Mann, *Die baltischen Länder in der deutschen Kriegszielpublizistik 1914–1918*, Tübingen, 1965, pp. 126–7.
50. Cited Grundmann, *Deutschtumspolitik*, p. 132.
51. K. Doss, *Reichsminister Adolf Köster 1883–1930. Ein Leben für die Weimarer Republik*, Düsseldorf, 1978, pp. 81–8.
52. Rüdiger, *Aus dem letzten Kapitel*, p. 33.
53. Doss, *Adolf Köster*, pp. 129–30.
54. Schiemann to Ruetz, 22.4.23. Schiemann Nachlass. Rigasche Rundschau. Briefe.
55. Rüdiger, *Aus dem letzten Kapitel*, p. 38.
56. Köster to Auswärtiges Amt, 10.1.1925. *Auswärtiges Amt files*, Akten betreffend Deutschtum im Ausland. Lettland 1, Politik 25 Politisches Archiv Bonn (PAB).
57. CGBP protocol 7.5.1923 LSPR. F. 2626. Apr. 1, L. 6. In general, Wachtsmuth, 1, pp. 79 ff.
58. Cf. CGBP Protocol of the Meeting of Riga's Welfare Institutions on 22 November 1922. LSPR. F.2626. Apr. 1, L.6.
59. Cf. CGBP protocol of 7.9.1923 deciding on the Central's composition. Ibid.
60. Schiemann, 'Die Tätigkeit des Ausschusses der deutsch-baltischen Parteien in Lettland', pp. 25 f.
61. Wachtsmuth, *Von deutscher Arbeit*, 3, pp. 164–5, and 2, p. 83.
62. Rüdiger, *Aus dem letzten Kapitel*, p. 42.
63. Grundman, *Deutschtumspolitik*, p. 151.
64. Cf. letters from Ruetz to Schiemann on 18.10.1925 and 25.10.1925. Both in Schiemann Nachlass. Rigasche Rundschau Briefe Nr 221–248. Cf. Schiemann comment in CGBP protocol 8.3.22 LPSR F. 2626 Apr. 1, L. 11.

65. On Samuel govt see CGBP protocol of 31.1.1924 LSPR. F. 2626, Apr. 1, L. 7.
66. 'Revolutionsabschluss', RR 5.4.1924. Donath, II, 7, pp. 1944–5.
67. CGBP protocol of 14.2.1924. LSPR F. 2626, Apr. 1, L. 7.
68. Ibid.
69. Ibid. Protocol of 25.1.1924.
70. Schiemann to Oscar von Schiemann, 1.10.1923. Schiemann Nachlass. Baltijas Centrala Biblioteka. Correspondence. Rigasche Rundschau 1921–1934.
71. CGBP protocol 8.3.1924, containing report of Fircks on Public Law Commission meeting. LSPR F. 2626 Apr. 1, L. 7.
72. 'Sylvester 1923. Gedanken über nationale Führerschaft', RR 31.12.1923. Donath, II, 7, pp. 1884–6.
73. See Report of Fircks to the CGBP on 14.2.1924, LSPR F. 2626 Apr. 1, L. 7.
74. Cf. Garleff, *Deutschbaltische Politik*, p. 118.
75. 'Unser Weg', RR 22.11.1924. Donath, II, 8, pp. 2254–5. Cf. his end of year editorial, 'Das Fest der Erfüllung', RR 24.12.24. Ibid., p. 2273.
76. See Schiemann's report to the CGBP, 9.12.1924, on his plans for talking to Celmiņš. LSPR F. 2626, Apr. 1, L. 7.
77. Cf. CGBP protocol of 30.1.1925 LSPR. F. 2626, Apr. 1, L. 8.
78. Cf. 'Ausgleich oder Kampfverewigung', RR 14.3.25.
79. 'Das deutsche Autonomiegesetz bis zum neuen Landtage verschoben', RR 29.4.1925.
80. Cf. discussion by the CGBP on 30 January 1925. LSPR. F. 2626, Apr. 1, L. 8.
81. Schiemann to Ago von Maltzan, 4.9.1920. A. A. Akten betreffend politische Beziehiehungen Deutschland zu Lettland. FO Film K2330/K663555–6.
82. 'Ums Gemeinwohl', RR 27.2.1925. Donath, II, 9, pp. 2487–8.
83. 'Deutsche Wahlbetrachtungen', RR 7.3.1925. Donath, II, 9, pp. 2491–2.
84. CGBP protocol 23.3.1925. LPSR. F. 4985, Apr. 1, L. 4.
85. CGBP protocol 20.11.1925 LSPR. F. 2626, Apr. 1, L. 8.
86. Protocol of meeting of the Committee of the German Balt Democratic Party, 1.12.1925. LPSR. F. 4985. Apr. 1, L. 4.
87. Keller Nachlass. Undated report: 'Die deutsche parlamentsfraktion (Juli 1919–Mai 1934)'.

Chapter 6 The Geneva Connection

1. O. Boelitz, *Das Grenz-und Auslandsdeutschtum. Seine Geschichte und seine Bedeutung*, Munich-Berlin, 1926, p. 97.
2. Schiemann, 'Die Tätigkeit des Ausschuss etc.', p. 23.
3. Schiemann, 'Die nationalen Minderheiten in Lettland', *Zeitschrift für Politik*, 14, 1925, p. 281.
4. 'Der deutsche Minderheitenkongress in Wien', RR 9.8.1924. Donath II, 8, p. 2205.
5. Wachtsmuth, *Wege, Umwege*, p. 188.
6. Nachlass Keller. Herder Institute. Baltikum Nr 289. 'Gedanken zur Erfassung des Deutschtums in Stadt und Land für die Bedürfnisse des Deutschtums'. 14.11.1925.

7. Cf. H. Pärn for details and scales. 'Die Einführung der Selbstbesteurung innerhalb der Volksgemeinschaft der Deutschtum in Lettland', *Jahrbuch des baltischen Deutschtums*, 1927, pp. 45–9.
8. Cf. Rüdiger, *Aus dem letzten Kapitel*, pp. 17 ff.
9. Ibid., p. 37.
10. Ruetz to Schiemann, 25.10.1925. Schiemann Nachlass. Rigasche Rundschau Briefe; Ruetz to Schiemann, 18.10.1925, ibid.
11. For a comprehensive overview of the Zentrale's activities, Wachtsmuth, *Von deutscher Arbeit*, 1, pp. 104 ff.
12. Ibid., p. 109.
13. Schiemann to Harry Michaelowsky, 26.11.1922. Schiemann Nachlass. Correspondence, RR 1921–34.
14. Ibid. Schiemann to Ruetz, 22.4.1923.
15. Cf. Paul Schiemann to *Frankfurter Zeitung*, 26.11.1922 and to Fritz Klein, *Deutsche Allgemeine Zeitung*, 12.2.1923. Both ibid.
16. CGBP Protocol of 5.11.1925 LPSR. F. 4985, Apr. 1, L. 4.
17. 'Sozialdemokratie und deutsche Fraktion', RR 26.9.25. Donath II, 9, pp. 2610–12.
18. CGBP Protocol of 5.12.1925. F. 2626, Apr. 1, L. 8.
19. K. Stavenhagen, *Das Deutschtum in Lettland. Taschenbuch des Grenz- und Auslandsdeutschtum*, Berlin, 1927, p. 15.
20. Bruns' 'Voraussetzungen und Wege für die deutsche Politik zum Schutz der deutschen Minderheiten in Polen'. 29.12.1920. Cited H. Pieper, *Minderheitenfrage und das Deutsche Reich 1919–1933/4*, p. 70.
21. Ibid., pp. 75 ff; Schot, *Nation oder Staat*, p. 142.
22. S. Bamberger-Stemmann, *Der Europäische Nationalitätenkongress*, pp. 162 ff.
23. Cf. Schot, *Nation oder Staat*, p. 147, citing memo.
24. Ibid., p. 147.
25. Hiden, *Baltic states and Weimar Ostpolitik*, pp. 172 ff.
26. Ibid., pp. 152–5, 160–1.
27. 'Wir und die deutsche Volksgemeinschaft', RR 4.6.1925. Donath, II, 9, pp. 2564–5. 'Die Autonomie ist die Voraussetzung der Staatlichkeit und die Staatlichkeit ist die Voraussetzung der Autonomie'.
28. 'Funf Jahre', RR 17.11.1923. Donath, II, 7, pp. 1869–70.
29. 'Weltpolitisches Gleichgewicht', RR 5.7.1924. Donath, II, 8, pp. 2201–2.
30. 'Jahresausschau', RR 3.1.1925. Donath II, 9, pp. 2463–4.
31. 'Staatliche Schicksalsgemeinschaft', RR 17.1.25. Donath, II, 9, pp. 2467–8.
32. 'Antiparlamentarismus', RR 28.6.1924. Donath, II, 8, pp. 2196–7.
33. Source, note 30.
34. 'Der baltische Zweibund', RR 3.11.1923. Donath II, 7, pp. 1864–5.
35. 'Helsingfors', RR 10.1.1925. Donath II, 9, pp. 2465–6.
36. 'Friedensgarantie', RR 30.8.1924. Donath II, 8, pp. 2214–5.
37. 'Europas Versagen', RR 8.8.1925. Donath II, 9, pp. 2588–9.
38. 'Leve Finland', RR 21.6.26. Donath II, 10, pp. 2902–3.
39. Bamberger-Stemmann, *Nationalitätenkongress*, p. 74.
40. Ibid., p. 94.

41. Cited Grundmann, *Deutschtumspolitik*, p. 286.
42. Bamberger-Stemmann, p. 88.
43. Nicolai von Berg to Schiemann, 28.1.1928. Schiemann Nachlass. Nicolai von Berg, 1922–36.
44. Cf. M. Garleff, 'Baltischen Minderheitenvertreter auf den Europäischen Nationalitätenkongress 1925–38', *Jahrbuch des baltischen Deutschtums*, 1986, pp. 119 ff, and 'Deutschbaltische Publizisten etc.', p. 191; Rothbath, 'Grenzrevision und Minderheitenfragen etc.', p. 13.
45. Bamberger-Stemmann, *Nationalitätenkongress*, p. 77.
46. Ibid., pp. 94 ff.
47. Ibid., p. 75.
48. 'Werden und Wesen der Nationalitätenbewegung', *Der Christliche Ständestaat*, no. 25, 23.6.1935.
49. Bamberger-Stemmann, *Nationalitätenkongress*, p. 91 ff.
50. CGBP protocol, 13.8.1925. LPSR. F. 4985, Apr. 1, L. 4.
51. M. Garleff, 'Baltische Minderheitenvertreter auf den Europäischen Nationalitätenkongressen', p. 119.
52. Garleff, 'Deutschbaltische Publizisten etc.', p. 200.
53. See next chapter.
54. Bamberger-Stemmann, *Nationalitätenkongress*, pp. 104, 116.
55. Schot, *Nation oder Staat*, p. 104.
56. CGBP Protocol of 5.11.1925. LPSR. F. 4985, Apr. 1, L. 4.
57. 'Die Genfer Minoritäten-Konferenz', RR 29.10.1925. Donath II, 9, pp. 2624–5.
58. Cf. K. Aun, *Der völkerrechtliche Schutz nationaler Minderheiten in Estland von 1917–1940*, Hamburg, 1951, pp. 25 ff.
59. R. Peters, 'Baltic states diplomacy and the League of Nations', p. 288.
60. Cf. 'Minderheitenrecht', RR 8.9.1923. Donath, II, 7, p. 1849.
61. Peters, 'Baltic states diplomacy', p. 293.
62. Aun, 'Der völkerrechtliche Schutz', p. 24.
63. Sitzungsbericht des Kongresses 25–27.8.1926, Vienna-Leipzig, 1927.
64. Schiemann, 'Die nationalen Minderheiten Lettlands etc.', pp. 276–81.
65. Schot, *Nation oder Staat*, pp. 16–17, 169.
66. Ibid., p. 290.
67. Cf. G. Bruns, 'Grundfragen der Minderheitenverträge unter besonderer Berücksichtigung der Praxis des Völkerbunds' in his *Gesammelte Schriften zur Minderheitenfrage*, Berlin, 1933, pp. 77 ff.
68. 'Minoritätenschutz und Nationalitätenrecht', RR 20.2.1926. Donath, II, 10, pp. 2859–60.
69. Source, note 63.
70. Cf. discussion of statistics by E. Ammende, 'Die Sprache der Zahlen', *Nation und Staat*, Heft 10/11, 1931, pp. 650–6.
71. R. Pearson, *National minorities in Eastern Europe*, London, 1983, p. 144.
72. Cf. Schot, *Nation oder Staat*, pp. 169–70.
73. Cited in AA Akten betreffend Sozialismus, Bolschevismus, Kommunismus. Randstaaten Bd 1. FO K2171/K601667–8.

74. See 'Das Auslandsdeutschtum und Schwarz-Weiss-Rot', RR 6.9.1924. Donath II, 8, pp. 2218 and ibid., pp. 2224–6 for Boehm's reply, 'Der unselige Farbenstreit', RR 18.9.1924.
75. CGBP protocol 20.9.1924 LSPR. F. 2626, Apr. 1, L. 7.
76. 'Solidarität und Parteigeist', RR 20.9.24. Donath II, 8, pp. 2228–9.
77. Cited in Grundmann, *Deutschtumspolitik*, p. 286.
78. Cf. Bamberger-Stemmann, *Nationalitätenkongress*, pp. 86–7, 135.
79. Letters cited in Grundmann, *Deutschtumspolitik*, pp. 287–8.
80. Ruetz to Schiemann, 18.10.1925. Schiemann Nachlass. Rigasche Rundschau Briefe.
81. Bamberger-Stemmann, *Nationalitätenkongress*, pp. 79–80.
82. Ibid., p. 81.
83. Rotbarth, 'Grenzrevision und Minderheitenfragen', p. 14.
84. Bamberger-Stemmann, *Nationalitätenkongress*, p. 82.
85. Cf. Schot's plausible arguments, *Nation oder Staat*, pp. 38 ff.
86. The protocol of the regional conference of minority representatives of the Baltic states on 16.1.26 confirms Schiemann's centrality in getting the nationalities movement underway in Germany. LSPR F. 2626, Apr. 1, L. 8.
87. Cf. Rotbarth, 'Grenzrevision und Minderheitenfragen', pp. 13–14.
88. Bamberger-Stemmann, *Nationalitätenkongress*, pp. 148 ff.
89. Protocol of DB Demokratische Partei 11.6.1925 LPSR. F. 4985, Apr. 1, L. 4.
90. 'Zum Tode Meierovics', RR 26.8.1925. Donath II, 9, pp. 2600–1.
91. Protocol of the DB Demokratische Partei 10.9.25. LPSR. F. 4985, Apr. 1, L. 4.
92. CGBP Protocol of 27.11.1922. LSPR. F. 2626, Apr. 1, L. 7.
93. CGBP Protocol of 30.9.1925. LSPR. F. 2626, Apr. 1, L. 8.
94. 'Anonyme Wahlagitation', RR 3.10.25. Donath II, 9, p. 2615.
95. 'Deutsche Minderheiten und Deutschlands Innepolitik', RR 7.10.1925. Donath II, 9, pp. 2616–7.
96. 'Staatsvolk und Minderheit', RR 8.5.1926. Donath II, 10, pp. 2881–4.
97. 'Vetrauensmandat oder Interessenmandat', RR 12.12.25. Donath II, 10, pp. 2824–5.

Chapter 7 Thinker of the Minorities Movement

1. M. Garleff, 'Baltische Minderheitenvertreter auf den Europäischen Nationalitätenkongressen, 1925–1938', *Jahrbuch des baltischen Deutschtums*, 1986, p. 119.
2. 'Der Entwicklung einer Ideologie', RR 5.9.1925, Donath, II, 9, pp. 2602–3.
3. Cf. M. Dörr, 'Paul Schiemanns Theorie vom "anationalen Staat"', *Geschichte in Wissenschaft und Unterricht*, 8, 1957, p. 407.
4. P. Schiemann, 'Werden und Wesen der Nationalitätenbewegung', *Der Christliche Ständestaat. Oesterreichishce Wochenhefte*, Nr 25.
5. Aun, *Der völkerrechtliche Schutz nationaler Minderheiten in Estland*, p. 9.
6. 'Der Entwicklung einer Ideologie', RR 5.9.1925.
7. P. Schiemann, 'Eine Krise des Staatsgedanken', RR Nr 6, 1926.
8. Sitzungsbericht des Kongresses der organisierten nationalen Gruppen in den Staaten Europas, 25–27.8.1926, Geneva, 1926, p. 39.

9. 'Volksgemeinschaft u. Staatsgemeinschaft', *Nation und Staat*, vol. 1, no. 1, p. 23.
10. A. Cobban, *The nation state and national self-determination*, London, Glasgow, 1969, pp. 35–6.
11. 'Drei Weltanschauungen und doch eine', RR 19.9.1931. Donath, II, 15, pp. 4420–2.
12. 'Liberalismus und Demokratie', RR 24.4.1924. Donath, II, 8, pp. 2177–8.
13. 'Eine Krisis des Staatsgedankens', RR Nr 6, 1926.
14. 'Europas Versagen', RR 8.8.1925. Donath, II, 9, pp. 2588–9.
15. 'Im Banne der Routine', RR 15.10.1927. Donath, II, 11, pp. 3251–2.
16. 'Liberalismus und Demokratie', RR 24.4.1924. Donath, II, 8, pp. 2177–8.
17. 'Volksgemeinschaft und Staatsgemeinschaft', p. 23.
18. 'Die nationale Minderheiten in Lettland', *Zeitschrift für Politik*, 14, 1925, p. 276.
19. 'Volksgemeinschaft und Staatsgemeinschaft', p. 21.
20. Ibid., pp. 22–3.
21. Ibid., p. 21.
22. 'Die nationalen Minderheiten in Lettland', p. 277.
23. *Ein europäisches Problem*, p. 40.
24. 'National-kulturelle Autonomie', RR 15.12.23. Donath, II, 7, pp. 1879–10.
25. 'Staat und Volkstum. Der Weg zum wahren Frieden'. Schiemann's opening speech at Geneva was reprinted in RR 29.10.1925, Donath, II, 9, pp. 2621–3.
26. Cf. remarks of H. Kause, 'Paul Schiemann (1876–1944), die Balten und ihre Zeitgeschichte. Zu Schiemanns 100. Geburtstag am 29 März 1976', *Jahrbuch des Baltischen Deutschtums*, 1976, p. 35.
27. Im Kerker des Nationalitätenvermerks', RR 5.9.1925. Donath, II, 9, p. 2604.
28. 'Staatsgemeinschaft und Volksgemeinschaft', RR 14.5.27.
29. 'Volksgemeinschaft und Staatsgemeinschaft', pp. 27–8.
30. 'Die nationalen Minderheiten in Lettland', p. 276.
31. The entire speech is in *Sitzungsbericht des Kongresses*, 25–27.8.1926, Vienna, 1927, pp. 34–45.
32. Internationale Presse und Minderheitenkongress', RR 7.9.1926. Donath, II, 10, pp. 2927–8.
33. Extracts in 'Der neue Weg zur Lösung des Nationalitätenproblems', RR 2.10.1926. Donath, II, 11, pp. 3125–6.
34. Source note 32.
35. 'Die Minderheiten. P. Schiemann über die Ergebnisse des Genfer-Kongresses', RR 4.9.1926. Donath, II, 10, pp. 2925–6.
36. See note 33.
37. Cf. Grundmann, *Deutschtumspolitik*, p. 348.
38. 'Die Minderheiten. P. Schiemann über die Ergebnisse des Genfer-Kongresses', RR 4.9.1926. Donath, II, 10, pp. 2925–6.
39. 'Glossen zur internationalen Minoritätenpolitik', *Nation und Staat*, vol. 1, no. 11/12, p. 778.
40. Ibid., pp. 778–9. Cf. 'Minoritätenschutz und Nationalitätsrecht', RR 20.2.1926. Donath, II, 10, pp. 2859–60.
41. J. Hiden, 'A voice from Latvia's past: Paul Schiemann and the freedom to practise one's culture', *Slavonic and East European Review*, vol. 77, no. 4, October 1999, p. 694.

42. 'Internationale Presse und Minderheitenkongress', RR 7.9.1926. Donath, II, 10, pp. 2927–8.
43. See interesting general discussion in M. Garleff, 'Nationalitätenpolitik zwischen liberalen und völkischen Anspruch' in *Reval und die Baltischen Länder. Festschrift für Hellmuth Weiss zum 80. Geburtstag*, edited Jürgen von Hehn, C. J. Kenez, 1980, pp. 113–32.
44. '*Sitzungsbericht des Kongresses der organisierten nationalen Gruppen in den Staaten Europas*', 22–24.8.1927, Geneva, 1928.
45. 'Der Konflikt im Minderheitenkongress. Abg. Schiemann über die Friesenfrage', RR 29.8.1927. Donath, II, 11, pp. 3244–5.
46. 'Streitfragen der Nationalitätenkongress', RR 1.10.1927.
47. 'Volksgemeinschaft und Staatsgemeinschaft', p. 38. Cf. Dörr, 'Paul Schiemanns Theorie vom "Anationalen Staat"', pp. 413 f and Feest, 'Abgrenzung oder Assimilation etc.', p. 513.
48. Cf. Grundmann, *Deutschtumspolitik*, pp. 345–6.
49. 'Rechtschutz des Volkstums', *Nation und Staat*, 9, 1930, p. 566.
50. See 'Staat und Volkstum. Der Weg zum wahren Frieden', RR 29.10.1925. Donath, II, 10, pp. 2621–3.
51. Sitzungsbericht des Kongresses, 22–24.1927, Vienna, 1928.
52. 'Die nationalen Minderheiten in Lettland.', p. 280.
53. 'Minderheitenziele', RR 23.4.1927.
54. 'Kulturstaat', RR 9.11.29.
55. Source note 53.
56. Cf. Garleff, 'Nationalitätenpolitik zwischen liberalen und völkischen Anspruch', p. 117.
57. 'Volksgemeinschaft und Staatsgemeinschaft', p. 28. On the international dimension, 'Zielsetzung der Minderheiten', *Der Deutsche in Polen*, 29.6.1936.
58. Cf. 'Das Wesen der Volksgemeinschaft', RR 2.7.1927. Donath, II, 11, pp. 3239–40.
59. Ibid.
60. 'Volksgemeinschaft und Staatsgemeinschaft', pp. 34–5.
61. See 'Ende der Nationalitätenbewegung?', *Der Deutsche in Polen*, 9.4.1939.
62. 'Volksgemeinschaft und Staatsgemeinschaft', p. 36.
63. Dörr, 'Paul Schiemanns Theorie etc.', p. 417; Grundmann, *Deutschtumspolitik*, pp. 344 ff; H. Kause, 'Die Jahre 1930 bis 1933 als Wende im Leben der deutschen volksgruppen in Lettland', *Jahrbuch des baltischen Deutschtums*, 1971, pp. 31–40.
64. 'Staatsgemeinschaft und Volksgemeinschaft', RR 15.5.1927. Cf. Dörr, 'Paul Schiemanns Theorie etc.', p. 416.
65. 'Volksgemeinschaft und Staatsgemeinschaft', p. 38.
66. Cf. 'Sitzungsbericht des Kongresses', 1927, pp. 79–82.
67. *Ein europäisches Problem*, p. 31; cf. Feest, 'Abgrenzung oder Assimilation', p. 513.
68. 'Das Minoritätenrecht als Grundlage des Friedens', RR 27.8.1927. Cf. D. Loeber, 'Paul Schiemann damals u. Heute', *Jahrbuch des baltischen Deutschtums*, 21, 1974, pp. 107–14.

69. Cf. 29.11.27 LPSR. F. 4985, Apr. 1, L. 4. Also RR 29.8.1927 'Der Konflikt im Minderheitenkongress. Abg. Schiemann über die Friesenfrage', Donath, II, 11, pp. 3244–5.
70. 29.11.1927 LPSR F. 4985, Apr. 1, L. 4.
71. 'Streitfragen der Natonalitätenkongress', RR 1.10.1927.
72. 'Die Wahlniederlage der nationalen Minderheiten Deutschlands', RR 2.6.1928.
73. 'Die Spaltung im Nationalitätenkongress', *Nation und Staat*, 1.3.1927, p. 160.
74. Ibid., pp. 168–9.
75. 'Herr L. Skala', RR 19.2.1929. Donath, II, 13, pp. 3813–4.
76. Bamberger Stemmann, *Nationalitätenkongress*, pp. 236–7.
77. Ibid., pp. 246–7.
78. See also Ibid., pp. 175–6.
79. Ibid., pp. 70–1.
80. Ibid.
81. Grundmann, *Deutschtumspolitik*, p. 375.

Chapter 8 The Return of the Right

1. Cf. Schiemann thanking Maltzan for his kindness during his Riga visit and for his 'complete understanding of the political situation here [in the Baltic]'. Schiemann to Maltzan, 4.9.1920. AA Akten betreffend politische Beziehungen Deutschland zu Lettland. FO Film K2330/K663555–6.
2. 'Gesandter Dr Adolf Köster gestorben', RR 19.2.30. Donath II, 13, p. 3992–4. Cf. Wallroth to Keller, 23.12.1922. Nachlass K. Keller, berufliche und politische Laufbahn 1906–1934, Herder-Institut Baltikum Nr. 283.
3. Cf. CGBP protocol 11.2.1926. LSPR. F. 2626. Apr. 1 L. 8.
4. Hiden, *Baltic states and Weimar Ostpolitik*, pp. 152–61.
5. 'Die gesprungene Feder', RR 16.10.1926. Donath II, 11, pp. 3127–8; 'Der Ruf nach dem Arbeitskabinett', RR 11.12.1926, ibid., pp. 3152–3.
6. P. Schiemann, 'Politische Jahresübersicht', *Jahrbuch des baltischen Deutschtums*, 1928, pp. 28–32.
7. For Fircks' speech, Saiema report 17 December 1926, in RR 18.12.1926, Donath II, 11, pp. 3175–6. Cf. Schiemann's 'Latvia: 1927. Eine bürgerliche Neujahresbetrachtung', RR 5.1.1927. No. 3. 1927.
8. 'Der neue Kurs', RR 18.12.1926. Donath, II, 11, pp. 3154–5.
9. Ostpolitik und Völkerbund, RR 24.3.1926. Donath, II, 10, pp. 2875–6.
10. Köster's report, 3.5.1926. Auswärtiges Amt, Akten betreffend politische Beziehungen Deutschland zu Lettland, vol 4 FO film K2331/K664223–6.
11. 'Russische Politik', RR 17.4.1926. Donath, II, 10, pp. 2877–8. For AA quote, *Akten zur deutschen Auswärtigen Politik 1918–1945*, (ADAP) Serie B, 1925–1933, vol. 1, Göttingen, 1966, P. 162.
12. 'Russland-Litauen und Lettland', RR 2.10.1926. Donath II, 11, pp. 3123–4.
13. CGBP protocol 22.2.1927 for Schiemann report on the tension in the foreign affairs commission. LPSR. F.2626. Apr. 1. L.9.
14. 'Friede im Osten', RR 26.2.1927. Donath II, 11, pp. 3212–3. Cf. 'Neutralität', RR 28.5.1927. Ibid., pp. 3235–6.

15. Cf. 'Lettland und Deutschland. Eine Antwort an den Abgeordneten Zeelen', RR 17.9.1932. Donath II, 19, pp. 6009–11.
16. Cf. CGBP protocols of 6.10.1927 and 12.10.1927. LPSR. F.2626. Apr. 1. L.9.
17. Ibid., account dated 18.10.1927.
18. 'Das russische Rätsel', RR 24.9.1927. Donath II, 11, pp. 3249–10.
19. W. von Fircks, 'Lettländische Innenpolitik und Wir', *Baltische Monatsschrift*, 3, 1927, p. 80.
20. Köster to Wallroth, 4.11.1927. Wallroth Handakten. FO film 5265H/E319679–80.
21. 'Um den Vertrag', RR 22.10.1927. Donath II, 11, pp. 3253–4.
22. 'Die Grossen und die Kleinen', RR 16.9.1927. Ibid., pp. 3247–8.
23. W. Wulffius, '1927. Rückblick und Ausblick', *Baltische Monatsschrift*, 62, 1931, p. 542.
24. Undated account, 'Streit in der deutschen Fraktion d. Lettl. Landtages wegen das Russland-Vertrages.' Keller Nachlass, Herder-Institut Baltikum Nr 288.
25. Cf. protocol of DB Demoktratische Partei committee, 11.1927. LPSR. F.4985. Apr. 1. L.4.
26. Protocol of CGBP 4.11.1927. Schiemann's report on the internal situation, LPSR. F.2626. Apr. 1. L.9.
27. Köster to Wallroth, 4.11.1927. Wallroth Handakten. FO film 5265H/E319679–80.
28. Wallroth to Köster, 9.11.1927. Ibid. See also Wallroth to Köster 19.12.1927, Ibid. 5265H/E319672
29. Source, note 15.
30. Cf. 'Im Banne der Routine', RR 15.10.1927. Donath II, 11, pp. 3251–2.
31. Köster to Wallroth, 11.11.1927. Wallroth Handakten. FO film 5265H/E319676–8.
32. Grundmann, *Deutschtumspolitik*, pp. 469–70. Cf. account of Keller's change of heart in a committee meeting of the German Balt Democratic Party on 17 F 4985. Apr. 1 L. 4. Protocol of DB Demoktratische Partei, LPSR F. 4985. Apr. 1. L. 4. On the prospects of a Schiemann-led cabinet, Dribins, 'Die Deutschbalten und die Idee vom nationallettischen Staat', p. 292.
33. Grundmann, *Deutschtumspolitik*, p. 464. See CGBP meeting of 24.11.27 for an example of Fircks pushing for the fall of the left wing government. LPSR F. 2626. Apr. 1. L. 9.
34. Köster to Wallroth, 11.11.1927. Wallroth Handakten. FO film, 5265H/E319676–8.
35. What follows is based on this undated assessment, written at some point in 1929: 'Schulen der Minoritäten in Lettland' in Nachlass K. Keller, *Das deutsche Bildungswesen in Lettland, 1919–1929*. Herder Institut Baltikum Nr 285.
36. Keller quote from undated 'Antwort auf die Fragen, wie sich das Mehrheitsvolk zu der Minderheitenfrage gestellt hat, und welchen Standpunkt die vershiedenen Minderheiten zu ihr einnehmen', Nachlass K. Keller, *Das deutsche Bildungswesen in Lettland, 1919–1929*. Herder Institut Baltikum Nr 285. Cf. P. Schiemann, 'Politische Jahresübersicht. 1928', pp. 28–32.

37. Cf. undated account, 'Die deutsche parlamentsfraktion' (Juli 1919–Mai 1934). Keller Nachlass. Herder Institute Marburg.
38. W. von Rüdiger, *Aus dem letzten Kapitel*, pp. 12–13.
39. See Schiemann's remark on the subject to his own party committee, 11.12.1929. LPSR F. 4885. Apr. 1. L. 5. Protocols of meetings of the Committee of the DB Demokratische Partei.
40. 'Mieter und Hausbesitzer innerhalb der deutsche Fraktion', RR 14.2.28. Donath II, 12, pp. 3505–6.
41. Cf. Kause, 'Die Jahre 1930 bis 1933 als Wende im Leben der deutschen volksgruppen in Lettland', *Jahrbuch des baltischen Deutschtums*, 1971, p. 35.
42. 'Verschiedene Warten', RR 28.5.1929. Donath II, 13, pp. 3845–6.
43. Kause, 'Der publizistische Widerstand Paul Schiemanns gegen den Nationalsozialismus in den deutschen Volksgruppen' in M. Garleff, ed., *Deutschbalten, Weimarer Republik und Drittes Reich*, Cologne, Weimar, Vienna, 2001, p. 200; Kause, 'Die Jahre 1930 bis 1933 etc.', p. 35.
44. F. Rosenberg, *Für Deutschtum und Fortschritt*, p. 8.
45. Cf. Schiemann's response to Rosenberg. 'Erinnerungen aus dem Jahre 1919', RR 10.1.1928. Donath II, 12, pp. 3487–8.
46. Cf. Protocols of DB Demokratische Partei committee, 18.1.1928 and 2.2.28. LPSR. F. 4985. Apr. 1. L. 5.
47. Protocol of 2.2.1928. Ibid.
48. Cf. W. Wulffius, '1927. Rückblick und Ausblick.' *Baltische Monatsschrift*, December 1927, p. 541.
49. 'Silvester', RR 31.12.1927. Donath II, 12, pp. 3452–3.
50. Feest, 'Abgrenzung oder Assimilation etc.', pp. 509–10.
51. Rüdiger, *Aus dem letzten Kapitel*, p. 12.
52. Hehn, *Umsiedlung*, p. 45.
53. 'Rechts und Links I', RR 7.1.1928. Donath II, 12, pp. 3487–9.
54. 'Rechts und Links II', RR 14.1.1928. Donath, ibid., pp. 3491–3.
55. 'Rechts und Links III. Die Politik der deutschen Fraktion', RR 16.1.1928. Donath, ibid., pp. 3494–6. RR. Cf. 'Das neue Kabinett', RR 23.1.1928. Donath, ibid., pp. 3497–8.
56. 'Das beunruhigte Europa', RR 21.4.1928. Donath II, 12, pp. 3517–8.
57. Cf. Rüdiger, *Aus dem letzten Kapitel*, pp. 12–13, on conservative attitudes to Schiemann.
58. Wallroth's memorandum of talk with P. S. von Kügelgen, Handakten Wallroth. Lettland. FO film, 5265H/E319667–8.
59. Feldmanis, 'Die Deutschbalten: Ihre Einstellung etc.', p. 368; Hehn, *Umsiedlung*, pp. 45–6. For Schiemann on Rautenfeld, protocol of DB Demokratische Partei committee, 31.3.1927. LPSR. F. 4985, Apr. 1, L. 4.
60. Cf. C. Siegert, 'Deutschbalten in Deutschland in der Zwischenkriegszeit.' p. 334.
61. Cf. Kause, 'Der publizistische Widerstand etc.', pp. 200–1 with G. von Rauch, *Baltic States*, pp. 166–7.
62. Printed as a pamphlet, Die kulturellen Aufgabe der deutschbaltischen Presse. Vortrag gehalten in der Gesellschaft 'Euphonie' in Riga am 15 November 1928. Riga, 1928. See also Donath II, 13, pp. 3775–96.

63. 'Die Baltische Monatsschrift und das Zeitungsproblem', RR 1929 Donath II, 13, pp. 3797–8.
64. 'Der Aufmarsch der Parteien', RR 18.8.1928. Donath, II, 12, pp. 3552–4.
65. Cf. 'Wahlrechtsreform', RR 27.11.1926. Donath II, 11, pp. 3142–3; 'Änderung des Wahlrechts', RR 15.12.1927. Donath, ibid., pp. 3446–7. Cf. Wachtsmuth, *Von deutscher Arbeit*, 3, pp. 410 ff.
66. 'Warum brauchen wir sechs Abgeordnete. Abg. Schiemann auf dem Diskutierabend des Gewerbevereins', RR 27.9.1928. Donath II, 12, pp. 3562–3. Cf. Schiemann's report to his party of 28.9.1928. LPSR. F. 4985, Apr. 1. L. 5.
67. 'Der dritte Landtag', RR 1.11.1928. Donath II, 12, pp. 3570–1.
68. Cf. his reports to his party on 24.11.1928 and 14.12.1928, LPSR. F. 4985, Apr. 1. L. 5. See also 'Sorgen des Tages', RR 15.12.1928. Donath II, 12, pp. 3579–80.
69. 'Silvester', RR 31.12.1928. Donath, ibid., pp. 3585–6; 'Volksgemeinschaft', RR 5.1.1929. Donath II, 13, pp. 3800–2.
70. Protocol of DB Demokratische Partei meeting 20.4.1929. LPSR. F. 4985, Apr. 1. L. 5.
71. Cf. account of meeting called by Schiemann on 24.1.1930 of enlarged CGBP to discuss relations with the government. LPSR. F. 2626, Apr. 1. L. 10 and 13.2.1930 protocol of his own party, LPSR. F. 4985, Apr. 1. L. 5.
72. Cf. Ibid., protocol of 8.1.1931.
73. Cited Wachtsmuth, *Von deutscher Arbeit*, 1, p. 119. Cf. Rüdiger, *Aus dem letzten Kapitel*, p. 17.
74. Feest, 'Abgrenzung oder Assimilation etc.', 517.
75. 'Sittlichkeit', RR 7.12.1929. Donath II, 13, pp. 3876–7.
76. Cf. protocols of DB Demokratische Partei 7.11.1929, 23.4.1930. LPSR. F. 4985, Apr. 1. L. 5.
77. 'Die Wahlniederlage der nationalen Minderheiten', RR 2.6.1928.
78. 'Die kollektivistische Gefahr', RR 18.1.1929. Donath II, 14, pp. 3975–6.
79. 'Der Europäische Gedanke und die Schule', RR 11.5.1929. Donath II, 13, pp. 3840–1.
80. Cf. 'Dr Gustav Stresemann der 50-Jährige', RR 11.5.1928, Donath II, 12, p. 3523.
81. Schot, *Nation oder Staat*, pp. 187–200.
82. 'Staatssicherheit und Minderheitenfrage. Die Rede des Abg Dr Paul Schiemann in Genf', RR, 3.9.1928.
83. Schot, *Nation oder Staat*, pp. 208–213.
84. 'Heilige Rechte', RR 22.12.1928.
85. Pieper, *Minderheitenfrage*, p. 168. Cf. W. Stresemann, *Mein Vater*, p. 547.
86. Schot, *Nation oder Staat*, pp. 234 ff.
87. Ibid., p. 238.
88. Ibid., p. 241.
89. Sitzungsbericht des Kongresses 26–28.8.1929 etc.' p. 52.
90. 'Genfer Eindrücke', RR 5.10.29 Donath II, 13, pp. 3852–5.
91. The description is taken from the title of Stresemann's most recent biographer, Jonathan Wright, *Gustav Stresemann: Weimar's greatest minister*, Oxford, 2002.
92. P. Schiemann, quoting his 1925 speech, in 'Drei Voraussetzungen. Theorie und Praxis des Minderheitenproblems', *Der Christliche Ständestaat. Oesterreichische Wochenhefte*, 12.9.37.

Chapter 9 The New Nationalist Wave

1. Wachtsmuth, *Von deutscher Arbeit*, 3, pp. 145–6.
2. Interview with Dr Freimane, Riga, 13.9.2001.
3. 'Ein Müdes Jahr', RR 11.1.1930. Donath II, 13, pp. 3973–4.
4. 'Die kollektivistische Gefahr', RR 18.1.1930. Donath, II, 13, pp. 3975–8.
5. 'Paneuropa, 'Nationalismus und Klassenbewusstsein', RR 17.5.1930.
6. 'Europäische Imperium', RR 27.6.1930.
7. 'Coudenhove und Rohan', *Nation und Staat*, 10/11, 1930, pp. 50–6.
8. 'Metternich', RR 16.6.1931. Donath II, 15, pp. 4379–81. Cf. undated 'Entwurf einer Stellungnahme zu Briands Denkschrift über einen Bund der europäischen Staaten'. Schiemann Nachlass. Div. Manuskripte zur deutschen Minderheiten.
9. 'Coudenhove und Rohan', p. 630. Cf. 'Weltkrisis und Lokalkrisis.' RR. 15.8.1931. Donath II, 15, pp. 4414–5.
10. Ibid., p. 631.
11. 'Das Problem der nationalen Minderheiten', *Europäische Revue*, June 1930.
12. 'Coudenhove and Rohan', p. 634.
13. 'Zwischeneuropa', RR 11.6.1932. Donath II, 18, pp. 5293–5.
14. On Gesamtdeutsch aspirations, Grundmann, *Deutschtumspolitik*, pp. 349, 364; Bamberger-Stemmann, *Nationalitätenkongress*, p. 69. Cf. M. H. Boehm, 'Ruf der Jungen. Zur Geschichte der deutschen Erneurungsbewegung', *Baltische Monatshefte*, 1933, pp. 674–9.
15. Bamberger-Stemmann, *Nationalitätenkongress*, p. 71.
16. Ibid., p. 188 ff
17. 'Gesandter Dr Adolf Köster gestorben', RR 19.2.1930. Donath II, 13, pp. 3992–4.
18. Rüdiger, *Aus dem letzten Kapitel*, p. 39.
19. Bruns letter to Schiemann, 26.2.1930. Schiemann Nachlass. Correspondence. Verband der deutschen Volksgruppen in Europa 1929/30. Cf. Ammende to Schiemann, 22.1.1930, on the 'catastrophe' of Köster's death for 'our work'. Ibid.
20. Cf. Bruns letter of 24.10.1927. Schiemann Nachlass. Correspondence. Verband der deutschen Volksgruppen in Europa, 1921–8.
21. 'Was ist Korruption? Rede des Abg. Paul Schiemanns auf der gestrige Parlamentssitzung', RR 15.3.1930. Donath II, 13, pp. 4003–5. Cf. discussion of credit policy of Bank of Latvia by Schiemann's own party's committee on 27 Feb. 1930. LPSR. F. 4985, Apr. 1, L. 5.
22. Dribins, 'Die deutschbalten etc.', p. 295.
23. 'In der Richtung des Krebses', RR 8.3.1930. Donath II, 13, pp. 3986–8. 'Staat und nationalität', RR 15.2.1930. Donath II, 13, pp. 3989–1.
24. Dribins, 'Die deutschbalten etc.', pp. 294 ff.
25. 'Ubernationale Staatsgemeinschaft', RR 27.2.1930. Donath II, 13, pp. 3995–6.
26. R. Wittram, 'Liberal und Konservativ als Gestaltungsprinzipien baltischer Politik', *Baltische Monatsschrift*, 1930, p. 228.
27. Cf. remarks of M. Garleff, ed., *Deutschbalten, Weimarer Republik und Drittes Reich*, Cologne, Weimar, Vienna, 2001. P. 1.

28. R. Wittram, 'Rückblick auf den Strukturwandel der deutsch-baltischen Volksgruppen im letzten Jahrzehnt vor der Umsiedlung' in P. Classen, P. Scheibert, eds, *Festschrift Percy Ernst Schramm zu seinem siebzigsten Geburtstag.* vol. 2, Wiesbaden, 1964, p. 232.
29. Feest, 'Abgrenzung oder Assimilation etc.', p. 516.
30. Feldmanis, 'Die Deutschbalten', pp. 368–9.
31. Cf. J. von Hehn, *Die Umsiedlung der baltischen Deutschen—das letzte Kapitel baltisch-deutscher Geschichte*, Marburg an der Lahn, 1982, p. 45.
32. 'Paneuropa, Nationalismus und Klassenbewusstsein', RR 15.5.1930.
33. Grosberg to Schiemann, 6.9.1930. Schiemann Nachlass. Rigasche Rundschau Briefe. Cf. Ruetz to Schiemann 25.8.30. Ibid. It seems that Schiemann had informed friends of the bad news in the last third of August.
34. Protocols of DB Demokratische Partei committee meetings 25.9.1930 and 29.9.1930. LPSR. F. 2626, Apr. 1, L. 10.
35. Rimscha to Schiemann, 19.10.30. Schiemann Nachlass. Correspondence. Rigasche Rundschau 1921–34.
36. Stieve to Schiemann, 20.11.1930. Schiemann Nachlass. Deutsche Gesandte Riga 1930/1 (Friedrich Stieve).
37. 'Nationalsozialismus I', RR 22.11.1930. Donath, II, 14, pp. 4116–18.
38. 'Nationalsozialismus II', RR 29.11.1930. Donath, ibid; pp. 4119–21.
39. 'Nationalsozialismus III', RR 6.12.1930. Donath ibid., pp. 4122–9.
40. Protocol of meeting of 1.12.1930. LPSR. F. 2626, Apr. 1, L. 10.
41. 'Nationalsozialismus V', RR 20.12.1930. Donath ibid., pp. 4130–3.
42. Ibid.
43. Sass to Schiemann 18.1.1931. Schiemann Nachlass. Aus der Arbeit der Rigaschen Rundschau'. The file has a detailed general account of the episode by E. Pabst, 'Bericht über stattgehabte und inzwischen beigelegte Differenzen zwischen den stellvertretenden Chefredakteur Dr K. Keller einerseits und den Redakteuren Oskar Grosberg, G. H. Eckhardt, Dr H. von Rimscha, C. Klassohn, Werner Grosberg und Baron W. v. Sass andererseits, 14.1.1931.
44. Rimscha to Schiemann 27.3.1931 refers to the open letter. Schiemann Nachlass. Correspondence. *Rigasche Rundschau*, 1921–34.
45. Grosberg to Schiemann, 10.1.1931. Schiemann Nachlass. Rigasche Rundschau Briefe.
46. Rimscha to Schiemann, 11.1.1931. Schiemann Nachlass Correspondence. Rigasche Rundschau, 1921–34.
47. The document, dated 7 January 1931, is with the file cited in note 43.
48. Wertheimer to Bleyer, 11.3.1930. Schiemann Nachlass: Volksgr ENK Korresp 1929/30.
49. Ibid., for a copy of Bleyer's letter dated 4.3.1930.
50. Ibid., Bruns to Schiemann, 1.12.1930.
51. Ibid., Graebe to Schiemann, 28.2.1931.
52. Ibid., Hasselblatt to Schiemann, 14.3.1931.
53. Ibid., letters from Ammende to Schiemann of 6.3.1931, 14.3.1931 and 19.3.1931. Ibid.
54. Hasselblatt to Schiemann, 14.3.1931. Ibid.

55. Bamberger-Stemmann, *Nationalitätenkongress*, p. 194.
56. Ibid., p. 189.
57. Hasselblatt to Schiemann, 14.3.1931. Schiemann Nachlass. Volksgr ENK Korresp 1929/30.
58. Schiemann to Graebe, 10.3.1931. Ibid.
59. Bamberger-Stemmann, *Nationalitätenkongress*, pp. 188–9.
60. Ibid., p. 155.
61. On his health, Ammende to Schiemann, 29.7.1930. Schiemann Nachlass: Volksgr ENK Korresp, 1929/30.
62. Bamberger-Stemmann, *Nationalitätenkongress*, pp. 278–9.
63. Cf. N. v. Berg to Schiemann, 28.1.1928, 2.7.1930. Schiemann Nachlass.: Nicolai v. Berg 1922–36.
64. Dribins, 'Die deutschbalten etc.', p. 297.
65. RR 9.3.1931. Donath II, 14, p. 4137.
66. The dispute is described in detail in Garleff, *Deutschbaltische Politik*, pp. 138–5.
67. Protocol of 9.7.1931 LPSR. F. 2626, Apr. 1, L. 10.
68. Grosberg to Schiemann, 7.4.1931. Schiemann Nachlass. Rigasche Rundschau Briefe.
69. Garleff, *Deutschbaltische Politik*, p. 155.
70. 'Die europäische Krise', RR 20.6.1931. Donath II, 14, pp. 4141–2.
71. Ruetz to Schiemann 4.3.31. Rigasche Rundschau Briefe; Hans Joachim Voss to Schiemann, Schiemann Nachlass Correspondence. *Rigasche Rundschau*, 1921–34.
72. Dribins, 'Die deutschbalten etc.', p. 297.
73. 'Das Herr in Lettland', RR 4.8.31. Donath II, 15, pp. 4405–7.
74. Schiemann to Nicolai von Berg, 21.12.31. Nachlass Schiemann. Nicolai v. Berg-P. Sch. 1922–36. Cf. Schiemann's report of a talk with Skujenieks in November 1931, LPSR. F. 2626, Apr. 1, L. 11.
75. 'Die Politik dieser Tage', RR 14.11.1931. Donath II, 15, pp. 4440–1; 'Die deutsche Fraktion gegen die neue Regierung', RR 8.12.1931, ibid., p. 4453.
76. See CGBP discussion of 21.12.31. LPSR. F. 2626, Apr. 1, L. 10.
77. Garleff, *Deutschbaltische Politik*, pp. 98 ff.
78. 'Die Tugend des Nationalismus', RR 4.7.31. Donath II, 15, pp. 4386–8.
79. Source, note 73.
80. Garleff, *Deutschbaltische Politik*, p. 99.
81. 'Das Herr in Lettland', RR 4.8.31. Donath II, 15, pp. 4405–7.
82. 'Antwort an Herrn E. M', RR 16.12.1931. Donath II, 15, pp. 4462–4. See also Schiemann to Munzinger, 10.12.1931. Schiemann Nachlass. Correspondence. *Rigasche Rundschau*, 1921–34. 1931/1932. National(-sozial)-ismus. On Ernst Munzinger see I. Feldmanis, 'Die Deutschbalten. Ihre Einstellung zum Nationalsozialismus etc.', p. 368.
83. 'Einheitskultur', RR 9.1.32. Donath II, 16, pp. 4715–7.
84. 'Hüben und Drüben', RR 30.1.1932. Donath, ibid., pp. 4723–4.
85. 'Deutsche und Letten. I', RR 5.2.32. Donath, ibid., pp. 4729–31.
86. 'Sprachenfrage in Lettland', RR 23.2.32.
87. Dribins, 'Die Deutschbalten etc.', p. 296.

88. Uexkull to Schiemann 23.1.32. Schiemann Nachlass. Volksgr ENK Korresp 1929/30.
89. Ibid., Schiemann to Terdenge (AA), 16.2.1932.
90. Ibid., Hasselblatt to Schiemann, 17.2.1932.
91. Cf. Berg to Schiemann, 27.10.1932 and 12.12.1932. Both in Nachlass Schiemann. Nicolai v. Berg-P. Sch. 1922–36.
92. Schiemann to Wilfan, 15.2.32. Schiemann Nachlass. Correspondence. Verband der deutschen Volksgruppen in Europa 1932.
93. Wilfan to Schiemann, 14.4.32. Ibid.
94. Hasselblatt to Schiemann, 29.3.32. Schiemann Nachlass: Volksgr ENK Korresp 1929/30.
95. Hasselblatt to Schiemann, 9.6.32. Schiemann Nachlass. Correspondence. Verband der deutschen Volksgruppen in Europa 1932.
96. Ibid., Ammende to Schiemann, 11.6.32.
97. Ibid., Ammende to Schiemann, 11.6.32.
98. Paul Schiemann, 'Die neue nationalistische Welle. Rede gelegentlich der Jahrestagung des Verbandes der deutschen Volksgruppen, Baden bei Wien, 26 June 1932', *Nation und Staat* sonderdruck aus 5 Jhrg, Sept 1932, Heft 12, 1–13.
99. Sitzungsbericht des Kongresses 29.6/1.7.1932, Vienna, 1933.
100. Bamberger-Stemmann, *Nationalitätenkongress*, p. 260.
101. Cf. Letters of 2.8.1932, 5.8.1932, 6.8.1932. Schiemann Nachlass. 3056: Gluckwünsche zur Verleihung der Goethe Medaille. 1932.
102. M. Garleff, 'Ein unbekannter Brief Thomas Manns an Paul Schiemann aus dem Jahre 1932', *Vierteljahrshefte für Zeitgeschichte*, vol. 4, 1969.

Chapter 10 Passage to Exile

1. 'Eine Niederlage des Rechtsgedankens. Betrachtungen zur gestrigen Parliamentssitzung', RR 5.11.32. Donath II, 19, pp. 6032–3.
2. 'Aufhebung der Unabhängigkeit unseres Richterstandes.' RR 13.12.1932. Donath II 20, p. 6313.
3. Cited in I. Butulis, 'Die Deutschbalten in der lettischen Presse in den Jahren 1930–1934', *Nordost-Archiv*, vol. 5, no. 2, p. 316.
4. Cf. G. von Rauch, *Baltic states*, pp. 151ff; A. Pabriks, A. Purs, *Latvia: the challenges of change*, London, 2001, pp. 20–1.
5. 'Unabhängige Staatsführung', RR 12.11.1932. Donath II, 19, pp. 6034–5.
6. Protocol of 10.11.1932. LPSR F. 2626, Apr. 1, L. 11.
7. R. Wittram, 'Umschau. Politische Führung', *Baltische Monatshefte*, 1933, pp. 179 ff.
8. Wachtsmuth, *Von deutscher Arbeit*, 3, p. 153.
9. Ibid., pp. 166–7.
10. 'Wilhelm Baron Fircks zum Gedächtnis', *Baltische Monatsschrift*, 1934, p. 28.
11. R. Wittram, 'Rückblick auf den Strukturwandel der deutsch-baltischen Volksgruppen im letzte Jahrzehnt vor der Umsiedlung' in *Festschrift für P. E. Schramm*, Wiesbaden, 1964, p. 241.
12. Cf. 'Deutsch-baltische Minderheitenpolitik', RR 4.1.1933. Donath II, 20, pp. 6421–3.

13. Cf. W. Fircks, 'Mitarbeit?', *Baltische Monatshefte*, 1933, p. 344.
14. 'Grenzziehung im Gemeinschaftsleben', RR 28.1.1933. Donath II, 20, pp. 6428–30.
15. Cf. Kause, 'Paul Schiemann (1876–1944) etc.', p. 33.
16. The following account draws on H. von Rimscha's 'Die Gleichschaltung der "Rigaschen Rundschau" im Jahre 1933. Aus meinen Erinnerungen', *Baltische Hefte*, 21, 1976/7, pp. 178–97, and on a CGBP meeting protocol of 8.3.1933. LPSR. F. 2626, Apr. 1, L. 11.
17. Schiemann to Winkler, 9.1.1933. Schiemann Nachlass. Rigasche Rundschau. Briefe.
18. Protocol of 8.3.1933. LPSR. F. 2626, Apr. 1 L. 11.
19. Rimscha, 'Die Gleichschaltung etc.', p. 192.
20. 'Das Ende des Kabinetts Breitsch', RR 4.2.1933. Donath II, 20, pp. 6431–2.
21. For a fuller account of what measures the German fraction deflected see Wachtsmuth, *Von deutscher Arbeit*, 2, pp. 99 ff. See also Garleff, *Deutschbaltische Politik*, pp. 177–9.
22. E. Kroeger, 'Über politische Inversion', *Baltische Monatshefte*, pp. 92 ff.
23. 'In eigener Verantwortung' RR 4.3.1933, Donath II, 20, pp. 6441–5.
24. 'Die Folgerungen sind Falsch', RR 18.3.1933. Ibid., pp. 6446–7.
25. Cf. Kause, 'Der publizistische Widerstand Paul Schiemanns gegen den Nationalsozialismus in den deutschen Volksgruppen' in Garleff, ed., *Deutschbalten, Weimarer Republik*, p. 205.
26. Rimscha, 'Die Gleichschaltung etc.,' p. 195.
27. Report of Liepens dated 20.6.1933. LPSR. F. 2575, Apr. 4, L. 5703. I am indebted to Valters Scerbinskis for this information.
28. Rimscha to Schiemann, 26.4.1933. Baltijas Centrala Biblioteka. Schiemann Nachlass. Aus der Arbeit der Rigaschen Rundschau. Korrespondenz.
29. Rimscha to Schiemann, 9.6.1933. Ibid.
30. Rimscha to Schiemann, 19.6.1933. Ibid.
31. E. Kroeger, 'Nationalpartei der deutschen Balten. Baltischer Landesdienst. Was wir wollen', *Baltische Monatshefte*, 1933, pp. 298–300.
32. W. Fircks, 'Mitarbeit', *Baltische Monatshefte*, 1933, pp. 344–50.
33. The first quote is from H. Stegmann, 'Aus meinen Erinnerungen, 1: Stadtverordneter in Riga (1920–1933)', *Baltische Hefte*, 7, 1960, p. 104; the second from 'Aus meinen Erinnerungen, II: Im sterbenden Parlament, der Saeima (1933–4)', Ibid., p. 156.
34. Feldmanis, 'Die Deutschbalten etc.', p. 369; Hehn, *Umsiedlung*, pp. 50 ff.
35. Protocol of 7.6.1933. LPSR. F. 4985, Apr. 1, L. 5.
36. Rimscha to Schiemann, 19.6.1933. Schiemann Nachlass. Aus der Arbeit der Rigaschen Rundschau. Korrespondenz.
37. Rimscha to Schiemann, 4.7.1933. Ibid.
38. See Kause, 'Die Jahre 1930 bis 1933 als Wende im Leben der deutschen volksgruppen in Lettland', *Jahrbuch des baltischen Deutschtums*, 1971, p. 40. See too Rimscha to Schiemann, 9.6.1933, 19.6.1933, 4.7.1933 and 25.7.1933. All in Schiemann Nachlass. Aus der Arbeit der Rigaschen Rundschau.' Korrespondenz.

39. Grosberg to Schiemann, 24.3.1934. Schiemann Nachlass. Rigasche Rundschau Briefe.
40. Cf. Rimscha to Schiemann 14.6.1934. Cf. Rimscha, 'Gleichschaltung etc.', p. 185.
41. Cf Stegman, II, p. 159; Wachtsmuth, *Von deutscher Arbeit*, 3, pp. 170 ff.
42. See materials cited in Garleff, *Deutschbaltische Politik*, p. 193.
43. Stegman, II, p. 159.
44. Lengthy extracts from the letters in Wachtsmuth, *Von deutscher Arbeit*, 3, pp. 178–80.
45. P. Schiemann, 'Baron Wilhelm Fircks', *Nation und Staat*, 7, 1933/4, pp. 268 f.
46. W. Wulffius, 'Wilhelm Baron Fircks zum Gedächtnis', *Baltische Monatshefte*, 1934, pp. 27–9.
47. Democratic Party Protocol of 4.4.1934. See also protocols of 14.12.1933, 23.1.1934 and 8.2.1934 .LPSR. F. 4985, Apr. 1, L. 5.
48. Feldmanis, 'Die Deutschbalten etc.', p. 380. Cf. J. von Hehn, *Die Umsiedlung*, p. 53. See too for further developments in the 1930s C. Siegert, 'Deutschbalten in Deutschland in der Zwischenkriegszeit. Versuch einer politischen Einordnung', *Nordost-Archiv*, Neue Folge, vol. 5, 2, 1996, pp. 325–48.
49. Rüdiger, *Aus dem letzten kapitel*, p. 58.
50. Erich Koch-Weser (former Reich Minister), 'Volkstum und Reich im deutschen Staatsangehörigkeitsgesetz', *Nation und Staat*, 8, 1932, pp. 526–31.
51. M. H. Boehm, *Das eigenständige Volk. Volkstheoretische Grundlagen der Ethnopolitik und Geisteswissenschaften*, Göttingen, 1932, p. 184.
52. 'Volk und Staat', RR 19.11.1932. Donath II, 19, pp. 6038–40.
53. 'Volk über den Staaten', RR 31.12.1932. Donath II, 20, pp. 6314 ff.
54. Source note 52.
55. Bamberger-Stemmann, *Europäische Nationalitätenkongress*, pp. 254 f.
56. Ibid., p. 278.
57. Ammende to Schiemann, 16.6.1934. Schiemann Nachlass. Volksgruppen 1933–5.
58. P. Schiemann, 'Ein Alter Streit', RR 8.10.1932. Cf. 'Sprachen im Judentum', RR 28.9.1932. Donath II, 19, p. 6016.
59. Cited Bamberger-Stamman, p. 288.
60. 'Missbrauchte Demokratie', *Allgemeines Jüdisches Familienblatt*, 3.2.1933. Re-printed D. Loeber, ed., *Pauls Šimanis. Raksti 1933–1940*, Riga 2000, p. 1.
61. 'Minderheitenbewegung und Judenfrage', *Der Christliche Ständestaat. Oesterreichische Wochenhefte*, 26.4.1936. Re-printed Loeber, ed., *Pauls Šimanis*, pp. 31–3.
62. Cited Bamberger-Stemmann, *Nationalitätenkongress*, p. 288.

Chapter 11 Full Circle

1. Schiemann Nachlass. Nicolai von Berg 1922–36.
2. Cf. Schiemann to Ammende 2.7.1935. Schiemann Nachlass. Korresp. 1932–7 (Oesterr.) 60. Geb. 1936.
3. Cf. remarks of H. Kause, 'Der publizistische Widerstand Paul Schiemanns gegen den Nationalsozialismus in den deutschen Volksgruppen', In M. Garleff, ed.,

Deutschbalten, Weimarer Republik und Drittes Reich, Cologne, Weimar, Vienna, 2001, p. 208.

4. Bamberger-Stamman, *Nationalitätenkongress*, p. 259.
5. Cf. account by Rüdiger, *Aus dem letzten Kapitel*, pp. 64 f.
6. 'Paul Schiemann scheidet von seinem Werk', *Der Deutsche in Polen*, 29.9.1935.
7. Bamberger-Stemmann, *Der Europäische Nationalitätenkongress*, pp. 267 f.
8. Rüdiger, *Aus dem letzten Kapitel*, pp. 49–50.
9. 'Bruderkampf im Auslandsdeutschtum', *Der Deutsche in Polen*, 9.1.1936.
10. Ibid.
11. Schiemann to Berg, 24.2.1936. Schiemann Nachlass. Nicolai von Berg 1922–1936.
12. 'Paul Schiemann-Sechziger', *Der Deutsche in Polen*, 5.5.1936.
13. Wachtsmuth to Schiemann, 3.4.1936. Schiemann Nachlass. Korrespondenz 1932–7 (Österr.)
14. R. Wittram, *Livland. Schicksal und Erbe der baltischen Deutschen*, Berlin 194, p. 83.
15. 'Dr Ammende verstorben', *Berliner Tageblatt und Handels-Zeitung*, 15.5.1936.
16. M. H. Boehm, 'Ewald Ammende als Mittler der europäischen Volksgruppen', *Jahrbuch des baltischen Deutschtums*, 10, 1963, pp. 55–60.
17. 'Minderheiten und Staat. Neue Grundlagen zur Sammlung des Deutschtums in Polen', *Der Deutsche in Polen*, 25.4.1937.
18. Cf. remarks of H. von Rimscha, 'Paul Schiemann als Minderheitenpolitiker', *Vierteljahreshefte für Zeitgeschichte*, 5, 1956, pp. 57–8.
19. 'Auslandsdeutsche Erneurung', *Der Deutsche in Polen*, 8.8.1937.
20. 'Um ein Gedankengut', *Der Deutsche in Polen*, 23.3.1937.
21. 'Das Schicksal der deutschen Minderheiten', *Neues Wiener Tagblatt*, 16.1.1936.
22. 'Volksgemeinschaft', *Neues Wiener Tagblatt*, 12.4.1936.
23. See P. Schiemann, *Ein europäisches Problem. Unabhängige Betrachtungen zur Minderheitenfrage*, Vienna, Leipzig, 1937, pp. 20–37, and 'Die Bedrohungen der Nationalitätenbewegung', *Der Deutsche in Polen*, 7.7.1935.
24. 'Kompromittierte Minderheitenpolitik', *Der Deutsche in Polen*, 13.2.1937.
25. 'Auslandsdeutsche Lebensfragen', *Neues Wiener Tagblatt*, 7.3.1937.
26. P. Schiemann, *Ein europäisches Problem*, p. 12.
27. 'Um ein Gedankengut', *Der Deutsche in Polen*, 23.3.1937.
28. Cf. 'Ende der Nationalitätenbewegung?', *Der Deutsche in Polen*, 9/4/1939. Cf. comments of Kause, 'Der publizistische Widerstand Paul Schiemanns etc.', p. 207.
29. 'Die europäischen Verfassungskrisen und die nationale Minderheiten', *Der Deutsche in Polen*, 10.6.1934.
30. 'Ein europäisches Problem', *Der Deutsche in Polen*, 27.9.1936.
31. '*Ein europäisches Problem. Unabhängige Betrachtungen*', p. 41.
32. Ibid., p. 42.
33. 'Werden und Wesen der Nationalitätenbewegung', *Der Christliche Ständestaat*, 23.6.1935.
34. Ibid.

35. See 'Staatsform und Minderheiten', 18.12.1937, and *Wirtschaft und Weltanschauung*, 29.1.1938 Both in *Der Oesterreichische Volkswirt*,
36. 'Europäische Imperium', RR 27.6.1930.
37. 'Die Abendländische Front', *Der Deutsche in Polen*, 23.5.1937.
38. 'Die Umsiedlung 1939 und die Europäische Minderheitenpolitik', *Jahrbuch des baltischen Deutschtums*, 21, 1974, pp. 99–106.
39. 'Die nationalen Minderheiten und die staatliche Kulturverwaltung', *Der Deutsche in Polen*, 3.6.1936.
40. 'Drei Weltanschauungen und noch eine', RR 9.9.1931. Donath, II, 14, pp. 4420–22.
41. Cf. remarks of H. Kause, 'Der publizistische Widerstand Paul Schiemanns etc.', pp. 208–9.
42. A copy of this report is in the collection of materials assembled by Mads Ole Balling for his reference work on interwar minority leaders. Institut für Zeitgeschichte, Munich, Mads Ole Balling ED 224/24 r-s.
43. H. Kause, 'Paul Schiemann (1876–1944), die Balten und ihre Zeitgeschichte. Zu Schiemanns 100. Geburtstag am 29 März 1976', *Jahrbuch des Baltischen Deutschtums*, 1976, p. 37.
44. H. Bosse, A. von Taube, *Baltische Köpfe*, p. 163.
45. Cf. R. Wittram, *Livland. Schicksal und Erbe der baltischen Deutschen*, Berlin, 1941, p. 84.
46. Institut für Zeitgeschichte, Munich, Mads Ole Balling ED 224/23.
47. 'Ein Führer starb', *Der Deutsche in Polen*, 13.11.1938.
48. 'Ende der Nationalitätenbewegung?', *Der Deutsche in Polen*, 9.4.1939.
49. Hehn, *Umsiedlung*, p. 61.
50. 'Ein Autonomieplan der deutschen Volksgruppe in Lettland um die Jahreswende 1938/9' in J. von Hehn, C. J. Kenez, eds, *Reval und die baltischen Länder. Festschrift für Hellmuth Weiss zum 80. Geburtstag*, Marburg/Lahn, 1980, pp. 171–80.
51. Hehn, *Umsiedlung*, pp. 75 f.
52. E. Kroeger, *Der Auszug aus der alten Heimat*, Tübingen, 1967, p. 45.
53. D. Loeber, *Diktierte Option. Die Umsiedlung der Deutsch-Balten aus Estland und Lettland*, Neumünster, 1972, p. 651.
54. D. Loeber, 'Deutsche Politik gegenüber Estland und Lettland. Die Umsiedlung der Volksgruppe im Zeichen der Geheimabsprache mit der Sowjetunion von 1939' in M. Funke, ed., *Hitler, Deutschland und die Mächte*, Düsseldorf, 1976, pp. 675–83.
55. Hehn, *Umsiedlung*, p. 102.
56. Paul Schiemann zur Umsiedlung. Ein Bericht des *Sydvenska Dagbladet* 'über ein Gespräch mit Paul Schiemann', reprinted in Hehn, *Umsiedlung*, pp. 208–9.
57. Kause, 'Der publizistische Widerstand Paul Schiemanns etc.', pp. 209, 215.
58. Hehn, *Umsiedlung*, p. 103.
59. Cited ibid, p. 103.
60. 'Die Umsiedlung 1939 und die europäische Minderheitenpolitik', *Jahrbuch des baltischen Deutschtums*, 21, 1974, pp. 99–106.
61. Ibid., p. 102.
62. Cited Hehn, *Umsiedlung*, p. 166.

63. 'Die Umsiedlung 1939', p. 106.
64. Egil Levits, 'Der Zweite Weltkrieg und sein Ende in Lettland', *Nordost-Archiv*, Neue Folge, 5, 1996, 1, pp. 39–40.
65. Hiden and Salmon, *Baltic Nations*, p. 114.
66. 'Ein Jahr Bolschewismus in Lettland 1940/1', printed as an appendix to P. Schiemann, *Zwischen zwei Zeitaltern*, p. 185.
67. Ibid., p. 186.
68. Ibid., p. 186.
69. Ibid., p. 187.
70. Ibid., p. 188.
71. Levits, 'Der Zweite Weltkrieg und sein Ende', pp. 40–1.
72. 'Ein Jahr Bolschewismus etc.', p. 193.

Chapter 12 Epilogue and Epitaph

1. Plakans, *The Latvians*, p. 149.
2. Cited in Y. Arad, *Ghetto in flames: The struggle and destruction of the Jews in Vilna in the Holocaust*, Jerusalem, 1980, pp. 37–8. See too C. Pajouh, 'Die Ostpolitik Alfred Rosenbergs 1941–1944' in Garleff, ed., *Deutschbalten, Weimarer Republik*, etc., pp. 170–1.
3. See Otto Bräutigam, *Ueberblick über die besetzten Ostgebiete während des Zweiten Weltkrieges*, Tübingen, 1954. An important study remains S. Myllieniemi, *Die Neuordnung der baltischen Länder, 1941–1944. Zum nationalsozialistischen Inhalt der deutschen Besatzungspolitik*, Helsinki, 1973.
4. On Lohse see A. Dallinn, *German rule in Russia, 1941–1945*, London, New York, 1957, p. 186.
5. Ibid., p. 174.
6. H. Wittrock, *Kommisarischer Oberbürgermeister von Riga, 1941–44. Erinnerungen*, Lüneburg, 1979, pp. 11–13.
7. Hiden, Salmon, *Baltic Nations*, p. 117.
8. Plakans, *The Latvians*, p. 149. R. Hilberg, *The destruction of the European Jews*, Chicago, 1961, pp. 190–208.
9. Kause, 'Der publizistische Widerstand Paul Schiemanns etc.' in Garleff, ed., *Deutschbalten, Weimarer Republik*, p. 210.
10. V. Freimane, 'Remembering Paul Schiemann', The manuscript, made available by its author, was originally published in a shorter form in *Literatur un Maksla*, Riga, 1994,
11. Kause, 'Der publizistische Widerstand etc.', p. 210.
12. W. von Rüdiger, 'Umsiedlung in den Warthegau 1940. Vier und ein halbes Jahr/Aug 1940 bis Anfang 1945', Copy of unpublished MS. sent to the author by Monika von Hirsteydt.
13. Rüdiger, *Aus dem letzten Kapitel*, p. 26.
14. Ibid.
15. Bosse and Taube, *Baltische Köpfe*, p. 163.
16. Freimane, 'Remembering Paul Schiemann.'

17. The remarks are from an interview the author had with Dr Freimane on 14 October 2001.
18. Ibid.
19. Interview with Dr Freimane.
20. Levits, 'Der Zweite Weltkrieg und sein Ende in Lettland', p. 46.
21. Interview with Dr Freimane.
22. Ibid.
23. Freimane, 'Remembering Paul Schiemann'.
24. Wittrock, *Kommisarischer Oberbürgermeister von Riga*, p. 106.
25. Communication of 25.8.1944. Schiemann Nachlass 3056. Paul Schiemann. Dokumente seines Lebenswegs. Aus seinem Nachlass zusammengestellt und geordnet von Otto Bong.
26. Ibid. Undated letter referring to a petition of 27.1.1954 on behalf of Schiemann's wife.
27. Letter from Helmuth Kause to author, 25.8.1996.
28. Otto Bong to Lotte Schiemann, 22.12.1968. Schiemann Nachlass. Paul Schiemann. Dokumente seines Lebenswegs.
29. Cf remarks of G. von Pistohlkors, 'Fünfzig Jahre Baltische Historikertreffen in Göttingen. Die Arbeit der Baltischen Historischen Kommission e.V.', *Jahrbuch der historischen Forschung in der Bundesrepublik Deutschland*, 1996/7, pp. 52–9.
30. Wachtsmuth letters of 2.5.1959 and 14.6.1959. Wachtsmuth, Wolfgang 1–36. Marburg 36: Briefwechsel Wolfgang Wachtsmuth (1876–1964) mit Wilhelm Schlau 1946–1964. On Wittram, H. -E. Volkmann, 'Von Johannes Haller zu Reinhard Wittram. Deutschbaltische Historiker und der Nationalsozialismus', *Zeitschrift für Geschichtswissenschaft*, 45, 1, 1997, pp. 52–46.
31. Wachtsmuth quote ibid., in his letter to Schlau of 10.6.1958. On Rimscha's role as chairman, Pistohlkors, '*Fünfzig Jahre etc.*' In general see also J. Hackmann, 'Contemporary Baltic History and German *Ostforschung*, 1918–1945: Concepts, Images and Notions', *Journal of Baltic Studies*, 30, 4, 1999, pp. 322–37.
32. Kause, 'Paul Schiemann (1876–1944), die Balten und ihre Zeitgeschichte etc.', p. 39.
33. Wachtsmuth, W., 'Recht geht vor Macht' in H. Bosse, A. Taube, *Baltische Köpfe. 24 Lebensbilder aus 8 Jahrhunderten deutschen Wirkens in den baltischen Ländern*, Bovenden, 1953, p. 163.
34. C. Moorehead, 'Small groups, big problems', *Times Higher Education Supplement*, 1.5.1998, p. 28.
35. S. Stroschein, S. Deets, 'Minorities, Kin States and the 2001 Hungarian Status Law', *Analysis of Current Events*, 14, 1, Feb. 2002, p. 14.
36. Ibid., p. 18.
37. Roy Hattersley, 'Why the nation state is now out of date', *Guardian*, 4.9.1997.
38. Cf unpublished paper of Jens Zvirgsdgrauds, 'Liberalism, pluralism, minorities and human rights', delivered at a conference on the 'The Value of Liberty: The Challenge of Isaiah Berlin', Riga, 25 September 1998.
39. Monika von Hirschhedt, '"Gerechte unter den Völkern". Israel ehrte Dr Paul und Charlotte Schiemann in Riga', *Baltische Briefe*, 53, 2000, 10.

Bibliography

UNPUBLISHED SOURCES

Latvian State Archive, Riga (LVVA)

F. 4985, Apr. 1, L. 1–5 and 10. Materials on Schiemann's own German Balt Democratic Party from its foundation, including the original statutes, membership lists and protocols of the regular meetings of the party leadership, 1920–34.

F. 2626 Apr. 1. L. 1–5. MS of W. Wachtsmuth's *Von deutscher Arbeit in Lettland* (see bibliography) under the pen-name Friedrich Just. There is also a copy of this in the Herder Institute at Marburg.

F. 2626 Apr. L. 6–15. Protocols and resolutions of the meetings of the Committee of German Balt Parties from 1920 onwards.

F. 2575, Apr. 20, L. 2. Declarations of the main German Balt political parties.

Bundesarchiv, Koblenz

Reichskanzlei Akten betreffend Auslandsdeutschtum, Auswärtige Angelegenheiten. R4 31/542–546.

Akten betreffend die Zusammenfassung der gesamten Pflege der Grenz- und Auslandsdeutschtums. R2/Zg29/1959/1059.

Politisches Archiv des Auswärtigen Amts, Bonn

Auswärtiges Amt, Akten betreffend Deutschtum im Ausland, Lettland, vol. 1 (Politik 25 Lettland).

Gesandtschaftsakten betreffend Reichsdeutsche Kolonie Riga, 1920–41 (Gg 16, Packet 39).

Foreign Office Library, London (Film)

Auswärtiges Amt, Akten betreffend politische Beziehungen Deutschland zu Lettland (K2330/K663458–668 and K2331/663689–4393).

Handakten Erich Wallroth, betreffend Lettland (5265H/E319666–828).

(For a fuller list of German archive materials bearing on many of the general questions raised in this book see bibliography in Hiden, *Baltic States and Weimar Ostpolitik*, Cambridge University Press., 1987)

Herder-Institut e.V., Marburg an der Lahn

Baltikum 10 and 11. Paul Schiemann.

Reden, Aufsätze und Leitartikel zum Minderheitenproblem (1919–33). 2 folders of Schiemann's typed leading articles and handwritten notes by Lothar Schoeler sent by Wolfgang Wachtsmuth. Baltikum 36. Wachtsmuth, Wolfgang

Briefwechsel Wolfgang Wachtsmuth (1876–1964) mit Wilhelm Schlau 1946–64.

Baltikum 279. Karl Keller
Rücktritt als Chef der Bildungsverwaltung, 1928

Baltikum 285. Karl Keller, Das deutsche Bildungswesen in Lettland 1919–29:
Die Tätigkeit der Verwaltung des deutschen Bildungswesens vom April 1920 bis Dezember 1921 (Sonderdruck aus der 'Libauschen Zeitung Nr 289 and 290 vom Jahre 1921.
Schulen der Minoritäten in Lettland.
Antwort auf die Fragen, wie sich das Mehrheitsvolk zu der Minderheitenfrage gestellt hat, und welchen Standpunkt die vershiedenen Minderheiten zu ihr einnehmen.
Die deutsche Parlamentsfraktion (Juli 1919–Mai 1934) 1.6.1934.

Baltikum 288. Karl Keller
Streit in der deutschen Fraktion d. Lettl. Landtages wegen das Russland-Vertrages—undated.

Baltikum 289. Karl Keller
Gedanken zur Erfassung des Deutschtums in Stadt und Land. 11.11.1925.

Baltijas Centrala biblioteka, Riga

Schiemann Nachlass
Correspondence. *Rigasche Rundschau*, 1921–34.
Correspondence. Verband der deutschen Volksgruppen in Europa, 1921–8, pp 1–76.
Correspondence. Verband der deutschen Volksgruppen in Europa, 1929/30
Correspondence. Verband der deutschen Volksgruppen in Europa, 1932.
Rigasche Rundschau. Briefe.
Briefe aus Riga. Lettland, 1930–4.

Div. Manuskripte z. d. Minderheiten.
Aus der Arbeit der Rigaschen Rundschau.
Aus der Arbeit 'RR' Red. Konflikte, Erklärungen etc. 1930/1.
Dt Gesandte Riga 1930/1 (Friedrich Stieve).
Nicolai v. Berg-Paul. Schiemann. 1922–36.
Three manuscripts, 1932–9.
3056. Gluckwünsche zur Verleihung der Goethe Medaille, 1932.
Aus der parlamentarischen Arbeit, 1920–33.
Volksgruppen, 1933–5.
Korresp. 1932–7 (Österr.) 60. Geb. 1936.
3056 Paul Schiemann. Dokumente seines Lebenswegs.

Institut für Zeitgeschichte, Munich

Reichskanzlei Akten betreffend Auslandsdeutschtum. Ausw Angel. MA 148.

Hentig, Dr Werner Otto v. Botschafter. Private Papiere 1914–81. Bestand ED 113, Bd 1–10.

Biographische Sammlung Mads Ole Balling: Deutsche Minderheiten-parliamentarier in Ostmittel-und Südosteuropa, 1919–45: ED 224/24—materials on Schiemann and ED 224/23 on Eduard Pant.

Manuscripts

Lotte Schiemann, 'Meine Reise von Riga nach Krementschug. Der Liebe Wegen.' Copy of ms given to author by Ruth Schiemann-Gostic.

Wilhelm von Rüdiger, 'Umsiedlung in den Warthegau 1940. Vier und ein halbes Jahr/Aug 1940 bis Anfang 1945.' Copy of unpublished ms given by Monika von Hirsteydt.

Valentina Freimane. Transcription of conversation with the author, Riga, 14 October 2001.

Hans Donath, 'Paul Schiemann—ein deutsch-baltischer Politiker. Was er den Letten heute sagen würde.' Lecture given at the Baltische Kulturtagen der 'Carl-Schirren Gesellschaft', 3 July 1994. Copy of MS. made available by Hans Donath's daughter, Ingeborg Baumann.

PUBLISHED SOURCES

Schiemann's own writing

A full listing of Schiemann's articles and speeches used in this study would take far too much space. Detailed citations are in the footnotes and what follows is a general overview. The major source, apart from his theatrical criticism for the *Revalsche Zeitung*, 1903–7, is Schiemann's political journalism for the *Rigasche Rundschau* between 1907–14 and 1919–33. One of Schiemann's former co-workers, Hans Donath, collected, edited and privately published a huge collection of Schiemann's writings:

Paul Schiemann: Leitartikel, Reden, Aufsätze in Auswahl, vol. 1 (four parts of which were published in Frankfurt am Main, between 1980 and 1991).

Paul Schiemann: Die Theaterkritiken in Riga. Eine Dokumentation. Ein kulturhistorischer Beitrag 30 Jahre vor dem Untergang (published in three parts in Frankfurt am Main, 1986).

Paul Schiemann: Leitartikel, Reden, und Aufsätze, 1919–1933 (published in 20 parts in Frankfurt am Main, 1986–92). M. Garleff and M. Imhoff have tackled shortcomings in the dating of some of the articles reproduced by Donath in their indispensable bibliographical article 'Paul Schiemanns Veröffentlichungen in der "Revalschen Zeitung" und "Rigaschen Rundschau"', *Jahrbuch des Bundesinstituts für Ostdeutsche Kultur und Geschichte*, 6, 1998, pp. 7–74. Schiemann also published extensively in other journals, notably *Nation und Staat, Jahrbuch des baltischen Deutschtums, Europäische Revue* and German newspapers including the *Berliner Tageblatt* and *Frankfurter Zeitung*. Another valuable listing can be found in M. Garleff, 'Deutschbaltische Publizisten. Ewald Ammende—Werner Hasselblatt—Paul Schiemann', *Berichte und Forschungen. Jahrbuch des Bundesinstituts für Ostdeutsche Kultur und Geschichte*, 2, 1994, pp. 217–24. The list also includes work Schiemann published in the 1930s for the anti-Nazi *Der Deutsche in Polen* as well as in *Der christliche Ständestaat. Oesterreichische Wochenhefte* and *Oesterreichische Volkswirt*. Those articles, often exceptionally difficult to read in the original, have been reprinted in D. Loeber, ed., *Pauls Šīmanis. Raksti 1933–1940*, Riga, 2000. *Der Deutsche in Polen* can also be read on microfilm in the Institut für Zeitgeschichte, Munich. See also the collection of writings edited by D. Henning, *Pauls Šīmanis. Eiropas Problēma. Rakstu izlase*, Riga, 1999.

Schiemann's important pamphlets include

Die Arbeiten des estländischen Provinzialrats. Ein Beitrag zur Zeitgeschichte der baltischen Landespolitik, Tallinn, Leipzig, 1907.

Massenland. Russische Erfahrungen und deutsche Besorgnisse, Berlin, 1918.

Das Fiasko der russischen Demokratie. Ein Beitrag zur Pyschologie der letzten Revolution, Berlin, 1918.

Die Asiatisierung Europas. Gedanken über Klassenkampf und Demokratie, Berlin, 1918.

'Die neue nationalistische Welle', *Nation und Staat*, 5, 12, pp. 1–13.

Ein Europäisches Problem. Die Minderheitenfrage. Unabhängige Betrachtungen zur Minderheitenfrage, Vienna, Leipzig, 1937.

His major speeches to the Nationalities Congress can be found in the published proceedings of each conference: *Sitzungsbericht des Kongresses der organisierten nationalen Gruppen in den Staaten Europas*, published yearly in Vienna from 1927.

Reference

M. O. Balling, *Von Reval bis Bukarest. Statistisch-Biographisches. Handbuch der Parlamentariar der deutsche Minderheiten in Ostmittel—und Südosteuropa 1919–1945*, Copenhagen, 1991.

W. Lenz, ed., *Deutschbaltisches Biographisches Lexicon 1710–1960*, Cologne, Vienna, 1970.

Peterson, C., R. Hermann, H. Schwalm, eds, *Handwörterbuch des Grenz- und Auslandsdeutschtums,*. vol 3: *Lettland*, Breslau, 1938, pp. 337–55.

Memoirs

Bischoff, M., *Die letzte Front. Geschichte der Eisernen Division im Baltikum*, Berlin, 1935.

Blankenhagen, H. von, *Am Rande der Weltgeschicht. Erinnerungen aus Alt-Livland 1913–1923*, Göttingen, 1966.

Blodnieks, A., *The undefeated nation*, New York, 1960.

Blücher, W. von, *Deutschlands Weg nach Rapallo*, Wiesbaden, 1951.

Boehm, M. H., 'Ruf der Jungen. Zur Geschichte der deutschen Erneurungsbewegung', *Baltische Monatshefte*, 1933, pp. 674–79.

Demme, F., 'Meine Erinnerungen an die Werdezeit der deutschen Schulen in Lettland', *Jahrbuch des baltischen Deutschtums*, 1930, pp. 90–2.

Duranty, W., *I write as I please*, London, 1935.

Fircks, W., *Meine Reisedecke. Erinnerungen*, ed., K. Stavenhagen, Riga, 1934.

Freimane, V., 'Remembering Paul Schiemann', unpublished ms.

Goltz, R. von, *Als politischer General im Osten*, Leipzig, 1936.

Goltz, R. von, *Meine Sendung im Finnland und im Baltikum*, Leipzig, 1920.

Gregory, J. D. *On the edge of diplomacy*, London, 1928.

Grosberg, Oskar, 'Begegnungen mit Paul Schiemann', Donath, I, 1, pp. xi–xii.

Kroeger, E., *Der Auszug aus der alten Heimat*, Tübingen, 1967.

Niessel, H., *L'evacuation des pays baltiques par les Allemands*, Paris, 1935,

Noske, G., *Von Kiel bis Kapp. Zur Geschichte der deutsche Revolution*, Berlin, 1920.

Ozols, C., 'Russia, Germany and the Baltic states', *International Affairs*, 13, 4, 1934, pp. 558–60.

[du] Parquet, Lt.-Col., *Der Drang nach Osten. L'Aventure allemande en Lettonie*, Paris, 1926.

Riesser, H. E., *Von Versailles zur Uno*, Bonn, 1962.

Rimscha, H. von., 'Die Gleichschaltung der *Rigaschen Rundschau* im Jahre 1933. Aus meinen Erinnerungen', *Baltische Hefte*, 21, 1976/7, pp. 178–97.

Rosenberg, E. von, *Für Deutschtum und Fortschritt im Lettland. Erinnerungen und Betrachtungen*, Riga, 1928.

Rüdiger, W. von, *Aus dem letzten Kapitel deutsch-baltischer Geschichte in Lettland, 1919–1939*, Hanover-Wülfel, 1955.

———, *Die Deutsch-Baltische Volksgruppe. Ausklang*, Hannover-Wülfel, 1937.

———, *Zur Abwehr in eigener Sache*, Riga, 1928.

Schiemann, P., 'Begegnungen vor dem Ersten Weltkrieg', ed Hans von Rimscha, *Baltische Hefte*, 1, 1954, pp. 10–17, and 2, 1955, pp. 18–22.

———, *Zwischen zwei Zeitaltern. Erinnerungen 1903–1919*, Lüneburg, 1979.

Stegmann, H., 'Aus meinen Erinnerungen: I. Stadtverordneter in Riga. Baltisches Schicksal um 1919. (1920–33)', *Baltische Hefte*, 7, 1960, pp. 91–113; II. 'Im sterbenden Parlament der Saeima (1933/4)', Ibid., pp. 156–79.

Tallents, S., *Man and Boy*, London, 1943.

Wachtsmuth, W. *Wege, Umwege, Weggenossen*, Munich, 1954.

———, *Von deutscher Arbeit in Lettland 1918–1934. Ein Taetigkeitsbericht. Materialen zur Geschichte des baltischen Deutschtums*, vol. 1: *Die deutsch-baltsche Volksgemeinschaft in Lettland, 1923–34*, Cologne, 1951; vol. 2: *Die autonome deutsche Schule in Lettland, 1920–34. Mit einem Anhang: Das Herder-Institut zu Riga*, Cologne, 1952; vol 3: *Das politische Gesicht der deutschen Volksgruppe in Lettland in der parlamentarische Period 1918–193*, Cologne, 1953.

Watson, H. A. G., *An account of a mission to the Baltic states in the year 1919*, London, 1957.

Wette, W., *Gustav Noske. Eine politische Biographie*, Düsseldorf, 1987.

Winnig, A., *Am Ausgang der deutschen Ostpolitik. Persönliche Erlebnisse und Erinnerungen*, Berlin, 1927.

———, *Heimkehr*, 1935.

Wittrock, H., *Kommisarischer Oberbürgermeister von Riga, 1941–4. Erinnerungen*, Lüneburg, 1979.

Other books and articles

Ahmann, R., 'The German Treaties with Estonia and Latvia of 7 June 1939—Bargaining Ploy or an Alternative for German-Soviet Understanding?', *Journal of Baltic Studies*, 20, 1989, pp. 337–64.

Ammende, E., 'Auf falschem Wege', *Nation und Staat*, 5, 9, 1932, pp. 594–8.

———, 'Die Sprache der Zahlen', *Nation und Staat*, 10/11, 1931, pp. 650–6.

———, 'Genf und die Nationalitäten', *Nation und Staat*, 7, 2, 1933, pp. 72–82.

———, 'Zwiespaltige Mentalität. Ein Beitrag zur Charakteristik der nationalen Krise', *Nation und Staat*, 1, 8, 1927/8, pp. 542–5.

———, *Die Nationalitäten in den Staaten Europas. Sammlung von Lageberichten*, Vienna, Leipzig, 1931.

Angelus, O., *Die Kulturautonomie in Estland*, Detmold, 1951.

Arad, Y., *Ghetto in flames: The struggle and destruction of the Jews in Vilna in the Holocaust*, Jerusalem, 1980.

Aun, K., *Der völkerrechtliche Schutz nationaler Minderheiten in Estland von 1917–1940*, Hamburg, 1951.

Bamberger-Stemmann, S. *Der Europäische Nationalitätenkongress 1925 bis 1938*, Marburg/Lahn, 2000.

Bauer, O., *Die Nationalitätenfrage und die Sozialdemokratie*, Vienna, 1907.

Baumgart, W., *Deutsche Ostpolitik. Von Brest-Litovsk bis zum Ende des Ersten Weltkrieges*, Vienna, Munich, 1966.

Benz, E., *Die Revolution von 1905 in den Ostseeprovinzen Russlands. Ursachen und Verlauf der lettischen und estnischen Arbeiter- und Bauernbewegung im Rahmen der ersten russischen Revolution*, Mainz, 1990.

Bilmanis, A., *A History of Latvia*, Princeton, NJ, 1951.

Boehm, M. H., *Das eigenständige Volk. Volkstheoretische Grundlagen der Ethnopolitik und Geisteswissenschaften*, Göttingen, 1932.

———, 'Vom Problem der Autonomie', *Baltische Monatsschrift*, 60, 1929, pp. 716–26.

———, 'Ewald Ammende als Mittler der Europäischen Volksgruppen', *Jahrbuch des baltischen Deutschtums*, 10, 1963, pp. 55–60.

Boelitz, O., *Das Grenz-und Auslandsdeutschtum. Seine Geschichte und seine Bedeutung*, Munich-Berlin, 1926.

Bosse, H., A. Taube, *Baltische Köpfe. 24 Lebensbilder aus 8 Jahrhunderten deutschen Wirkens in den baltischen Ländern*, Bovenden, 1953.

Bräutigam, O., *Ueberblick über die besetzten Ostgebiete während des Zweiten Weltkrieges*, Tübingen, 1954.

Bruns, G., *Gesammelte Schriften zur Minderheitenfrage*, Berlin, 1933.

Buelow, F. W. von, 'Social aspects of agrarian reform in Latvia', *International Labour Review*, 20, 1929, pp. 35–66.

Butulis, I., 'Die Deutschbalten in der lettischen Presse in den Jahren 1930–1934', *Nordost-Archiv*, 5, 2, pp. 301–24.

Carsten, F. L., *Reichswehr und Politik*, Cologne-Berlin, 1964.

Cobban, A., *The nation state and national self-determination*, London, Glasgow, 1969.

Conze, W., 'Nationalstaat oder Mitteleuropa? Die Deutschen des Reiches und die Nationalitätenfragen Ostmitteleuropas im ersten Weltkrieg' in W. Conze, ed., *Deutschland und Europa*, Düsseldorf, 1951.

Crohn-Wolfgang, H. F., *Lettlands Bedeutung für die Oestliche Frage*, Berlin, Leipzig, 1923.

Dallinn, A., *German rule in Russia, 1941–1945*, London, New York, 1957.

Dehio, G., *Livland und Elsass*, Berlin, 1918.

'Der Bericht der Genralleutnants Walter von Eberhardt "Meine Tätigkeit im Baltikum"', *Zeitschrift für Ostforschung*, 13, 1964, pp. 728–33.

Donath, H., 'Paul Schiemann—ein deutsch-baltischer Politiker. Was er den Letten heute sagen würde'. Photocopy of lecture in author's possession.

Dopkewitsch, H., *Die Entwicklung des lettländischen Staatsgedenken bis 1918*, Berlin, 1936.

———, 'Zur englischen Politik im Baltikum 1918–1919', *Deutsche Archiv für Landes-und Volksforschung*, 6, 1942, pp. 119–47.

Dörr, M., 'Paul Schiemanns Theorie vom "anationalen Staat"', *Geschichte in Wissenschaft und Unterricht*, 8, 1957, pp. 407–21.

Doss, K., *Reichsminister Adolf Köster, 1883–1930. Ein Leben für die Weimarer Republik*, Düsseldorf, 1978.

Drews, H., *Die lettische Revolution und das Baltentum*, Riga, 1927.

Dribins, L., 'Die Deutschbalten und die Idee vom nationallettischen Staat (1918–1934)', *Nordost-Archiv*, 5, 1996, pp. 277–99.

Dziewanowski, M. K., *Joseph Pilsudski: A European federalist 1918–1922*, Stanford, CA, 1969.

E., 'Nationalpartei der deutschen Balten. Baltischer Landesdienst. Was wir wollen', *Baltische Monatshefte*, 1933, pp. 298–300.

Elvert, J., *Deutsche Pläne zur europäischen Neuordnung 1918–1945*, Stuttgart, 1999.

Epstein, K., *Matthias Erzberger and the dilemma of German democracy*, Princeton, NJ, 1959.

Ezergailis, A., and G. Pistohlkors, ed., *Die baltischen Provinzen Russlands zwischen den Revolutionen von 1905 und 1917*, Cologne, 1983.

Fechner, H., 'Das Ende der deutschen Ostpolitik im Baltikum', *Ostbrief: Mitteilung der Ostdeutschen Akademie*, Lüneburg, 11, pp. 233–7.

Feest, D., 'Abgrenzung oder Assimilation. Ueberlegungen zum Wandel der deutschbaltischen Ideologien 1918–1939 anhand der 'Baltischen Monatsschrift', *Zeitschrift f. Ostmitteleuropa-Forschung*, 45, 4, 1996, pp. 505–43.

Feldmanis, I., 'Die Deutschbalten. Ihre Einstellung zum Nationalsozialismus und ihr Verhältnis zum Staat Lettland (1933–9)', *Nordost-Archiv*, 5, 2, 1966, pp. 363–86.

Fircks, W., 'Innenpolitische Jahresübersicht', *Jahrbuch des baltischen Deutschtums*, Riga, 1926.

———, 'Minderheitenautonomie in Lettland' in K. C. von Loesch, ed., *Bücher des Deutschtums*, vol. 2, Berlin, 1926, pp. 164–72.

———, 'Lettlands Innenpolitik und Wir', *Baltische Monatsschrift*, 3, 1927, pp. 178–85.

———, 'Volkstum und Bodenständigkeit', *Baltische Monatsschrift*, 58, 1, 1927, pp. 35–43.

———, 'Mitarbeit', *Baltische Monatsschrift*, 1933, pp. 344–50.

Frauenstein, A. M., *Die Zentraleuropäischen Randstaaten mit besonderer Berücksichtigung des Baltischen Dreibund-Problems Lettland, Estland und Litauen*, Riga, 1921.

Garleff, M., 'Ein unbekannter Brief Thomas Manns an Paul Schiemann aus dem Jahre 1932', *Vierteljahrshefte für Zeitgeschichte*, 4, 1969, pp. 450–3.

———, *Deutschbaltische Politik zwischen den Weltkriegen*, Bonn, Bad Godesburg, 1976.

———, 'Paul Schiemanns Minderheitentheorie als Beitrag zur Lösung der Nationalitätenfrage.' *Zeitschrift für Ostforschung*, 25, 4, 1976, pp. 632–60.

———, 'The politics of coalition.' In V. S. Vardys, R. J. Misiunas eds., *The Baltic states in peace and war 1917–1945*, Pennsylvania-London, 1978.

———, 'Autonomiemodelle in den baltischen Staaten zur Zeit ihre Selbständigkeit.' *Jahrbuch des baltischen Deutschtums*, 1980, pp. 150–6.

———, 'Nationalitätenpolitik zwischen liberalen und völkischen Anspruch' in Jürgen von Hehn, C. J. Kenez, eds, *Reval und die Baltischen Länder. Festschrift für Hellmuth Weiss zum 80. Geburtstag*, 1980, pp. 113–32.

———, 'Baltische Minderheitenvertreter auf den Europäischen Nationalitätenkongress 1925–8', *Jahrbuch des baltischen Deutschtums*, 1986, pp. 117–31.

———, 'Deutschbaltische Publizisten. Ewald Ammende-Werner Hasselblatt-Paul Schiemann.' 'Berichte und Forschungen', *Jahrbuch des Bundesinstitut für Ostdeutsche Kultur und Geschichte*, 2, 1994, pp. 189–229.

———, ed., *Deutschbalten, Weimarer Republik und Drittes Reich*, vol. 1, Cologne, Weimar, Vienna, 2001.

Gernet, B., 'Lettlands auswärtige Handelsbeziehungen', *Lettlands Oekonomist*, Riga, 1929, pp. 22–45.

Grimm, C., *Jahre deutscher Entscheidung im Baltikum*, Essen, 1939.

Grundmann, K. -H., *Deutschtumspolitik zur Zeit der Weimarer Republik. Eine Studie am Beispiel der deutsch-baltischen Minderheit in Estland und Lettland*, Hannover-Döhren, 1977.

Hackmann, J., 'Contemporary Baltic History and German *Ostforschung*', *Journal of Baltic Studies*, 30, 4, 1999, pp. 322–37.

Hagen, M., 'Die Deutschbalten in der III Duma', *Zeitschrift für Ostforschung*, 23, 1974, pp. 577–97.

Haltzel, M., *Der Abbau der deutschen ständischen Selbstverwaltung in den Ostseeprovinzen Russlands*, Marburg/Lahn, 1977.

Handrack, H., *Die Bevoelkerungsentwicklung der deutschen Minderheit in Lettland*, Jena, 1932.

Hasselblatt, W., 'Gedanken über Sicherung des baltischen Raumes', *Baltische Monatsschrift*, 1928, pp. 12–23.

———, 'Die deutschen Minderheiten in Europa', *Süddeutsche Monatshefte*, 26, 1928/9, pp. 726–8.

Hehn, J. von, *Die Entstehung der Staaten Lettland und Estland. Der Bolschewismus und die Grossmächten*, Berlin, 1956.

———, *Lettland zwischen Demokratie und Diktatur*, Munich, 1957.

———, 'Das Herder-Institut zu Riga, 1921–1939', *Zeitschrift für Ostforschung*, 30, pp. 494–526.

———, 'Die Lage des Deutschtums in den baltischen Staaten am Vorabend der nationalsozialistischen Machtergreifung', *Zeitschrift für Ostforschung*, 28, pp. 602–55.

———, 'Ein Autonomieplan der deutschen Volksgruppe in Lettland um die Jahreswende 1938/9' in J. von Hehn, C. J. Kenez, eds, *Reval und die baltischen Länder. Festschrift für Hellmuth Weiss zum 80 Geburtstag*, Marburg/Lahn, 1980, pp. 171–80.

———, 'Vom baltischen Deutschtum in den letzten 20 Jahren (Bemerkungen zu seiner Geschichte in der Nachweltkriegszeit und zur Umsiedlung', *Deutsches Archiv für Landes- und Volksforschung*, 5, 1941, pp. 216–41.

———, 'Zum Deutsch-Lettischen Verhältnis im Jahr 1939', *Zeitschrift für Ostforschung*, 23, 4, pp. 661–75.

———, and H. Rimscha, *Von den baltischen Provinzen zu den baltischen Staaten. Beiträge zur Entstehungsgeschichte der Republiken Estland und Lettland, 1917–1918*, Marburg/Lahn, 1971.

———, *Die Umsiedlung der baltischen Deutschen-das letzte Kapitel baltischdeutscher Geschichte*, Marburg, 1982.

Henning, D., 'Letten und Deutsche. Aspekte einer schwierigen Nachbarschaft.' *Nordost-Archiv*, 5, 2, 1996.

Heyking, A. von, *The main issues confronting the minorities of Latvia and Estonia*, London, 1922.

Hiden, J., 'The Baltic Germans and German policy towards Latvia after 1918', *Historical Journal*, 13, 2, 1970, pp. 295–317.

———, 'A voice from Latvia's past: Paul Schiemann and the freedom to practise one's culture', *Slavonic and East European Review*, 77, 4, 1999, pp. 680–99.

———, 'Baltic gold and Latvian privatisation', *Journal of Baltic Studies*, 23, 1, pp. 63–72.

———, 'The significance of Latvia. A forgotten aspect of Weimar Ostpolitik', *Slavonic East European Review*, 53, 132, 1977, pp. 295–317.

———, 'The Weimar Republic and the problem of the Auslandsdeutsche', *Journal of Contemporary History*, 12, 1977, pp. 273–89.

———, *The Baltic states and Weimar Ostpolitik*, Cambridge, 1987.

———, 'Paul Schiemann on reconciling "nation" and "state"' in M. Leskelä, ed., *Constructing Identities in an integrating Europe*, Turku, 1999, pp. 217–233.

———, and P. Salmon, *The Baltic nations and Europe*, London, 1991.

Hilberg, R., *The destruction of the European Jews*, Chicago, 1961.

Hoetsch, O., 'The Baltic states, Germany and Russia', *Foreign Affairs*, 10, 1, p. 120–33.

Hoover, K. D., 'The Baltic re-settlement of 1939 and National Socialist racial policy', *Journal of Baltic Studies*, 8, 1, pp. 79–89.

Hovi, K., *Cordon sanitaire or barrière de l'est: The emergence of the new French East European Alliance policy, 1917/19*, Turku, 1976.

Janssen, K. -H., 'Die baltische Okkupationspolitik des deutschen Reiches' in J. von Hehn *et al.*, *Von den baltischen Provinzen zu den baltischen Staaten*, Marburg/Lahn, 1971.

Johnsson, S. H., 'The coup d'etat that failed', *Baltic Review*, 22, 1961, pp. 49–53.

Jones, L. E., *German liberalism and the dissolution of the Weimar party system 1918–1933*, Chapel Hill, NC, 1988.

Kahn, E., *Die Agrarstruktur Lettlands bis 1939*, Königsberg, 1942.

Kause, H., 'Die Einstellung Paul Schiemanns (1876–1944) zur deutsch-baltischen Politik vor 1914' in A. Ezergailis, G. von Pistohlkors, eds, *Die baltischen Provinzen Russlands zwischen den Revolutionen von 1905 und 1917*, Cologne, Vienna, 1982, pp. 155–72.

———, 'Paul Schiemann (1876–1944), die Balten und ihre Zeitgeschichte', *Jahrbuch des baltischen Deutschtums*, 1976, pp. 32–9.

———, 'Der publizistische Widerstand Paul Schiemanns gegen den Nationalsozialismus in den deutschen Volksgruppen' in M. Garleff, ed., *Deutschbalten, Weimarer Republik und Drittes Reich*, Cologne, Weimar, Vienna, 2001.

———, 'Die Jahre 1930 bis 1933 als Wende im Leben der deutschen Volksgruppen in Lettland', *Jahrbuch des baltischen Deutschtums*, 1971, pp. 31–40.

———, 'Es ist eine Lust zu leben. Einige Bebachtungen zur Stellung Paul Schiemanns (1876–1944) in deutschbaltischen Oeffentlichkeit vor und nach dem Ersten Weltkrieg' in J. v. Hehn, C. J. Kenez, eds, *Reval und die baltischen Länder. Festschrift für Hellmuth Weiss zum 80 Geburtstag*, Marburg/Lahn, 1980, pp. 106–112.

———, 'Paul Schiemann (1876–1944), die Balten und ihre Zeitgeschichte. Zu Schiemanns 100. Geburtstag am 29 März 1876', *Jahrbuch des Baltischen Deutschtums*, 1976, pp. 32–9.

Keller, K., 'Unsere deutschen Schulen', *Jahrbuch des baltischen Deutschtums*, 1927, pp. 33–5.

Kitchen, M., 'Hindenburg, Ludendorff and the Baltic', *East European Quarterly*, 11, 4, pp. 429–44.

Kluge, P., 'Das lettländische Geldwesen und die Tätigkeit der Bank von Lettland', *Osteuropa*, 2, 1926/7, pp. 517–27.

Knorre, W. von, 'Vom Wirtschaftsleben des baltischen Deutschtums' in M. H. Boehm, H. Weiss eds., *Wir Balten*, Salzburg-Munich, 1951, pp. 112–16.

Koch-Weser, E., 'Volkstum und Reich im deutschen Staatsangehörigkeitsgesetz', *Nation und Staat*, 8, 1932, pp. 526–31.

Koehl, R. L., 'The Nazi 'resettlement' swindle', *Journal of Baltic Studies*, 4, 3, 1973, pp. 244–69.

Komjathy, A., and R. Stockwell, *German minorities and the Third Reich: Ethnic Germans of East Central Europe between the wars*, New York, London, 1980.

Krastins, J., *Riga. Art Nourveau Metropolis*, Riga, 1996.

Krekeler, N., *Revisionsanspruch und geheime Ostpolitik. Die Subventionierung der deutschen Minderheit in Polen*, Stuttgart, 1973.

Kroeger, E., 'Nationalpartei der deutschen Balten. Baltischer Landesdienst. Was wir wollen', *Baltische Monatshefte*, 1933, pp. 298–300.

———, 'Ueber politische Inversion', *Baltische Monatshefte*, 1933, pp. 92 ff.

Kroeger, G., 'Zur Situation der baltischen Deutschen um die Jahrhundertwende', *Zeitschrift für Ostforschung*, 17, 1968, pp. 601–32.

Lange, F., 'Die Deutschbalten—Hindernis für eine Annäherung zwischen Lettland und dem Dritten Reich?', *Nordost-Archiv* 5, 2, 1996 pp. 349–62.

Lemburg, E., 'Zur Geschichte der deutschen Volksgruppen in Ost-Mitteleuropa', *Zeitschrift für Ostforschung*, 1, 3, 1952, pp. 321–45.

———, *Ostmitteleuropa zwischen den beiden Weltkriegen 1918–1939. Stärke und Schwäche der neuen Staaten, nationale Minderheiten*, Marburg, 1997.

Lenz, W., 'Deutsche Machtpolitik in Lettland im Jahre 1919. Ausgewählte Dokumente des von General Rüdiger von der Goltz geführten Generalkommandos des VI Reservekorps,' *Zeitschrift für Ostforschung*, 36, 1987, pp. 523–76.

———, 'Die Umsiedlung der Deutschen aus Lettland', *Jahrbuch des baltischen Deutschtums*, 1964, pp. 80–7.

———, 'Vom politschen Schicksal des baltischen Deutschtums. Welches Mass an Freiheit besassen die beiden letzten baltischen Generationen?', *Jahrbuch des baltischen Deutschtums in Lettland und Estland*, 1959, pp. 62–9.

———, *Der baltische Literatenstand*, Marburg/Lahn, 1953.

———, 'Paul Schiemann in Memoriam', *Baltische Hefte*, 7/8, 1969.

———, 'Zur britischen Politik gegenüber den baltischen Deutschen 1918–1919' in Thaden, Pistohlkors, eds, *Das Vergangene und die Geschichte*, Göttingen, 1973, pp. 272–82.

Levits, E., 'Der Zweite Weltkrieg und sein Ende in Lettland', *Nordost-Archiv*, 5, 1996, pp. 37–62.

Liulevicius, V. G., *War land on the Eastern Front: Culture, national identity and German occupation in World War 1*, Cambridge, 2000.

Loeber, D., 'Deutsche Politik gegenüber Estland und Lettland. Die Umsiedlung der Volksgruppe im Zeichen der Geheimabsprache mit der Sowjetunion von 1939' in M. Funke, ed., *Hitler, Deutschland und die Mächte*, Düsseldorf, 1976, pp. 675–83.

———, *Diktierte Option. Die Umsiedlung der Deutsch-Balten aus Estland und Lettland*, Neumünster, 1972.

———, 'Paul Schiemann damals und Heute', *Jahrbuch des baltischen Deutschtums*, 21, 1974, pp. 107–14.

———, '*Die Minderheitenschutzverträge—Entstehung, Inhalt und Wirkung*' in H. Lemberg, ed., *Ostmitteleuropa zwischen den beiden Weltrkiegen*, 1918–1939, Marburg, 1997, pp. 189–200.

Loit, A. ed, *The Baltic countries, 1900–1914*, Stockholm, 1990.

Lundin, C. L., 'The road from Tsar to Kaiser: the changing loyalties of the Baltic Germans, 1905–1914', *Journal of Central European Affairs*, 10, 1950, pp. 223–55.

Macartney, C. A., *National states and national minorities*, London, 1934.

Mann, B., *Die baltischen Länder in der deutschen Kriegszielpublizistik 1914–1918*, Tübingen, 1965.

Maydell, K., 'Die Baltendeutschen vor ihrer Umsiedlung. Ein statistischer Rückblick', *Jomsburg*, 4, 1940, pp. 59–90.

Meissner, B., ed., *Die baltischen Nationen. Estland, Lettland, Litauen*, Cologne, 1990.

Mendelsohn, E., *The Jews of East Central Europe between the two world wars*, Bloomington, IN, 1987.

Meyer, K., *Theodor Schiemann als politischer Publizist*, Frankfurt am Main, 1956.

Meyer, P., *Die Industrie Lettlands*, Riga, 1925.

Mintz, M., *Die nationale Autonomie im System des Minderheitenrechtes unter besondere Berücksichtigung der Rechtsentwicklung in den baltischen Staaten*, Riga, 1927.

Myllieniemi, S., *Die Neuordnung der baltischen Länder 1941–1944. Zum nationalsozialistischen Inhalt der deutschen Besatzungspolitik*, Helsinki, 1973.

———, *Die baltische Krise 1938–1941*, Stuttgart, 1979.

Noltein, E. von, *Die Umsiedlung der Deutschen aus Lettland, 1939*, Munich, 1979.

———, 'Die Umsiedlung der Deutschen aus Lettland 1939 im Spiegel der Rigaer deutschen Presse. Ein Ueberblick', *Acta Baltica*, 19/20, 1981, pp. 182 ff.

Nottbeck, Bernard von, *Vorgeschichte einer Schlacht von Libau nach Wenden*, Tallinn, 1992.

Nottbeck, E. von, 'Organization und Verlauf der Umsiedlung der Deutschen aus Estland', *Baltische Hefte*, 1971.

Pajouh, C., 'Die Ostpolitik Alfred Rosenbergs während des Zweiten Weltkrieges', in M. Garleff, ed., *Deutschbalten, Weimarer Republik und Drittes Reich*, vol. 1, Cologne, Weimar, Vienna, 2001, pp. 37–62.

Pärn, H., 'Die Einführung der Selbstbesteurung innerhalb der Volksgemeinschaft der Deutschtum in Lettland', *Jahrbuch des baltischen Deutschtums*, 1927, pp. 45–9.

Pearson, R., *National minorities in Eastern Europe*, London, 1983.

Peters, R. P., 'Problems of Baltic Diplomacy in the League of Nations.' *Journal of Baltic Studies*, 14, 1983, pp. 128–49.

———, 'Baltic states diplomacy and the League of Nations' in J. Hiden, A. Loit eds, *The Baltic in international relations between the two world wars*, Stockholm, 1988, pp. 281–302.

Pieper, H. *Minderheitenfrage und das Deutsche Reich, 1919–1933/4*, Frankfurt/M, 1974.

Piip, Ants, 'Baltic states as a regional unity', *Annals of American Academy of Political and Social Sciences*, CLXVIII, 1933, pp. 171–7.

Pistohlkors, G. von, 'Führende Schicht oder nationale Minderheit', *Zeitschrift für Ostforschung*, 21, 1972, pp. 601–18.

———, 'Russifizierung und die Grundlagen der deutschbaltischen Russophobie.' *Zeitschrift für Ostforschung*, 1976, pp. 618–31.

———, *Ritterschaftliche Reformpolitik zwischen Russifizierung und Revolution. Historische Studien zum Problem der politischen Selbsteinschätzung der deutschen Oberschicht in den Ostseeprovinzen Russlands im Krisenjahr 1905*, Göttingen, 1978.

———, *Baltische Länder*, Berlin, 1994.

———, 'Fünfzig Jahre Baltische Historikertreffen in Göttingen. Die Arbeit der Baltischen Historischen Kommission e.V.', *Jahrbuch der historischen Forschung in der Bundesrepublik Deutschland*, 1996/7, pp. 52–9.

Plakans, A., 'Peasants, intellectuals and nationalism in the Russian Baltic provinces', *Journal of Modern History*, 46, 3, pp. 445–75.

———, *The Latvians: a short history*, Stanford, CA, 1995.

Purs, A., *Latvia. The challenges of change*, London, 2001.

Radecki, M., 'Unsere Schulen', *Jahrbuch des baltischen Deutschtums*, 1925, pp. 34–9.

Rauch, G. von, 'Der Revaler Kommunistenputsch', *Baltische Hefte*, 1955.

———, *The Baltic states: Estonia, Latvia, Lithuania: the years of independence 1918–1940*, London, 1975.

———, *Aus der baltischen Geschichte. Vorträge, Untersuchungen, Skizzen aus sechs Jahrzehnten*, Hannover-Döhren, 1980.

———, ed., *Geschichte der deutsch-baltischen Geschichtsschreibung*, Cologne-Vienna, 1986.

Rexheuser, R., 'Die Umsiedlung der Deutschbalten 1939. Versuch einer historischen Einordnung', *Jahrbuch des baltischen Deutschtums*, 1989, pp. 9 ff.

Ribhegge, W., *August Winnig—eine Historische Persönlichkeitsanalyse*, Bonn, 1973.

Rimscha, H. von, *Die Staatswerdung Lettlands und das baltische Deutschtum*, Riga, 1939.

———, 'Paul Schiemann', *Jahrbüchher für Geschichte Osteuropas*, 2, 4, 1954, pp. 475–8.

———, 'Die Politik Paul Schiemanns während der Begründung der Baltischen Staaten', *Zeitschrift für Ostforschung*, 5, 1956, pp. 68–82.

———, 'Paul Schiemann als Minderheitenpolitiker', *Vierteljahrshefte für Zeitgeschichte*, 4, 1956, pp. 43–61.

———, *Die Umsiedlung der Deutschbalten aus Lettland im Jahre 1939. Eine Betrachtung von Hans von Rimscha*, Hannover-Döhren, 1960.

———, 'Die Baltikumpolitik der Grossmächte', *Historische Zeitschrift*, vol. 177, 1973, pp. 281–309.

———, 'Die Eingliederung der deutschen Volksgruppe als nationale Minderheit in den Staat Lettland', *Jahrbuch des baltischen Deutschtums*, 1976, pp. 129–34.

Robinson, J., 'Die Juden Osteuropas als nationale Minderheit', *Nation und Staat*, 1, 1927/8, pp. 98–104.

Rodgers, H. I., *Search for security: a study in Baltic diplomacy, 1920–1934*, Hamden, CT, 1975.

Rolnik, H., *Die baltischen Staaten. Litauen, Lettland und Estland und ihre Verfassungsrecht*, Leipzig, 1927.

Rotbarth, M., 'Kontroversen im Europäischen Minderheitenkongress', *Studien zur Geschichte der deutsch-polnischen Beziehungen*, 3, Rostock, 1980, pp. 49–62.

———, 'Grenzrevision und Minderheitenfragen. Zur Funktion des Europäischen Minderheitenkongresses in der Ostpolitik des deutschen Imperialismus', *Studien zur Geschichte der deutsch-polnischen Beziehungen*, 6, 1982, pp. 5–30.

Rothfels, H., 'The Baltic provinces. Some historic aspects and perspectives', *Journal of Central European Affairs*, 4, 2, 1944, pp. 117–46.

Rüdiger, W. von, 'Deutsch-baltische Volksgemeinschaft in Lettland', *Jahrbuch des baltischen Deutschtums*, 1929, pp. 17–19.

Rutenburg, G., *Die baltischen Staaten und das Völkerrecht*, Riga, 1928.

Salts, A., *Die politische Parteien Lettlands*, Riga, 1925.

Samts, J., 'The achievements of Meierovics' last European trip', *Journal of Baltic Studies*, 7, 3, 1976, pp. 247 ff.

Schirren, C., *Livländische Antwort an Herrn Juri Samarin*, Leipzig, 1869.

Schlau, W., ed., *Die Deutschbalten*, Munich, 1995.

Schot, B., *Stresemann, der deutsche Osten und der Volkerbund*, Wiesbaden, 1984.

———, *Nation oder Staat. Deutschland und der Minderheitenschutz*, Marburg/ Lahn, 1988.

Schwabe, A., *Histoire agraire de la Lettonie*, Riga, 1929.

Scupin, H. U., *Die neuen lettländischen Wirtschaftsgesetze in ihrer Auswirkung auf die deutsche Volksgruppe in Lettland*, Hamburg, 1936.

Seraphim, H. J. and H. Wollenweber, *Ergebnisse einer Studienreise durch Lettland*, Berlin, 1933.

Siegert, C., 'Deutschbalten in Deutschland in der Zwischenkriegszeit. Versuch einer politischen Neuordnung', *Nordost-Archiv. Zeitschrift für Regionalgeschichte*, 5, 2, 1996, pp. 325–8.

Siew, B., *Lettlands Volks und Staatswirtschaft*, Riga, 1925.

Šilde, A., 'Die Entwicklung der Republik Lettland' in B. Meissner, ed., *Die baltischen Nationen. Estland, Lettland, Litauen*, Cologne, 1990, pp. 63–74.

Stavenhagen, K., 'Das Deutschtum in Lettland', *Taschenbuch des Grenz- und Auslandsdeutschtums*, 20, Berlin, 1927.

Stegman, H., 'Rechtsgrundlagen der deutschen Kulturautonomie in Lettland', *Baltisches Recht*, 1, 1962, pp. 9–16.

Stern-Rubath, E., *Graf Brockdorff-Rantzau. Wanderer zwischen zwei Welten*, Herford and Bonn, 1968.

Stupperich, R., 'Siedlungspläne im Gebiet des Oberbefehlshabers Ost während des Weltkrieges.' *Jomsburg*, 5, 1941, pp. 348–67.

Sullivan, C. L., 'The German role in the Baltic campaign Spring 1919', *Baltic Review*, 36, 1969, pp. 40–62.

———, 'German Freikorps in the Baltic 1918–1919', *Journal of Baltic Studies*, 7, 2, 1976, pp. 124 ff.

Tarnowski, A., *Two Polish attempts to bring about a Central East European organization*, London, 1943.

Taube, A. von, 'Das Auswärtige Amt und die estnische Frage', *Jahrbücher für die Geschichte Osteuropas*, 17, 1969, pp. 542–80.

———, 'Der Reichskommissar Graf Robert Keyserlingk und die deutsche Politik in Livland und Estland im März/April 1918', *Zeitschrift für Ostforschung*, 19, 4, 1970, pp. 601–31.

Thadden, E. C., ed., Russification in the Baltic provinces 1855–1914. Princeton, 1981.

Thadden, R. v, G. von Pistohlkors, H. Weiss, eds, *Das Vergangene und die Geschichte. Festschrift für Reinhard Wittram zum 70 Geburtstag*, Göttingen, 1973.

———, ed., *Russification in the Baltic provinces and Finland, 1855–1914*, Princeton, NJ, 1981.

Unfug, D., 'The Baltic policy of Prince Max of Baden', *Journal of Central European Affairs*, 23, 1963, pp. 152–65.

Vardys, V. S., and R. Misiunas, eds, *The Baltic states in peace and war, 1917–45*, London, 1978.

Vietsch, E. von, *Wilhelm Solf. Botschafter zwischen den Zeiten*, Tübingen, 1961.

Vockrodt, P., 'Die deutsche Schulautonomie in Lettland', *Nation und Staat*, 3, 1929/30, pp. 218–23.

Volkmann, H. E., *Die deutsche Baltikumpolitik zwischen Brest-Litovsk und Compiegne*, Cologne, Vienna, 1970.

———, 'Oekonomie und Machtpolitik. Lettland und Estland im politisch-ökonomischen Kalkül des Dritten Reiches', *Geschichte und Gesellschaft* 2, 4, 1976, pp. 471–500.

———, 'Von Johannes Haller zu Reinard Wittram. Deutschbaltische Historiker und der Nationalsozialismus', *Zeitschrift für Geschichtswissenschaft*, 45, 1, 1997, pp. 21–46.

Wachtsmuth, W., 'Recht geht vor Macht' in *Baltische Köpfe. 24 Lebensbilder aus 8 Jahrhunderten deutschen Wirkens in den baltischen Länden*, Bovenden, 1953.

Walters, M., *Lettland. Seine Entwicklung zum Staat und die baltischen Fragen*, Rome, 1923.

———, *Baltengedanken und Baltenpolitik*, Paris, 1926.

Weiss, H., 'Zum Geschichtsbewusstsein in den baltischen Ländern', in E. Birke, E. Lemberg, eds, *Geschichtsbewusstsein in Ostmitteleuropa*, Marburg/Lahn, 1961, pp. 131–8.

———, 'Der deutsch-baltische Beitrag zur Lösung der Minderheitenfrage in der Zeit zwischen den beiden Weltkriegen' in E. G. Schulz, ed., *Leistung und Schicksal. Abhandlungen und Berichte über die Deutschen im Osten*, Cologne/Graz, 1967, pp. 88–91.

Wertheimer, F., *Von deutschen Parteien und Parteiführern im Ausland*, Berlin, 1930.

———, 'Umschau. Politische Führung.' *Baltische Monatshefte*, 1933, pp. 179–80.

Wittram, R., 'Liberal und Konservativ als Gestaltungsprinzipien baltischer Politik', *Baltische Monatsschrift*, 1930, pp. 213–32.

———, 'Das Reich und die baltischen Deutschen. Beiträge zur Vorgeschichte der Umsiedlung' in *Das Reich. Idee und Gestalt. Festschrift für Johannes Haller*, Stuttgart, 1940, pp. 304–47.

———, *Livland. Schicksal und Erbe der baltischen Deutschen*, Berlin, 1941.

———, 'Die Schulautonomie in Lettland', *Zeitschrift für Ostforschung*, 1, 1952, pp. 256–61.

———, *Das Nationale als europäisches Problem. Beiträge zur Geschichte des Nationalitätenprinzips*, Göttingen, 1954.

———, 'Rückblick auf den Struktur-Wandel der deutsch-baltischen Volksgruppen im letzten Jahrzehnt vor der Umsiedlung' in *Festschrift P. E. Schramm*, vol. 2, Wiesbaden, 1964, pp. 231–50.

Wrangell, W., 'Ausschnitte aus der estnischen Politik, 1918–1920', *Baltische Monatsschrift*, 1930, pp. 521–42.

Wright, J., *Gustav Stresemann: Weimar's greatest minister*, Oxford, 2002.

Wulffius, W., 'Rückblick und Ausblick', *Baltische Monatsschrift*, 62, 1931, pp. 540 ff.

———, 'Wilhelm Baron Fircks zum Gedächtnis', *Baltische Monatshefte*, 1934, pp. 26–30.

Zetterburg, S., *Die Liga der Fremdvölker Russlands, 1916–1918*, Helsinki, 1978.

Zinghaus, Viktor, *Führende Köpfe in den baltischen Staaten*, Kaunas, Leipzig, Vienna, 1938.

Index